Childhood Poverty

Palgrave Studies on Children and Development

Series editors:

Michael Bourdillon, Emeritus Professor, Department of Sociology, University of Zimbabwe.
Jo Boyden, Director of Young Lives, Department of International Development, University of Oxford, UK.

There has been increased attention to children and development, and children's development, in international policy debates in recent years, reflected in the United Nations Convention on the Rights of the Child and the child-centred focus of United Nations' Millennium Development Goals. This is based first on the interests of children according to their human rights, and second, a recognition of the importance of children for societal development. However, despite this increasing focus on policies and programmes (and budgets) to support children, relatively little has been written to draw together the lessons of development policy and practice as well as research into children's development over the life-course.

This series will start off with a mini series of three books from Young Lives, a unique 15-year longitudinal study of childhood poverty in developing countries. It will also incorporate other edited or single-author volumes, from a range of disciplines, which relate to and reflect the work being done by Young Lives on children and development, but broaden debates into the wider childhood studies field. A particular strength will be the ability to bring together material that links issues from developed and developing countries, as they affect children. As such the series will present original and valuable new data for an important and growing field of scholarship.

Forthcoming titles:

Growing Up in Poverty: Findings from Young Lives
Towards a Better Future: Lessons from Young Lives

Palgrave Studies on Children and Development
Series Standing Order ISBN 978–0–230–31924–0 (hardback) and
978–1–137–00619–6 (paperback) 978–1–137–00620–2 (ebook)

You can receive future titles in this series as they are published by placing a standing order. Please contact your bookseller or, in case of difficulty, write to us at the address below with your name and address, the title of the series and one of the ISBNs quoted above.

Customer Services Department, Macmillan Distribution Ltd, Houndmills, Basingstoke, Hampshire RG21 6XS, England

Childhood Poverty

Multidisciplinary Approaches

Edited by

Jo Boyden
Director, Young Lives, University of Oxford, UK

and

Michael Bourdillon
Emeritus Professor of Sociology, University of Zimbabwe

KH

First published 2012 by
PALGRAVE MACMILLAN

Palgrave Macmillan in the UK is an imprint of Macmillan Publishers Limited,
registered in England, company number 785998, of Houndmills, Basingstoke,
Hampshire RG21 6XS.

Palgrave Macmillan in the US is a division of St Martin's Press LLC,
175 Fifth Avenue, New York, NY 10010.

Palgrave Macmillan is the global academic imprint of the above companies
and has companies and representatives throughout the world.

Palgrave® and Macmillan® are registered trademarks in the United States,
the United Kingdom, Europe and other countries.

ISBN 978–0–230–31924–0

This book is printed on paper suitable for recycling and made from fully
managed and sustained forest sources. Logging, pulping and manufacturing
processes are expected to conform to the environmental regulations of the
country of origin.

A catalogue record for this book is available from the British Library.

A catalog record for this book is available from the Library of Congress.

10 9 8 7 6 5 4 3 2 1
21 20 19 18 17 16 15 14 13 12

Printed and bound in the United States of America

5/1/13

Contents

v

Tables

Figures

Boxes

Acknowledgements

We would like to thank the many people who assisted in the writing of this book. The chapters presented here are a combination of recent findings from the Young Lives study, together with papers from international experts in childhood studies who attended a conference held by Young Lives in 2009. Maggie Black and Bill Myers reviewed the papers and provided useful comments on early drafts.

In particular we wish to thank the Young Lives children and their families for generously giving us their time and cooperation. They willingly shared with us a great deal of detailed personal information about their daily lives, and we have a responsibility to protect their confidentiality and ensure that their identities remain protected. For this reason, the names of the children and their communities have been changed.

Young Lives is a collaborative partnership between research and government institutes in the four study countries and the University of Oxford, together with Save the Children UK. Young Lives is core-funded from 2001 to 2017 by UK aid from the Department for International Development (DFID), and co-funded from 2010 to 2014 by the Netherlands Ministry of Foreign Affairs.

Contributors

Jere R. Behrman is the W.R. Kenan, Jr. Professor of Economics and Sociology and Research Associate of the Population Studies Center at the University of Pennsylvania. His research is in empirical microeconomics, economic development, labour economics, human resources (education, training, health, nutrition), economic demography, household behaviours, life-cycle and intergenerational relations, and policy evaluation. He has published more than 330 professional articles and 33 books. He has been a research consultant with a number of international organizations, involved in research or lecturing in over 40 countries, a principal investigator on over 70 research projects, and received a number of honours for his research.

Michael Bourdillon studied Social Anthropology at Oxford University, and taught for over 25 years in the Department of Sociology at the University of Zimbabwe, where he is now Emeritus Professor. For the past 20 years, he has been involved with street and working children, both as an academic and a practitioner. Recent among his many publications is the co-authored book, *Rights and Wrongs of Children's Work* (2010).

Jo Boyden is an anthropologist and Director of Young Lives and a Reader in Development Studies in the Department of International Development at the University of Oxford. Her work with Young Lives since 2005 has focused on children's experiences of poverty, particularly the relationship between poverty and other forms of childhood risk, the political–economic processes that underpin the distribution of risk, the role of subjective perceptions in mediating outcomes, and children's contributions to household risk reduction. Her previous research centred on child labour and young people living with armed conflict and forced migration.

Karen Brock is a social scientist, writer, and editor, focusing on natural resource management issues, development policy processes, social accountability, and participatory governance. Her publications include *Knowing Poverty: Critical Reflections on Participatory Research and Policy* (2002) and *Unpacking Policy: Knowledge, Actors and Spaces in Poverty Reduction in Uganda and Nigeria* (2004).

Laura Camfield is Lecturer in the School of International Development at the University of East Anglia. She specializes in research methods to understand and measure well-being in developing countries, including the way people experience poverty and develop resilience. Laura holds an ESRC Comparative Cross-National Research Methods grant (2010–14) to develop and share methods for the collection of data on these topics based on her earlier work with Young Lives and the Well-being in Developing Countries research group (www.welldev.org.uk).

Santiago Cueto is Senior Researcher at GRADE (the Grupo de Análisis para el Desarollo), Lima in the areas of education and human development, and coordinator of the Young Lives study for Peru. He is also Professor at the Pontificia Universidad Católica del Perú (PUCP), President of the Peruvian Society for Educational Research, and a member of the National Council of Education in Peru.

Gina Crivello is a Research Officer with Young Lives. She has a PhD in Anthropology from the University of California, where her research focused on the role of gender in youth migration from Morocco to Europe. In Young Lives, she has explored children's mobilities and migration in relation to their experiences of school and work, and the responsibilities they have within their families.

Andrew Dawes is an applied developmental psychologist with affiliations to the Universities of Cape Town and Oxford. He has a long-standing interest in the development of an evidence-base for policies and interventions to improve the situation of children who are rendered vulnerable to poverty and violence.

Stefan Dercon is Professor of Development Economics at the University of Oxford, and leads the poverty dynamics research stream within Young Lives. He has worked extensively on risk and poverty in Ethiopia, Tanzania, and India, using longitudinal and long-term cohort data. His work on children has focused on risk, nutrition, schooling, and psychosocial competencies, and their role in the persistence of poverty.

Patrice Engle is Professor of Psychology and Child Development at Cal Poly State University. She specializes in care practices and child nutrition, responsive feeding, HIV and AIDS, and women's empowerment from the perspective of early childhood development. She has worked for the World Health Organization, and for UNICEF in India and New York. She has recently prepared an updated review on the effectiveness of programmes to improve early child development in low- and middle-income countries and is currently developing assessment tools for child development for Latin America and for East Asia.

Deborah Ewing is a consultant and specialist in child-focused methodologies.

Paul Glewwe is Professor at the University of Minnesota's Department of Applied Economics. Earlier he was a research economist at the World Bank. His research focuses on economics of education, poverty, and inequality in developing countries. His recent publications have appeared in many reputable journals and volumes, including the *Economics of Education Review, Handbook of Development Economics, Handbook of the Economics of Education, International Encyclopedia of Education, Journal of Development Economics, The Lancet,* and *World Bank Economic Review*.

Gabriela Guerrero is Associate Researcher at GRADE and a doctoral candidate in Educational Sciences at the Catholic University of Leuven in Belgium.

John Hoddinott is Deputy Division Director at the International Food Policy Research Institute, a think-tank based in Washington DC. His research focuses on the long-term consequences of early childhood malnutrition, the causes of poverty, and the evaluation of interventions designed to reduce poverty. In addition to living in a hut in Kenya for six months, he has worked in a number of developing countries, including Ethiopia, Guatemala, Mali, and Zimbabwe. Born in Canada, he has a doctorate in Economics from the University of Oxford.

Caroline Knowles is Communications Manager for Young Lives and has a background in development publishing and research communication.

Anuradha Komanduri is Professor of Social Work at Sri Padmavati Women's University (SPMVV), Tirupati, India and Assistant Qualitative Researcher for Young Lives in Andhra Pradesh. A social work educator and researcher for the past 21 years, her research interests include child mental health, social work methodologies, and children in difficult circumstances.

Juan León is a doctoral student in the Department of Educational Theory and Policy Analysis at Pennsylvania State University.

Susan Levine is Senior Lecturer in Social Anthropology at the University of Cape Town. She specializes in child agricultural labour in South Africa.

Gillian Mann is a freelance child protection consultant. She trained in education at Harvard University and in anthropology at the London School of Economics and Political Science, where her PhD thesis was entitled 'Being, Becoming and Unbecoming a Refugee: The Lives of Congolese Children in Dar es Salaam'. In addition to her academic work, she has conducted research, evaluation, and training for a broad range of agencies on issues related to children's experiences of forced migration, displacement, family separation, HIV/AIDS, and poverty.

Virginia Morrow is Senior Research Officer with Young Lives and leads the study's work on research ethics. She also works with the qualitative research teams, advising on methods for research with children. She holds a Master's in Sociology of Childhood and Children's Rights at the Institute of Education, University of London. Her recent book *The Ethics of Research with Children and Young People* (2011, co-authored with Priscilla Alderson) covers ethics at every stage of research.

Ismael Muñoz is Research Assistant at GRADE, Lima.

Kate Orkin is a DPhil student in the Department of International Development at the University of Oxford. Her research uses qualitative and econometric methods to analyse home and school factors that affect the school attendance and achievement of rural Ethiopian children. A Young Lives Research Associate, she worked on the survey of schools attended by Young Lives children conducted in Ethiopia in 2010. She is a South-Africa-at-large Rhodes Scholar and won a Skye Foundation grant and the Frankel Studentship in Economics at Oriel College, Oxford.

Elisa Seguin works for the Human Development Department in the Lima office of the World Bank. Previously she was a research assistant in the area of education and human development at GRADE. .

Judith Streak is an economist with particular expertise in child poverty measurement and the analysis of budgetary provision for children. Having worked in South Africa for most of her career, she is now based at the University of Adelaide.

Uma Vennam is Professor of Social Work at SPMVV with 27 years of teaching and research experience. The focus of her research has been rural poverty, NGOs and rural development, and children in difficult situations (including trafficking). She is currently the Lead Qualitative Researcher for Young Lives in Andhra Pradesh, India.

Theodore D. Wachs is Professor of Psychological Sciences at Purdue University, working on risk factors and infant and child development. His research interests are in the areas of chaotic family environments and infant micro-nutrient deficiencies, and their impact on early social–emotional development. He has undertaken studies in these areas with colleagues in Egypt, Jamaica, Pakistan, and Peru. Previously he was a Golestan Fellow at the Netherlands Institute for Advanced Studies and a Fulbright Distinguished Scholar in residence at the Centre for International Child Health, London.

Tassew Woldehanna is Associate Professor in Economics at the School of Economics, Addis Ababa University, Senior Research Fellow at the Ethiopian Development Research Institute, and Principal Investigator for Young Lives in Ethiopia. He is a development economist mainly interested in child welfare, poverty, and related research, including the economics of education and health.

Martin Woodhead is Professor of Childhood Studies at The Open University and leads the education research stream within Young Lives. His research relates to early childhood development, education, and care, including theoretical and policy studies and extensive international work. He has also carried out research on child labour and children's rights and was Special Advisor to the UN Committee on the Rights of the Child, in preparation of *General Comment 7: Implementing Child Rights in Early Childhood* (2005).

Introduction

Michael Bourdillon

This book is the first of a series of three books arising from, *Young Lives Research on Children and Poverty*, a Young Lives study on how poverty affects children's lives at the beginning of the twenty-first century, both their current experience of it and the way it will shape their future life trajectories. At least since the work of Amartya Sen in the early 1980s, it has been accepted that poverty cannot be understood simply in terms of income. Adequate livelihood includes people's 'entitlement' to necessary goods and empowerment to exercise some control over their own life. Crises that damage lives and result in inadequate livelihoods affect people differentially, and may continue to affect them years after the initial shock. Analysis that can effectively guide policy towards enabling poor people to improve their circumstances and opportunities must disaggregate poverty and examine the detail of who is affected and how, as well as the factors that promote or constrain personal and/or structural change.

According to UNICEF, a billion children are severely deprived of at least one of the essential goods and services they require to survive, grow, and develop.[1] Further, children are generally more vulnerable, and the effects of poverty in childhood are frequently lasting, sometimes permanently affecting children's growth and cognitive development (Grantham-McGregor et al. 2007). The children of poor families are more likely to end up being poor, for these reasons and on account of factors in the social environment that put them at a disadvantage. So giving priority to children and the alleviation of childhood poverty is not just about reducing suffering; it is about breaking poverty cycles that trap whole families, communities, and countries in the long term.

There has been considerable growth in recent years in research into the different ways in which children experience poverty, the mechanisms by which this may have long-term detrimental effects on their lives, as well as the protective factors that can promote their resilience. Despite the welcome growth in child poverty research, most studies have limited ability to address fundamental questions by virtue of their narrow geographical focus (notably poverty in rich societies), by their specific methodologies (ranging from large-scale surveys through to in-depth ethnographies), and by their design (most often cross-sectional accounts of poverty at the time of data collection).

The Young Lives study is a step towards filling this lacuna and establishing this priority, by following two cohorts of children in poor communities in four developing countries over a period of 15 years.

The volume introduces issues of central concern to Young Lives through a number of chapters by distinguished scholars who have researched and published on them. It also shows how some of these issues appear in practice through essays reporting on early rounds of the Young Lives research and related research in other contexts and countries. This first book of the Young Lives research series covers the earliest phases of data collection, when the two Young Lives cohorts were growing through early and middle childhood (up to age 12). Future volumes in the series will look at later phases of the life cycle, including the outcomes of poverty in early adulthood.

Children and poverty in a historical context

In nineteenth-century Europe and North America, there was growing concern for children of the poor, together with attempts to provide them with education to enhance their constructive role in society. Early in the twentieth century, Eglantyne Jebb inspired the globalization of the 'child-saving' movement, and since then there has been growing attention to children in international policy debates, reflected in recent decades by the International Year of the Child in 1979, the UN Convention on the Rights of the Child (CRC) in 1989, and the Millennium Development Goals (MDGs) in 2000. This has resulted in a greater focus on children in development cooperation, massive investment in services for children in developing countries, and the establishment of a children's rights framework. There are two aspects to this attention: one is the interests of children according to their human rights; a second is recognition of the importance of children for societal development.

Rights and protection

A key step in this process was the acceptance of the United Nations Convention on the Rights of the Child (CRC) in 1989 and its rapid ratification by virtually every country in the world. Although Young Lives was conceived within this context, it was designed as a study concerned with childhood poverty rather than directly with child rights: analysis and conclusions are based on empirical data collected, rather than on predetermined norms. Poverty, however, directly impinges on many fundamental rights, such as rights to nutrition, shelter, and education.

Concerns about children's poverty are consequently closely linked to concerns about children's rights, which therefore must be central to the work of Young Lives. The programme's approach to understanding childhood poverty draws on the four guiding principles of the CRC: the best interests of the child as a primary consideration in all matters concerning children; their rights to life, survival, and development; no unjustified discrimination; and respect for the views of the child.

The interpretation and application of the CRC influence the design and impact of rights-based interventions in the lives of children and their families. While human rights are universal, the CRC also emphasizes the importance of traditions and cultural values. Young Lives is in a particularly strong position to evaluate how policies and their application based on particular interpretations of children's rights affect the lives of children in specific contexts. This will encourage interventions based on evidence rather on than assumed norms.

Concern for the rights of children also affects how research is conducted, as discussed in the chapter by Virginia Morrow (Chapter 2). In particular, Young Lives places children's views at the centre of its research and recognizes children as active social agents. The Young Lives study highlights questions of children's experiences, well-being, and the inequalities between different groups of children.

Children and societal development

Attention to children is crucial to the development of a productive society. If their physical development is impeded, the productive capacity of the future workforce will diminish, and society is likely to incur additional costs. Similarly, impeding children's cognitive development diminishes their life chances and future productivity, especially in contemporary economies that are increasingly reliant on ever more complex technology (see Qvortrup 2001). As populations expand and cultures mingle, it can no longer be taken for granted that children will pick up the social skills necessary for constructive interaction from their immediate environment. Since many parents do not have all the resources necessary to ensure that their children achieve their full potential, attention to children of poor families becomes a key issue in societal development.

Much public attention and literature, however, has focused on policy (World Bank 2007; UNICEF 2007). There has been less attention to understanding the situations of children in particular contexts and the political economy of these contexts. Although support has been provided for education and health and some child welfare, these involve government ministries with little control over finance, and even this is threatened by the current global economic crisis. The MDGs have indeed improved the volume and quantity of international aid, but questions remain about how appropriate and sustainable this is, and how we should address fundamental inequalities that persist. The emphasis of the MDGs on increasing coverage has not been matched by attention to quality: in particular, the health and education services available to poorer children are often of an inadequate standard, and attention has largely focused on areas that are relatively easy to assess and address, such as health for children under 5 years old and primary education for those aged 6 to 12. Gains in child survival have been dramatic and important but a narrow focus on survival, protection, and schooling neglects other dimensions of children's lives and development. A further challenge is to move beyond the critical threshold: reaching the last 20 per cent of children costs as much as providing for the first 80 per cent, and is far more complex. Related to this is frequent failure to deal adequately with bias towards urban areas or with gender inequalities.

The MDGs are a form of high-level monitoring of macro trends. But because they are about incidence and averages, they miss vital information about inequality and how the poorest and most vulnerable populations are doing. Elaborate research tools monitoring macro-level inputs and outputs rely heavily on broad and general indicators that often miss the specific situations of children in poor communities. And specific issues facing children are often lost when national data sets are used that consider only households, and fail to consider inequalities within them (see, for example, Saporiti 1994). The dominance of cross-sectional studies of 'vulnerable' groups gives little sense of life trajectories and the processes by which people live with risk and respond to adversity. Similarly, large-scale studies often neglect the ways in which different cultures mediate decisions and expectations concerning children, children's own beliefs, aspirations, and decisions, and the way 'modern' childhoods co-exist with more traditional influences.

To support development interventions and policy, research is needed that links the daily situation of poor communities to macro-economic and political structures, in order to identify the causes and effects of poverty within a life-course framework. Research must take into account the complex processes, dynamics, and multiple influences in children's lives, learning from the children's own knowledge and perspectives. Such research can provide a bridge between generalized analysis of large-scale data and specific interpretations appropriate to the contexts in which children live, which in turn can feed into policies that might help to break cycles of poverty.

Young Lives

Young Lives[2] is a study that seeks to improve understanding of the causes and consequences of childhood poverty, and of the factors that contribute to breaking cycles of poverty and to reducing the inequality that underpins poverty. It is designed to provide credible evidence to inform the development and implementation of future policies and practices for children.

The study is based in four countries: Ethiopia, India (in the state of Andhra Pradesh), Peru, and Vietnam. In each country, 20 sites were selected to reflect diversity, including urban and rural areas, communities with different livelihoods, and sites with different ethnic groups. Although the study sites include a range of wealth levels, the focus is on relatively poor communities and therefore the sample is not representative of the country as a whole. In each site, roughly equal numbers of randomly selected boys and girls participate. In each country, the study incorporates two cohorts of children: 2,000 children born in 2001–02, and 1,000 children born in 1994–95. The study will have five major survey rounds following the children at three-year intervals. Survey questionnaires were designed to provide material that can easily be compared both between the four countries and over time. They collect a wide variety of indicators on these children's well-being over time, as well as information on their caregivers and the circumstances they face. The first survey round took place in 2002, Round 2 in 2006, and Round 3 in 2009, which was being analysed as this book was being compiled. Two further rounds are planned for 2013 and 2016.

Soon after the study started, it became clear that more intensive qualitative research was needed to complement the quantitative survey data. Starting in 2007, detailed studies have been carried out in selected sites, and sub-studies prompted by questions raised by the survey data.

Research thus incorporates methods from different disciplines, including both numerical analysis of survey data (dominant in economics and some psychology) and detailed studies of children and communities using ethnographic and related techniques. The next chapter in this volume (Chapter 1), by Brock and Knowles, outlines the methodology of Young Lives.

A feature of this research programme is its multidimensional view of poverty and holistic understanding of children's well-being and development. Many studies focus on particular aspects of life, such as nutrition, health, education, income, or psychological development. Such approaches are facilitated by the fact that each dimension is largely the interest of a particular discipline, with its appropriate methodology; but they can easily miss the connections between the domains of children's development or aspects of their lives. Bringing the different dimensions together, however, requires combining disciplines with their sometimes very different methodologies and different forms of expression and communication: in particular, it is a challenge to make numerical data analysis accessible to those used to more observational research methods.

Emerging narratives

Although only half the expected survey rounds have been completed at this stage, there are four key narratives emerging from the ongoing research.

The first concerns the *multifaceted outcomes of deprivation in early childhood*. Negative effects of undernutrition and other adversities early in childhood are persistent (to at least the age of 12) across diverse domains of children's development: these include physical growth, cognitive development (especially as measured by school performance), and factors relating to psychosocial well-being (such as a sense of self-efficacy and self-esteem). While this persistence is well known and widely researched (see chapters by Engle (Chapter 8), Wachs (Chapter 9), Behrman (Chapter 6), and Hoddinott (Chapter 3) in this volume), Young Lives is looking at links between developmental domains that have received little, if any, attention elsewhere: for example, Stefan Dercon and Alan Sanchez (forthcoming) link early nutrition problems, as reflected in stunting, with later impairment in cognitive skills and psychosocial competencies – in this case self-efficacy, self-esteem, and educational aspirations.

Second, in relation to *informal and formal learning*, Young Lives researchers are tracing important processes that focus on competencies such as social skills, life skills, and collective morality, recognizing that these informal processes offers a more holistic picture of children's learning and development than would come from studying their formal learning alone. At the same time, Young Lives research reveals just how significant formal school learning has become during the first decade of the twenty-first century, in terms of near universal access to primary school for most of the sample. The importance of tracking the implementation of MDGs and Education-For-All goals within the sample is reflected in priorities for data collection, which now includes a further component to assess the features and quality of schools attended by Young Lives children. The school data will combine with household data, including child interviews and cognitive and educational achievement tests to provide a rich mine of education data, comprehensively capturing the changing and varied role of school in the lives of children and families. Parents' hopes for their children's education are remarkably high, but with a wide gulf between aspirations, the poor quality of schools that many are able to access, and the consequent variability in learning outcomes. Commitment to school attendance incurs financial costs for households, even where children attend government schools. Children also face dilemmas, as they struggle to keep up with family and work alongside their schooling. The evidence around these struggles and issues of school quality highlights the dilemmas for many children and families, around how far investing in school will deliver the promise of 'a better life'. These dilemmas also raise the question how far spending the precious years of childhood in inadequate or inappropriate formal education may be de-skilling children, by weakening their knowledge of traditional livelihoods while failing to deliver skills needed for modern economies, especially where there are limited employment opportunities.

The third narrative emerging is about persistent poverty and inequality (Dornan 2010a, 2010b; Pells 2010). The early rounds of research covered periods of macro-economic growth (2002–2007), when the whole sample benefited (to some degree) from improved services and infrastructure. Nevertheless, inequality persists and households with certain characteristics are becoming increasingly trapped in poverty. Differences based on ethnicity and caste, urban or rural residence, region, and family wealth affect children's life-chances and the effectiveness of policy in delivering better outcomes for all children. Young Lives research is producing considerable information about the processes whereby inequality becomes perpetuated across life cycles, domestic cycles, and generations. In Vietnam, for example, households with low maternal education are becoming increasingly concentrated among the poorest quintile (Le Thuc, 2008: vii). In this volume, Santiago Cueto et al. (Chapter 15) show how indigenous language speakers are disadvantaged in Peru's education system, which overlaps with disadvantages experienced by people in rural areas. Jo Boyden and Gina Crivello (Chapter 10) consider disadvantages relating to tribe and caste in Andhra Pradesh; they show that relations of power affect experiences of risk; and rural–urban inequalities in Ethiopia appear in the chapter by Tassew Woldehanna (Chapter 7). Round 3 data will add to this a discussion of the impacts of the recent and current global economic crisis.

Fourth, there is a growing narrative on the relationship between poverty and other forms of risk. In this volume, Theodore Wachs (Chapter 9) shows in general how poverty can result in cumulative risk with detrimental consequences for children, and Jo Boyden and Gina Crivello (Chapter 10) examine risk in Andhra Pradesh, relating it to structures of power and considering children's experiences and responses. This important narrative will receive more attention in future rounds, paying attention to levels of both household and individual children. Poverty and related deprivations comprise significant sources of risk for children worldwide. Poorer households in the Young Lives sample experience a higher burden of risk and a greater diversity of forms of risk than those that are better off: in particular, they suffer more frequently and more seriously from illness (which sometimes results in the death of a parent), and are more vulnerable to environmental hazards. Often the development and well-being of poor children is doubly compromised by the interaction of multiple hardships. Household risks clearly interact with and exacerbate poverty, and Young Lives data can establish some causality in this process. At the same time, research can assess whether social protection has beneficial effects and in what ways. We shall also be looking at whether household risk correlates significantly with child protection concerns, although the latter can only be analysed through qualitative research.

Key themes

The Young Lives programme has identified three major areas of focus that provide structure to the research and policy analysis, and indeed to this volume. The themes are not mutually exclusive. Many topics and research projects impinge on more than one of them, and each incorporates a variety of disciplines and methodologies. But they do focus on different levels of analysis, and different areas of policy and intervention.

The first theme is *poverty dynamics and mobility,* introduced and illustrated in the second part of this volume. The theme includes measuring different dimensions of poverty and examining correlations and interactions between them, focusing on the levels of family and community rather than that of the individual. It considers how households become trapped in or escape from poverty, and the importance of social protection measures. Survey data and statistical analysis are the dominant methods in this theme, although as the chapter by Stefan Dercon (Chapter 4) illustrates, surveys and their analysis need to be informed by detailed qualitative research.

The second theme, *children's experiences of poverty,* the subject of Part III, explores the outcomes of childhood poverty at the level of the children themselves. It looks at how poverty and risk affect their physical and psychosocial well-being. However, the well-being of children is not simply about the presence or scarcity of material resources. The social environment influences how available resources meet children's expectations, and how children learn to make the best use of what resources are available. This theme therefore includes children's responses to poverty. Understanding their experiences of poverty requires detailed knowledge of their lives and their worlds; it also requires researchers to find ways of encouraging the children to express their own perspectives. The illustrative chapters on this theme show detailed ethnographic research, often supported by survey data, which indicate the prevalence of issues raised.

The third theme is *learning, time use, and life transitions.* Much of the data on this theme recount children's progress through formal systems of pre-school and school, but the theme includes other activities that contribute to social and cognitive development and learning various life skills. The theme also examines how the choices made by children and their families around children's use of time affect their transitions through childhood and into adulthood. There are four chapters in the fourth section of this book on this theme, which will receive more emphasis in later volumes reporting on children as they grow older and move through school.

Policy

Research into children's poverty is of little use if it is unable to influence policy and intervention. For this, it must produce evidence that is convincing and accessible both to policymakers and to the general public, and that responds to their current interests and priorities. Young Lives research spans aspects of children's lives that are key priority areas for international and national policy, and the programme is concerned to bring its findings to the attention of policymakers, particularly when they challenge orthodoxies and open up new questions for debate.

The contexts for policy in each of the four study countries, as well as internationally, are constantly evolving over the 15-year life span of the Young Lives study. The context of economic growth in the early rounds of research raised questions about inequality. Two rounds of research later, the study countries, along with much of the rest of the world, are experiencing the shocks of a global financial crisis with ramifications for food prices, household incomes, aid budgets, and public spending. Round 3 is revealing that overall conditions for children have continued to improve despite the crisis, but inequality remains (and is growing in some cases) and vulnerability to shocks is very evident – with possible long-term consequences. Nevertheless, new questions arise. What are the impacts of this global crisis on children and young people? How will it affect global targets for poverty reduction over the medium and longer term? To be useful, collection and analysis of the data must respond to these shifting conditions, and to the priorities that they demand.

The timeframe of the Young Lives research mirrors that of the MDGs and the global targets of the movement to provide Education For All. By taking a multi-sector approach, the programme collects evidence that can both challenge and support progress in many of these global priority areas, as well as highlighting vital interconnections that are often missed.

From addressing child malnutrition and mortality, to improving education quality, a consistent message arising from the Young Lives research is that a focus on children and equity, along with a multidimensional understanding of poverty, can help to tackle overall poverty and move towards more equitable development and growth.

Part I: methodology

The volume begins with four chapters on methodology. In Chapter 1, Karen Brock and Caroline Knowles explain how and why the approach of Young Lives was constructed.

While much attention has been given to developing ethical guidelines for research, there is little literature on their practice. In Chapter 2, Virginia Morrow recounts difficulties that arose when accepted ethical guidelines were applied in the Young Lives field research. She shows that ethics need to be applied contextually. Misunderstanding between researchers and informants, together with changing circumstances in the communities, mean that approaches must be constantly adapted between rounds.

There are so many dimensions of poverty impeding all spheres of child development that it is difficult to determine causal relationships between an early privation and later growth. In Chapter 3, John Hoddinott discusses statistical techniques that can help to establish such relationships, and in particular, how they have enabled researchers to draw conclusions from past studies about the deleterious effects of early childhood under-nutrition.

Before moving into dynamics of childhood poverty, we consider the methodological problem of measuring poverty, which is more difficult than the uncontroversial nature of the concept might suggest. It is relatively simple to estimate formal income, by counting, for example, those openly receiving less than $1.25 a day – one of the measures used by the World Bank. However, informal or illegal income is often omitted from such counting; indeed it is often deliberately kept hidden. Besides, earnings do not always reflect consumption and are not therefore a reliable guide on whether or not children are deprived in any way. The last argument applies also to measurements of wealth or assets. Initially, Young Lives developed an index of poverty based on assets, which it still uses in some analysis; but the relevance of assets is not readily comparable between countries nor between, say, rural and urban areas. So Young Lives, has largely replaced this measure of wealth by attention to household consumption and expenditure as a more appropriate indicator of poverty. This is calculated as the sum of the estimated value of food and non-food items (including what is bought and home-grown, and gifts and exchanges, but excluding capital items and one-off expenditures); the total is divided by the number of people in the household. Even this calculation takes little account of experience and expectations, of inequalities within households, and of dimensions of agency by which people can control and improve their lives. Measures of income or expenditure can provide a gross indication of progress (or lack of it) in fighting poverty, but poverty has many dimensions, and counting by any one dimension excludes some people who are deprived in other ways.

In the fourth methodology chapter, Stefan Dercon uses Young Lives data to argue that even complex multidimensional measures are unreliable for purposes of policy or intervention. If many dimensions are included, the target population becomes too large; if dimensions are limited for counting purposes, some people in need of support are excluded. In particular, children's experiences and perceptions of poverty comprise important dimensions for the outcomes of poverty; they are difficult to count and do not correlate exactly with dimensions that are easier to count. Multidimensional data such as those collected in Young Lives research are essential to understanding the interaction between dimensions, which in turn can indicate where policy and intervention might focus; but target groups need to be identified by more focused measures, which are also needed for accurate monitoring.

Notes

1. http://www.unicef.org/mdg/poverty.html (accessed 26 January 2011).
2. Young Lives is located within the Department of International Development at the University of Oxford. It is a consortium of research partners in the four study countries, supported by an international advisory board of experts.

References

Dercon, Stefan and Alan Sanchez (2011) *Long-term Implications of Malnutrition on Non-Cognitive Skills: Evidence from Four developing Countries*, Working Paper 72, Oxford: Young Lives.

Dornan, Paul (2010a) *Children and the Millennium Development Goals: Fragile Gains and Deep Inequalities*, Policy Paper 2, Oxford: Young Lives

Dornan, Paul (2010b) *Understanding the Impacts of Crisis on Children in Developing Countries*, Round 3 Preliminary Findings, Oxford: Young Lives.

Grantham-McGregor, S., V.B. Cheung, S. Cueto, P. Glewwe, L. Richter, B. Strupp and the International Child Development Steering Group (2007) 'Child Development in Developing Countries: Development Potential in the First Five Years for Children in Developing Countries', *The Lancet* 369: 60–70.

Le Thuc, Duc, Nguyen Phuong Ngoc, Tran Minh Chau, Nguyen Van Tien, and Vo Thanh Son (2008) *Vietnam Country report: Young Lives: Vietnam Round 2 Survey*, Oxford: Young Lives.

Pells, Kirrily (2010) *Inequalities, Life Chances and Gender*, Round 3 Preliminary Findings, Oxford: Young Lives.

Qvortrup, Jens (2001) 'School-work, Paid Work and the Changing Obligations of Childhood' in Philip Mizen, Christopher Pole, and Angela Bolton (eds), *Hidden Hands: International Perspectives on Children's Work and Labour*, London: Routledge.

Saporiti, Angelo (1994) 'A Methodology for Making Children Count', in Jens Qvortrup, Mariatta Bardy, Giovanni Sgritta and Helmut Wintersberger (eds), *Childhood Matters: Social Theory, Practice and Politics*, Aldershot: Avebury.

Sen, Amartya (1981) *Poverty and Famines: An Essay on Entitlement and Deprivation*, Oxford: Oxford University Press.

UNICEF (2007) *Children and the Millennium Development Goals: Progress Towards A World Fit for Children*, New York: UNICEF.

World Bank (2007) *World Development Report 2007: Development and the Next Generation*, Washington DC: World Bank.

Part I
Methodology

1
Doing Longitudinal Research: Opportunities and Challenges in a Study of Childhood

Karen Brock and Caroline Knowles

Young Lives has been introduced as a longitudinal study that follows two cohorts of children in poor communities in Ethiopia, India, Peru, and Vietnam as they grow into young adults. In this chapter, after pointing to the importance of longitudinal studies in the social sciences, we use the experience of designing and implementing Young Lives to reflect on some issues surrounding the process of such studies, and on the use of their findings to inform policy.

The power, potential, and challenges of longitudinal research

The power of longitudinal research lies in its capacity to illuminate patterns of change in the lives of selected groups of people. Making repeated, structured observations about the same group over time allow the exclusion of unobservable individual characteristics that do not change over time (for example, an adventurous personality with a tendency to take risks) and the identification of short- and long-term patterns of change. A classic example of this can be found in the British Doctors Study, a longitudinal study which surveyed 40,000 British doctors six times between 1957 and 2001, and found the first statistical proof that tobacco smoking increases the risk of lung cancer (Doll et al. 2004).

In the social sciences, longitudinal research can be divided into repeated cross-sectional and cohort studies. The former sample a cross-section of the population and survey it at given points in time. The latter track a group of people (a 'panel') selected because they have experienced the same event – typically birth – during a specified time period. Studies of these types can provide a glimpse into both the life histories of the individuals who make up a segment of the population, and the broader patterns of change that make up the social landscape.

Cohort studies have been particularly useful and important for understanding children and childhood across many disciplines and have used a range of qualitative and quantitative methods. An early example of a cohort study from the USA (Elder 1974) tracked the lives of children born in 1920 and 1928 through the years of the Great Depression, and had a profound influence in changing the way in which the impact that unemployment, parental absence and death have on children was understood (Bronfenbrenner 1999). The UK has three national birth cohort studies[1] and their findings have contributed to debates in many areas of social policy that are crucial for children.

Cohort studies can also be important in influencing popular understanding of lifecycle issues, including childhood. Two contemporary British TV series – *Seven-Up* and *Child of our Time*[2] – use cohort studies as the basis for periodic documentaries. *Seven-Up* set out to explore the assumption that children's futures are pre-determined by their social class, while *Child of our Time* posed the question, 'Are we born, or are we made?' The success of these two series is an example of the compelling nature of the information that can be generated by cohort studies, and how it can be used to stimulate debate on issues of child development and its social context.

The large datasets collected in developing countries have tended to focus on producing nationally representative quantitative data using surveys. They are usually cross-sectional rather than cohort studies, with the sample of people studied changing between rounds and relatively little information about individuals. The World Bank's Living Standards Measurement Study, for example, has since 1980 supported the production of national household survey data across the developing world (Grosh and Glewwe 1995), while the USAID-supported Demographic and Health Surveys project has since 1984 collected data on population, health, HIV, and nutrition through more than 200 surveys in more than 75 countries.[3] Initiatives like these reflect the power of long-term research to provide policymakers with quantitative data that measure not only rates of phenomena like unemployment, poverty, or HIV infection, but also shed light on the determinants of these outcomes.

In contrast to these nationally representative survey-based studies, some longitudinal research makes considerable use of qualitative research methods, including participatory and action research approaches, alongside survey techniques. Inherent in high-quality participatory research is an ethical obligation to feed findings back to participants and their communities. Inherent in action research is the notion that enquiry, learning, and action are equal parts of a research process. One example of a study design with these features is the Busselton Health Study, which has since 1966 involved the residents of an Australian town in a series of health surveys. The study was established with the intention of carrying out health research in a community setting that would provide epidemiological data, but also with the explicit intention of empowering participants to take an active role in their own health and well-being. This study alerts us to the possibility that longitudinal research can have an intended, direct effect on the lives of its participants. Challenges may arise from longitudinal studies, however, if the effects on participants are either unintended or negative, or go unnoticed.

As even this briefest of overviews illustrates, the power of longitudinal studies and their potential to provide information about change and how it happens are considerable. Longitudinal studies are also, however, both expensive and difficult to conduct, and bring with them a host of methodological, logistical, and analytic challenges. Despite these challenges, and the ethical issues around working with children and bringing well-resourced and educated researchers into poor communities,[4] Young Lives was designed as a longitudinal cohort study because the major funder (the UK Department for International Development) wanted a study that could examine the factors and policies that make a difference in children's lives over time. Their intention was to provide evidence to help policymakers analyse and address the challenges they face in alleviating childhood poverty in developing countries. The following section discusses the methodology of the Young Lives study and outlines some of the emerging challenges.

Young Lives research design and emerging methodological challenges

The twin objectives of Young Lives are to improve understanding of the causes and consequences of childhood poverty, and to inform the development and implementation of future policies and practices that will reduce childhood poverty. The first step in designing a longitudinal study to meet these objectives was to identify a conceptual and analytical framework for the enquiry.

Young Lives has adopted a multidimensional view of poverty in which income is one aspect among many others (as explained in the Introduction). This view emphasizes that poverty is a complex, dynamic phenomenon subject to both contextual specificity and multiple, inter-acting contributory factors. Providing a comprehensive picture of the experience of poverty thus demands many variables and an analytical framework encompassing many components. The Young Lives analyti-cal framework integrates the outcomes of child poverty, the means by which poverty shapes children's transitions and trajectories through childhood, the intergenerational dynamics of poverty, and the impact of public policies and programmes designed to protect children and facilitate their progress.

As mentioned in the Introduction, this framework generated three research themes: the dynamics of poverty and uncertainty; children's experiences of poverty and its outcomes in their lives; and children's learning, their changing responsibilities, and their use of time. To provide information on these themes, Young Lives is tracking 12,000 children in the four study countries. In each country, there are 2,000 children who were born in 2000–01 and 1,000 born in 1994–95, with roughly equal numbers of boys and girls in both cohorts.

A multi-stage sampling methodology known as the sentinel site sur-veillance system was used to select a sample of poor children in each country (Wilson, Huttley, and Fenn 2006). The concept of a sentinel site comes from health studies and is a form of purposive sampling in which the site or cluster is deemed to represent a certain type of popu-lation or area, and is expected to show early signs of trends affecting those particular people or areas. For example, monitoring a typical slum area of a given city may help detect events and trends which will have an impact on most slums in that city.

In India, Ethiopia and Vietnam, sites were purposively sampled according to predetermined criteria, which differed from country to country. In India, selection criteria were agro-climatic areas and a number of development indicators, while in Ethiopia and Vietnam they were regional and rural/urban diversity and poverty ranking. The Peru study was slightly different, in that clusters of equal population were randomly selected across the country, but then excluding districts located in the richest 5 per cent of a national poverty map. Once study sites had been selected, in all four countries, households with children in the right age group were randomly sampled. The result of this process is a pro-poor, clustered sample.

The study comprises five cohort survey rounds: the first carried out in 2002 and the last in 2016, the structure of which is shown in Table 1.1. Between these survey rounds, four rounds of qualitative research involving a mix of collective and individual methods are being carried out with a sub-sample of children and adults.

The cohort survey at the heart of Young Lives consists of community, household, and child questionnaires. The community questionnaire is designed to provide background information about the social, economic, and environmental context of each community. The household and child questionnaires gather information on topics such as household composition, livelihood and assets, food and non-food consumption and expenditure, socioeconomic status, social capital, economic changes and recent life history, childcare, child health and access to basic services, parental background, and the child's education. We also collect detailed time-use data for all family members, and information about the children's weight, height, and their comprehension of maths and language. The survey further asks the children about their daily activities and experiences, attitudes to work and school, likes and dislikes, and hopes and aspirations for the future.

The qualitative research that supplements the survey data is building a set of 200 case studies, the main focus of which is children's own experiences and the circumstances of their daily lives. In each country, 50 case study children have been selected and five rounds of data collection will document the changing trajectories of their individual lives in the contexts of their families and communities. These children were enabled to express their views individually in interviews and in group discussions; carers and teachers were also interviewed; and several activities observed. In addition to this, there are also shorter enquiries focused on context-specific issues, for example orphanhood in Ethiopia and the impact of the National Rural Employment Guarantee Scheme in India.

Table 1.1   The structure of the panel in the study countries

	Younger cohort (2,000 children)	Older cohort (1,000 children)
Round 1 (2002)	6 to 18 months	7 to 8 years
Round 2 (2006)	4 to 5 years	11 to 12 years
Round 3 (2009)	7 to 8 years	14 to 15 years
Round 4 (2013)	11 to 12 years	18 to 19 years
Round 5 (2016)	14 to 15 years	21 to 22 years

The survey work and the qualitative research feed into each other. Analysis of survey data points to research subjects and topics for more intensive research and provides patterns into which more detailed information is likely to fit. Particularly when data do not conform to established academic models, qualitative work is necessary to identify further research issues that could be included in later surveys and possible new models for analysing survey data (see Chapter 17 by Kate Orkin for an example of this process). Further, survey analysis can test the extent to which we can generalize qualitative findings. This interaction between different types of data and different kinds of analysis is a continuous process throughout the Young Lives programme.

The design of Young Lives has been shaped by the recognition that childhood poverty is a complex issue best described and analysed by integrating multiple disciplines and approaches. This multidimensional and multi-method approach is producing a unique dataset, which situates children's experiences of poverty in relation to the people around them, and the sociocultural context, institutions, services, and policies that shape their lives and opportunities. At the same time, it is producing a series of challenges arising from the collection, analysis, and use of data.

In common with all longitudinal studies, Young Lives has collected, archived, and analysed huge quantities of data. Implementing this kind of study is a long-term process and its centre is the integrity of the cohort. Ensuring low attrition rates requires building strong and lasting relationships of trust between researchers and children with their families, and investment of time in tracking children in the sample. To achieve this, wherever possible Young Lives has supported field teams to stay together and placed a strong emphasis on ethical issues in fieldworker training.

Using Young Lives findings to influence policy and practice

Informing policies and practices that will reduce childhood poverty is the underlying driver of Young Lives. A large and diverse literature however suggests that using research to influence policy is far from straightforward, especially when the research subject is complex and multidimensional (Jones 2009).

An important step in using research findings to influence policy is to be clear about what they can and cannot be used for. Young Lives data cannot be used to compare communities or countries, or to monitor poverty. The Young Lives children and their communities are not a nationally representative sample, and this shapes the kind of narratives of childhood poverty that researchers can construct from the emerging data.

Although the Young Lives data cannot indicate, for example, the percentage of children in Peru who attend a poor-quality school, it is possible to compare the outcomes for children in the Peru sample who live in a poorer household and attend a poor-quality school with the outcomes of those children who live in a better-off household and attend a poor-quality school. It is this possibility of disaggregation according to factors of social difference – whether wealth, gender, ethnicity, or caste – that makes the Young Lives dataset particularly valuable for policymakers who aim to deliver equitable development outcomes and effectively to meet the needs of different kinds of children. For example, one broad narrative to have emerged from the research is that poverty persists in families with poorly educated parents, and that children of better-educated parents are more likely to escape poverty. This can be further refined at the country level: in Vietnam for example, maternal education below primary completion is increasingly linked to extreme poverty among the children in the sample (Le Thuc et al. 2008). Such findings can be used both internationally and within countries to justify continued investment in girls' education as an effective intervention to break intergenerational poverty cycles.

The Young Lives data can also make a valuable contribution to understanding the impact of particular policies on children. Analysis of the effect of three different social protection schemes on children in Andhra Pradesh, Ethiopia, and Peru suggests that while social protection brings benefits for many children and is an important part of anti-poverty strategies, children benefit unevenly (some hardly at all), and there can be unintended consequences such as children having to do more work, which in turn can affect their school attendance and performance (Porter and Dornan 2010). Findings like these have resulted in recommendations to decision-makers about refining the design of ongoing programmes to make them more supportive of children.

The timing of data collection, as well as its subject and structure, influences how it can be used. As Young Lives runs from 2002 to 2016, the final round of data collection will take place the year after the Millennium Development Goals (MDGs) will have succeeded or failed to meet their targets. Young Lives findings are well placed to contribute detailed sub-texts to unpack widely publicized headlines, particularly regarding education. For example, the second and third MDGs concern the achievement of universal primary education and the elimination of gender disparities in education, towards which considerable progress has been achieved on a global scale. Indeed, among the Young Lives children, levels of enrolment in primary school were typically high and rising, and the difference in enrolment rates between boys and girls at 12 years old was encouragingly small. However, this positive progress has not necessarily been matched in terms of either attendance or quality. Data on the ability of 12-year-olds to read a simple sentence show clear differences in literacy levels between richer and poorer households in each country (Dornan 2010). These findings resonate with those on social protection in that they point to the importance of the quality of services as a policy issue. For services that support children to break out of poverty, part of this quality can be understood as interventions that match the realities of children's lives.

As well as running in parallel with the final years of the MDG target period, the period covered by Young Lives research has seen modest economic growth replaced with a worldwide economic instability. Comparing data from the first three rounds – 2002, 2006, and 2009 – will result in a detailed picture of how the food price crisis is affecting children and reveal changes in the frequency of different kinds of shocks experienced by Young Lives families. The character of current economic shocks draws our attention to the power of the unforeseen in longitudinal surveying. It presents Young Lives researchers with the constant challenge of creating narratives about child poverty that are relevant to contemporary policy questions in a period of rapid change, and prioritizing pathways of data analysis that will provide the most policy-relevant information quickly enough for it to be put to the best possible use.

Notes

1. The National Child Development Study (1958), the British Cohort Study (1970), and the Millennium Cohort Study (2000), all housed at the Centre for Longitudinal Studies.
2. *Seven-Up* has interviewed 14 children (selected to represent different social classes) every seven years since 1964, when the children were 7. *Child of our Time* is following 25 children (selected to represent a range of genetic, social, geographic and ethnic backgrounds) who were born around 2000 until they are 20.
3. http://www.measuredhs.com
4. See chapter 2 by Virginia Morrow for a full discussion of the ethical challenges of working with children and families in the Young Lives research.

References

Bronfenbrenner, U. (1999) 'Foreword' in G. Elder, *Twenty-fifth Anniversary Edition of Children of the Great Depression*, Boulder CO: Westview Press.

Doll, R., R. Peto, J. Boreham and I. Sutherland (2004) 'Mortality in Relation to Smoking: 50 Years' Observation on Male British Doctors', *British Medical Journal* 328: 1519.

Dornan, P. (2010) *Children and the Millennium Development Goals: Fragile Gains and Deep Inequalities*, Policy Paper 2, Oxford: Young Lives.

Elder, G. (1974) *Children of the Great Depression: Social Change in Life Experience*, Chicago IL: University of Chicago Press.

Grosh, M. and P. Glewwe (1995) *A Guide to Living Standards Measurement Study Surveys and Their Datasets*, Living Standards Measurement Study Working Paper 120, Washington DC: World Bank.

Jones, H. (2009) *Policy-making as Discourse: A Review of Recent Knowledge-to-Policy Literature*, IKM-Emergent/ODI Working Paper 5, London: Overseas Development Institute.

Le Thuc, Duc, Ngyuen Phuong Ngoc, Tran Minh Chau, Nguyen Van Tien and Vo Thanh Son (2008) *Country Report 2: Vietnam Round 2 Survey*, Oxford: Young Lives.

Porter, C. and P. Dornan (2010) *Social Protection and Children: A Synthesis of Evidence from Young Lives Longitudinal Research in Ethiopia, India and Peru*, Policy Paper 1, Oxford: Young Lives.

Wilson, I., S. Huttley and B. Fenn (2006) 'A Case Study of Sample Design for Longitudinal Research: Young Lives', *International Journal of Social Research Methodology* 9.5: 351–65.

2

The Ethics of Social Research with Children and Families in Young Lives: Practical Experiences[1]

Virginia Morrow

Introduction

Research ethics exist to ensure that the principles of justice, respect, and the avoidance of harm are upheld, by using agreed standards. These principles are universal, though there many subtleties and diversities, and how principles are understood, interpreted, and practised can vary from place to place (Ulrich 2003). Following controversies involving deception and political involvement by researchers in the social sciences, ethical codes building on these principles were developed. These codes built on earlier ones developed for medical research on humans in the Nuremburg Code (1947, following the war crimes trials) and the Declaration of Helsinki (1964). The governance of research has expanded and now includes ethical practices in social research in general (ESRC 2005, 2010) and with children in particular (Alderson and Morrow 2011; Schenk and Williamson 2005). A burgeoning literature describes the processes, practices, and difficulties that occur in social research (see, for example, Armbruster and Laerke 2008; Iphofen 2009; Mertens and Ginsberg 2009; van den Hoonard 2002).

In medical research, cases have been reported of drug companies exploiting desperate communities, without adequate attention to consent, communication, controls, and risks (see, for example, McGregor 2006). While social research, like that of Young Lives, does not pose the same kinds of physical risks as medical research, it may seriously damage people's lives, futures, reputations, and relationships, through unwanted publicity and through influence (or lack of needed influence) on policies and practices. Although informed consent and Research

Ethics Committee review may be vague and even alien concepts to many people, and burdensome to many researchers (Hammersley 2009; Dyer and Demeritt 2009), they gain clear meaning after harm occurs.

Young Lives values high-quality research, while respecting the key principles of justice, respect, and the avoidance of harm. Starting from approaches that Young Lives has adopted, this chapter identifies fundamental ethics questions and contributes to current debates about research practices, the ethics of longitudinal research with children, and research with communities in developing countries, in a spirit of shared enquiry and learning. It discusses some of the difficulties encountered in fieldwork and strategies for attempting to resolve them. The chapter concludes that an understanding of local context is central to explanations of how research participants respond to being involved in a longitudinal data-gathering exercise like Young Lives, and that some adaptation and fluidity is necessary at the local level.

Seeking research ethics approval

The academic consortium that initiated Young Lives in 2000 was attentive to research ethics within the epidemiological/medical paradigm, which is now broadly accepted in social research. For example, it developed an ethics committee in Vietnam and obtained approval from the Research Ethics Committee at the Instituto de Investigación Nutricional (IIN) in Peru, which was established in 1971, as well as from the ethics committee of the Social Science Division at the University of Oxford in 2006, for the whole study. Young Lives has utilized guidelines from the University of Oxford's Department of International Development, which are adapted from the ethical guidelines of the Association of Social Anthropologists of the Commonwealth and are based on the Helsinki guidelines as well as the Child Protection Policy of Save the Children UK (Save the Children 2003).

Young Lives' qualitative, quantitative, and policy teams have discussed research ethics in order to develop a shared understanding within the whole study. This was a complex task, involving differing academic traditions and disciplines (economists, educationalists, social anthropologists, developmental psychologists, epidemiologists, nutritionists, social work specialists, sociologists, and political scientists), and differing power dynamics within and between research teams and communities studied. Working with in-country teams may reduce 'stranger involvement', but there may remain stark social differences between researchers and respondents: there are important power dynamics when professionals of a higher social class interact with very poor research participants, and further power dynamics reflecting social divisions along the lines of gender, ethnicity, and caste (the last two highly sensitive and political issues in some countries and sites). There is also the power differential of age when adult research teams work with children as young as six or seven. Furthermore, there are differing understandings of children in each country, reflecting the different cultural, religious, and historical constructions of childhood.

Approaches to ethics questions in Young Lives have been developed in collaboration with the country research teams. The survey and the qualitative research teams undergo training sessions at which ethics are discussed, and fieldwork manuals contain detailed ethics guidance (referred to in the section on consent below). Following piloting of the qualitative research methods in 2007, a memorandum of understanding for fieldworkers was developed in collaboration with qualitative research teams, which set out some basic guidance about research procedures and respectful communication with research participants.[2] This is now being used with the survey teams too.

Experiences relate to both the household and child surveys and to the qualitative research. There is an important relationship between the two components, which from the point of view of participating families and children may not be obvious, especially as the survey round and qualitative research happen separately, with several months between them. Ethics questions can differ between the two research processes, in so far as qualitative research allows more time to build trust, learn about respondents' concerns, and so on. Young Lives qualitative data are all transcribed and coded, and include a category on participants' comments about 'relationship to Young Lives'. Thus all data from participants about their experiences of being involved in the Young Lives study, their views about the questions, and their questions to researchers can be analysed. Qualitative fieldworkers record ethics questions in their field notes as they arise and discuss these with lead researchers. These processes mean that Young Lives has already collected considerable data relating to the ethics of the research (Ames 2009; Tafere et al. 2009; Truong 2009; Vennam 2009). Survey enumerators also record questions related to ethics, and systematic analysis of these will take place in future survey rounds. In Peru, for example, survey fieldworkers are all experienced enumerators and are required to report any cases that give cause for concern – for example, relating to child protection or children's health/medical condition – to their supervisors immediately, who will try to resolve the situation with the fieldworker. The supervisors then also bring questions for discussion by the lead researchers. In some cases, direct help has been provided, but mostly people are directed to specific services or sources of advice relevant to the question. The ethics committee of IIN is also informed of these specific cases.

Consent: informed and understood, freely given, adapted in local contexts

Researchers in Young Lives must obtain the informed consent of parents or caregivers, and of children who have the capacity to consent. In Peru, for example, the IIN ethics committee recommends that, in addition to parents' or caregivers consent, 'children aged seven and older give their assent to participate' (Creed-Kanashiro et al. 2005: 926). Research teams are required to ensure that the purpose of the research is clearly explained, and that children and adults understand what they agreeing to. The fieldworker manual for the Round 3 survey states:

> No project staff should pressurize, coerce or deceive respondents in an effort to ensure their participation. Staff should also try to ensure that respondents are not pressurized by other family or community members. ... The respondents will have at least 24 hours to consider whether they want to take part and will be free to withdraw from the study at any time.

In relation to consent from children, the manual emphasizes care 'to explain in ways that they can understand why you are there, why you are interviewing them and what the information is to be used for'. It points out that children are generally taught from a very young age that they must obey adults, making it difficult for them to refuse researchers. So it must be made clear that there will be no adverse consequences for them if they refuse to take part.

Young Lives fieldworkers are clear about the limitations of the research in terms of its capacity to bring about change in research participants' lives. For example, qualitative research teams use local translations and relevant versions of the following statement when explaining the research to children:

> Young Lives is a study of children growing up in four countries – India, Peru, Vietnam and Ethiopia – taking place over 15 years. We are trying to find out about children's everyday lives: the things you do, and the important people in your life, and how these things affect how you

feel. Bits of what you say/write/draw will be used in reports that we write that we hope will be helpful to local and national governments when making plans or planning services for children in the future. Our research may not change things in the short term, because that depends on local and national governments. (Young Lives 2009)

In many parts of the world, however, people do not necessarily have any experience or understanding of what research is. Many Young Lives respondents are illiterate or semi-literate (in the case of parents) or have basic literacy (in the case of children). People who have minimal basic education and no exposure to formal manipulation of knowledge cannot be expected to fully understand the parameters of a research study of this kind.

Further, there may be differing understandings of and approaches to 'informed consent'. The ESRC Research Ethics Framework (2005) recognized that, in developing countries:

> The conventional meaning of informed consent may be problematic because the conventional model of consent rests on 'the primacy of the individual'. The individual is seen as both the owner of rights and the bearer of reciprocal duties to the rights of others. This emphasis on the individual can seem inappropriate or meaningless in some cultural contexts, where the individual may take less precedence than broader notions of kin or community. (ESRC 2005: 24. See also Brown et al. 2004)

There is a danger here of a false dichotomy between 'developing' and 'developed' countries in relation to ethics. The emphasis on the individual may seem inappropriate in some cultural contexts, but when something goes wrong and people are damaged, the focus will rightly be drawn to the interests of the individual. Second, in developed countries, children are also seldom seen as completely separate persons, since they are connected to parents/carers.

Young Lives attempts to ensure that reasonably equal minimum standards are met in relation to seeking informed consent. Research teams initially approached community leaders and then individual parents and children (similar practices operate in developed countries where negotiations take place with several 'gatekeepers' before children can be approached to be invited to participate in research; see Alderson and Morrow 2011). Informed consent is sought and recorded from parents and children by enumerators and fieldworkers at the beginning of each visit, again at the start of each session or activity, and ideally again at the end of the session in relation to how the data will be used or regarding participation in future activities. Where appropriate, researchers provide contact details of the research teams and detailed leaflets that they can read out to ensure minimum standards of information.

Within the qualitative research, there is a constant process of attempting to check participants' understandings. Some teams have found that signing a paper consent form is not acceptable for various reasons, mostly because people are wary of putting their signature on forms, and so they have voice-recorded verbal consent with the digital recordings being stored (but not transcribed). Other teams have found it inappropriate to use voice-recorders, but are recording their experiences of the consent process in their field notes. Consent is understood to be an ongoing process. A fieldworker in Vietnam noted that 'local people ask lots of questions about us as researchers and the research, and we always take time and interest not only to satisfy their curiosity but also to get their feedback about the research itself'.

The following example from India illustrates the consent process, with one of the qualitative research team explaining the study to an Older Cohort girl:

> We are coming from *Young Lives*. We told you about this study in detail in the morning. While we were conducting the group activity, we told you why we came to your village, and what we wanted to know about you. Now the interview which we are going to do is totally about your personal information. [A list of examples follows.] We came here to know all these things. So now we are going to start our interview. If it is a long interview and if you feel like stopping it you can ask us to stop, we shall stop there, ... we shall continue tomorrow. You can also stop me if you don't understand any of the questions that I ask. OK! Shall we begin?[3]

In the second round of the qualitative research in Ethiopia, an Older Cohort child declined to participate, despite his parents' willingness for him to do so. 'There was some speculation from the caregiver that the boy had heard a rumour from his friends that Young Lives has a mission to convert children to Protestantism' (Tafere et al. 2009). This demonstrates differences in views between parents and children, though of course parents may have had similar fears. That children's views about participation are respected must be understood positively as informed consent operating in practice. Further, this situation may change on the next visit, in which case, children's or adults' previous refusal could be explored with them if they were willing.

In Young Lives, research relationships have to be sustained over a long period of time and informed consent has to be renewed, which is difficult if the research is not promising to improve people's lives. Notwithstanding the emphasis on continual consent, the loss of participants from the samples in Young Lives has been less than 2 per cent per annum, and is usually due to the death of children (see Outes-Leon and Dercon 2008 for a detailed analysis and comparison with other longitudinal studies in developing countries).

Research in very poor communities

As noted, it is inevitably difficult for people to understand the parameters of a complex study like Young Lives. Many of the study sites are recipients of a range of intervention projects, both governmental and non-governmental, that offer services and may sometimes make unrealistic promises (see, for example, Olivier de Sardan 2005). Frequently, participants assume that Young Lives is an intervention from which benefits can be extracted or expected (see also Nyambedha 2008). Requests for personal assistance from members of poor communities to visitors of all kinds are so common, despite constant explanations, that this is likely to be a generic situation. In some communities, research teams have found widely differing conceptions about the purpose of the research. These are usually locally specific, linked to a history of interventions, and difficult to modify through conventional ethics procedures. For example, in Ethiopia, the interviewer asked the caregiver of a Younger Cohort girl if she had any questions or suggestions:

> *Caregiver*: What I want to request is if you have something to help me with her education. Maybe if you have something to help me, especially the payment...

In Peru, parents associated Young Lives with aid interventions. Even though fieldworkers explained that there are no material benefits other than gifts for their children (that is, books and crayons), parents remained hopeful: 'Maybe one day you bring some help/benefit for us [laughter]'; 'Maybe when he's studying, you [Young Lives] can help me with it'.

> *Fieldworker*: And your father approved of Niños del Milenio [Young Lives]?
> *Older Cohort boy*: Yes, because he said it could bring some aid.

In another example from a group discussion in Peru, a professional asked the fieldworker about the purpose of the study. The fieldworker started to explain, but another professional interrupted and mentioned that there was a problem with the programme *Juntos* (a government-run conditional cash transfer programme). He claimed that fieldworkers from Young Lives had told him that all children who participated in the study would become direct beneficiaries of the *Juntos* programme. Other families confused Young Lives with non-governmental organizations (NGOs) like Intervida, which sponsors children and communities.

Despite explanations, the idea that Young Lives is associated with the government remains. This perception is partly accurate in Vietnam and Ethiopia, where government departments are involved in data collection. Further explanations for it may lie in the use of a clearly recognizable logo and also the involvement of Save the Children UK (an international aid agency) in the study.

There are often gaps between what is supposed to happen, the procedures put in place to ensure that it does happen, the way these procedures are actually implemented by fieldworkers, how fieldworkers describe this, and how people interpret interventions (see Fairhead et al. 2005: 106, discussing a vaccine trial in The Gambia). Although these disjunctions occur in all kinds of research, they are particularly likely in a large, longitudinal, interdisciplinary, international study with vulnerable groups such as very disadvantaged children. There may be a 'therapeutic misconception' that arises when people expect some benefits to come from their involvement. The research teams ask detailed questions about household expenditure, and some people living in poverty may understandably take every opportunity to ask for help and money, especially when they want to spend their limited time and resources on activities that will bring them direct benefits. In poor communities, it is likely that any outsiders who are not strictly government representatives providing government services will become the objects of speculation, and in this process, it is difficult for people to distinguish research from intervention.

A problem has sometimes arisen in translation, and particularly in the use of the term 'project' (see Olivier de Sardan 2005: 179). For example, a fieldworker in Vietnam noted:

> both at provincial and local levels, the term 'project' has become loaded with expectations for material and financial benefits, sometimes an instant remuneration. A research project without direct material benefits like Young Lives requires significant efforts to

explain itself against the grain. ... [We were warned] about this aspect quite early before the field research started. We later found [the] warning described the expectations of officials, teachers, education administrators and village cadres more closely than those of the ordinary people. (Truong 2009)

In Ethiopia, however, Young Lives is known as a *tinat*, which means 'study'. In Peru, the word *estudio* is used, which also translates as study. The word for research is avoided, because it can be translated as *inves tigación*, which may be confused with the word the police use for an investigation. The research teams emphasize that Young Lives is not an intervention or a programme evaluation. Peru teams do also use the word *proyecto*, but this is followed by a description that explains that it is a study.

Reciprocity in research: rewards, compensation, and giving something back

Compensating or paying research participants raises ethics questions. Payments can be made to reimburse expenses; to compensate for time, inconvenience, and possible discomfort; to show appreciation for participants' help; or to pay for people's help. According to the ESRC Framework for Research Ethics 2010, a balance has to be struck between coercion and 'incentivization'.

There should be no coercion of research participants to take part in the research. Adult research participants, however, may be given small monetary reimbursement for their time and expenses involved. ... Where children are involved, it is often appropriate to acknowledge their help with gifts to participating schools and/or personal gifts. In short, incentives may be permissible, but anything which implies coercion is not. (ESRC 2010: 29–30)

This has implications for informed consent. As Creed-Kanashiro et al. (2005: 925) suggest, 'cultural context may limit truly independent consent and may also be distorted through the giving of incentives in populations in limited economic circumstances'. Payments to encourage people to take part may in such cases contravene Nuremberg standards against persuasion or pressure of any kind on participants (Alderson and Morrow 2011; see also Wendler et al. 2002). On the other hand, the Association of Social Anthropologists of the UK and Commonwealth guidelines (ASA 1999) recommend, 'There should be no economic exploitation of individual informants, translators and research participants; *fair return* should be made for their help and services' (emphasis added). Others may rightly challenge the differential treatment of children and adults advocated by the ESRC guidance, which suggests that children should not be paid.

Each country research team deals with this in locally specific ways, reflecting cultural contexts about the value of people's time, their willingness to undertake research activities 'for the common good', and the reality of poverty and not having the capacity to miss a day's wages to spend time talking with researchers. Some country teams pay respondents, including children, for their participation. Others give small gifts as a 'thank you'. Norms and patterns of reciprocity, notions of community, and/or doing what the government tells you (for example, in Vietnam where government census enumerators are administering the survey) are likely to affect people's participation. However, paying respondents (adults and Older Cohort children) to compensate them for their time may cause some confusion, as the following example shows.

In Ethiopia, children were encouraged to use the money they received for participating to buy school materials. During the first round of qualitative research, the Ethiopian research team noted that, in the situation of extreme poverty, people perceived Young Lives as an aid agency and money received as aid. In the second round, researchers paid more attention to explaining that Young Lives does not provide any aid to the community in general nor to the research households in particular (Tafere et al. 2009).

Other country research teams (Peru, for example) are giving small gifts as a 'thank you', as well as some supplies to local schools. In India, research teams provide some resources to schools (for example) as requested by local community leaders to benefit all children in the locality, and up to 2009, were not making direct payment to research participants. However, in some cases, research respondents consider it unfair that they are giving up their time but benefits are for everyone in the community.

The question of remuneration to Young Lives' research respondents is becoming increasingly important as economies become more market-oriented. For example, in Andhra Pradesh, the National Rural Employment Guarantee Scheme, which pays household members at least Rs. 80 (the equivalent of £1) for a morning's work, has recently been implemented. Whereas in the past, the opportunity cost of spending time talking to a researcher may have been zero, or negligible, since respondents could carry out domestic chores or work on the farm while researchers talked to them, they are now becoming more aware of the financial value of their time and are more likely to expect monetary compensation. Thus the decision has been made to compensate respondents for their time in subsequent research rounds. Similar patterns might apply in the other countries. Young Lives may run a risk of people refusing to participate in future: fieldworkers report that, especially in urban areas, it is already difficult to persuade people to continue to be involved. This is not to suggest that people should not be paid when they most need it – after all, the duress to accept monetary incentives is created by poverty, not by the incentives. Rather, it is to suggest that care has to be exercised here, and awareness that it may be difficult for low-status people living in poverty to refuse requests to participate in the research.

As the research progresses, Young Lives is developing ways to give something back to communities, and people are eager to know what happens to the information they provide. Preliminary findings are reported to the communities involved in the research at meetings in a manner that is accessible to them and highlights the usefulness of the data they are providing. In some countries, this is accompanied by further useful information, about, for example, nutrition in Peru and local services in Ethiopia. However, there remains a need to produce research summaries or short reports in language appropriate to the dif-fering groups, according to age or culture. Reports to communities also explain how Young Lives is taking messages to governments and is advo-cating for change. However, this raises questions about the likelihood of governments (or local policymakers) taking notice of research findings, and in the case of longitudinal research, the time taken for research findings to work their way into the policy domain. It was noted in Peru that while families react positively to the explanation that Young Lives is a study to gather information to inform public policy targeted at all children, 'they are distrustful of any real impact of the information Young Lives provides in improving the current situation of poverty, because they distrust the government and feel abandoned by it' (Ames 2009).

Further work can reveal what information people would find useful, rather than presenting very general findings about the whole country. For example, in Peru, fieldworkers noted that parents said that they would like to learn more about their own children and, since they attended the group sessions and talked to the fieldworkers, perhaps they could get more information about their children's behaviour and feelings, and so on. In one site in Peru, parents were worried about the presence of gangs and wanted to know about their children's whereabouts. They saw Young Lives activities as a way of obtaining advice on this issue. However, even this poses problems since researchers promise children they will not tell others what they say and emphasize that children's confidentiality must be respected: with such small numbers in each community it would be difficult to mask identities.

In some cases, community representatives and professionals such as teachers expressed expectations about the research. For example, in one site in Peru, a group of participating teachers said that they would like Young Lives to explain to parents about the benefits of early childhood education and persuade them to bring their children to kindergarten. Other teachers asked about fieldworkers' observations in the classrooms: they wanted to know how the children in their class were doing and also to receive some advice. All of this needs consideration against the risk that Young Lives could come to be seen as 'intervention' or 'evaluation', which has implications for further rounds of data collection.

A further benefit to local communities from the research process may be the encouragement of reflection, mentioned in the section below on the effects of research. This is particularly relevant to children who are encouraged to speak about matters that affect them.

The need for reciprocity is acknowledged in Young Lives research, but the level and type of reciprocity is decided by the country teams. Results have varied and Young Lives is cataloguing each country's approach to enable local adaptation while respecting key principles.

Child protection and parents' fears

Research teams are encouraged to discuss concerns with lead quantitative or qualitative researchers, whilst the research team based at Oxford provides guidance and support following internationally accepted protection policies. There is growing sensitivity as children mature about having gender-balanced field teams where possible, which is partly a child protection question and partly an attempt to respect local norms related to gender-appropriate behaviour (that is, men and women being together).

In some sites, although parents have very high expectations of the research, they also have fears about what might happen to their children, some of which relate to child protection. In Ethiopia, for example, some parents believed their children might be taken abroad (to the USA) to be educated, and some felt worried about this. One mother preferred to stay with her child during the interview and later revealed to the researcher that she was guarding her child because she feared that he might be taken abroad for adoption. Research teams are consequently careful to reassure parents and other adults in the community that children will not be taken away.

In Peru also, among some indigenous highland communities and other rural communities located in the poorest regions, parents are frightened that Young Lives children will be taken away by outsiders. These fears relate to local myths about indigenous people being abducted and murdered for their 'fat', which have a very long history and relate to any outsiders The myths have arisen in the long history of discrimination from the earliest years of Spanish colonization: it was rumoured that Spanish conquerors and missionaries wanted the fat of native people for all kinds of purposes (Vasquez del Aguila 2007). Besides, newspapers in Peru have made much of child kidnapping in the context of hostility to inter-country adoptions. A local authority worker in a group discussion in Peru commented that there were rumours in the community that Young Lives were going to take children away. When the fieldworker reassured them, a questioner wanted further assurance that the field team were all Peruvians.

This is a positive reflection of the research relationship, suggesting that people feel they can express their fears and concerns to fieldworkers. While these are different versions of stranger-danger myths from those in Ethiopia, underlying them all may be similar ideas about powerful people coming into communities who will 'change our lives' for good or ill.

Explaining archiving

Archiving data is a relatively new requirement. Although there are rigorous controls on access to archived data, archiving any form of data presents difficulties for notions of informed consent, because the later uses of the research data cannot be anticipated and so cannot be explained to people (Alderson 1998). The Economic and Social Data Service (the UK data archive organization) has guidance on how to seek consent from adults for their data to be archived, indicating who will have access to the information and how it will be used. In relation to children, it recommends that 'storage of data should be explained in a way that children can understand' (ESDS n.d.). But the document does not provide examples of how to do this (see Goodenough et al. 2003; Alderson 1998). Young Lives research teams explain what archiving is and reassure participants that anonymity will be preserved and identifying features (of places, people, organizations) disguised when data are sent for archiving.

In Peru, the term *un archivo* is understood, since almost all villages and communities own publicly accessible archives with documentation regarding the village. In India, researchers suggested 'stored in a computer'. In Vietnam, researchers noted:

> We used the word 'storage' (pack and store away), pointing to a cupboard or wardrobe or trunk if any of those are available in the house, or simply a box or a bag. Since we brought our laptop to the field, children saw us typing notes. We showed them what we typed – excerpts of transcripts of what they said (even if some can't read) – and pictures (of their house, no person). We also replayed a short part of the tape so that they could hear their voice. We then explained that all of these will be kept in Hanoi and England for many years but nobody will know that these words are theirs or go after them because of what they said. The children and their family members were quite excited, some were scared at first, then became very proud. (Truong 2009)

The effects on children and families of being involved in the research: prolonged contact

In Peru, some parents were not sure about the length of the study. Some thought it was going to follow up children until they were 15, others until they were 20 years old. Other parents expressed their wish to keep in touch after the study was over.

> *Fieldworker*: The project is supposed to last until children are 15, then it is over, and then we'll leave you in peace.
> *Caregiver*: Hmm, and that's it then. And, what if one day they study and became professionals and remember they're Niños del Milenio? Where can they reach you?

There are likely to be both short- and long-term effects on children, their families, and their communities because of their involvement in the research since the study asks questions that encourage reflection and might affect (for example) educational motivation. Some participants may continue to welcome the research, while others may resent the continued involvement. As one Ethiopian caregiver (of an Older Cohort boy) reflects:

> Your follow-up is good. In earlier times we didn't know if the support was going to start or not. ... You have identified the children who have lost parents and who have parents. And it is for the future of the lives of children. ... So I have positive comment on Young Lives, I am happy about it. The child also has been filled with hope because of this study. All I have is this and I thank you.

In the second round of qualitative data collection in India, at the end of a group discussion, Older Cohort boys reflected on the research:

> I have not seen any time [before] children meeting together and discussing about their matters. Till now no one has discussed like this with children. We feel happy that [research] team members mingle with us. Earlier we never spoke [up] in front of anybody. But now we are able to speak out in front of people like you without any fear, and this helped us in having courage, and now I know what I will become in my future. Within these two years, we have come to know how to speak with elders.

Suggestions for future rounds of research

Young Lives will continue to develop its memorandum of understanding (Young Lives 2009; referred to above) with research teams and fieldworkers, adapting it as we learn more about doing longitudinal research with children and families. Questions about informed consent and managing raised expectations clearly need constant reflection and development. The possible effects on children and families of being involved in such detailed research also need to be monitored over time.

A great advantage of long-term research is that it provides time to learn and adapt methods and standards to fit people's views more closely. Some of the research activities may be experienced as time-consuming and difficult. Some of the questions in the surveys are complex (for example, asking people to recall very precise amounts of foodstuffs, or asking children to write about unfamiliar concepts) and children and adults may have difficulty answering them. In developing the Round 3 survey, certain sensitive and intrusive questions were discussed in depth and dropped or refocused in particular country contexts, in case they cause distress or difficulties. For example, in Ethiopia, because of the political situation, it would be insensitive to ask about participation in political protests. Subsequent rounds of the survey have been adapted to minimize these difficulties, but there is a clash here with the need for continuity of data and questions.

Such factors may change from one year to the next. For example, in two of the sites in recent qualitative research in Peru, levels of distrust seem to be higher than they were on the previous visit, despite the explanations provided. However, the fact that these fears were shared openly could arise from greater trust in the field team. In one site, there seemed to be a decline in trust in general within the community towards local organizations and services because of an unsettling incident involving the arrest of a local leader (Ames 2009). When research teams visit, they are not going into neutral situations – situations change very rapidly and these changes themselves need careful research and documentation.

Conclusion

This chapter has shown how Young Lives has paid attention to the general principles of research ethics. Matters like consent and reciprocity are not straightforward when people meet from different social and cultural backgrounds, with different class and educational status, and with unbalanced power relations (especially those relating to age). The principles of research ethics, therefore, have to be adapted and applied to particular situations and particular times. Locally appropriate codes of practice require input from all stakeholders. Moreover, they require careful communication of the nature of the research, and realistic expectations of what it can offer, to the people who provide information. This adaptation and communication in turn requires knowledge and experience of local situations.

This chapter has shown that attention to research ethics needs to be on-going, requiring continual learning at all levels. Long-term research poses difficulties in establishing relationships with communities that are both ethical and enable the research to continue. It also offers the opportunity to learn about relationships between researchers and researched and how to fine-tune these according to sound ethical principles.

This process also requires learning on all sides. While researchers explain to those being researched, the nature and purpose of the research, researchers must also be learning from those they are researching. Ethical research must take into account the understanding and values in communities being studied. Reciprocity requires learning from them what they find useful. Lessons arising from the experiences in particular locations and attempts to solve problems may help researchers in other situations to improve their practices. This requires communication and learning at a further level: between country research teams, aided by the central co-ordinating team. The central team takes guidance from its own researchers as well as from a range of bodies outside the project, including academic bodies, international NGOs, and national and local bodies governing ethics. Ideally the lessons learned can be reported back to such bodies, and this can help research governance bodies to understand the possibilities of local adaptation based on specific conditions and cultures.

Notes

1. The author would like to thank the children and families and communities; fieldworkers for faithfully recording their observations; Young Lives staff in the study countries for their invaluable experiences and insights from fieldwork; and Maggie Black, Caitlin Porter, and Young Lives staff in Oxford, who all provided many helpful comments.
2. http://www.younglives.org.uk/what-we-do/research-methods/ethics
3. Interviews transcribed here are from the second round of qualitative research conducted in 2007/08.

References

Alderson, P. (1998) 'Confidentiality and Consent in Qualitative Research', *BSA Network* 69: 6–7.
Alderson, P. and V. Morrow (2011) *The Ethics of Research with Children and Young People: A Practical Handbook,* London: Sage.
Ames, P. (2009) 'Peru Data Gathering Report: Second Qualitative Round of Data Collection in 2008', internal document, Oxford: Young Lives.
Armbruster, H. and A. Laerke (2008) *Taking Sides: Ethics, Politics and Fieldwork in Anthropology,* Oxford: Berghahn.
ASA (Association of Social Anthropologists) (1999) *Ethical Guidelines for Good Research Practice,* www.theasa.org (accessed 8 April 2010).
Brown, N., M. Boulton, G. Lewis and A. Webster (2004 version 2) *Social Science Research Ethics in Developing Countries and Contexts,* ESRC Research Ethics Framework Discussion Paper 3, www.esrc.ac.uk (accessed 7 April 2009).
Creed-Kanashiro, H., B. Ore, M. Scurrah, A. Gil and M. Penny (2005) 'Conducting Research in Developing Countries: Experiences of the Informed Consent Process from Community Studies in Peru', *Journal of Nutrition* 135: 925–8.

Dyer, S. and D. Demeritt (2009) 'Un-Ethical Review? Why it is Wrong to Apply the Medical Model of Research Governance to Human Geography', *Progress in Human Geography* 33.1: 46–64.

ESDS (Economic and Social Data Service) (n.d.) *Legal and Ethical Issues in Interviewing Children*, www.esds.ac.uk (accessed 12 April 2008).

ESRC (Economic and Social Research Council) (2005) *Research Ethics Framework*, www.esrc.ac.uk (accessed 7 April 2009).

ESRC (Economic and Social Research Council) (2010) *Framework for Research Ethics*, www.esrc.ac.uk (accessed 8 April 2010).

Fairhead, J., M. Leach and M. Small (2005) 'Public Engagement with Science? Local Understandings of a Vaccine Trial in the Gambia', *Journal of Biosocial Science* 38: 103–16.

Goodenough, T., E. Williamson, J. Kent and R. Ashcroft (2003) '"What Did You Think About That?" Researching Children's Participation in a Longitudinal Genetic Epidemiological Study', *Children and Society* 17.2: 113-25.

Hammersley, M. (2009) 'Against the Ethicists: On the Evils of Ethical Regulation', *International Journal of Social Research Methodology* 12.3: 211–25.

Iphofen, R. (2009) *Ethical Decision-Making in Social Research*, Basingstoke: Palgrave Macmillan.

McGregor, J. (2006) 'Does the Use of Human Subjects in Research in Developing Nations Violate Their Human Rights? If So, Are Reparations an Appropriate Response?', *Journal of Social Philosophy* 37.3: 441–63.

Mertens, D. and P. Ginsberg (2009) *The Handbook of Social Research Ethics*, London: Sage.

Nyambedha, E. (2008) 'Ethical Dilemmas of Social Science Research on AIDS and Orphanhood in Western Kenya', *Social Science and Medicine* 67: 771–9.

Olivier de Sardan, J.P. (2005) *Anthropology and Development. Understanding Contemporary Social Change*, London: Zed Books.

Outes-Leon, I. and S. Dercon (2008) 'Survey Attrition and Attrition Bias in Young Lives', Technical Note 5, Oxford: Young Lives.

Save the Children (2003) *Child Protection Policy*, www.savethechildren.net/alliance/resources/child_protection.pdf (accessed 21 July 2009).

Schenk, K. and J. Williamson (2005) *Ethical Approaches to Gathering Information from Children and Adolescents in International Settings: Guidelines and Resources*, Washington DC: Population Council.

Tafere, Y., W. Abebe and A. Assazinew (2009) 'Ethiopia Data Gathering Report 2008: Second Qualitative Round of Data Collection', internal document, Oxford: Young Lives.

Truong, H.C. (2009) 'Qualitative Sub-Study on Ethnic Minority Education in Vietnam: Data Gathering Report', internal document, Oxford: Young Lives.

Ulrich, G. (2003) 'Charges and Counter-charges of Ethical Imperialism: Towards a Situated Approach to Development Ethics' in P. Quarles van Ufford and A.K. Giri (eds) *A Moral Critique of Development: In Search of Global Responsibilities*, London: Routledge.

Van den Hoonard, A. (2002) *Walking the Tightrope: Ethical Issues for Qualitative Researchers*, Toronto: University of Toronto Press.

Vasquez del Aguila, E. (2007) 'Myth, Rumor, Resistance and Structural Inequalities in Colonial and Modern Peru', Unpublished paper, Sociomedical

Sciences and Anthropology, Columbia University–Mailman School of Public Health, New York, http://interculturalidad.org (accessed 19 May 2009).

Vennam, U. (2009) 'Andhra Pradesh, India, Data Gathering Report 2008: Second Qualitative Round of Data Collection', internal document, Oxford: Young Lives.

Wendler, D., J. Rackoff, E. Emanuel and G. Grady (2002) 'Commentary: The Ethics of Paying for Children's Participation in Research', *Journal of Pediatrics* 141.2:166–71.

Young Lives (2009) 'Memorandum of Understanding for Young Lives Field Researchers. Key Points: Respecting Children in Research', internal document, Oxford: Young Lives.

3
Uncovering the Consequences of Pre-School Malnutrition[1]

John Hoddinott

Introduction

Researchers involved in Young Lives will have obtained data on the nutritional status of children as pre-schoolers. Subsequent rounds of data collection have generated more information on the human capital of these individuals, including school attainments and measures of cognitive ability such as reading scores and tests of vocabulary. A natural research topic is the exploration of the consequences of pre-school nutrition on these outcomes; this work would join the numerous cross-sectional studies that document associations between pre-school nutritional status and subsequent attainments such as schooling and cognitive development. However, it is important to recognize that these are *associations,* not necessarily *causal* relationships, because pre-school nutritional status and subsequent attainments *both* reflect household decisions regarding investments in children's human capital.

Suppose we divide a child's life into two periods. Period 1 is the period of investment in the child in the pre-school years, while period 2 is the time during which parents make investments in the child's schooling. An outcome of period 1 is a child's nutritional status (measured by their height for age) that reflects *observable* parental decisions on investing in his or her health, *observable* child characteristics and *unobservable* parental and child characteristics. An outcome of period 2 could be an aspect of cognitive ability. This too will be a function of *observable,* and *unobservable,* parental and household characteristics. For example, faced with a short child in period 1, parents might subsequently allocate more food and other health resources to that child, or perhaps encourage greater school effort on the presumption that the child is unlikely to be successful in manual labour as an adult.

Because of these correlated unobservable characteristics, associations in cross-sectional data may substantially overstate or understate true causal effects.

Understanding the causal links between malnutrition and later life attainments – the question of whether the past history of these children determines their destiny – is at the heart of the Young Lives research programme. This chapter provides a formal explanation of the complexities associated with modelling the causal links between pre-school malnutrition and subsequent outcomes and suggests empirical strategies that Young Lives and other researchers might use to address these complexities.

The problem

In technical terms, the estimation problem can be interpreted as one in which the researcher wishes to model the determinants of a vector of outcomes (here, levels of children's human capital). These are the result of the child's family solving a dynamic programming problem, subject to the constraints imposed by the characteristics of the child and resources available to the family and the community in which they reside. In less technical terms, for purposes of exposition, we divide a child's life into two periods.[2] Period 1 is the period where parents make 'investments' in the child. In the Young Lives context, we could think of this period as the time when the child is a pre-schooler and the investments are those that affect his or her nutritional status as represented by his/her height given his/her age (H_{1k}). Period 2 is some subsequent point in time when we again observe this child. Height for age in period 1 reflects factors such as the prices of goods and services that affect child height (for example, the price of food and access to health care), child characteristics (such as age and sex), and household characteristics such as education, age, and wealth. We represent these factors by the term – strictly speaking a vector – (Z_{1k}) and write the determinants of height as[3]:

$$H_{1k} = \alpha_{Z1}Z_{1k} + v_{1k} \qquad (1)$$

The term v_{1k} captures those factors that affect height but are not observed by us, the social scientists. We can think of it as having three additive components ($v_{1k} = \varepsilon_H + \varepsilon_k + \varepsilon_I$) where ε_H represents unobserved characteristics of the home environment that do not change over time and are common to all the children in the home; ε_k reflects child-specific

characteristics that do not change over time, such as their genetic potential for growth; and ε_1, reflects purely random unobserved factors.

In the second period, the outcome from (1), H_{1k}, appears on the right-
hand side of the function:

$$A_{2k} = \alpha_H H_{1k} + \alpha_{Z2}Z_{2k} + v_{2k} \qquad (2)$$

If A_{2k} represents, say, the educational attainment of the child, then
equation (2) states that this is affected by his/her nutritional status (specifically her height) t, which we observed in period 1, plus a vector,
Z_{2k}, of those factors – prices, child and household characteristics – that
affect academic performance. Some of the components of Z_{2k}, but not
necessarily all, will be those found in Z_{1k}. Again we have a term, like
v_{1k}, v_{2k}, with three components: η_H, representing aspects of the home
environment which influence schooling and are common to all children in the household (this would capture, for example, parents' attitude towards schooling); η_k, which captures child-specific effects, such
as innate ability and motivation, that are not controlled by parents;
and η_2, a purely random term. The basic difficulty with ordinary least
squares (OLS) regression of (2), as noted by Behrman (1996) is the likelihood that $E(H_{1k}v_{2k}) \neq 0$ because of possible correlation between H_{1k}
and η_H or between H_{1k} and η_k mediated through either the correlation
of household effects or individual effects or both. That is, either $E(\varepsilon_H\eta_H)$
$\neq 0$ or $E(\varepsilon_k\eta_k) \neq 0$.

Such correlations could arise for several reasons. For example, a child
with high genetic growth potential will be, relative to his/her peers,
taller in both periods 1 and 2. Conversely, children with innately poor
health may be more likely to die between periods 1 and 2, leaving a
selected sample of individuals with, on average, better genetic growth
potential. Parents observing outcomes in period 1 may respond in a
variety of ways. For example, faced with a short child in period 1, parents might subsequently allocate more food and other health resources
to that child, or perhaps encourage greater school effort on the presumption that the child is unlikely to be successful in manual labour
as an adult. In any of these cases, estimates of α_H using ordinary least
squares will be biased.

Possible solutions

Where Young Lives' surveys have collected sibling data, it is possible
to estimate equation (2) using a household, or maternal, fixed-effects

model (also described as a siblings-difference model). Loosely put, in this approach, the dependent variable becomes the difference in outcomes between siblings, and the variables used as regressors are the differences between siblings in the variables that are found in Z_{2k}. As η_H does not vary across children in the same household, it (the characteristics common to all children within the household that do not change over time) effectively drops out of the regression. This purges the parameter estimates of the correlation between H_{1k} and η_H. However, as Glewwe et al. (2001) note, this leaves unresolved the correlation between H_{1k} and η_k.

An estimation strategy that does break the correlation between H_{1k} and η_k is the use of instrumental variables. At the heart of this approach is the search for variables ('instruments') that affect H_{1k} but do not affect A_{2k}. In the econometrics literature, these are referred to as the criteria of 'relevance' and 'uncorrelatedness', respectively. By relevance, we mean that the instrument has a measurable effect on H_{1k}. By uncorrelatedness, we mean that it has no effect on A_{2k} over and above the effect working through H_{1k}. Both relevance and uncorrelatedness can be tested using the battery of diagnostic statistics described in Baum et al. (2003). What makes this strategy difficult to execute is the need to satisfy both criteria. In our example above, mother's schooling would seem to satisfy the relevance criteria, given the plethora of studies showing a positive impact of maternal education on child anthropometric status. But it is also likely to have a direct effect on children's educational attainment and thus will not satisfy the uncorrelatedness requirement.

This estimation strategy was used by Behrman et al. (2008) in their analysis of the determinants of cognitive skills in adulthood. As part of their analysis, they explored the impact of pre-school nutritional status on adult cognitive skills. They used, as an instrument, whether the individual was exposed, between birth and the age of 36 months, to a community-level nutrition intervention – a nutritious supplement called *atole* that had been randomly allocated across the localities where these individuals had resided as pre-schoolers.[4] The supplement improved the nutritional status of these individuals and Behrman et al. could show therefore that it was 'relevant'. But because the supplement was randomly assigned, it was not correlated with v_{2k}. Put more precisely, this instrument is a cohort-specific shock, which is uncorrelated with η_H and η_k (because of random assignment) and is individual specific (because exposure to the supplement depends on the timing of the availability of the intervention and the child's date of birth). Note that Behrman et al. use exposure to, not actual take-up of, the supplement, as their intervention. Take-up reflects, in part, parental decisions regarding investments in their children which may, as discussed above, be responsive to η_k and thus would not be a valid instrument.

Not all, and indeed perhaps none, of the Young Lives study sites have a randomized intervention present to use in this way. What other variables could be considered as instruments? Alderman et al. (2006) combined maternal fixed-effects estimation with instrumental variables to sweep out correlation between H_{1k} and η_k. Given the nature of the data collection undertaken in the Young Lives studies, this represents a potentially feasible approach and so here we describe it in some detail.

Alderman et al. (2006) used longitudinal data of households and children residing in three resettlement areas of rural Zimbabwe, specifically data collected in 1983/84, 1987, and 2000. The 1983/84 and 1987 rounds obtained valid measurements on heights of all children who were offspring of the household head and aged 6 months to 6 years. In 2000, these individuals were traced and data were collected on their height and schooling attainments. As we, the authors, note, the fact the initial surveys were spread out over time leads to a wide range of birth dates, from September 1978 to September 1986. This was a tumultuous period in Zimbabwe's history. Children born in the late 1970s entered the world during a vicious civil war. Nearly half the sample was born into families that, during this period, were housed in what were euphemistically described as 'protected villages'. In areas where conflict was most intense, residents were forced to abandon their homesteads and move to these hastily constructed villages, with no amenities and with restrictions on physical movement. The transition to majority rule was complete by mid-1980, and in 1981 households in this sample began the process of resettlement, in which they acquired access to considerably larger land holdings than they had enjoyed in the pre-independence period. However, almost immediately afterwards, they were affected by two back-to-back droughts, in 1982–83 and 1983–84. Circumstances began to improve substantially in the years that followed, with better rainfall levels and improvements in services such as agricultural extension and health facilities.

There are two features of these data which, from a Young Lives perspective, are noteworthy. First, there are observations on two or more children within the same household (as pre-schoolers and as young adults); indeed in nearly all cases, these are offspring of the same mother. As a result, estimating model (2) using maternal fixed-effects eliminates the impact of η_H on their estimates. A further attractive feature of this approach is that it sweeps out any effects of selective attrition at the household level.

Second, we argued that these shocks – the war and the drought – are plausible instruments for initial nutritional status. Specifically, we constructed two 'child-specific' shock variables. The first is the logarithm of the number of days a child was living prior to 18 August 1980. This captures all the 'shocks' associated with the war and the immediate post-independence period. The second is a '1982–84 drought shock' dummy variable. Recall that the drought was spread out over a two-year period and that the first survey was spread out over 1983 and 1984. Hoddinott and Kinsey (2001) demonstrated that in rural Zimbabwe, the age range of 12–24 months is where drought shocks seem to have their greatest impact on children's height for age. Given the dates of the first survey, this variable equals 1 if the child was observed in 1983 and was aged between 12 and 24 months or was observed in 1984 and was aged between 12 and 36 months, and equals 0 otherwise.[5]

Table 3.1 summarizes the results of this estimation strategy for two outcomes: height and grade attainment at follow up. The ordinary least squares (OLS) estimates that ignore the econometric problems discussed above are shown in columns (1) and (3). The maternal fixed effects – estimates of instrumental variables that Alderman et al. claim resolve these – are found in columns (2) and (4). The striking feature here is that the OLS estimates dramatically *underestimate* the effects of early life nutritional status on long-term outcomes.

Are these results credible? At the heart of this approach are two assumptions: these shocks are of sufficient magnitude and persistence to affect a child's stature and sufficiently transitory *not* to affect the

Table 3.1 Maternal fixed effects: Instrumental variables estimates of the determinants of height and grade attainment

	Height at follow-up		Grades attained at follow-up	
	(1)	(2)	(3)	(4)
	OLS estimates	Instrumental variables, maternal fixed effects	OLS estimates	Instrumental variables, maternal fixed effects
Child height for age	1.730	2.677	0.222	0.678
z-score	(8.38)**	(1.98)**	(3.64)**	(2.13)**

Notes: See Alderman et al. (2006), Tables 4 and 5 for full specification details. Numbers in parentheses are absolute values of t statistics (columns 1 and 3) and z-statistics (columns 2 and 4). ** Significant at the 5% level.

siblings' stature. That is, they need to find instruments that affect H_{1k} vary across children within the same household, and are sufficiently transitory *not* to affect A_{2k}; that is, they must meet the criteria of instrument relevance and instrument uncorrelatedness. We argue that while all household members face the shock at the same time, not all children face the shock at the same age: consequently these variables differ for the purpose of identification since they specify the identifying variables in terms of a shock at a given age for the individual. Further, we show that these instruments satisfy the relevance assumption. More controversial is our assumption that the uncorrelatedness property holds. Strauss and Thomas note that the impact of the drought is likely to have lasted several years through its impact on grain storage and prices and on livestock holdings and prices: it could thus have effects on human capital accumulation beyond those captured by Z_{1k}. Similarly, the civil war could have had emotional or social consequences that affected children beyond their pre-school years. In our paper, we show that these variables pass the uncorrelatedness test. This gives some reassurance that these are indeed valid instruments.

Concluding remarks

In the context of the Young Lives study, the use of cohort-specific, community-level shocks that are uncorrelated with unobservable child characteristics represents a feasible estimation strategy for uncovering the long-term effects of poor nutritional status in early life.[6] However, these must be shocks that occurred when the children were aged 6–24 months or perhaps 6–36 months. Why? Children are at most risk of malnutrition in the early years of life, particularly between the ages of 1 and 3. During this period, children are no longer exclusively breast-fed, they have high nutritional requirements because they are growing quickly, and they are susceptible to infection because their immature immune systems fail to protect them adequately (Martorell 1997). From the age of 3 onwards, there is no evidence that children either catch up lost growth or fall further behind (Martorell 1999). These shocks and their interaction terms must have an effect on pre-school nutritional status; in the language of instrumental variables, they must be 'relevant'. Further, they must have an effect only on pre-school nutritional status and not on the outcome of interest, that is, they must satisfy the 'uncorrelatedness' requirement of an instrument.

Understanding how pre-school nutritional status affects subsequent outcomes represents an important topic of study for Young Lives. In particular, such analyses will contribute to a growing body of evidence that transitory events can have long-term impacts. In turn, such findings can inform policy discussions, particularly those surrounding actions that reduce the likelihood that such events occur and/or reduce their impact. However, in examining this issue, it is vitally important that researchers are careful to distinguish between associational and causal relations. This chapter has outlined the nature of this problem and the challenges that researchers will face when attempting to solve it.

Notes

1. A number of the arguments presented here have benefited from earlier collaborations with Harold Alderman, Jere Behrman and Stefan Dercon and it is a pleasure to acknowledge them here. Errors are my own.
2. This discussion draws heavily on work by Alderman et al. (2001), Alderman, et al. (2006), Behrman et al. (2008) and Glewwe et al. (2001). Cunha et al. (2004) and Strauss and Thomas (2008) provide detailed expositions of models of this form.
3. This is called a 'reduced form demand function' by economists.
4. The intervention was fielded across four villages between 1969 and 1977. Residents in all villages were given access to free preventative medical care and all mothers were given both ante-natal and post-natal medical services. In two villages, randomly selected, *atole,* a protein-dense drink called was made available. In the other two villages, a less calorie-dense drink called *fresco* was provided. Martorell et al. (2005) provide further details.
5. The use of the age range 12–36 months here is necessary because there are some children who were aged between 24 and 36 months in 1984 (and who thus experienced the 1982–83 drought when they were aged between 12 and 24 months).
6. Alderman et al. (2001) use information on current prices at the time of measurement as the instrument or 'shock' variable for pre-school height for age. By interacting these with levels of parental education, they induce variability in these shocks at the household level. They find 'fairly substantial effects of pre-school nutrition on school enrollments' (p. 26).

References

Alderman, H., J. Behrman, V. Lavy and R. Menon (2001) 'Child Health and School Enrollment: A Longitudinal Analysis', *Journal of Human Resources* 36.1: 185–205.

Alderman, H., J. Hoddinott and B. Kinsey (2006) 'Long Term Consequences of Early Childhood Malnutrition', *Oxford Economic Papers* 58.3: 450–74.

Baum, C., M. Shaffer and S. Stillman (2003) 'Instrumental Variables and GMM: Estimation and Testing', *Stata Journal* 3.1: 1–31.

Behrman, J., (1996) 'The Impact of Health and Nutrition on Education', *World Bank Research Observer* 11.1: 23–37.

Behrman, J., J. Hoddinott, J. Maluccio, E. Soler-Hampejsek, E. Behrman, R. Martorell, M. Ramirez-Zea, and A. Stein (2008) *What Determines Adult Cognitive Skills? Impacts of Preschooling, Schooling and Post-Schooling Experiences in Guatemala*, Washington, DC: International Food Policy Research Institute.

Cunha, F., J. Heckman, L. Lochner and D. Masterov (2004) 'Interpreting the Evidence on Life Cycle Skill Formation' in E. Hanushek and F. Welch (eds) *Handbook of the Economics of Education, Vol. 2*, New York: North-Holland.

Glewwe, P., H. Jacoby and E. King (2001) 'Early Childhood Nutrition and Academic Achievement: A Longitudinal Analysis', *Journal of Public Economics* 81: 345–68.

Hoddinott, J., and B. Kinsey (2001) 'Child Growth in the Time of Drought', *Oxford Bulletin of Economics and Statistics* 63: 409–436.

Martorell, R. (1997) 'Undernutrition during Pregnancy and Early Childhood and Its Consequences for Cognitive and Behavioural Development' in M.E. Young (ed.) *Early Childhood Development: Investing in our Children's Future*, Amsterdam: Elsevier.

Martorell, R. (1999) 'The Nature of Child Malnutrition and its Long-Term Implications', *Food and Nutrition Bulletin* 19: 288–92.

Martorell, R., J. Behrman, R. Flores and A.D. Stein (2005) 'Rationale for a Follow-Up Study Focusing on Economic Productivity', *Food and Nutrition Bulletin* 26 (Suppl 2): S5–S14.

Strauss, J. and D. Thomas (2008) 'Health Over the Life Course' in T. Paul Schultz and John Strauss (eds)., *Handbook of Development Economics, Vol. 4*, New York: North-Holland.

4
Understanding Child Poverty in Developing Countries: Measurement and Analysis

Stefan Dercon

Introduction

Childhood, and the extent and consequences of childhood poverty, have a central place in the study of development. In many economies of Asia and Latin America, where growth has picked up considerably in recent years, the patterns of growth and the extent and nature of inclusion of poor people are crucially important for the type of society that will be produced for the next generation. More specifically, the educational and health opportunities for children who are currently poor, as well as the nature of their social inclusion and their general well-being, will determine their chances of partaking fully in this future society. In several sub-Saharan African countries, despite recent growth successes, sustained growth is still largely elusive, and current child poverty, with its cumulative effects on destitution, may undermine the possibility of economic growth in the future. Recent research has highlighted the cumulative consequences of childhood poverty and deprivation. For example, a meta-analysis of the effects of early childhood nutritional deficiency and poverty has highlighted its serious consequences for a variety of outcomes, including school achievement and earning potential in later life (Grantham-McGregor et al. 2007).

Although there are many current initiatives focusing on child well-being, there are crucial information gaps and areas of uncertainty. In particular, there is much yet to be learnt about the circumstances that influence childhood poverty, and children's experiences of and responses to poverty, as well as the multiple and diverse ways in which poverty affects children in specific countries, regions, and communities, not only in infancy and early childhood but also throughout childhood and adolescence.[1] As a consequence, the evidence provides only a limited basis for the development of effective poverty reduction and social policies.

Childhood well-being has multiple dimensions, including nutrition, educational opportunities, a child's experience of material poverty, and its general psychosocial status. Children can be deprived in these and other dimensions, implying that a comprehensive concept of child poverty has to be multidimensional. But does this imply that analysis of child poverty requires a multidimensional measurement to express the incidence and extent of child poverty? As will be developed in the section of this chapter on measuring multidimensional poverty, different dimensions combined may offer a set of powerful general patterns ('stylized facts') but they may also confuse and distract from the more fundamental questions of policy, which require an understanding of the causes and consequences of the various dimensions of child poverty. Deprivations in different dimensions may be caused in complex ways by a variety of factors at various times during childhood and aggregating dimensions may obscure rather than illuminate them.

This chapter uses Young Lives data from Peru, Ethiopia, Vietnam, and the state of Andhra Pradesh in India to illustrate these arguments. We focus on the data and analysis of Rounds 1 and especially 2 in 2002 and 2006. In the next section, we introduce the data and present descriptive analysis of some key dimensions of poverty. In the following section ('Measuring multidimensional poverty'), we discuss multidimensional poverty indexes and illustrate the possibilities offered by the Young Lives data. In the subsequent section, we discuss some of the limitations of this approach and various ways in which causes and consequences of poverty can be researched using longitudinal data such as those collected by Young Lives, which allow us to investigate some of the dynamic processes of child poverty. The nature of such data has limitations but also important advantages. It is not intervention-based or experimental, so causal inference using statistical tools is at times problematic. Nevertheless, the chapter will argue that by using careful non-experimental statistical methods, we can offer substantive new insights into child poverty and its causes and consequences. We will use some examples from recent work using the Young Lives data to illustrate this potential.

The Young Lives study: some descriptive analysis

Young Lives is tracking the development of 12,000 children in four country sites through quantitative and qualitative research over a

15-year period (as outlined in the Introduction to this volume) to gain understanding of the multiple dimensions of childhood poverty, along with the multiple life trajectories of poor children.

The samples are relatively small in comparison with the population in each of the selected countries and regions, and poorer children are purposively oversampled. Consequently, the samples are not appropriate for monitoring poverty levels in a country: basic descriptive data such as poverty levels in the sample do not represent poverty levels in the country as a whole.[2] Reweighting could be considered but the relatively small sample would make even a reweighted sample unlikely to reflect the exact levels of national poverty. Nevertheless, compared to larger representative samples such as the Demographic Health Surveys, the Young Lives samples have been shown to cover the broad range of characteristics and attributes of the population of children of this age group (Outes-Leon and Sanchez 2008; Escobal and Flores 2008; Nguyen 2008; Kumra 2008). While not designed to specifically monitor child poverty in a country, the data are suitable for analytical work on child poverty in each of the countries: they may not be suitable to indicate the number of poor children but could help to illuminate patterns and differences between various groups and over time. As questionnaires are virtually identical across countries, comparative work is possible, highlighting any differences and similarities in the processes determining child poverty and its consequences.[3] Although there is also a qualitative component, this chapter is restricted to a discussion of some of the quantitative data.

In coverage of different dimensions of child well-being, Young Lives instruments go beyond what is usually included in standard household survey instruments, such as the Living Standard Measurement Study (LSMS) survey instruments favoured by the World Bank or what is covered by Demographic and Health Surveys (DHS) or UNICEF Multiple Indicator Cluster Surveys (MICS). The LSMS instruments are commonly used to measure household income or consumption and these, and more generally household budget and expenditure surveys, lie at the basis of standard monetary poverty measures, such as those linked to the first Millennium Development Goal of halving poverty by 2015. Nevertheless, LSMS surveys include typically also what DHS and MICS surveys cover. The latter feed recent UNICEF efforts to measure child poverty based on deprivations in the spheres of access to clean water, good sanitation, shelter, basic health and nutrition, food, and education. These are no doubt important dimensions of a child's life – but it would be wrong to reduce a child's life to these dimensions: children have agency and are not just passive recipients of goods and services. The Young Lives data go further and include child-centred information on typically less studied dimensions related to children's psychosocial well-being and their subjective assessment of their well-being. In dimensions related to education, poverty is not just about school enrolment and grade achievement, but also about the quality of the schooling received and actual cognitive achievements, again dimensions Young Lives can consider. Similarly, on other issues, Young Lives can add a more comprehensive view of a child's life, such as more detailed experiences related to work within and outside the family, the risks he or she faces, his or her vulnerabilities, and his or her aspirations, as well as a richer description of caregivers' living conditions and experiences.

Below we introduce a selection of these. The selection is not comprehensive nor does it exploit the full potential of the data. This touches on a first key issue in any multidimensional poverty measurement: in most cases, the dimensions included in the analysis are opportunistic, simply using what is available. For example, DHS-style surveys have good coverage of health, nutrition, and demography, but information on children is restricted to certain key factors that are the focus of public health literature, such as access to health care and water, immunization, mother's education, and health information. Children's well-being consequently tends to be reduced to dimensions of health and nutrition for children up to the age of 5, and of education after that age. Teenage nutrition and any form of psychosocial well-being are ignored simply because data are not collected.[4] In sum, the dimensions covered by most existing surveys are important, but cannot be considered complete for a full understanding of childhood poverty. Young Lives does better, but the limitations of statistical data collection using structured survey instruments imply that completeness is hardly possible.

Tables 4.1 to 4.3 offer, nevertheless, interesting data from the Young Lives survey. We use data on the Older Cohort (born around 1995) since they include self-reported data from children. Table 4.1 presents some of the standard indicators for 2006: data on school enrolment (at the age of 12), stunting (that is, low height for age), and consumption poverty. The stunting data were collected in 2002, when this cohort was between 6.5 and 7.5 years of age. By then, height deficits would have been accumulated and catch-up is not generally considered possible; the data are comparable to stunting data of children at 5 years of age commonly found in general nutrition statistics. The data are presented in unweighted form and should not be compared directly to national

Table 4.1   Poverty and deprivations of children aged 12 in Young Lives data (%)

	Ethiopia	AP (India)	Vietnam	Peru
Stunting				
Moderate and severe stunting (age 7)	29	33	32	30
Enrolment				
Not enrolled in school (age 12)	3	10	3	1
Poverty				
Consumption poverty (< 50% of median)	10	7	9	12
Consumption poverty (< $1.25 a day in PPP)	32	41	11	4
Consumption poverty (< $2 a day in PPP)	45	56	20	7

Note: Moderate and severe stunting is defined as having a z-score for height-for-age below −2. Enrolment is recorded as a positive answer to whether a child is attending school. Consumption poverty uses total food and non-food expenditure per capita per month with three alternative definitions of the poverty line. The first is relative poverty, counting the percentage of people with consumption levels below 50% of the median consumption level in the data. The second and third consumption poverty measures first transform poverty in terms of Purchasing Power Parity corrections for 2006 to express consumption per capita in PPP US dollars, by using the corrections from the International Price Comparisons Global Report 2005. In particular, using nominal exchange rates for 2006, a further correction for purchasing power is used that suggests that prices in Peru are 45% of US prices. The corresponding percentages for Andhra Pradesh, Ethiopia, and Vietnam are 33%, 26%, and 30% respectively. The poverty lines are the standard poverty lines used by the World Bank: below US$1.25 a day per person and below US$2 a day per person.

poverty-monitoring statistics. We will nevertheless comment on their relationship with national statistics.

Table 4.1 shows that in each of the country samples, stunting is still considerable. It is in line with stunting in national data, with the exception of Ethiopia, where official statistics suggest still higher stunting in 2005. Enrolment rates of 12-year-olds are now impressive, and especially in Ethiopia, reflect recent gains. Relative poverty (consumption poverty as defined by consumption level relative to a poverty line of 50 per cent of the median within the sample) may appear surprisingly low in Andhra Pradesh and Ethiopia, and high in Peru, but the measure reflects as much inequality as poverty per se. The final two rows offer in that respect a more direct comparison between the countries, as the measure of consumption and the poverty line are now expressed in US dollars and in constant purchasing power. It reflects what is generally known about monetary poverty levels in these countries, with Ethiopia and Andhra Pradesh having significantly higher levels of poverty than the other countries; all this is similar to other international comparative databases.[5] Again, these data are not intended for poverty monitoring, but the patterns are broadly in line with comparative monitoring datasets for these indicators.

Tables 4.2 and 4.3 offer some alternative indicators, broadly linked to the same three dimensions of health and nutrition, education, and poverty in general. In Table 4.2, we offer data collected from the main caregiver of the 12-year-olds involved; in Table 4.3, we present data collected directly from the children.

The first row presents answers to a health question: whether the caregiver considers the particular child to have worse health than children

Table 4.2 Household-level perceptions of child health, overall well-being and poverty (% of children aged 12 living with a particular deprivation)

	Ethiopia	AP (India)	Vietnam	Peru
Child of worse health than others of same age	11	13	28	7
Position on ladder of life (at or below 3)	46	62	29	25
Consider household struggling, poor, or destitute	55	49	23	67

Table 4.3 School achievement, nutrition and child-level perceptions of overall well-being and poverty (% of children aged 12 living with a particular deprivation)

	Ethiopia	AP (India)	Vietnam	Peru
Low score on maths test (less than 4 out of 9)	31	17	5	12
Not able to read simple sentence properly	39	18	3	3
Not able to write simple sentence properly	43	30	6	14
Position on ladder of life (at or below 3)	37	51	20	11
Thinness (BMI z-score < –2)	36	34	17	1
Obesity (BMI z-score > 2)	0	1	1	5

Note: BMI is the Body Mass Index, which is weight in kg, divided by the square of height in metres. It is transformed in a standardized age-specific distribution using international benchmarks from the World Health Organization.

of a similar age in the community. The other questions refer to overall poverty perceptions. The general 'ladder of life' question is familiar to much research on subjective well-being, such as the World Value Study. People are asked to consider their overall life circumstances and to place themselves on an imaginary ladder with nine steps. The table gives the percentage of people placing themselves low steps of 3 or below. Although some use these indicators for comparisons across countries, these should only be made very cautiously. The results from our sample are nevertheless interesting, with most people in the Indian sample, and about half in the Ethiopian sample placing themselves at low values, compared to about a quarter in Vietnam and Peru. One can doubt the 'accuracy' of this information, but key here is how people perceive themselves, which can hardly be ignored in poverty debates. The next row offers further information, with questions framed much more in a specific poverty and deprivation framework. People were asked to judge their household's circumstances on a scale of 6 from very rich or rich (1 or 2), comfortable (3), a fourth level (struggle, never quite enough), to poor (5) and destitute (6). Again, in each context they are likely to have *relative* meaning but such indicators contain suggestive information.[6] More than half the sample in Ethiopia and about half in India classified themselves as struggling, poor, or destitute; in Vietnam this was true for just under a quarter of the households involved. Possibly reflecting much higher economic and social inequality in Peruvian society, about two-thirds considered themselves struggling or poor.

Table 4.3 includes more specific information collected directly from the children. While Table 4.1 showed that most children were in school at the age of 12 in the sample, Table 4.3 shows that there are vast differences in performances in some basic tests. A simple standardized mathematics test saw much lower performance in Ethiopia than in Vietnam, where performance was excellent. Similar patterns appeared in tests exploring whether the child can read or write a simple sentence correctly. Even though the type of tests used are intended to be comparable across contexts, some caution is due in practice (for more information on the tests and comparability, see Cueto et al. 2009).[7]

Table 4.3 also includes the child's answers regarding his or her position on the ladder of life, offering again a clear distinction between the Indian and Ethiopian samples on the one hand, and those of the other countries on the other, not dissimilar (although by no means identical) to what the caregiver judged to be the position on the ladder.[8] Finally, recent World Health Organization standards to define under-nutrition (in terms of obesity and thinness) for children above the age of 5, such as our sample of 12-year-olds, reveals considerably low body mass index (BMI) in India and Ethiopia, and virtually no thinness in Peru, which shows emerging problems of obesity, virtually non-existent elsewhere.

While by no means complete, these data show some dimensions of child well-being not usually measured in the main international datasets used for child poverty discussions. The information contained can contribute to child poverty discussions, and there is no obvious superiority of one set of indicators over others. In the next section, we discuss some of the key issues related to the measurement of child poverty using a single indicator.

Measuring multidimensional poverty

Although surveys we have mentioned contain a wealth of information on child poverty, the tables deriving from them fail to answer directly the question: how many children are poor? Policy debates often centre on whether poverty is increasing or decreasing, or whether poverty is higher under one policy regime than under another. One of the key achievements of the World Bank's poverty measurement is to offer a simple, reasonably transparent way of measuring poverty in the world as the number of people living on 'less than a dollar a day', offering a new impetus to discussions on the geographical spread of poverty, even while accuracy and relevance of this measurement have been questioned. Many other UN agencies have followed in trying to formulate definitions of poverty related to their specific objectives, leading to measures of the 'hungry' (Food and Agriculture Organization), or 'child poverty' (UNICEF). In principle, they aim to offer a basis for policy analysis and evaluation. In practice, they are rarely used for this purpose; we explore why this is the case at the end of this section. First, using the type of data offered in the previous section, we critique ways in which some people have tried to develop measures of child poverty.

The simplest way of using these data is to count numbers of deprivations and count the number of children experiencing these deprivations. This is the core of the method used by UNICEF, partly building on Gordon et al. (2003), who considered seven deprivations, and classified children as poor if they experienced at least one deprivation, and in absolute poverty if they suffered at least two deprivations. Such counting approaches are simple and intuitive, and therefore appealing for policy discourse, but they suffer from some weaknesses. For example, the extent of deprivation is not taken into account, while anyone suffering, say, five deprivations is treated in the same way as someone with two.

Alkire and Foster (2009) offer a more sophisticated measure, which is applied by UNDP for the Human Development Report 2010. For their multidimensional poverty index (MPI), they consider three core dimensions: health, education, and standard of living (drawing inspiration from the dimensions embedded in indicators such as the Human Development Index), each of which can be measured by various indicators. Their MPI is then constructed in two steps. The first step is not dissimilar to the earlier approach: only those people who are deprived in at least a particular number of deprivations will be counted as poor. For example, if six indicators are considered, only those deprived according to, say, at least three are counted. However, rather than just counting the number of poor people, an additional feature is that the authors adjust (or weigh) the head count by the percentage of deprivations experienced by each of these people included. This means that those with many deprivations are given a higher weight than those close to the cut-off point.

Table 4.4 gives some results from multidimensional poverty indicators, based on the data in Tables 4.1 to 4.3. The findings are intended to be suggestive for the type of issues involved in presenting such indicators. We consider deprivations in three dimensions: health, education, and the overall standard of living, and offer aggregate indicators for the Young Lives sample of 12-year-olds using relatively standard methods. First, we use three key indicators that are commonly used for much poverty measurement: attending school, being stunted, and monetary poverty. For the latter, we use as before both poverty defined relative to the median and poverty based on US$1.25 per day per person (in PPP terms).

The first five rows of Table 4.4 offer standard poverty indicators based on these three dimensions. Many children are deprived in at least one of these – when using the World Bank's 'dollar-a-day' poverty line, a half or more in the samples from Ethiopia and India, and above a third in Vietnam and Peru. Using the relative poverty indicator reduces child poverty (and even changes the order of the four countries). It may however make sense to use a stricter definition of child poverty and count only those who are deprived in at least two dimensions as poor. With most children aged 12 enrolled in school, both in the Young Lives data and in the national data for these countries, and with only three indicators considered in total, this focuses attention on the overlap between stunting and living in a monetary poor country. The overlap

Table 4.4 Multidimensional Child Poverty Indicators using counting and adjusted headcount (MPI) approach, 2006 (%)

	Ethiopia	AP (India)	Vietnam	Peru
A. Standard approach (three dimensions)				
Counting at least one (enrolment, stunting, monetary poverty $1.25 per day)	50	60	38	34
Counting at least one (enrolment, stunting, monetary poverty relative to median)	35	42	37	39
Counting at least two (enrolment, stunting, monetary poverty $1.25 per day)	12	21	8	1
Counting at least two (enrolment, stunting, monetary poverty relative to median)	5	7	7	4
Adjusted headcount at least two (enrolment, stunting, monetary poverty $1.25 per day)	8	14	5	1
B. Standard plus child cognitive achievement and subjective well-being (as reported by caregiver)				
Counting at least two (enrolment, stunting, monetary poverty $1.25 per day, subjective health, subjective well-being, write a sentence)	50	59	31	20
Adjusted headcount	21	27	13	7
C. Child focused only (all data measured for the child and obtained from the child if relevant)				
Counting at least two (enrolment, stunting, subjective child well-being, write a sentence, thinness or obesity)	45	49	19	10
Adjusted headcount	22	27	9	4
Identification differences between counting approaches				
Poor in caregiver questions (B) not in child (C)	14	17	15	9
Poor in child (C) not in caregiver (B)	10	6	3	3
Poor in both (C) and (B)	36	42	16	7
Poor in both, as % of sum of poor in either or both	60	64	47	35

is remarkably low, and child poverty levels now appear to be at most 21 per cent (in India) and considerably lower in Peru and Vietnam, in line with lower monetary poverty levels in these countries. With relative poverty definition, child poverty is considerably lower also in India and Ethiopia. A child MPI based on Alkire and Foster (2009), weighting the number of deprivations, brings the count of child poverty down further if few people are deprived in many dimensions. With respect to the Young Lives data, such an indicator would suggest low child poverty with an adjusted headcount of at most 14 per cent (in India).

A second set of poverty measures builds essentially on some of the more detailed data collected by Young Lives. It still focuses on the same three dimensions of health, education, and standard of living, but adds alternative indicators: cognitive achievement (measured by functional literacy in the form of writing a sentence) and two subjective well-being indicators, one in health (assessing child's health) and one a ladder of life, as defined above, collected from the main caregiver. Adding more measures of deprivation for the same dimensions of well-being but retaining the same cut-off point of at least two deprivations has strong implications for the child poverty measure. Now, we find that both in India and Ethiopia, more than half the sample of children is poor, and almost a third and a quarter in Peru and Vietnam, respectively. Poor subjective health in Vietnam and poor functional literacy in Peru seem to be important in this relative increase in poverty.[9] The adjusted headcount is now considerably higher.

The last set of data in the table offers a unique child poverty index that can be offered by the type of data Young Lives has available: a child poverty index entirely based on child-focused indicators, without any data collected at the household or caregiver level. In particular, we give actual child outcomes and data on the child's experiences of poverty. The data cover the same three dimensions: health (stunting but also thinness or obesity), education (enrolment but also functional literacy), and standard of living (child-level data on subjective well-being using the ladder of life). For both the counting measure and the adjusted headcount (MPI), the data for India and Ethiopia appear similar, while child poverty is lower in Vietnam and Peru than appeared from the caregiver data. Overall, these results are striking: using only child-focused information on various dimensions of poverty and the way children experience this poverty, close to half the children in the Ethiopian and Indian samples appear as poor. Despite its reported progress on poverty of children, a third of the children in the Vietnam sample are still poor; despite the country's considerably higher GDP per capita compared to the other countries, a quarter of the Peruvian children in the sample are also poor.

There are some surprisingly strong differences between these various measures. The final four rows in Table 4.4 present differences in identification between the two counting approaches with extended measures: the one based on the caregiver's experiences of poverty and the other based on the child's experiences. These child poverty definitions are not equivalent: even in India and Ethiopia, less than two-thirds of the children are identified as poor by both measures. In Vietnam and especially Peru, the figure is even lower, and only partly explained by the lower incidence identified by the child-focused measure.[10]

So what have we learned? First, all of these 'child poverty' measures would great make great headlines ('50 per cent or 45 per cent or 55 per cent of 12-year-olds in Ethiopia are poor using a new multidimensional poverty measure'). But each identifies different children as being poor depending on which dimensions are included. This should not surprise the researcher interested in multidimensional poverty measurement: one of the key motivations for a multidimensional focus is that different dimensions are *not* perfectly correlated. They matter in different ways to children, and this needs to be researched. If these different dimensions were perfectly correlated, then multidimensional child poverty measures would identify the same children as poor, but then also, there would be no point in developing a multidimensional measure: one dimension would suffice!

A key implication is that 'opportunistic' measures that simply use available data, which is the practice for most measures, are not convincing since the inclusion of other dimensions would change the findings. One alternative would be to state that all dimensions included are essential and being deprived in any defines a child as poor, while acknowledging that other dimensions may matter too. While child poverty measured by a given number of dimensions might be relatively low, if data on other dimensions become available, further children will be classified as poor, or at least, the number of poor children will never go down. This can become meaningless: by adding more dimensions, measured child poverty will go up, eventually classifying virtually all children as poor. For example, using the six 'child-focused' indicators on the Indian data, more than 80 per cent of the children appear deprived in at least one and would be classified as poor if being deprived in at least one dimension is deemed sufficient for such classification. Adding further dimensions increases this number: if the caregiver's experiences of poverty and monetary poverty were also considered, more than 90 per cent of children would be classified as poor. Aiming for completeness by adding more dimensions could still be a solution if at the same time we increase the number of dimensions in which a child must be deprived; but this could make it harder for a child to be recognized as poor as more information about the lives of children becomes available.

The problem is not only about identifying poor people, but also about how to act on this information. It would not be sound to recommend to a policymaker that they target children by any of the above measures, since different definitions would result in different children being included and excluded. It may nevertheless be argued that a measure could be useful in policy analysis and design: we could, for example, choose between policies on the basis of their impact on child poverty, as measured by a multidimensional definition of poverty.

Even this is questionable since the information contained in a multidimensional poverty index is composite. In the examples above, indexes mix outcomes that can only be affected in the long run or at very specific periods in life (such as stunting) with outcomes that could be changed relatively quickly and at any point in time (such as monetary poverty); they mix flows (such as the current level of monetary poverty or current enrolment) with stocks, that is, the result of cumulative processes (such as stunting or cognitive achievement). Other indexes mix inputs (such access to particular services) with outcomes (such as stunting or cognitive development). To change overall multidimensional child poverty, many different things may need to change, but none of these measures give any sense of how to address child poverty. A multidimensional measure can confuse the design of policies: one needs to unpack the different dimensions to judge how progress in each can be achieved. The index may give an overall indication of achievement, by which progress can be judged. But since this indication depends on what privations are included, the composite measure remains of dubious utility.

Multidimensional poverty analysis

Does this argument mean that one should not be concerned with child poverty as a multidimensional set of deprivations? Not at all. Instead of constructing a composite *measure,* which in fact is likely to prove irrelevant to the understanding of child poverty, multidimensional poverty analysis appears most fruitful when one tries to understand the causal factors behind particular deprivations and the interactions between dimensions of child poverty. This is not straightforward to implement, and in this section we discuss some of the issues surrounding such analysis and the way longitudinal data, such as those generated by Young Lives, can help.

A common technique used in quantitative poverty analysis is the construction of a 'poverty profile'. This essentially provides a set of correlates of those identified as poor using geographical, family, or community characteristics. Examples include whether poor people are more likely to be found in rural or urban areas, how poverty correlates to local services and infrastructure, and how it correlates with wealth or other family characteristics. Using a multidimensional framework to analyse poverty, children may be poor in particular dimensions and it would be possible to construct multidimensional poverty profiles. Given the drawbacks of working with multidimensional poverty indexes, constructing a profile for those identified as poor may be misleading; nevertheless, a profile of who is deprived dimension-by-dimension may still contain useful information.

Finding correlates is not the same as establishing causality. This is not a problem of univariate analysis only. The *multivariate* alternative involves correlating different dimensions of well-being or poverty with a set of geographical, community, household, and individual factors, usually using a multivariate regression model.[11] Multivariate analyses are helpful to guard against misleadingly simplistic interpretations, but they are still seriously problematic if used to draw policy conclusions. The key problem is inference of *causality*: for example, finding via a multivariate poverty profile that poverty in the data is correlated with living in an area with only a state-owned but no private school does not *show* that not having a private school *causes* poverty. There are more insidious examples; finding that the presence of a child nutrition programme is correlated with lower child poverty does not confirm the effectiveness of the programme in alleviating poverty, since it could be that richer communities are more able to attract programmes. Extreme caution must be applied in drawing conclusions from correlations.

To be sure of the causal chain in child poverty, or to gain understanding on how to change child poverty, one can design specific intervention-based studies, typically in the form of randomized controlled trials in which a particular group is subject to an intervention. There have been some intervention-based studies (also referred to as experimental) focusing on children's nutrition at an early age and its consequences,[12] as well as a rising number of intervention-based studies focusing on cognitive achievement or other learning outcomes.[13] Some also look at the interaction of these dimensions of learning and nutrition, and its long-term consequences.[14] However, since many child outcomes and deprivations are the consequence of long-term processes in many dimensions, it is unlikely that enough evidence can be gathered in the short term on the causes and consequences of child poverty by using experimental data only.

Other attempts at establishing causal links in quantitative data may also be faulty. The key to non-experimental analysis is to establish convincingly that there is exogenous variation in a potentially causal factor, either between children ('in the cross-section') or over time, so that any inference related to the role of this causal factor is not affected by other factors that could be correlated with both the variable of interest (the outcome) and this causal factor. In practice, such other factors often intervene. For example, finding a correlation between maternal education and child health outcomes may have little to do with maternal education itself, but could just reflect that wealthier families are better educated and can also afford to create conditions for good child health. Similarly, finding that stunted children perform less well in school may not mean that it is stunting that is causing poor school performance: stunted children may simply live in poorer families, who may find it harder to support their children in homework or may require their help with caring for siblings or even their work for cash to support the family. Proving the link between education and health outcomes is therefore harder than may appear at first.

These examples also illustrate how multidimensional poverty analysis is so much more than measuring deprivations. A key feature is that different dimensions of poverty affect each other in causal ways, making it important to unpack the processes and interactions between dimensions. Some of the emerging work using the Young Lives data is beginning to illustrate this further. Other work has conclusively established that deprivation in early childhood nutrition leads to stunting and that this stunted development has long-term implications on cognitive development (Grantham-McGregor et al. 2007). Outes-Leon et al. (2010) confirm this causal process using comparisons between siblings in the Young Lives sample in Peru, showing that those stunted in early childhood have lower cognitive achievement at the age of 7 to 8.

Other analyses of Young Lives data highlight further interactions. Sanchez (2009) shows that household-level shocks via extreme cold events in Peru when children are young have long-term implications for cognitive development, working not only through nutrition, but more generally through overall pressure on the family at critical times in children's cognitive progress. Le Thuc (2009) shows that the link between cognitive development and early childhood nutrition is weaker in the Vietnam sample, but that deprivations in early childhood, possibly owing to parental skills, matter for poor performance in cognitive tests later on. Dercon and Krishnan (2009) show that in all the four countries, psychosocial skills, especially self-esteem and educational aspirations are at the age of 12 strongly associated with general material poverty, controlling for parental education and a host of other attributes. Dercon and Sanchez (forthcoming) show that beyond material poverty, a child's stunting has an additional effect on these psychosocial skills across all four countries, and that this effect persists, controlling for many attributes that may be correlated with both stunting and psychosocial skills, such as the caregiver's education and the caregiver's own psychosocial skills.

These are some of the studies illustrating that unpacking the causal processes underlying child poverty and the interactions between deprivations offers a richer analysis of the multidimensionality of child poverty than does any measurement exercise. Such unpacking also offers steps towards identifying ways in which child poverty can be addressed.

Conclusion

This chapter used Young Lives data to illustrate some of the problems of identifying poor children using multidimensional poverty indicators. While seemingly providing richer information, such indicators are very sensitive to the specific dimensions included, resulting in considerable errors of exclusion or inclusion. Furthermore, to understand the multidimensional processes underlying poverty, multidimensional measures may obscure more than they illuminate. Understanding child poverty requires multidimensional poverty analysis, not in establishing one or more measures, but rather in unpacking relations between dimensions.

Notes

1. In different disciplines, there is much research on specific aspects of child poverty, such work on the economic constraints on human capital accumulation by poor people in developing countries (see for example, Glewwe and Kremer 2006).
2. The dataset from Peru forms the important exception, as it constructed a two-stage random sample of the entire population of households with children

of the specific age group, although this is still not a random sample of all individuals, households, or children at any point of time (Escobal and Flores 2008).

3. Details on the instruments can be found at www.younglives.org.uk.

4. Income poverty of the family is ignored since such measures commonly reduce socioeconomic dimensions to an index based on the ownership of a small set of durable goods, usually ownership of a car, a bicycle, phone, television and furniture, and access to safe sanitation, water and electricity. The relevance of the asset index is disputable: there is no doubt that it reflects some differences in socioeconomic status but its comparability across contexts even within the same country could be questioned; for instance, between rural and urban areas, or between mountainous and flat rural areas. For example, access to electricity and ownership of electric appliances in a remote area where generators are required could be a much more significant sign of wealth than access and ownership to the same appliances in an urban area.

5. The higher poverty in Andhra Pradesh relative to Ethiopia using PPP comparisons may seem slightly puzzling, but different sampling procedures make the Andhra Pradesh sample more 'pro-poor'. This is also due to a PPP correction for Ethiopia that appears high, as it is suggesting that Indian prices are a third higher than in Ethiopia, which seems somewhat unlikely to those familiar with price levels for poor people in each of these countries. Not too much should be read into this, as neither sample is intended for monitoring poverty; we use them here to illustrate issues related to poverty measurement.

6. Subjective poverty and well-being are often considered to give information on individual positions *relative* to their respective contexts; that is, people consider themselves satisfied with life or poor by assessing their position relative to others around them.

7. In any case, the correlation in performance on the writing and maths test is very high – with correlation coefficients between 0.45 and 0.56.

8. The correlation coefficient between children's and caregivers answers in the raw indicator is above 0.5 for all but Peru, where it is approximately 0.3.

9. Using this indicator, more than 80 per cent of the Ethiopian and Indian samples were poor in at least one deprivation, and about half the Peruvian and Vietnamese sample.

10. When we repeated this exercise by comparing the first counting measure using standard poverty measures as in set A with the child-focused measures, we found it similarly resulted in the identification of different children – with only at most 58 per cent of children counted in either or both measures counted by both measures in India, and fewer in other countries.

11. For a detailed description on how to make poverty profiles, including how to establish multivariate profiles and an overview of their use, see World Bank Institute (2005), chapters 7 and 8, http://siteresources.worldbank.org/PGLP/Resources/PovertyManual.pdf.

12. Many of the relatively limited number of studies are reviewed in Grantham-McGregor et al. (2007).

13. For a review, see Glewwe and Miguel (2007).

14. An example is Hoddinott et al. (2010) on Guatemala.

References

Alkire, Sabina and James Foster (2009) *Counting and Multidimensional Poverty Measurement*, Working Paper 32, Oxford: Oxford Poverty and Human Development Initiative.

Cueto, Santiago, Juan Leon, Gabriela Guerrero and Ismael Muñoz (2009) *Psychometric Characteristics of Cognitive Development and Achievement Instruments in Round 2 of Young Lives*, Technical Note 15, Oxford: Young Lives.

Dercon, Stefan and Alan Sanchez (in preparation) 'Long-term Implications of Malnutrition on Non-cognitive Skills: Evidence from Four Developing Countries'.

Dercon, Stefan and Pramila Krishnan (2009) 'Poverty and the Psychosocial Competencies of Children: Evidence from the Young Lives Sample in Four Developing Countries', *Children, Youth and Environments* 19.2: 138–63.

Escobal, Javier and Eva Flores (2008) *An Assessment of the Young Lives Sampling Approach in Peru*, Technical Note 3, Oxford: Young Lives.

Glewwe, Paul and Michael Kremer (2006) 'Schools, Teachers, and Education Outcomes' in E. Hanushek and F. Welsh (eds) *Handbook of the Economics of Education*, Vol. 2, Oxford and Amsterdam: North-Holland.

Glewwe, Paul and Edward A. Miguel (2007) 'The Impact of Child Health and Nutrition on Education in Less Developed Countries' in T. Paul Schultz and John A. Strauss (eds), *Handbook of Development Economics*, Vol. 4, Oxford and Amsterdam: North-Holland.

Gordon, D., S. Nandy, C. Pantazis, S. Pemberton and P. Townsend (2003) *Child Poverty in the Developing World*, Bristol: Townsend Centre for International Poverty Research.

Grantham-McGregor, S., V.B. Cheung, S. Cueto, P. Glewwe, L. Richter, B. Strupp and the International Child Development Steering Group (2007) 'Child Development in Developing Countries: Development Potential in the First Five Years for Children in Developing Countries', *The Lancet* 369: 60–70.

Hoddinott, John, John A. Maluccio, Jere R. Behrman, Rafael Flores and Reynaldo Martorell (2008) 'Effect of a Nutrition Intervention during Early Childhood on Economic Productivity in Guatemalan Adults', *The Lancet* 371: 9610: 411–16.

Kumra, Neha (2008) *An Assessment of the Young Lives Sampling Approach in Andhra Pradesh, India*, Technical Note 2, Oxford: Young Lives.

Le Thuc, Duc (2009) *The Effect of Early Age Stunting on Cognitive Achievement Among Children in Vietnam*, Working Paper 45, Oxford: Young Lives.

Nguyen, Ngoc P. (2008) *An Assessment of the Young Lives Sampling Approach in Vietnam*, Technical Note 4, Oxford: Young Lives.

Outes-Leon, Ingo and Alan Sanchez (2008) *An Assessment of the Young Lives Sampling Approach in Ethiopia*, Technical Note 1, Oxford: Young Lives.

Outes-Leon, Ingo, Catherine Porter, Alan Sanchez, Santiago Cueto, Stefan Dercon and Javier Escobal (2010) 'Early Nutrition and Cognition in Peru: A Within-Sibling Investigation', Washington DC: Inter-American Development Bank.

Sanchez, Alan (2009) *Early Nutrition and Cognitive achievement in Preschool Children in Peru*, Working Paper 57, Oxford: Young Lives.

UNICEF (2009) *The State of the World's Children 2009: Maternal and Newborn Health*, New York: UNICEF.

World Bank Institute (2005) *Introduction to Poverty Analysis,* Washington DC: World Bank.

Part II
Dynamics of Childhood Poverty

This theme covers ways in which different dimensions of poverty overlap and interact; it incorporates attention to the levels of household and environment, to conditions behind movement into and out of poverty, and to the mechanisms of intergenerational poverty. We consider the interaction between poverty and other household adversities, such as sickness, crop failure, or other forms of loss of income. Although researchers in these fields cannot afford to ignore issues raised by qualitative research (as Dercon demonstrated in Chapter 4), this section deals mainly with broad patterns that emerge from survey data. Here we are dealing with statistical probabilities rather than the actual outcomes for children that are discussed in Part III, where we consider children's experiences.

The methodological problems in measuring poverty discussed in the last chapter lead directly into this theme. In the introduction to methodology, we pointed out the problems of measuring poverty in terms of wealth or income, and indicated how Young Lives has tried to overcome these by using instead measures of expenditure and consumption. In Chapter 4, Stephan Dercon discussed in some detail the difficulty of measuring poverty as such for the purposes of policy or intervention. In this part of the volume we find a limited use of certain indices and focused measures.

Notwithstanding the limitations of generalized measures, in the first chapter of this section of the volume (Chapter 5), Paul Glewwe uses a number of indicators to assess whether poor people in Vietnam are benefiting from that country's economic growth. Generally, economic growth has increased household incomes among the poor, which in turn appears to have increased school enrolment and reduced children's work. But there was little evidence that improved incomes significantly reduced under nutrition or improved the survival of children. Moreover, the general trends of improved income and school enrolment do not indicate the different ways in which children of poor people benefit or the extent of such benefits when they occur; nor do the general trends indicate the specific conditions under which benefits can be maximized. Glewwe shows that government programmes designed specifically to help poor people have not successfully focused on the poorest families, and he argues for research to ensure that the poorest children are reached more effectively.

This follows the point made earlier by Dercon. Glewwe uses general indices to offer guides on the overall success of policy. If, however, policy and intervention are to help those most in need, research is needed to focus on specific problems they face and processes that might alleviate these. There is growing evidence of the importance of the first five years of life for subsequent childhood development, as indicated by the chapters by Engle (Chapter 8) and Wachs (Chapter 9) in Part III of this volume, and by Young Lives data generally. This has provoked massive investment in pre-school institutions to prepare children (and particularly those from deprived households) for entry into the school system by providing constructive learning environments (UNESCO 2006). Besides the strong evidence of the beneficial impact of stimulation for learning, there is also growing evidence that early under-nutrition can have permanent effects on both physical development and school attainment. Jere Behrman, after discussing research techniques for establishing causes and effects, presents evidence on the disadvantages of early malnutrition. He discusses strategies for improving the nutrition of children and argues that investment in this area is particularly rewarding. Policy on early childhood development should, therefore, extend beyond learning centres and education: it should integrate the efforts of a number government ministries to ensure a sound start to young lives in both cognitive and material spheres.

Tassew Woldehanna (Chapter 7) picks up this theme, analysing data from two rounds of Young Lives research in Ethiopia. Following the Younger Cohort of children over four years, he considers how pre-natal and post-natal economic shocks relate to the later physical growth of children, and argues that what appears as a temporary setback may have long-term consequences for a family. Pre-natal shocks are significantly related to poor growth at five years, although some children have been able later to recover from early stunting. Woldehanna uses simulation exercises to indicate the benefit of social assistance programmes responding to area-wide shocks, such as drought. He points out, however, that shocks particular to specific families, such as illness or death of the bread winner, are also significant; since these are not at present adequately covered by social assistance in Ethiopia, the analysis suggests an expansion of current policy.

Data that we present in this volume underline the importance for policy of early childhood nutrition (Chapters 3, 6, and 7, reinforced by Chapters 8 and 9 to come). As we pointed out in the introduction, Young Lives data reveal broader consequences of early under-nutrition in the psycho-social realm, which will be reported in further volumes of this series. The next section points to a broader range of early childhood risks.

References

UNESCO (2006) *Strong Foundations: Early Childhood Education and Care*, Education For All Global Monitoring Report 2007, Paris: UNESCO.

5
'Pro-Poor' Growth and Children in Developing Countries: The Case of Vietnam

Paul Glewwe

Introduction

Economists often claim that economic growth in developing countries leads to a better quality of life for virtually everyone in those countries. Presumably this claim includes children as well as adults. The extent to which economic growth improves children's welfare may depend on the nature of that growth. This has led some economists to investigate 'pro-poor growth', that is, economic growth that is particularly favourable to the well-being of poor people, including children.

This chapter examines the extent to which economic growth improves the quality of life of children in developing countries, especially poor children. It begins by clarifying the concept of pro-poor growth, and then discusses the relationship between economic growth and child well-being. Finally, recent data from Vietnam are used to investigate whether recent economic growth in that country can be characterized as pro-poor. The conclusion summarizes the results and presents suggestions for future research.

What is 'pro-poor' growth?

In the 1950s and 1960s, most economists assumed that economic growth would reduce poverty, which was defined in terms of individual or household income. Yet this assumption was criticized in the 1970s and 1980s. First, some critics charged that income growth for the economy as a whole did not necessarily imply income growth among poor people. (Fishlow (1980) argues that economic growth did not reduce

75

poverty in Brazil during the 1960s.) Second, others argued that focusing on income was misleading because higher income does not guarantee a higher quality of life.

Responding to the first criticism, economists investigated whether economic growth in developing countries raises the incomes of poor people. This literature on this topic started appearing in the 1970s (for example, Chenery et al. 1974). In the last one to two decades, with more abundant and higher-quality household surveys from developing countries, economists have found that economic growth usually, but not always, increases the incomes of poor people (Ravallion 1995; Dollar and Kraay 2002). Moreover, economic growth is usually accompanied by a higher quality of life for poor households, as measured by education, health, and dwelling characteristics.

Yet these findings that economic growth usually raises poor people's incomes and quality of life also show wide variation in those improvements. In particular, poor people may experience a much smaller rate of income growth than do the rest of the population. This has led to interest into what makes economic growth more 'pro-poor', that is, which policies or conditions generate rates of income growth among poor people that are similar to those enjoyed by the rest of society.

Some economists have proposed precise definitions of pro-poor growth that compare the rate of income growth of poor people with that of non-poor people (see Ravallion 2004). This chapter proposes no precise definition, since arbitrariness is unavoidable regarding where to draw the line when comparing the growth rates of the incomes of poor people and non-poor people. Instead, pro-poor growth is loosely defined as a rate of income growth for poor people that is approximately equal to or greater than the rate for the rest of the population.

The rest of this paper discusses whether pro-poor growth, or more generally economic growth, benefits children in developing countries. The focus is on poor children, since these children have the lowest quality of life and thus would potentially benefit the most from economic growth.

Does economic growth benefit poor children?

The notion that economic growth benefits poor children *if and only if* it is 'pro-poor' is overly simplistic, for two reasons. First, even if economic growth were concentrated among non-poor households, it could still benefit poor people if it increased government revenues *and* those revenues were spent to help poor people. Second, a poor household whose income increases may not spend that increase on children in that household. Thus the relationship between economic growth and children's well-being is more complicated than may first appear. This section provides a framework for evaluating whether economic growth improves child welfare.

Figure 5.1 shows the different pathways by which economic growth can increase child welfare. The first, and most obvious, question is whether economic growth has occurred. If not, there is no possibility for any benefits that such growth may bring.[1] If it has occurred, the second question is whether that growth has increased the incomes of poor people. If the answer is 'yes', one must ask whether this income growth has benefited the children in poor households; this is the third question in Figure 5.1.

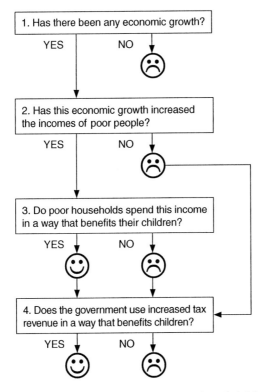

Figure 5.1   The relationship between economic growth and child welfare

Economists and others have studied the impact of increased income on children in poor (and non-poor) households since the early 1990s. It is rare to see no benefit, but there is ample evidence that the benefits depend on which household members' incomes increased. In particular, children appear to benefit more if their mothers' incomes increase than if their fathers' incomes increase (see King and Mason 2001: 154–64, for a recent review). Another issue is whether the increased income is perceived as permanent or temporary. Increases perceived as permanent are likely to be spent, while increases viewed as temporary may increase saving more than spending, postponing most of the benefits to children (and to other household members) until sometime in the future.

Even if poor people's incomes were not directly increased by economic growth, or if they were increased but poor households do not spend the money to benefit their children, poor children would still benefit if economic growth raises tax revenues, and some of those revenues are spent to benefit poor children. This is the last question in Figure 5.1. Indeed, when poor households do spend part or all of any increases in their income to benefit their children, there may be additional benefits through the government revenue and spending channel. When government revenues increase, there are many ways those funds could be spent to benefit poor (and non-poor) children, such as improved schools, better health clinics, and early childhood development programmes. Even building new roads and increasing agricultural services could eventually benefit poor children because such activities may raise their parents' incomes (assuming that at least some of that increased income is spent to benefit children).

How does higher family income benefit poor children?

There is now strong evidence that general economic growth increases the incomes of poor families. How do such increases improve the lives of children in those families? This section reviews four pathways.

The first two pertain to child health. Parents may spend some of their increased income on additional food for their children, and they could also purchase more medicine and medical services for their children. Both actions will improve their children's health and nutritional status. This not only brings immediate health benefits, but also improves educational performance (see Glewwe and Miguel 2008 for a review of the evidence).

A third way that increased parental income could benefit children is through higher spending on education. This can be done by paying for additional years of schooling, buying educational items such as textbooks and other school supplies, and even paying for a higher-quality education. The last can be achieved by paying for private schooling, sending children to tutoring classes, or by paying transportation and/or housing fees that enable children to attend a more distant, but better, school.

A fourth avenue by which increased household income could benefit poor children is by reducing child labour.[2] While child labour may increase funds available for schooling and provide useful work experience (that will make children more productive when they are adults), it may interfere with their schooling and, in some cases, compromise their health. Thus, reductions in child labour may benefit poor children.

Economists and other social scientists have accumulated extensive evidence on whether higher household incomes in developing countries benefit children by these four pathways. While many studies that have shown that increased income improves children's health status, some have questioned the methodologies used in those studies (Deaton 2007). Even so, several studies have shown that negative income 'shocks' can impair child health (Ferreira and Schady (2009) and section 4.4 in Strauss and Thomas (2008) provide recent reviews). Several studies have also shown that income, especially income shocks, can have large impacts on education outcomes (Orazem and King 2008, section 5.2). Finally, Edmonds (2008, section 4.4) reviews studies of child labour and finds that increases in household income lead to substantial reductions in child labour, although some estimation methods may lead to biased results. Overall, there is substantial evidence that rising household incomes lead to higher school enrolment rates and less child labour, while the plausible positive impact on child health has less empirical support.

Evidence from Vietnam

The rest of this chapter examines the relationship between economic growth and child well-being for Vietnam. Vietnam provides a very interesting case study. First, it has experienced rapid economic growth for the last two decades. Second, by some (though not all) measures child welfare in Vietnam was already quite high despite its low income; in particular it has had unusually high school enrolment and low infant and child mortality rates. Third, there are detailed data from Vietnam, especially household survey data, that can be used to assess the impact of economic growth on child welfare, and many researchers have used those data for that purpose.[3]

Has Vietnam's recent economic growth been 'pro-poor'?

Although data on economic growth in Vietnam in the 1980s and earlier are unreliable, since about 1990 the data are of much better quality and clearly show higher rates of economic growth from 1990 to 2008. More specifically, the average growth rate in GDP per capita from 1990 to 2008 was 6.0 per cent.[4]

Nationally representative household survey data are available from Vietnam for 1992/93, 1997/98, 2002, 2004, 2006, and 2008. Household expenditure data from those surveys, which are more comparable and less prone to errors than household income data,[5] reveal a small increase in inequality, but in general the expenditure data indicate that incomes among poor people have increased at almost the same rate as those of non-poor people. This is seen in Table 5.1, which shows growth rates in real per capita expenditure for the poorest 20 per cent of the population, the poorest 40 per cent, and the entire population from 1992/93 to 2008.

According to household survey data, real per capita expenditure for Vietnam as a whole increased at an annual rate of 7.4 per cent between 1992/93 and 1997/98. This is a very rapid increase and is slightly higher than the increases of 6.4 per cent (6.2 per cent) for the poorest 40 per cent (20 per cent) of the population over that same time period. Thus the growth rate of per capita expenditure was almost as high for poor people as it was for the population as a whole, which implies that Vietnam's economic growth in the 1990s was 'pro-poor'. Similar findings hold from 1997/98 to 2008, although the period from 1997/98 to 2002, when economic growth was low, shows lower growth in expenditure for the

Table 5.1 Per capita expenditure levels and annual growth rates of real per capita expenditure in Vietnam, 1992/93–2008

Year	Per capita expenditure, nominal (000s of dong)			Annual growth rate of real per capita expenditure (since previous survey) (%)		
	National average	Poorest 40%	Poorest 20%	National average	Poorest 40%	Poorest 20%
1992/93	1,314.9	679.7	552.2			
1997/98	2,855.4	1,436.7	1,159.4	8.1	7.5	7.3
2002	3,472.5	1,617.7	1,290.6	2.8	0.8	0.5
2004	4,456.2	2,039.0	1,587.3	9.4	8.4	7.1
2006	5,855.2	2,730.5	2,099.0	4.9	5.9	5.3
2008	7,889.1	3,766.6	2,896.9	5.5	6.5	6.5

poorest 20 per cent and poorest 40 per cent (relative to average growth). One intriguing finding since 2004 is higher-than-average growth for poor people; the annual growth in per capita expenditure for the poorest 40 per cent (5.9 per cent) and the poorest 20 per cent (5.3 per cent) between 2004 and 2006 were slightly *higher* than that for the country as a whole (4.9 per cent), and this pattern continued from 2006 to 2008.

While the data in Table 5.1 suggest that Vietnam's economic growth from 1992/3 to 2008 has been fairly pro-poor, in another sense, it is even more pro-poor. This is because the comparisons in that table implicitly assume that poor people always remain poor, that is, the poorest 20 per cent (or 40 per cent) in an earlier year are also the poorest 20 per cent (40 per cent) in later years. In fact, at least some, and maybe quite a few, of the households in the bottom 20 or 40 per cent in the earlier year were no longer in that group in a later year, so *for the same households* over time the growth rate of the bottom 20 or 40 per cent is even higher than the figures in Table 5.1.

Comparisons *of the same households* from 1992/93 to 1997/98, based on Glewwe and Dang (2011), are shown in Table 5.2. The data suggest that, when comparing the same households over time, the annual growth rate of real per capita expenditure from 1992/93 to 1997/98 of the poorest 20 per cent of households in 1992/93 (quintile 1) is almost twice as high as that for Vietnam as a whole (13.9 per cent vs. 7.5 per cent) and about three times higher than the growth for the wealthiest 20 per cent of households (4.6 per cent). While this 'super pro-poor

Table 5.2 Pro-poor growth in Vietnam when comparing the same households, 1992/93 and 1997/98

	Annual growth rate of per capita expenditure (%)		
		1992/93 quintile	
	Current quintile	Uncorrected	Correcting for measurement error
All Vietnam	7.5	7.5	7.3
Quintile 1 (poorest 20%)	6.6	13.9	11.1
Quintile 2	6.7	10.5	9.4
Quintile 3	6.7	9.6	8.1
Quintile 4	7.0	7.5	7.1
Quintile 5 (wealthiest 20%)	7.6	4.6	5.1

growth' is exaggerated by measurement error in the expenditure data, correcting for that error (last column of Table 5.2) still shows a growth rate of expenditure of the poorest 20 per cent of Vietnamese in the 1990s to be well above the national average and more than twice that of the wealthiest 20 per cent of the population.[6]

More recent data are available to examine growth rates by quintile from 1997/98 to 2008, but it is difficult to use those data to follow the same households over time, so only analyses of the type presented in Table 5.1 can be shown; analyses of the type presented in Table 5.2 are not available. Thus Table 5.3 presents results analogous to those in Table 5.1, but for two more recent time periods: 1997/98 to 2002 and 2002 to 2008. As seen above, the relatively slow growth from 1997/98 to 2002 was particularly hard for poor people; for example, per capita growth was 1.0 per cent per year or less for both quintiles 1 and 2, compared to 2.8 per cent for the general population. In contrast, from 2002 to 2008 annual per capita expenditure growth for the poorest 20 per cent of the population (not necessarily the same households over time) was almost as high as the rate for the population as a whole (6.3 and 6.5 per cent, respectively), and was higher than that for the wealthiest 20 per cent (5.5 per cent).

In summary, household survey data indicate that Vietnam's economic growth from 1992/93 to 2008 was widespread, with per capita expenditure growth rates among the poorest households similar to those for Vietnam as a whole (except for the 1997/98 to 2002 period), and even higher than the overall growth rate when one compares the same households over time. Clearly, economic growth in Vietnam has increased the incomes of poor Vietnamese households. This raises the question of whether this growth benefited the children in those households.

Table 5.3 Pro-poor growth in Vietnam, 1997/98–2008 (current quintile only)

	Annual growth rate of per capita expenditure (%)	
	1997/98–2002	2002–2008
All Vietnam	2.8	6.5
Quintile 1 (poorest 20%)	0.5	6.3
Quintile 2	1.0	7.4
Quintile 3	1.7	7.8
Quintile 4	3.0	7.3
Quintile 5 (wealthiest 20%)	3.9	5.5

Child welfare and economic growth since 1992/93

This section first examines how children have fared during Vietnam's period of high economic growth. Overall, the evidence indicates large improvements in child welfare. It then examines whether these improvements are due to income growth, which is more difficult to verify. Almost all the studies that examine this question rely on data from the 1992/93 and 1997/98 surveys.

Table 5.4 presents several child welfare indicators for 1992/93, 1997/98, and 2006. More specifically, it examines primary and secondary school enrolment, stunting and wasting (measures of children's nutritional status), child labour, and infant and child mortality. The primary school enrolment rate in 1992/93 was nearly 100 per cent for children aged 6 to 10 years, and it exceeded 100 per cent in 1997/98 and 2006. This reflects Vietnam's almost universal primary school enrolment; rates above 100 per cent indicate that some 'over-age' children were still in primary school due to repetition or late initial enrolment. Secondary school enrolment increased dramatically from 1992/93 to 2006, rising from 41 to 85 per cent of children aged 11 to 17. This was paralleled by reduced child labour, which suggests that children increased the time they spent in school by reducing their time spent working. More specifically, the percentage of 6- to 15-year-old children who report (or whose parents report) that they worked in the preceding 12 months declined from 34 per cent in 1992/93 to 25 per cent in 1997/98, and dropped to only 9 per cent by 2006.

Turning to child health, presented in Table 5.4, stunting among children aged 6 months to 60 months declined dramatically from 1992/93

Table 5.4   Indicators of child welfare in Vietnam, 1992/93–2006 (%)

	1992/93	1997/98	2006
Primary school enrolment rate	96	113	105
Secondary school enrolment rate	41	63	85
Child labour force participation	33.9	25.2	8.9
Child stunting rate (HAZ < –2)	54.2	38.3	33.1
Child wasting rate (WHZ < –2)	6.2	11.0	11.0
Infant mortality rate	34	25	15
Under-5 mortality rate	45	36	17

Note: Child stunting and wasting rates refer to children between the ages of 6 and 60 months. Child labour force participation refers to children between the ages of 6 and 15 years.

Source: All 1992/93 and 1997/98 figures were calculated from household surveys for those years. Figures for 2006 are from the household survey for that year, except that infant and child mortality rates are taken from World Bank (2008: Table 2.21).

to 1997/98, from 54 to 38 per cent, an unusually rapid decline.[7] By 2006, the rate had fallen further, to 33 per cent. While wasting increased somewhat over this period (from 6 to 11 per cent), its prevalence is much lower than that of stunting. Improvements in child health are also seen in reduced infant mortality rates: both infant and child mortality rates fell by more than half from 1992/93 to 2006.

Virtually all indicators of child welfare in Table 5.4 show dramatic improvements since the early 1990s, suggesting that economic growth *caused* these improvements. Yet causal interpretations must be made cautiously, since they require careful examination of the data. The most direct causal pathway is via increased household income; higher household incomes enable parents to provide better for their children's welfare, for example, by purchasing additional schooling and medical care. The rest of this sub-section presents results from several studies that attempt to assess whether increased household incomes are the primary cause of improvements in child welfare in Vietnam.

Glewwe et al. (2004) examined the impact of household income (measured by household expenditure) and other factors on child stunting (measured by height for age). Using several estimation methods, they find that increased income reduces stunting, but the estimated effects are small. In particular, estimated effects using several estimation methods account for only a small fraction of the reduction in stunting from 1992/93 to 1997/98. Wagstaff and Nguyen (2004), who investigated the determinants of child survival (the 'opposite' of infant and child mortality) using 1992/93 and 1997/98 household survey data, obtained similar results. Specifically, they found no significant impact of household expenditure on child survival in either year, although they found some evidence that that impact may be increasing over time.

Turning to education, Glewwe (2004) examined the impact of household income (measured by household expenditure) and other factors on primary school and lower secondary school completion in 1997/98. He found that household expenditure had a strong impact on both. Using panel data, Glewwe and Jacoby (2004) found similar results for changes in school enrolment from 1992/93 to 1997/98.

A final indicator of child welfare is child labour. As explained above, it is declining over time in Vietnam. Edmonds (2005) investigated whether this drop is due to increased household income, and found a large effect. Overall, there is little evidence that increased household income in the 1990s led to improvements in child health, but there is evidence that it increased in school enrolment and reduced child labour.

Government expenditure and child welfare

Almost all government expenditure on education, by definition, benefits children. In 1995, Vietnam spent about 2.9 per cent of its GDP on education. By 2008, this figure had almost doubled, reaching 5.3 per cent.[8] Given Vietnam's high rate of economic growth since the late 1980s, total spending on education has increased rapidly since 1995. While it is difficult to determine how much of this spending reaches poor children, two things suggest that much of it does. First, virtually all children, poor and non-poor, are enrolled at the primary and lower secondary levels; specifically, the primary and lower secondary gross enrolment rates in 2006 were 105 and 96 per cent, respectively, and the net enrolment rates of 89 and 79 per cent were also quite high (General Statistics Office 2007: 67–8). Second, unlike other developing countries, spending per pupil is relatively even across the primary, secondary, and tertiary levels. In particular, per pupil government spending in 2008 (as a percentage of GDP per capita) was 19.7, 17.2, and 61.7 per cent at the primary, secondary, and tertiary levels, respectively.

Unfortunately, it is difficult to find data on government spending in Vietnam on health that focus on children. However, there is a substantial upward trend in government health spending. Specifically, in the early 1990s, government spending on health services was about 1.1 per cent of GDP (World Bank 1998), but this figure had reached 1.7 per cent by 2003 and 2.8 per cent by 2007.[9] Given that Vietnam's GDP per capita has more than doubled (in real terms) since the early 1990s, absolute levels of government health spending have more than quadrupled. Finally, studies of the incidence of the Vietnamese government's health care expenditure show that much of it benefits poor people (although none of these studies distinguishes between poor adults and poor children). For example, O'Donnell et al. (2007: 100) estimate that the poorest 20 per cent of the population receive 14.8 per cent of Vietnam's health care subsidies. While this distribution of public subsidies is not 'equal', it is much more equal than the proportion of household expenditure made by the poorest 20 per cent in Vietnam (which the authors estimate to be 8.8 per cent).

The Vietnamese government also spends substantial sums on programmes intended to assist poor people directly. There is little research on the effectiveness of government programmes in improving child welfare, but van de Walle (2004) presents sobering evidence on the impact of Vietnam's poverty reduction programmes on poor people. She finds that these programmes are generally ineffective; many of the benefits go to non-poor households and many poor people do not benefit from the programmes.

Perhaps the most important reason why these programmes fail to reach poor people is that many were not designed to do so. For example, the largest programmes in place in 1998, which van de Walle calls 'social insurance funds', include pensions to veterans and retired civil servants, who are unlikely to be poor. Smaller, more focused poverty programmes were better targeted towards poor people in 1998, but there is much room for improvement: only 42 per cent of those benefits reached the poorest 20 per cent of the population, although 67 per cent reached the poorest 40 per cent. Van de Walle cites many problems with these programmes, including inadequate data to measure poverty at the commune and household level, and weak coordination among programmes.

Van de Walle uses data from the 1990s, yet a more recent study, based on 2002 and 2004 data, finds similar results. Cuong (2008) finds that a government-operated micro-credit programme designed to benefit poor people was not well targeted. Non-poor households accounted for the majority of the beneficiaries, and participating non-poor households received larger amounts of credit than did participating poor households. Clearly, more research is needed on this issue, especially analyses of the effectiveness of government programmes directed at poor children.

In summary, government health and education spending has increased substantially since Vietnam's economic growth rapidly increased in the late 1980s, and poor children almost certainly benefit from this spending. Yet many programmes intended to assist poor families are not well targeted. Thus while poor children benefit from government spending over and above the benefits received via their parents' higher incomes, these benefits could be increased if poverty programmes were better targeted.

Conclusion

Economic growth has great potential to improve the well-being of children in developing countries. Since the poorest children in those countries have the lowest quality of life, many hope that 'pro-poor' growth will greatly improve the well-being of those children. This chapter has explained the pathways by which economic growth could benefit poor children in those countries. There is compelling evidence that general economic growth raises the incomes of poor people, and thus has the potential to improve the lives of poor children. Whether higher household income benefits children depends on the type of benefit.

This chapter has examined data from Vietnam, and there is ample evidence that the rapid economic growth that has prevailed in Vietnam since the late 1980s has greatly increased the incomes of poor households. Moreover, this increase in household incomes appears to have increased school enrolment and reduced child labour, although the effects on child health are smaller. Finally, government spending on health and education has rapidly increased as Vietnam's economy has grown, which has almost certainly benefited poor children. In contrast, government spending on programmes designed to assist poor people often benefit the non-poor population.

Further research is needed in several areas. First, more analysis is needed on the impact of household income on health. This research should examine not only whether increased income improves these outcomes, but also the conditions that strengthen those impacts. Second, for all government programmes that could benefit children, research is needed on their effectiveness; randomized trials of a variety of programmes should provide a clearer picture of the impacts of those programmes. Finally, for Vietnam, more research is needed on how government health care expenditure can benefit children and how to improve the design of government poverty alleviation programmes.

Notes

1. It is possible for the incomes of poor people to increase even without economic growth; this could occur if income inequality decreased (without average income changing). However, this occurs relatively rarely; it is much more common for poor people's incomes to increase from general economic growth (Ravallion 1995; Dollar and Kraay 2002).
2. Child labour refers to any work by children that generates income for their families.
3. This analysis is limited to child welfare indicators available from nationally representative data. While this includes many commonly used indicators, it excludes other dimensions of children's welfare that may be of interest, such as mental health.
4. This growth rate was calculated using the World Bank's World Development Indicators database (series NY.GDP.PCAP.KN).
5. See Deaton and Grosh (2000: 93–5) for a thorough discussion of the advantages of (consumption) expenditure data over income data when analysing household surveys. The two main advantages are that (1) expenditure data are less prone to errors and (2) households' current well-being is more closely tied to expenditure than to income. Note that analyses of inequality within any country require household survey data.
6. The intuition for why random measurement error exaggerates income growth among the poor is as follows. In some initial time period, some of

the households whose incomes appear to put them in, say, the bottom 40 per cent of the income distribution are, in fact, households whose incomes (if correctly measured) put them in the top 60 per cent of the income distribution. In the next time period, assuming that measurement errors are uncorrelated over time, most households who were really in the top 60 per cent of the income distribution but were mistakenly assigned to the bottom 40 per cent in the initial time period will be in the top 60 per cent and thus will display unusually large increases in income. Thus random measurement error will exaggerate the (measured) growth of the poorest group but (assuming that the measurement errors' mean is zero) will not affect the measurement of average income for the whole population.

7. The age range does not go down to 0 months because the 2006 data measured children a few months after the interviews, and many children born after the interview were not measured.

8. These figures are from the World Bank's World Development Indicators database (series SE.XPD.TOTL.GD.ZS). The per pupil spending figures in this paragraph are from the same source (series SE.XPD.PRIM.PC.ZS, SE.XPD.SECO.PC.ZS and SE.XPD.TERT.PC.ZS).

9. The 2003 and 2008 figures are from the World Bank's World Development Indicators database (series SH.XPD.PUBL.ZS).

References

Chenery, Hollis, Montek Ahluwalia, Clive Bell, John Duloy and Richard Jolly (1974) *Redistribution with Growth*, Oxford: Oxford University Press.

Cuong, Nguyen Viet (2008) 'Is a Governmental Micro-Credit Program for the Poor Really Pro-Poor? Evidence from Viet Nam', *The Developing Economies* 46.2: 151–7.

Deaton, Angus (2007) 'Global Patterns of Income and Health: Facts, Interpretations, and Policies', WIDER Annual Lecture 10, UNU-WIDER, Helsinki, 29 September 2007.

Deaton, Angus, and Margaret Grosh (2000) 'Consumption' in M. Grosh and P. Glewwe (eds) *Designing Household Survey Questionnaires for Developing Countries: Lessons from 15 Years of the Living Standards Measurement Study*, Oxford: Oxford University Press.

Dollar, David, and Aart Kraay (2002) 'Growth is Good for the Poor', *Journal of Economic Growth* 7.3: 195–225.

Edmonds, Eric (2005) 'Does Child Labour Decline with Improving Economic Status?', *Journal of Human Resources* 40.1: 77–99.

Edmonds, Eric (2008) 'Child Labour' in T.P. Schultz and J. Strauss (eds) *Handbook of Development Economics*, vol. 4, Oxford and Amsterdam: North-Holland.

Fishlow, Albert (1980) 'Who Benefits from Economic Development? Comment', *American Economic Review* 70.1: 250–56.

Ferreira, Francisco, and Norbert Schady (2008) 'Aggregate Economic Shocks, Child Schooling, and Child Health', *World Bank Research Observer* 24.2: 147–81.

General Statistics Office (2007) *Result of the Viet Nam Household Living Standards Survey 2006*, Hanoi: Statistical Publishing House.

Glewwe, Paul (2004) 'An Investigation of the Determinants of School Progress and Academic Achievement in Vietnam' in P. Glewwe, N. Agrawal and D. Dollar (eds) *Economic Growth, Poverty and Household Welfare in Vietnam*, Washington DC: World Bank.

Glewwe, Paul, and Hai-Anh Dang (2011) 'Was Vietnam's Economic Growth in the 1990s Pro-Poor? An Analysis of Panel Data from Vietnam', *Economic Development and Cultural Change* 59.3: 588–608.

Glewwe, Paul, and Hanan Jacoby (2004) 'Economic Growth and the Demand for Education: Is There a Wealth Effect?' *Journal of Development Economics* 74.1: 33–51.

Glewwe, Paul, Stefanie Koch and Bui Linh Nguyen (2004) 'Child Nutrition, Economic Growth, and the Provision of Health Care Services in Vietnam' in P. Glewwe, N. Agrawal and D. Dollar (eds) *Economic Growth, Poverty and Household Welfare in Vietnam*, Washington DC: World Bank.

Glewwe, Paul, and Edward Miguel (2008) 'The Impact of Child Health and Nutrition on Education in Less Developed Countries' in T.P. Schultz and J. Strauss (eds) *Handbook of Development Economics*, vol. 4, Oxford and Amsterdam: North-Holland.

King, Elizabeth, and Andrew Mason (2001) *Engendering Development through Gender Equality in Rights, Resources and Voice*, Oxford: Oxford University Press.

O'Donnell, O., E. van Doorslaer, R.P. Rannan-Eliya, A. Somanathan, S.R. Adhikari, D. Harbianto, C.G. Garg, P. Hanvoravongchai, M.N. Huq, A. Karan, G.M. Leung, C.-w. Ng, B.R. Pande, K. Tin, L. Trisnantoro, C. Vasavid, Y. Zhang and Y. Zhao (2007) 'The Incidence of Public Spending on Healthcare: Comparative Evidence from Asia', *World Bank Economic Review* 21.1: 93–123.

Orazem, Peter, and Elizabeth King (2008) 'Schooling in Developing Countries: The Roles of Supply, Demand, and Government Policy' in T.P. Schultz and J. Strauss (eds) *Handbook of Development Economics*, vol. 4, Oxford and Amsterdam: North-Holland.

Ravallion, Martin (1995) 'Growth and Poverty: Evidence for Developing Countries in the 1980s', *Economics Letters* 48.3–4: 411–17.

Ravallion, Martin (2004) *Pro-Poor Growth: A Primer*, Policy Research Working Paper 3242, Washington DC: World Bank.

Strauss, John, and Duncan Thomas (2008) 'Health over the Life Course', in T.P. Schultz and J. Strauss (eds) *Handbook of Development Economics, Volume 4*, Oxford and Amsterdam: North-Holland.

van de Walle, Dominique (2004) 'The Static and Dynamic Incidence of Vietnam's Public Safety Net' in P. Glewwe, N. Agrawal and D. Dollar (eds), *Economic Growth, Poverty and Household Welfare in Vietnam*, Washington DC: World Bank.

Wagstaff, Adam, and Nga Nguyet Nguyen (2004) 'Poverty and Survival Prospects of Vietnamese Children under *Doi Moi*' in P. Glewwe, N. Agrawal and D. Dollar (eds) *Economic Growth, Poverty and Household Welfare in Vietnam*, Washington DC: World Bank.

World Bank (1998) *1998 World Development Indicators*, Washington, DC: World Bank.

World Bank (2008) *2008 World Development Indicators*, Washington, DC: World Bank.

6
Evidence on Early Childhood Development Investment Returns

Jere R. Behrman

An estimated 220 million pre-school-age children in the developing world fail to reach their development potential because of four major factors: stunting, iron deficiency, iodine deficiency and lack of cognitive and social-emotional stimulation (Grantham-McGregor et al. 2007). This undoubtedly has a large human cost. But possibly, in addition, it has a large productivity cost, which is the focus of this chapter. The question is: what are the potential productivity gains from increased investments in early childhood development (ECD) in the developing world?

This chapter considers selected evidence from recent studies on impacts of ECD investments in developing countries. By investments I mean the use of current resources such as food, time, and health services to increase productivity in the future – in this case, later in the life cycles of current pre-school-age children. The explicit focus is on very young lives, namely, children of pre-school ages back to conception. The focus is also on various components of a holistic view of ECD, one that includes nutrition and stimulation, because in poorly nourished and otherwise poor environments in developing countries, both are likely to be important. I explicitly note this broad definition here because nutritional considerations are excluded from many discussions of ECD. A number of the points about the challenges in evaluating the impacts of ECD investments, however, carry over for analysing investments in older children as well, and thus are of interest from the point of view of the broader age range covered by Young Lives. The first section below discusses the evaluation of impacts of investments in ECD. The second section summarizes some evidence on impacts of ECD investments in developing countries. The third section considers added evidence on impacts of nutritional components. The fourth section turns to the relative importance of ECD versus other investments. The fifth section presents conclusions.

Evaluation of impacts of ECD investments

To evaluate impacts of ECD investments, ideally one wants to compare outcomes for infants and toddlers (or older individuals who were affected by specific ECD investments when they were infants and toddlers) in whom specific ECD investments were made with *identical* infants and toddlers in whom *at the same time* these specific ECD investments were *not* made. Because such a comparison is not possible, analysts must use data and statistical methods to approximate this comparison.

Before summarizing the approaches used to approximate such comparisons, it is useful to consider some dimensions of the contexts in which ECD investments are made because these contexts make estimating the impacts of ECD investments challenging. Caregivers (often, but not always, parents) make choices that determine what these ECD investments are, whether these investments are made directly by the parents in the form, for example, of nutrients provided to the children or time spent on stimulating activities with the children, or indirectly through enrolling the children in pre-school programmes. The caregivers make these choices in light of the resources and options available to them, the caregivers' preferences regarding the use of these resources and alternative uses of these resources, and the characteristics of the children. There are many factors involved in these decisions by caregivers about ECD investments.

When analysts attempt to estimate the impact of ECD investments on subsequent outcomes, they have information that typically includes observations on a number of important characteristics of households, the children, and the communities in which they live such as: age and gender of the caregivers, and often their school attainment and occupation; age, gender, and birth order of the children; and the availability of ECD programmes and health clinics in the community. The basic problem, however, is that there are inevitably many possibly important factors underlying the ECD investment decisions that may also have impact on subsequent outcomes for the children through other channels than the specific ECD investment being evaluated, but on which analysts do not have information, including caregivers' preferences, innate abilities, and some dimensions of their resource constraints; children's innate abilities and innate health; and many dimensions of the physical, policy, and market environments of the communities.

This is a problem because these unobserved factors may both determine the ECD investment in the child and subsequent outcomes of the child, so in empirical estimates, the specific ECD investment under examination may represent not only its true effect but also the effects of such unobserved factors. To illustrate this problem, suppose that parents decide to invest more in children through sending their children to pre-school programmes, if and only if their children have relatively great innate ability and social skills, child characteristics that are not observed in the data available for analysis. If analysts then attempt to estimate the impact of ECD investments in pre-school programmes on subsequent tests of cognitive development and psychosocial skills, it will be a challenge to separate the true impact of the pre-school programmes from the impacts of the unobserved innate ability and social skills of the children who are selected to be enrolled in such programmes. There may be strong positive associations between attendance in pre-school programmes and subsequent tests of cognitive development and psychosocial skills even if the pre-school programmes do little or nothing to improve tests of cognitive development and psychosocial skills. Thus such *associations* may be very misleading as measures of the *causal impacts* of the ECD investments in pre-school programmes. In this example, the associations give an overestimate, perhaps a considerable overestimate, of the impacts of this particular ECD investment on cognitive development and psychosocial skills. But in other cases, the associations may give underestimates of the impacts of ECD investments – for example, if enrolment in an ECD programme depended on the children lagging in their development or being deprived in ways that are not observed in the data that analysts are able to use to estimate ECD investment impacts. Thus simple associations between ECD investments and subsequent outcomes may be misleading in either direction regarding the true impacts of the ECD investments.

The challenge for estimating the impact of ECD investments, therefore, can be viewed primarily as finding a way through research design and analysis to break the correlation between the empirical representation of the ECD investment being considered and the various unobserved factors that both affect the ECD investment and subsequent outcomes of interest through other channels.

Randomized controlled trials (RCTs) are generally considered to be the 'gold standard' for estimation of the impacts of such investments. In controlled double-blind randomized trials, baseline distributions of observed and unobserved characteristics are identical for those who receive the 'treatment' or the 'treated' (that is, those sent to pre-school in the example above) and those who do not receive the treatment or the 'control' group (that is, those not sent to pre-school in the example above). If the ECD investment is assigned randomly, it is not associated with unobserved family, child, or community characteristics. Therefore the associations between the ECD investments and subsequent outcomes of interest are not likely to be contaminated by correlations between the investments and unobserved characteristics, particularly in large samples. Although it would be desirable to have increased uses of experimental evaluations for investments related to ECD, they can raise the question of whether it is ethical to withhold the investment from a random group of children. But often in developing countries, ECD programmes and other forms of ECD investments are not instituted universally instantaneously, but phased in. Therefore some children will receive the ECD investment earlier than others, and in such cases, it would seem that random assignment of entry is likely to be a fairer and therefore more ethical procedure than the usual alternatives, such as responding to political pressures. The random assignment facilitates better evaluation of the ECD investment, thus providing an important public good in the form of information about the efficacy of the investment and on what conditions this efficacy depends.

However, RCTs do not solve all problems. They often are costly (perhaps in a political sense). They are difficult for ethical and cost reasons to keep going long enough to provide information on long-term effects. Some of the sample also may drop out of the study over time for reasons that affect inferences about the outcomes, such as failure at school and movement elsewhere. For such reasons alternative approaches are often used to try to assess the impact of ECD investments:

1. Difference-in-difference (Diff-in-Diff) estimates compare changes over time in outcomes for specific children in whom the ECD investments are made and other children in whom the investments are not made, thereby controlling for unobserved fixed characteristics such as innate child and parental ability. But Diff-in-Diff estimates do not control for unobserved factors that change over time, such as changes in particular household circumstances.
2. Propensity score matching (PSM) compares children in whom the ECD investments are made with those in whom the same investments are not made: both groups have similar observed characteristics, showing no particular bias for or against the investment. PSM results may, however, be affected by unobserved and differing characteristics of the children, their families, and their communities.

Marginal PSM makes comparisons between children who are similar apart from the investments, but focuses on changes over time for both groups: this effectively controls for unobserved fixed characteristics, but, like Diff-in-Diff, it fails to control for unobserved time-varying factors.

3. Regression discontinuity estimates compare those just above and below cut-offs for receiving the ECD investment in cases in which, for example, only children from families below the poverty line or only children in certain age ranges receive the specific ECD investments of interest. If the unobserved characteristics of children, their families, and their communities are very similar just above and just below the cut-off, this provides good estimates of programme effects for children close to the cut-off – though probably not for those far from the cut-off, such as the ultra poor if the cut-off is the poverty line.

4. Instrumental variables (IV) can sometimes provide evidence of the causal nature of statistical associations (examples are discussed by Hoddinott in this volume), but to be effective they must fulfil strict conditions and it is not always possible to find valid instruments. Valid instruments must both predict well the variable being instrumented (that is, the ECD investment in this case) and not have direct effects on the child outcome of interest, but only effects through the ECD investment being instrumented.

5. Structural models first estimate the underlying relations that determine behaviour like family ECD investments. Conditional on these estimated relations, they then explore hypothetical situations that suggest the effects of including or excluding elements of ECD investment (what economists, historians, and others call counterfactual experiments).

These options other than RCTs generally require stronger assumptions than do RCTs, but still may be preferable in certain situations if analysts are careful and explicit about what assumptions are being made and what are the implications of those assumptions for interpretation of the estimates. Despite these assumptions, one or more of these alternatives may be preferable over RCTs in specific situations because they may be much cheaper if the data are available for other reasons, particularly for longer-run effects. The last option listed, structural models, has the added advantage of permitting explorations of counterfactual ECD investments (that is, hypothetical variations on what actually took place) within a framework with heterogeneous individuals (avoiding possible effects of any common characteristics or associations). The estimates discussed below, as indicated, are based on a number of these different options.

Evidence on impacts of ECD programmes

ECD programmes are important vehicles for a number of ECD investments. What ECD programme interventions have worked at reasonable scale to reduce the loss of developmental potential for infants and toddlers in developing countries from the four major factors noted above? Engle et al. (2007) answer this question by reviewing 20 studies that satisfied the following criteria:

- Conducted since 1990
- RCT or matched groups (for example, marginal PSM)
- Intervention before children reached 6 years of age
- Focused on effectiveness or programme evaluation
- Child development assessed
- Focus on disadvantaged children in developing countries.

Engle et al. were able to find only 20 such studies for all the developing world with its varied contexts over a decade and a half. Table 6.1 summarizes the effects of interventions on cognitive and social-emotional development for three types of providers of ECD services: centre-based programmes, parent-training programmes, and comprehensive programmes. These studies indicate significant and substantial positive effects in the vast majority of cases for all three types of programmes.

Figure 6.1 summarizes the results from one of these studies, from the Philippines, that utilizes marginal PSM to obtain the estimates of improved cognitive skills arising from ECD programmes. The size of the effects of programmes may (and in this case does) depend importantly on the age of children and the duration of exposure. In particular, in

Table 6.1 Effects of ECD interventions in developing countries on cognitive and social-emotional development of children under 6 years

Type of intervention	Significant evaluations out of total	Effect sizes
Mainly centre-based	8 of 8	0.23–1.40
Mainly parent–child and parenting	5 of 6	0.45–0.8
Comprehensive	5 of 6	0.37–1.80

Source: Based on Engle et al. (2007).

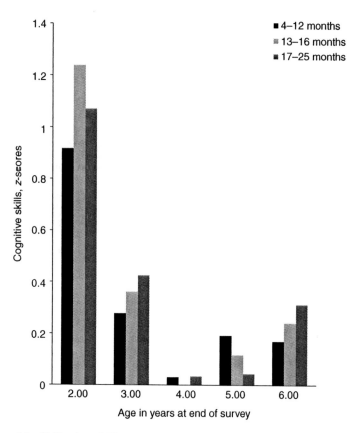

Figure 6.1   Philippines ECD programme effects on child cognitive skills related to children's age at evaluation and the months they were in ECD programme

Source: Based on marginal PSM estimates in Armecin et al. (2006).

this case, the effect sizes are much larger for children exposed to the programme during their first two years of life, second largest for those aged 3 at the time of the final survey, and third largest for those aged 6 at the time of the final survey, suggesting a U-shaped programme effect with age. Increasing the duration of exposure to the programme from less to more than a year also increases programme impact for these three age groups. Increasing duration of exposure beyond 16 months for very young children (aged 2 after the programme exposure) does not result in further gains; however, such an extension of exposure does increase programme impact for children aged 3 and 6 years at the final survey.

Table 6.2 illustrates two other important points from a study from Guatemala: the impacts of pre-school cognitive skills and nutritional status may be multiple and may occur over the life cycle (and, indeed, across generations, although this is not included in this table). These points mean that to capture the full impact requires data that covers multiple possible effects and that follows infants and toddlers for decades or, less satisfactorily but less costly, particularly in terms of elapsed time, pieces together life cycle segments from different birth cohorts.

Engle et al. conclude from the studies they review that the characteristics of successful ECD programmes include the following:

- Being comprehensive, including a range of components related to stimulation and nutrition
- Targeting disadvantaged children
- Beginning with younger children
- Having sufficient intensity and duration
- Being high quality, including having well-trained staff
- Having partnerships with families
- Including evidence-based monitoring and evaluation.

Table 6.2 IV estimates of impacts of pre-school cognitive skills and height over the life cycle in Guatemala

	Pre-school cognitive skills	Pre-school height
Schooling attainment (grades)	0.39	
	1.73	
Adult reading-comprehension skills	0.54	
	2.94	
Adult nonverbal skills	0.72	0.39
	2.62	*2.03*
Adult BMI	−0.47	−0.37
	−1.64	*−1.69*
Adult total labour income (ln)	0.06	
	2.58	
Total hours worked (ln)	0.22	
	5.81	

*t-statistics are in italics beneath point estimates. Coefficient estimates for pre-school cognitive skills and height that are not significantly nonzero at the 0.25 level are constrained to zero. All estimates also controlled for parental assets, parental education, community in which childhood was spent and gender.

Source: Based on Behrman et al. (2008a).

This provides a useful checklist for considering ECD programmes in developing countries. But it is very general and based on the relatively few studies that could be located that satisfied the criteria for inclusion in this review. Furthermore, despite the authors' careful review, the evidence for the importance of these characteristics varies significantly. For all of these reasons, careful consideration needs to be given to the implications of these general recommendations for any specific ECD programme in that specific context. Also it is very desirable, in the cases of ECD programmes that are implemented, to monitor them carefully and to consider careful systematic evaluation because almost any programme, no matter how carefully thought out in advance on the basis of previous experiences, can be improved with more knowledge about what is and what is not working well in that particular context.

Further evidence on impacts of nutritional components

As is well known, gestation and the first two to three years of life have the characteristics of high nutritional requirements, rapid growth and development, great susceptibility to infections, and almost complete dependence on others for care. These make children's development particularly vulnerable at this stage in life. In many developing countries, the initial period of life also is a time during which many children fall behind international standards in terms of nutritional indicators. Therefore the nutritional component of ECD investments may be critical, particularly in poorly nourished populations, which are substantial in many developing countries.

In a recent *Lancet* article, Victora et al. (2008) present new estimates based on five cohort studies (Brazil, Guatemala, India, Philippines, and South Africa) and review previous studies of associations between infant and child nutritional status and outcomes over the infants' and children's life cycles, which are summarized in Table 6.3. This table indicates important associations, though the studies did not use data and methods that establish causal connections.

Recently various colleagues and I have been involved in assessing the long-term effects of a nutritional intervention in early childhood in Guatemala. Briefly, in 1969–77 nutritional supplements that were better in terms of protein and calories (*atole*) and less good (*fresco*) were randomly available in four village centres in the well-known Institute of Nutrition for Central America and Panama (INCAP) longitudinal study. We conducted follow-up surveys in 2002–04 and 2006–07 of individuals who were 0–7 years of age in 1969–77 (and 25–42 years old

Table 6.3 Summary of selected associations between infant anthropometric measures and adult outcomes

Adult height increases by:	3.2 cm for 1 HAZ at age 2 years 0.7–1.0 cm for 1 cm at birth
Completed schooling attainment increases by:	0.5 grades for 1 HAZ at age 2 years 0.5 grades for 1 WAZ at age 2 years 0.3 grades for 1 kg at birth
Adult labour income increases by:	8% for 1 HAZ at age 2 years for males 8–25% for 1 HAZ at age 2 years for females

Note: HAZ is the height-for-age z-score. WAZ is the weight-for-age z-score. The z-scores give the number of standard deviations above or below the median for international standards for healthy children. They are particularly useful for comparisons of distributions measured in different units (such as height and weight).

Source: Based on Victora et al. (2008).

in 2002–04) and their children. Based on the experimental assignment of the nutritional supplements, exposure to the better nutritional supplement early in life had some significant and substantial effects about three decades later:

Exposure to improved nutrition from 0–3 years of age improved education (Maluccio et al. 2009):

- Schooling increased by 1.2 grades (0.36 Standard Deviation (SD) units) for women only
- Inter-American Reading scores improved by 0.28 SD units for both men and women
- Raven's Progressive Matrices cognition scores improved by 0.24 SD units for both men and women.

Exposure to improved nutrition before, but not after 3 years of age, improved wages (income/hour) by US$ 0.67 or 45 per cent of SD for men but not women. (Hoddinott et al. 2008)

Exposure for females when under 7 years of age (but not for males) affected their children 0–12 years of age 29–38 years later with significant increases in birth weight of 119 g, height of 1.3 cm, height-for-age z score (HAZ) of 0.26 and weight-for-age z score (WAZ) of 0.20. (Behrman et al. 2009)

These studies provide important evidence of substantial and significant long-term causal impacts of improved early life nutrition on a range of outcomes of interest later in the life cycle and across generations in the context of a poor developing country with substantial undernourishment.

Relative importance of ECD versus other investments

That ECD investments probably have significant effects in a number of developing country contexts is in itself not sufficient to make a compelling case for investing more resources in ECD. There may also be large effects of other investments, such as formal schooling or health programmes. In this section, I turn to some evidence on the relative returns to ECD investments as compared with some alternatives.

Relative effectiveness in Guatemala

Table 6.4 gives the estimated causal impacts of improved pre-school cognitive skills, based on IV estimates, on outcomes over the life cycle in comparison with associations with parental characteristics and wealth. (Many other studies suggest that the associations with parental characteristics are likely to overstate the causal effects of parental characteristics because of inter-generationally correlated endowments.) The effect sizes for most of the outcomes are larger for child pre-school cognitive skills than for parental characteristics, including maternal schooling, which has been heavily emphasized in the literature and in policy discussions. Moreover, changing parental characteristics such as those in this table would probably require much greater time lags before any effect was felt by children. Therefore these comparisons suggest

Table 6.4 Estimated effect sizes of better pre-school cognitive skills compared with better family background in Guatemala

	Pre-school cognitive skills	Mother's schooling	Father's schooling	Household assets
Schooling attainment (grades)	0.39	0.19	0.19	0.23
Adult reading-comprehension skills	0.54	0.17	0.15	0.18
Adult non-verbal skills	0.72	0.17	0.09	0.09
Adult BMI	−0.47	0.00	−0.04	−0.04
Adult total labour income (ln)	0.06	0.11	0.05	0.10
Total hours worked (ln)	0.22	0.10	0.03	0.01

Source: Based on Behrman et al. (2008a).

that ECD investments, such as increasing pre-school cognitive skills by directly investing in the children, may be more effective than investments to improve family background through, say, increasing schooling of those who are to become parents.

Cognitive achievement production functions indicate how cognitive skills are produced for these Guatemalan adults as dependent on pre-schooling, schooling, and adult experiences, with each of the experiences determined endogenously.[1] Figure 6.2 illustrates the relative impacts on adult reading comprehension scores of pre-school and school-age experiences. This figure also illustrates the importance of controlling for behavioural decisions and of including multiple life-cycle experiences, not just one. The first pair of estimates includes those that are obtained if there is no control for the experiences being behavioural and if only one particular experience is included at a time ('OLS by self' referring to standard ordinary least squares estimates). The second pair of columns gives the estimated impact if all experiences (that is, pre-school, schooling, and post-schooling experiences) are included and all are treated as behaviourally determined using instrumental variables (see above). This figure illustrates that schooling is significantly associated with cognitive skills, but the estimated causal effect of schooling with control for the behavioural determination of the experiences and the inclusion of all three experiences is only half as

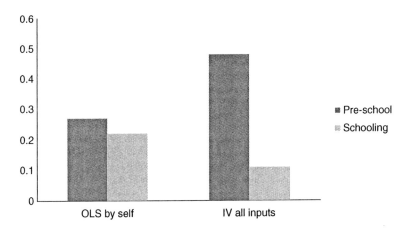

Figure 6.2 Impact on adult reading comprehension score (standard deviations) for pre-school-age child not being stunted or another grade of school (Guatemala)

Source: Based on Behrman et al. (2008b).

large for the reading comprehension test (and no longer significant for non-verbal skills in estimates not presented). In contrast, the estimated impact of pre-school stunting is larger and important relative to schooling with the inclusion of all three behaviourally determined experiences. These preferred estimates, for example, suggest that the causal impact on adult reading comprehension tests of moving a child from the pre-school experience of being stunted to not being stunted is equal to about the impact of four additional grades of schooling.

Economic benefits relative to economic costs

One of the challenges of estimating the benefits of ECD investments is that there are likely to be multiple impacts over the life cycle and across generations, and these impacts are conditional on survival probabilities. To calculate the benefits of investments it is important to (1) estimate benefits, not simply associations (as emphasized in the section on evaluation and illustrated in the previous section); (2) avoid double counting (for example, if part of the benefit is to increase schooling and part of the benefit of schooling is to increase post-schooling productivity, that part of schooling that increases productivity should not be counted twice as a benefit); (3) place monetary values on each benefit (which is a challenge for some benefits such as increasing the probability of survival); and (4) adjust for the different timing of benefits to reflect that a given monetary value of benefits is greater if it is received sooner because the proceeds can be reinvested (in technical terms, obtain present discounted values (PDVs) of benefits).

Table 6.5 illustrates from a very early ECD investment, better nutrition in the womb, the PDVs of various benefits from moving one baby out of low-birth-weight status (below 2.5 kg) in a low-income developing context such as South Asia. Often the benefits of increasing survival and reducing infant morbidity are emphasized in discussions of the benefits of reducing low birth weight. But even with discounting at 5 per cent, these estimates suggest that there are much bigger gains from productivity increases through the adult working years. Also these estimates illustrate the sensitivity to the discount rate used, with the PDV decreasing by half if the discount rate used is 10 per cent rather than 5 per cent.

But having good estimates of the absolute magnitudes of the benefits of ECD programmes (as in the section on impacts of nutritional components or Table 6.5) or even their relative magnitudes (as in the previous section) does not by itself determine whether the ECD programmes should be high or low among policy priorities in terms of

Table 6.5 Estimates of present discounted values of seven major benefits of moving one infant out of low-birth-weight status in a low-income country, at different discount rates

	Values (US$)		
	Annual discount rate		
Benefit	3%	5%*	10%
1. Reduced infant mortality	95	99	89
2. Reduced neonatal care	42	42	42
3. Reduced costs of infant and child illness	36	35	34
4. Productivity gain from reduced stunting	152	85	25
5. Productivity gain from increased cognitive ability	367	205	60
6. Reduced costs of chronic diseases	49	15	1
7. Intergenerational benefits	92	35	6
Total	832	510	257
Share of total at 5% discount rate	163%	100%	50%

*The 5% discount rate, shown in bold, is the base case estimate.

Source: Alderman and Behrman (2006).

their productivity impacts or resources saved. To establish such priorities, the economic costs of various programmes must be considered in addition to the benefits. The economic costs include costs of private and public resources, including administrative costs such as those necessary for creating incentives for use of resources by poor people, but do *not* include transfers of funds or materials (which remain available for use in the economy).The economic resource costs may be very different from the governmental budgetary costs, which do not include private costs but may include large transfers (for example, in conditional cash transfer programmes which have spread rapidly throughout the world). The costs, like the benefits, may also occur over time, so the present discounted value of costs needs to be obtained for comparison with the present discounted value of the benefits.

Table 6.6 provides some examples of estimates that combine the estimated PDV of benefits relative to the PDV of costs for a number of interventions related to improved nutrition, primarily for infants and toddlers or their mothers. Note that many of these interventions appear relatively attractive because the benefits are considerably greater than the costs (ranges are given to reflect alternative assumptions). Such estimates permit the comparison of these interventions with others. These estimates were made as an input into the 2004 Copenhagen Consensus at which interventions in ten broad policy areas were ranked by eight leading economists (including four Nobel

Table 6.6 Combining benefits and costs for nutritional interventions for women and children for 2004 Copenhagen Consensus

Opportunities and targeted populations	Benefits/ Costs	Size of targeted populations
1. Reducing LBW for pregnancies with high probabilities LBW (especially in South Asia)		12 million LBW births per year
1a Treatments for women with asymptomatic bacterial infections	0.6–4.9	
1b Treatment for women with presumptive STD	1.3–10.7	
1c Drugs for pregnant women with poor obstetric history	4.1–35.2	
2. Improving infant and child nutrition in populations with high prevalence of child malnutrition (fairly widespread in poor populations)		162 million stunted children
2a Breastfeeding promotion in hospitals where norm has been promotion of use of infant formula	4.8–7.4	
2b Integrated childcare programmes	9.4–16.2	
2c Intensive pre-school programme with considerable nutrition for poor families	1.4–2.9	
3. Reducing micronutrient deficiencies in populations in which they are prevalent		2 billion people with iodine deficiencies
3a Iodine (per woman of child-bearing age)	15–520	128 million pre-school children
3b Vitamin A (per child under 6 years)	4.3–43	3.5 billion people,
3c Iron (per capita)	176–200	including
3d Iron (pregnant women)	6.1–14	estimated 67 million pregnant women

Source: Based on Behrman et al.

Prize winners) on the basis in part of such benefit–cost ratios (Lomborg 2004). The interventions relating to nutrition in early life and of mothers rank fair to high among a wide range of interventions (Table 6.7). Unfortunately comparable estimates for types of ECD interventions other than these nutritional interventions were not made for the 2004 Copenhagen Consensus, nor have many been made to my knowledge by others. One possible exception is the estimate of benefit to governmental resource costs (but not including private resource costs) of 1.4 to 3.7 for the Bolivian PIDI (Proyecto Integral de Desarrollo Infantil [Integrated Child Development Programme]) pre-school programme

Table 6.7 Ranking of nutritional interventions for children and mothers in low-income countries among wide range of alternatives

Project ranking in Copenhagen Consensus

Project rating		Challenge	Opportunity
Very Good	1	Diseases	Control of HIV/AIDS
	2	**Malnutrition**	Providing of micronutrients
	3	Subsidies and trade	Trade liberalization
	4	Diseases	Control of malaria
Good	5	**Malnutrition**	Development of new agricultural technologies
	6	Sanitation and water	Small-scale water technology for livelihoods
	7	Sanitation and water	Community-managed water supply and sanitation
	8	Sanitation and water	Research on water productivity in food production
	9	Government	Lowering the cost of starting a new business
Fair	10	Migration	Lowering the barriers to migration for skilled workers
	11	**Malnutrition**	Improving infant and child nutrition
	12	**Malnutrition**	Reducing the prevalence of low birth weight
	13	Diseases	Scaled-up basic health services
Bad	14	Migration	Guest worker programmes for the unskilled
	15	Climate	Optimal carbon tax
	16	Climate	The Kyoto Protocol
	17	Climate	Value-at-risk carbon tax

Source: Based on Behrman et al. (2004) 'Hunger and Malnutrition' in Bjørn Lomborg (ed.) *Global Crises, Global Solutions*, © Environmental Assessment Institute 2004, published by Cambridge University Press, reproduced with permission.

(Behrman et al. 2004). But the limited available estimates do suggest a mismatch between, on the one hand, current investment patterns that focus on schooling and other investments later in the life cycle and, on the other, opportunities for early life investments of the sort emphasized recently particularly by Heckman and collaborators for the United States (Heckman 2006).

Conclusions

There is a rapidly increasing body of evidence regarding substantial impacts of ECD investments over the life cycle, relating to physical growth as much as to the kind of development commonly associated

106 *Jere R. Behrman*

with pre-school services. There is also some evidence regarding these benefits relative to benefits from other interventions. On the basis of such information, what Nobel Laureate James Heckman (2006) said for ECD investments in the USA is also probably true for most developing countries: 'It is a rare public policy initiative that promotes fairness and social justice and at the same time promotes productivity in the economy and in society at large. Early interventions targeted at disadvantaged children have much higher returns than later investments'.

The evidence, therefore, favours expanding ECD investments, with policies that better integrate ministries, are comprehensive (including cognitive and social stimulation, nutrition, and health), have increased incentives for providers and for families, and incorporate the development of better indicators for comparisons and evaluation together with ongoing monitoring and systematic evaluation. The collection of information and careful analysis of that information is critical because, while there is increasing evidence of high impacts of some ECD investments in some contexts, such results are likely to be very context-dependent and the existing evidence covers relatively few programmes in relatively few contexts. Moreover, such evidence is not generally integrated well with estimates of resource costs to help establish relative priorities. Therefore, despite the considerable challenges, there are likely to be high social returns to more systematic evaluations of varieties of ECD investments in different developing country contexts. Such efforts are likely to be critical for improving ECD investment programmes and for justifying the use of public resources for them.

Note

1. Production functions show how outcomes (for example, agricultural production of crops) depend on production inputs (for example, water, land, labour, fertilizer) in a technical production process. In this case the outcomes are adult cognitive achievement scores and the inputs are indicators of individual experiences when of pre-school age, of school age, and of post-school age.

References

Alderman, Harold and Jere R. Behrman (2006) 'Reducing the Incidence of Low Birth Weight In Low-Income Countries has Substantial Economic Benefits', *World Bank Research Observer* 21.1: 25–48.
Armecin, Graeme, Jere R. Behrman, Paulita Duazo, Sharon Ghuman, Socorro Gultiano, Elizabeth M. King, Nanette Lee, and The Office of Population Studies, University of San Carlos ECD Team (2006) 'Early Childhood Development

through Integrated Programs: Evidence from the Philippines', Cebu City, New York, Philadelphia and Washington: Universities of Pennsylvania and San Carlos (Office of Population Studies), Population Council and World Bank.

Behrman, Jere R., Harold Alderman and John Hoddinott (2004) 'Hunger and Malnutrition' in Bjørn Lomborg (ed.) *Global Crises, Global Solutions*, Cambridge: Cambridge University Press.

Behrman, Jere R., Maria Cecilia Calderon, Samuel Preston, John Hoddinott, Reynaldo Martorell and Aryeh D. Stein (2009) 'Nutritional Supplementation of Girls Influences the Growth of their Children: Prospective Study in Guatemala', *American Journal of Clinical Nutrition* 90 (November 2009): 1372–9.

Behrman, Jere R., Yingmei Cheng and Petra Todd (2004) 'Evaluating Preschool Programs when Length of Exposure to the Program Varies: A Nonparametric Approach', *Review of Economics and Statistics* 86.1 (February): 108–32.

Behrman, Jere R., Suzanne Duryea and John Maluccio (2008a) 'Addressing Early Childhood Deficits in Guatemala', Washington, DC: Inter-American Development Bank.

Behrman, Jere R., John Hoddinott, John A. Maluccio, Erica Soler-Hampejsek, Emily L. Behrman, Reynaldo Martorell, Manuel Ramirez and Aryeh D. Stein (2008b) *What Determines Adult Cognitive Skills? Impacts of Pre-School, School-Years and Post-School Experiences in Guatemala*, Discussion Paper No. 826, Washington, DC: International Food Policy Research Institute (IFPRI).

Engle, Patrice L., Maureen M. Black, Jere R. Behrman, Meena Cabral de Mello, Paul J. Gertler, Lydia Kapiriri, Reynaldo Martorell, Mary Eming Young, International Child Development Steering Committee, (2007) 'Strategies to Avoid the Loss of Potential Among 240 Million Children in the Developing World', *The Lancet* 369 (January): 229–42.

Grantham-McGregor, Sally M., Yin Bun Cheung, Santiago Cueto, Paul Glewwe, Linda M. Richter and Barbara J. Strupp (2007) 'Over Two Hundred Million Children Fail to Reach Their Developmental Potential in the First Five Years in Developing Countries', *The Lancet* 369 (January): 60–70.

Heckman, James J. (2006) 'Skill Formation and the Economics of Investing in Disadvantaged Children', *Science* 312 (30 June): 1900–2.

Hoddinott, John, John A. Maluccio, Jere R. Behrman, Rafael Flores and Reynaldo Martorell (2008) 'The Impact of Nutrition During Early Childhood on Income, Hours Worked, and Wages of Guatemalan Adults', *The Lancet* 371 (February): 411–16.

Lomborg, Bjørn (ed.) 2004, *Global Crises, Global Solutions*, Cambridge: Cambridge University Press.

Maluccio, John A., John Hoddinott, Jere R. Behrman, Agnes Quisumbing, Reynaldo Martorell and Aryeh D. Stein (2009) 'The Impact of Nutrition During Early Childhood on Education among Guatemalan Adults', *Economic Journal* 119 (Issue 537): 734–63.

Victora, Cesar G. , Linda Adair, Caroline Fall, Pedro C. Hallal, Reynaldo Martorell, Linda Richter and Harshpal Singh Sachdev, on behalf of the Maternal and Child Undernutrition Study Group (2008) 'Undernutrition 2: Maternal and Child Undernutrition: Consequences for Adult Health and Human Capital', *The Lancet* 371 (Issue 9609): 340–57.

7
Do Economic Shocks Have a Long-Term Effect on the Height of 5-Year-Old Children? Evidence from Rural and Urban Ethiopia

Tassew Woldehanna[1]

Introduction

Reductions in child mortality and illness are often considered the main indicators of social development. As a result, one of the targets of the Millennium Development Goals is reducing child and infant mortality rates by two-thirds. In the Ethiopian context, the target set by the national survival strategy is to reduce the under-five mortality rate from 140 to 85 per 1,000 births and the infant mortality rate from 97 to 45 per 1,000 births by 2015 (MoFED 2006a, 2006b: 117). The nutrition of children is key to reducing these mortality rates since malnutrition is currently the leading cause of disease globally (Ezzati et al. 2002) and has been identified as the underlying factor in about 50 per cent of deaths of children under five years of age in developing countries (Frimpong and Pongou 2006: 3; Black et al. 2003). Ethiopia's Health Sector Development Program (FMoH, 2005: 39) lists malnutrition as one of the major causes of child mortality, together with pneumonia, neonatal conditions, malaria, diarrhoea, measles, and HIV/AIDS.

In Ethiopia, households are commonly hit by shocks which are area-wide, such as drought and crop failure, and idiosyncratic shocks, such as the illness and death of household members, increases in food prices, and loss of employment. While these shocks are common in Ethiopia, there is no clear evidence to show how far they affect children's nutritional status and whether the effects persist.

In developing countries, economic shocks or crises have been shown to impact negatively on child health (Paxson and Schady 2004: 1–5,

12, 39; Hill et al. 1993: 1; Pongou et al. 2005). Many studies have been mainly concerned with the short-term effects of economic downturns on health (for example, Dercon and Hoddinott 2003; and at household level, Behrman and Rosenzweig 2004 and Haddad et al. 2003). Obviously shocks can have short-term effects on child growth, but as long as social assistance is in place and effective (Yamano et al. 2005), a one-off economic shock should not have a long-term impact on children's nutrition and growth. There are no studies so far conducted in Ethiopia regarding the long-term consequences of shocks while social assistance programmes are in place.

Literature suggests that human capital formation is a multistage process (Cunha et al. 2006), in which early childhood malnutrition could have a strong effect on malnutrition of children at a later stage of their development. Alderman et al. (2006) examine the long-term consequences of early malnutrition and the possibilities of recovery and catch-up growth, using data from school-age children in Zimbabwe. They found limited long-term consequences and a possibility of recovery (pp. 469–70). However, assessment of the long-term consequences of, and recovery from, malnutrition is obviously dependent on environmental factors and the age of the children chosen for assessment.

The main objectives of this chapter are to investigate sustained consequences of early childhood malnutrition and recovery from this, and to assess the long-term effects of pre-natal and post-natal economic shocks on child health and nutrition, using standardized height measurements. Further objectives are to examine the relative significance of area-wide (co-variant) and idiosyncratic economic shocks for the growth of 5-year-old children and to identify implications for the social protection policy of Ethiopia.

We employed multivariate analysis using two rounds of Young Lives Survey data on the Younger Cohort, who were around 1 year old in Round 1 and 5 years old in Round 2. Both Round 1 (conducted in the last quarter of 2002) and Round 2 data (collected in the last quarter of 2006) contain information on height for age of the 1-year-old and 5-year-old children, respectively, and on the incidence of economic shocks that hit households up to five years before the surveys.

Method, data source, and description of data

Statistical model

We take increases in height of 5-year-olds as an indicator of nutrition and health status. We calculated the main indicators used in the literature to measure malnutrition among children, namely, height for age and stunting, for the Younger Cohort (1- and 5-year-old children). We used a table of distribution of children's height for age developed recently by the World Health Organization (WHO 2007; WHO Multicentre Growth Reference Study Group 2006) and based on Brazil, Ghana, India, Norway, Oman, and the USA as a reference population to calculate the mean and the standard deviation.

To explain children's nutrition, we developed a model where the dependent variable is height or increase in height at the age of around 5 years. We used a number of measures for this model. Z-scores of height for age were calculated both at 1 year and 5 years: since these are based on standard deviations from the mean rather than on any particular units, they are useful for comparative purposes. To see the sensitivity of the results, we also measured nutrition by taking a logarithm of height in centimetres in order to standardize height. For probit analyses that require counting rather than measurements, we used the categories of *stunting* (between 2 and 3 standard deviations below the mean of height for age) and *severe stunting* (more than 3 standard deviations below the mean).

The pre-natal and post-natal economic shocks are included as explanatory variables because they are expected to affect health and nutrition inputs and household income. In order to have a clear picture of the effect of shocks on children's recovery from their stunting, we also analysed the changes in both measures of nutritional status (height for age and log of height) between the ages of 1 and 5 years. In addition to the pre-natal and post-natal economic shocks (that is, shocks that hit families before and after the birth of the child), various other independent variables are also used as controlling factors, including initial nutritional status (assessed at age 1), household wealth and household composition in Round 1.

Data source and description of datasets

We used longitudinal survey data from the Young Lives study collected in 2002 and 2006. At the time of Round 2 (2006), the survey included 1,860 children of 4.5 to 5.5 years old, of whom 1,119 were living in rural areas while 741 were living urban areas. The pre-natal economic shocks were logged during the Round 1 survey while the post-natal economic shocks are from the Round 2 survey.

Wealth and asset indexes

Table 7.1 presents levels of household wealth and percentage changes between Rounds 1 and 2, measured by asset and wealth indexes

Table 7.1 Household wealth, *R1–R2*, in urban/rural areas (by wealth and asset index)

	Rural			Urban			Total		
	R1	*R2*	% change	*R1*	*R2*	% change	*R1*	*R2*	% change
Wealth index	0.08	0.13	60.39	0.33	0.37	12.84**	0.18	0.23	25.42
Asset index	0.21	0.26	21.34	0.12	0.16	26.93**	0.18	0.21	21.02

Note: % change refers to *(R2–R1)/R1*100*; ** $p < 0.01$.

(see Woldehanna et al. 2008a for the construction of these indexes). Household wealth increased according to both indexes in both urban and rural areas. The increments are statistically significant for both indexes at less than a 1 per cent level of probability, although the magnitude of the change was higher for the wealth index than for the asset index.

The percentage of children in the Younger Cohort living in households with a wealth index below 0.2 decreased from 42.0 to 32.4, which represents an improvement over time of about 23 per cent. This difference is statistically significant at less than 1 per cent.

Malnutrition

As can be seen in Table 7.2, stunting and severe stunting declined, although the decline in stunting in urban areas was not significant by the standards of the *t*-tests used. Severe stunting has declined substantially. This is an impressive accomplishment, which can be attributed to an improvement in the wealth level of households and increased access to health services. These measures, however, were quite high in Round 1. Thus, what we observe could easily be recovery of child nutritional status. Table 7.3 also shows that, of the children who were not stunted at the age of 1 year, few became stunted by the age of 5 years. On the other hand, 41 per cent of the children who were stunted at the age of 1, and 75 per cent of those severely stunted recovered. The rate of recovery is considerably higher than the rate of deterioration in both categories of stunting.

Severe stunting showed an improvement for both genders while stunting declined only for boys (Table 7.4).

Economic shocks

As part of the Round 1 and the Round 2 surveys, Young Lives recorded economic shocks that affected household well-being. Round 1 recorded

Table 7.2 Malnutrition among 1-year-old and 5-year-old children (percentage of children stunted or severely stunted)

	Total			Rural			Urban		
	R1	*R2*	% change	*R1*	*R2*	% change	*R1*	*R2*	% change
Stunted	34.84	31.33	−10.0*	41.34	36.41	−11.92*	25.03	23.65	−5.51
Severely stunted	15.46	8.22	−46.80**	19.2	10.63	−44.64**	9.83	4.6	−53.19**

Note: % change = $((R1–R1)/R1))*100$; ** $p < 0.01$, * $p < 0.05$.

Table 7.3 A matrix of recovery of children from stunting and severe stunting between 2002 and 2006 (%)

	Status in 2006			
	Not stunted	Stunted	Total (%)	Total *N*
Not stunted (2002)	85	15	100	960
Stunted (2002)	41	59	100	508
Total	70	30	100	1,468

	Not severely stunted	Severely stunted	Total (%)	Total *N*
Not severely stunted (2002)	95	5	100	1,295
Severely stunted (2002)	75	25	100	173
Total	93	7	100	1,468

Source: Own computation; in order to reduce the measurement errors, we excluded observations whose z-score growth was below −2 and above 2.

Table 7.4 Changes in the proportion of children malnourished by gender of child, *R1–R2*

	Male			Female		
	R1	*R2*	% change	*R1*	*R2*	% change
Stunted	0.39	0.33	−16.4**	0.3	0.29	−0.6
Severely stunted	0.18	0.08	−54.4**	0.12	0.08	−33.7**

** $p < 0.01$.

shocks that had affected households in the previous five years, for the most part before the child was born. They are therefore classified here as pre-natal shocks. Shocks recorded during the Round 2 survey are those that occurred after the child was born, but before he/she reached the age of 5. These shocks are referred to as post-natal shocks. The incidence of these pre-natal and post-natal economic shocks included in our econometric analysis[2] appear as dummy variables because they are categorical in nature. The highest incidence of shocks reported before the child was born was of decreases in food availability, followed by crop failure, and for urban areas, job loss. Among the shocks that occurred after the child was born, drought, crop failure and pests and diseases have a higher incidence of occurrence.

Results and discussion

We first examined the sustained effects of early childhood malnutrition and the recovery of children from their early childhood malnutrition. Next, we assessed the long-term effects of pre-natal and post-natal economic shocks on children's height. In the estimation of the models, we employed ordinary least square (OLS) and instrumental variables (IV) estimation or generalized method of moments (GMM) methods. The instrumental variables used for early childhood malnutrition are dummy (or indicator) variable whether the child had a long-term illness and dummy variable for whether the household head was severely ill before the child was born.[3] We estimated probit model of stunting and severe stunting on the same set of explanatory variables. We use several methods of estimation techniques in order to check the robustness of our result.

We found the instrument variables were not correlated with initial z-score of height for age. We also conducted a test to see if z-score height for age and log of height in Round 1 were endogenous and we failed to reject that the z-score of height for age in Round 1 was exogenous. However, in the estimation of log of height for age, we found that log of height for age in Round 1 was endogenous. The summaries of the OLS and IV estimation results are provided in Tables 7.5 and 7.6. The results from both IV and OLS have similar signs, but the magnitude of the coefficients from IV estimation is slightly higher than that of OLS estimation.

For both rural and urban areas, the data fits well in all the OLS and probit regressions. In our regression of z-score of height for age, R^2 was 23 per cent, while it was 26 per cent in the regression of log of height for age. In the probit regressions, the Pseudo-R^2 is 11 and 15 per cent for rural and urban areas, respectively.

The association between early malnutrition and the height of 5-year-olds is summarized in Table 7.5. As expected, the z-score of height for age at the age of 1 year (initial nutritional status) has a positive and statistically significant effect on height for age at the age of 5 years, but is very low in magnitude, implying a very high potential for recovery of children between the age of 1 and 5 years. But this also suggests that there may be permanent consequences from stunting at the age of 1 year. The same pattern was observed when the dependent variable was log of height in centimetres. These results also hold when we control for community fixed effects, with the exception that the IV estimation method fails to show sustained effects of initial height for rural areas. We see more sustained effects of malnutrition and less recovery in urban areas than in rural areas.

Using our alternative specification where the dependent variable is change in z-score of height for age, we estimated negative and significant effects of initial score on the changes between Round 1 and Round 2 (Table 7.5). The magnitude of the coefficient in absolute value confirms what was shown in the regressions comparing stunting and severe stunting between the two rounds: the recovery of children from stunting is high and there is some sustained reduction in height. The results in general imply that efforts to achieve better nutritional status

Table 7.5 Effects of initial z-score of height for age or log of height in centimetres

Method of estimation	Dependent variable = z-score of height for age		Dependent variable = log of height in centimetres	
	Rural	Urban	Rural	Urban
OLS	0.223**	0.252**	0.280**	0.347**
Community fixed effect, OLS	0.250**	0.280**	0.353**	0.385**
IV estimation	0.046	0.514**	0.000	0.366**
Community fixed effect, IV	0.290	0.590**	0.437*	0.338**
	Dependent variable = changes in z-score of height for age of 5-year-old child		Dependent variable = changes in logarithm of height of 5-year-old child	
	Rural	Urban	Rural	Urban
OLS	−0.777**	−0.748**	−0.688**	−0.656**
IV estimation	−1.122**	−0.936**	−1.000**	−0.634**

$** p < 0.01, * p < 0.05$.

for children should start at an early stage of child development, perhaps during pregnancy or at least from the birth of the child.

Other factors found to correlate with growth at the age of 5 years include initial household wealth. Consistent with many findings and previous Young Lives results (Mekonnen et al. 2005), for both rural and urban children, and irrespective of the number of dependent persons in the household, initial household wealth has statistically significant and positive effects on height for age and change in height for age at 5 years (Table 7.6). The squared wealth index is found to have a statistically

Table 7.6 The effect of wealth index, household composition, and gender of child on z-score of height for age in *R2*

	OLS		IV	
	Rural v1	**Urban v1**	**Rural v1**	**Urban v1**
Length/height-for-age z-score in *R1*	0.223**	0.252**	0.046	0.514**
	(14.270)	(10.887)	(0.300)	(3.161)
Wealth index for 1-year-olds in *R1*	4.055**	2.082*	4.662**	0.799
	(3.915)	(2.379)	(3.887)	(0.652)
Square of wealth index in *R1*	−7.237***	−1.325	−7.872*	−0.060
	(−1.960)	(−1.104)	(−2.020)	(−0.039)
Dummy for male	0.022	−0.195**	−0.082***	0.008
	(0.367)	(−2.638)	(−1.926)	(0.137)
Number of household members below 7 and above 65 years	−0.073***	0.002	0.048***	−0.007
	(−1.821)	(0.043)	(1.735)	(−0.227)
Number of children between 7 and 17 years	0.032	0.012	−0.075	−0.061
	(1.412)	(0.419)	(−1.036)	(−0.990)
Number of male household members above 17 and below 65 years	−0.040	−0.016	−0.047	0.110*
	(−0.636)	(−0.344)	(−0.594)	(2.231)
Number of female household members above 17 and below 65 years	−0.025	0.112*		
	(−0.341)	(2.422)		
Other outputs omitted				

$**\ p < 0.01, *\ p < 0.05, ***\ p < 0.1.$

significant negative effect on height for age and change in height for age at the age of 5 years, indicating that the effect of household wealth on nutritional status of children is non-linear, in the sense that height for age ceases to increase when wealth increases beyond certain level. Wealth index also relates to stunting and severe stunting at the age of 5 years for both rural and urban children, statistically significant at 1 per cent for children living in both rural and urban areas. However, the square of wealth index was not statistically significant for both stunting and severe stunting and for both rural and urban children, indicating perhaps that the effect of the wealth index is constant, not changing as the wealth index changes.

Economic shocks and child height

Controlling for the early nutritional status of children, and initial household wealth and composition, we found that height was affected negatively (and stunting and severe stunting affected positively) by the pre-natal and post-natal economic shocks that affected households. The effects of these shocks remain statistically significant when we drop initial wealth only and both initial wealth and malnutrition, but the magnitude of the effects of pre-natal economic shocks became slightly higher, indicating that the shocks have affected the wealth and initial height.

Post-natal economic shocks

For rural children, among those shocks that occurred after the child was born, natural disaster including drought, crop failure, and pests and diseases have significant and negative effects on height and positive effects on stunting of the 5-year-old children (see Table 4.3 in Woldehanna 2010). These negative effects became lower in magnitude when initial wealth and dependent variables were included, indicating very strong lingering and persistent effects of postnatal economic shocks. The effects of these shocks on stunting and severe stunting are also statistically significant. Unexpectedly, a decrease in agricultural output prices affected the nutritional status of children positively and stunting and severe stunting negatively. Given that many of the rural households in Young Lives sites are poor and are perhaps net buyers of food, a decrease in output price reduces the price of food and affects many households positively, rather than being a negative economic shock from loss of income. Illnesses of household members also correlate negatively with height and positively with stunting and severe stunting; but the correlations are statistically significant only when initial wealth is excluded from the models, indicating that illness affects children's height only in poor households. Such effects of postnatal economic shocks are still significant when we use the instrumental variables estimation method (see Table 4.3 in Woldehanna 2010) and account for community fixed effect.

In urban areas, we found some economic shocks – namely divorce or separation within the family, and natural disasters including crop failure owing to drought or pests and diseases – to have negative effects on the height of 5-year-old children only when initial conditions were excluded from the model, indicating a very weak effect. However, theft is found to have a more negative effect on height, even when initial malnutrition and wealth are included, indicating a strong effect. When we consider stunting of the 5-year-old children, it is affected only by the death of livestock, while severe stunting of the 5-year-old children is not affected by any of the economic shocks that affect the household after the birth of the child, indicating that the effects of livestock death are limited.

Pre-natal economic shocks

Shocks that hit the household before the child was born are found to be more damaging to children than the shocks that affected the households after the child was born in both rural and urban areas. In rural areas, controlling for initial wealth and malnutrition, decreases in food availability and the death of household members, divorce or separation of family members affected z-score of height for age and log of height negatively, which is statistically significant (see Table 4.4 in Woldehanna 2010). The magnitude of these negative effects increased slightly when lagged wealth and dependent variables were dropped, indicating very strong lingering and persistent effects of pre-natal economic shocks. These results held also true when we used the instrumental variables estimation method accounting for community fixed effect, indicating the robustness of the results. However, when we consider the category of stunting, of the pre-natal shocks, only decreases in food availability and divorce or separation of family have a significant effect on the probability of a 5-year-old being stunted, while the only pre-natal shock to have a significant effect on the severe stunting of 5-year-old children was divorce or separation in the family.

These results in general imply that idiosyncratic shocks can have long-term consequences for child welfare, owing to the fact that they are not covered by any of the government and non-governmental social assistance programmes. If the idiosyncratic shocks are not to be covered by social assistance programmes, current crises such as unemployment and inflation will have consequences for the growth and development of our children and future generations.

In urban areas, the only pre-natal economic shocks to have statistically significant negative effects on height were crop failure and lack of availability of food (and then only under IV estimation). These results are robust when we control for initial wealth and malnutrition as well as for community fixed effects. Unexpectedly, divorce or separation in families before the birth of the child affects height positively at five years, a statistically significant result that requires further investigation.

Policy implications

What are the policy options that would help improve the nutritional status of children or reduce malnutrition of children in rural and urban Ethiopia? Since malnutrition relates to household poverty or wealth and household wealth has the greatest effect on stunting of all variables studied, the first and most important policy option is to increase the wealth status of households substantially. Moreover, increasing household wealth will reduce households' vulnerability to a variety of economic shocks, which have short- and long-term consequences on growth of children. However, given the frequency of shocks, especially area-wide shocks, that hit rural and urban Ethiopia, it is unlikely that increasing income alone will be sufficient to eliminate malnutrition. In many cases, household wealth itself is highly vulnerable to area-wide and idiosyncratic economic shocks. Over the last 15 years, Ethiopia has experienced area-wide economic shocks every four or five years. Not only poor households, but also richer ones, are vulnerable to area-wide economic shocks such as drought and pests. Households are also frequently hit by a variety of idiosyncratic economic shocks such as the illness of household members, breadwinners, and caregivers, as well as separation or divorce. Surprisingly, a substantial number of households (more than half those in the study) are vulnerable to these idiosyncratic economic shocks. Therefore, strengthening the social assistance programmes aimed at reducing households' vulnerability to both area-wide and idiosyncratic economic shocks seems to be another way of reducing the malnutrition of children in Ethiopia. To assess this latter option, we conducted simulation exercises on the effectiveness of reducing household vulnerability to area-wide shocks only, and to both area-wide and idiosyncratic economic shocks, by strengthening social assistance programmes.

The first simulation exercise comes from the fact that government and non-governmental organizations can strengthen their social assistance programmes to reduce household vulnerability to area-wide shocks such as drought, pests, and crop diseases by increasing resources for emergency relief, productive safety net programmes, and other food security programmes such as resettlement and household packages. Currently, about 63 per cent of the Young Lives rural households are vulnerable to natural disasters. At the national level, about 12 per cent of households are vulnerable to the effects of drought (Woldehanna et al. 2008b). The second simulation exercise estimated what would happen to z-score of height for age, stunting, and severe stunting if households' vulnerability to both area-wide and idiosyncratic economic shocks was reduced by making social assistance programmes cover both kinds of shocks. The results of the simulation exercises are presented in Table 7.7.

For rural areas, reducing area-wide shocks such as drought from 63 to 10 per cent, z-score of height for age could increase by 6.2 per cent.

Table 7.7 Effects on stunting of reducing area-wide and idiosyncratic economic shocks on z-score of height for age

	Total	Rural	Urban
Z-score of height for age R1	−1.257	−1.463	−0.945
Z-score of height for age R2	−1.452	−1.629	−1.185
Z-score of height for age R2 if area-wide shocks is reduced[a]	−1.352	−1.529	−1.17
Z-score of height for age R2 when area-wide shocks and idiosyncratic shocks are reduced[b]	−1.283	−1.46	−1.149
Stunting R1	34.84	41.39	24.93
Stunting R2	31.33	36.41	23.65
Stunting if drought shock reduced	28.09	33.57	22.83
Stunting if drought shock and idiosyncratic shocks reduced	25.89	31.04	22.18
Severe stunting R1	15.46	19.36	9.57
Severe stunting R2	8.22	10.63	4.6
Severe stunting if drought shock reduced	6.85	8.7	4.46
Severe stunting if drought shock and idiosyncratic shocks reduced	6.12	7.65	4.46
Number of observations	1,863	1,121	761

[a]Percentage of people affected by area-wide shocks such as drought reduced from 63% to 10% for rural areas and from 7.22% to 2% in urban areas.
[b]Percentage of people affected by idiosyncratic shocks reduced (for rural areas, death from 7% to 5%, food availability from 50% to 10%, and divorce from 4% to 2%; for urban areas, crop failure from 7.5% to 2%).

If, however, we also reduce idiosyncratic shocks from death from 7 to 5 per cent, from food availability from 50 to 10 per cent and from divorce from 4 to 2 per cent, height for age can be increased by 10.4 per cent. For urban areas, reducing area-wide shock such as drought from 7.2 to 2 per cent increased height for age by 1.3 per cent while reducing both the area-wide shocks and idiosyncratic shocks (crop failure shock from 7.5 to 2 per cent) increased height for age by 3.1 per cent.

Consequently, if rural households' vulnerability to only area-wide shocks is reduced, Round 2 stunting in rural areas declines from 36 to 33 per cent, while Round 2 severe stunting in rural areas declines from 11 to 9 per cent. If however, the social protection programmes are designed to mitigate both area-wide and idiosyncratic shocks, stunting in Round 2 declines from 36 to 31 per cent and severe stunting from 11 to 8 per cent. In urban areas, reducing households' vulnerability to area-wide shock only reduces Round 2 stunting from 23.7 to 22.8 per cent and severe stunting from 4.6 to 4.5 per cent. On the other hand, if social assistance programmes are made more effective and reduce the vulnerability of urban households to both area-wide and idiosyncratic shocks, Round 2 stunting declines from 23.7 to 22.2 per cent and severe stunting from 4.6 to 4.5 per cent, indicating the relative important of area-wide shocks.

This implies that although area-wide economic shocks such as drought are very significant and government needs to focus more on them, support against idiosyncratic shocks has considerable potential for the improvement of children's height for age and consequently for the reduction of stunting and severe stunting in Ethiopia. It would therefore be worthwhile if government assistance programmes covered idiosyncratic shocks such as the death and illness of household members (especially breadwinners and caregivers) and break up of families.

Summary and conclusions

Our results showed both sustained consequences of, and the recovery of some children from, early childhood malnutrition. When we compare our results with the study made by Alderman et al. (2006) on 17-year-old Zimbabwean children, our results shows more recovery and less sustained effects of very early malnutrition, perhaps because of the smaller age group we considered and the improved wealth status of households.

Pre-natal economic shocks are found to have significant effects on the 5-year-old children's nutritional status. In rural areas, decreased output prices were associated positively with children's nutrition, while a reduction in food availability, the death of the head of household, and divorce occurring before the child was born reduced children's growth. Natural disasters, including drought, that hit the households after the birth of the child also reduced children's growth. In urban areas, only crop failure that occurred before the child was born and natural disasters including drought that occurred after the child was born reduced children's z-score of height for age, while the separation of mothers and fathers and increases in input prices affected children's nutritional status positively. Similar results were found when we assessed the effects of these shocks on stunting, showing the robustness of the result. We found consistent results from both OLS and IV estimations, controlling for community fixed effect.

Simulation exercises indicate that social assistance programmes reducing the vulnerability of households to area-wide economic shocks, such as drought, are very important; providing additional focus on idiosyncratic shocks will also help reduce malnutrition in children, especially in rural areas. Therefore, to improve children's nutritional status, government and non-governmental organizations should strengthen social assistance programmes such as emergency relief, productive safety net programmes, household food security packages, and resettlement programmes.

The fact that idiosyncratic shocks can have long-term impacts on child growth indicates that social assistance programmes should cover not only area-wide shocks, but also individual idiosyncratic shocks, if they are to protect children from being affected by shocks in the future. Therefore, government and non-governmental organizations in Ethiopia should revise their social assistance programmes to make them cover idiosyncratic shocks, which frequently affect households and consequently children.

Notes

1. I would like to thank Young Lives colleagues, Stefan Dercon, John Hoddinott and two anonymous reviewers for insightful comments on the paper. I would also like to thank Asmelash Haile and Mahderekal Fiseha for providing me with support to complete the paper. However, the errors are mine.
2. We also included interaction of these shocks with the initial wealth index. However, none of the interaction was found to have significant influence on child growth. The interaction variables increased the level of multicolinearity among the regressors measured by condition index (Belsely et al. 1980) and variable inflating factor (VIF). Initially, we also included mother's

and father's education as explanatory variables, but we dropped the education variables from the estimation because none of these coefficients were different from zero at any reasonable level of significance.

3. First, we ran an instrumental variables estimation and generalized method of moments (GMM) estimation methods (using ivreg2 command in Stata version 11). We conducted various tests including under-identification, weak identification, over-identification and relevance tests. The instrument variables used are dummy variable whether the child had a long-term illness and dummy variable for whether the household head was severely ill before the child was born. We found that these instruments were relevant and passed the under-identification and weak identification tests as well as addressing over-identification problems. Specifically, we found these instrument variables are not correlated with Round 2 z-score of height for age, but strongly correlated with initial z-score of height for age, indicating the relevance of the instrument and uncorrelated nature of the instrument with the dependent variable (see Table Appendix A in Woldehanna 2010, for details of the estimation and testing results). Although, however, I strongly believe that the instruments can be reasonably thought to satisfy the exclusion restrictions, we need to be cautious in our interpretation of the causal link between early malnutrition and subsequent malnutrition, and to the extent early childhood nutrition is mediated via illness of children and parents, the association between initial malnutrition and height of 5-year-olds appears strong, which is in line with expectations.

References

Alderman, H., J. Hoddinott and W. Kinsey (2006) 'Long Term Consequences of Early Childhood Malnutrition', *Oxford Economic Papers* 58.3: 450–74.

Behrman, Jere R. and Anil B. Deolalikar (1998) 'Health and Nutrition' in H. Chenery and T.N. Srinivasan (eds) *Handbook of Development Economics*, vol. 1, Oxford and Amsterdam: North-Holland.

Behrman, Jere R. and Mark R. Rosenzweig (2004) 'Returns to Birthweight', *The Review of Economics and Statistics* 86.2: 586–601.

Belsley, D., E. Kuh and R. Welsh (1980) *Regression Diagnostics*, New York: Wiley.

Black, R.E, S.S. Morris, J. Bryce (2003) 'Where and Why are 10 Million Children Dying Every Year?', *The Lancet* 361.9376: 2226–34.

Carter, Michael R., and John A. Maluccio (2003) 'Social Capital and Coping with Economic Shocks: An Analysis of Stunting of South African Children', *World Development* 31.7: 1147–63.

Christiaensen, Luc and Harold Alderman (2004) 'Child Malnutrition in Ethiopia: Can Maternal Knowledge Augment the Role of Income?', *Economic Development and Cultural Change* 52.2: 287–312.

Cunha, F., J. Heckman, L. Lochner and D. Masterov (2006) 'Interpreting the Evidence on Life Cycle Skill Formation' in E. Hanushek and F. Welch (eds) *Handbook of the Economics of Education*, Oxford and Amsterdam: North Holland.

Dercon, Stefan and John Hoddinott (2003) *Health, Shocks and Poverty Persistence*, Helsinki: World Institute of Development Economics Research.

Ezzati M., A.D. Lopez, A. Rodgers, S. Vander Hoorn and C.J. Murray (2002) 'Selected Major Risk Factors and Global and Regional Burden of Disease', *The Lancet* 360 (9343): 1347–60.

Federal Ministry of Health (FMoH) (2005) *Health Sector Strategic Plan (HSDP-III) 2005/6–2009/10*, Planning and Programming Department: Addis Ababa.

Frimpong, Jemima A. and Roland Pongou (2006) *Impact of Macro-Level Economic Improvement on Child Health: Childhood Malnutrition in Ghana, 1988–2003*, Demographic and Health Survey (GDHS): Key Findings, 2003.

Haddad, L., H. Alderman, S. Appleton, L. Song and Y. Yohannes (2003) 'Reducing Child Malnutrition: How Far Does Income Growth Take Us?', *World Bank Economic Review* 17.1: 107–31.

Hill, K., G. Adansi-Pipim, L. Assogba, A. Foster, J. Mukiza-Gapere and C. Paxson (1993) 'Demographic Effects of Economic Reversals in Subsaharan Africa', Washington, DC: National Academies Press.

Mekonnen, Alemu, Bekele Tefera, Tassew Woldehanna, Nicola Jones, John Seager, Tekie Alemu and Getachew Asgedom (2005) *Child Nutritional Status in Poor Ethiopian Households: The Role of Gender, Assets and Location*, Working Paper 26, Oxford: Young Lives.

MoFED (2006a) *Ethiopia: Building on Progress. A Plan for Accelerated and Sustained Development to End Poverty (PASDEP) (2005/06–2009/10)*, Addis Ababa: Ministry of Finance and Economic Development.

MoFED (2006b) *Ethiopia: Building on Progress. A Plan for Accelerated and Sustained Development to End Poverty (PASDEP) (2005/06–2009/10). Volume II: Policy Matrix*, Addis Ababa: Ministry of Finance and Economic Development.

Paxson C. and N. Schady (2004) *Child Health and the 1988–1992 Economic Crisis in Peru*, World Bank Policy Research Working Paper 3260, Washington, DC: World Bank.

Pongou R., M. Ezzati, J.A. Salomon (2005) *Economic Crisis and Declining Child Nutrition in Cameroon During the 1990s: The Mediating Role of Household Effects*, Working Paper Series 2005, 15.2, Boston, MA: Harvard Center for Population and Development Studies.

Woldehanna, Tassew, Alemu Mekonnen and Tekie Alemu (2008a) *Young Lives: Ethiopia Round 2 Survey Report*, Oxford: Young Lives.

Woldehanna, Tassew, John Hoddinott, Frank Ellis and Stefan Dercon (2008b) 'Dynamics of Growth and Poverty Reduction in Ethiopia: (1995/96–2004/05). A Report for Development Planning and Research Department', Addis Ababa: Ministry of Finance and Economic Development.

Woldehanna, Tassew (2010) *Do Pre-Natal and Post-Natal Economic Shocks Have a Long-Lasting Effect on the Height of 5-Year-Old Children? Evidence From 20 Sentinel Sites of Rural and Urban Ethiopia*, Working Paper 60, Oxford: Young Lives.

WHO (2007) *WHO Child Growth Standards: Head Circumference-for-Age, Arm Circumference-for Age, Triceps Skinfold-for-Age and Subscapular Skinfold-for-Age: Methods and Development*, Geneva: World Health Organization.

Yamano T. H. Alderman, and L. Christiaensen (2005) 'Child Growth, Shocks, and Food Aid in Rural Ethiopia, *American Journal of Agricultural Economics*, 87.2: 273–88.

Part III

Children's Experiences of Poverty

In this part, we consider outcomes of poverty in children's lives, paying particular attention to how boys and girls experience poverty and related adversities and how they respond. The previous part discussed poverty at the levels of family and community; here we consider how poverty entails privations and risks that have outcomes, sometimes serious and long term, in the lives of children. In particular, poverty is a major source of risk in children's lives and well-being is compromised by the multiple privations and risks associated with poverty. Ethnographic studies have shown, however, that given the right social and cultural environments, it is possible for children to develop cognitively and socially notwithstanding severe poverty (for example, on highland Peru, see Bolin 2006).

We start with two chapters that bring together current knowledge of general patterns of how poverty can affect children's lives. Subsequent chapters bring out nuances and complexities that appear in case studies arising from ethnographic research.

In Chapter 8, Patrice Engle brings together current knowledge on what influences the developmental potential of children. At the individual level, children are affected by biological factors (genetics, health, and nutrition) and environmental conditions (families, communities, and schools). There are also influences that affect whole families and communities, such as opportunities for school or work, expectations, and social exclusion. Apart from genetics, these factors are all related to dimensions of poverty: damage in early childhood can affect development permanently and the influence can persist to future generations. The various factors interact with each other and with moderating positive factors in children's lives; Engle presents a variety of models of how this happens. She points out that while some effects of poverty are external to individuals, life trajectories are also determined by responses to the situation, a topic that is pursued in later chapters in this section. Again we see the importance of social factors in understanding poverty, and the variety of ways in which poverty can affect the lives of children.

One of the points presented by Engle is that while mild or moderate stress is not necessarily harmful to children in the long term, 'toxic stress' can be very damaging. This relates to the accumulation of risk discussed in the following chapter by Theodore Wachs (Chapter 9), which further illustrates the importance of understanding specific mechanisms operating between poverty and child development. Wachs points out that growing up in poverty has consistently been linked to impeded cognitive and psychosocial competence, which in turn reduces readiness for school. He presents evidence, mostly but not only from high-income countries, of the deleterious effects of risks, especially when risks accumulate as they so often do in the lives of poor people. He concludes that interventions to alleviate poverty must impact directly on poverty-related risks if they are to be effective in improving child development. Second, a focus on reducing specific risks is unlikely to have a strong effect when children are exposed to multiple risks, and it is not possible to devise programmes to cover all risks that can damage children's development. The evidence he presents points to the critical importance of intervening early in a child's life, before he or she is exposed to multiple cumulative risks.

Risk does not, however, always and necessarily result in damage. Jo Boyden (2009) has pointed out that childhood is a highly diverse phase of life. Although physical, biological, and psychological (factors discussed by Berhman, Woldehanna, Engle, and Wachs) have a significant influence in shaping lives, personality and the environment are at least as important. Some cultures, or social contexts, encourage problem-solving initiatives on the part of children, which develop competencies and enable children to respond positively to some risks. Even in times of great adversity, children (and others) may consciously act upon and influence the environment in which they live. Thus through adversity, it is possible to learn how to deal with it – what in some circles is referred to as developing resilience.

In her cross-cultural studies of child development, Barbara Rogoff points out that there are different ways of protecting children from danger (2003: 5–7). One is to remove them from dangerous situations; another is to introduce them to dangerous situations, and particularly the use of dangerous implements, carefully and under supervision, so that they learn how to deal with them. Intervention to protect children from all risk is not necessarily the best way to prepare them for a future in which they are going to have to face adversity. Indeed, children sometimes experience child protection as a negative, restrictive feature in their lives (for example, Sinclair et al. 2002: 8). While intervention is sometimes necessary to remove or minimize particularly harmful features in the lives and environment of children and their families, effective intervention should also provide them with support in their own attempts to deal with adversities they have to face. This requires detailed empirical knowledge of their particular contexts rather than an abstract set of universal norms.

The later rounds of Young Lives research will provide information on how children have fared after being subject to a variety of risks and privations. Meanwhile, from the first two rounds of data, Jo Boyden and Gina Crivello show how ethnicity and caste can increase poverty and risk in Andhra Pradesh. Families in Scheduled Castes and Scheduled Tribes are more likely to be poor and experience shocks, and their children are likely to have lower readiness for school and drop out earlier. The experience of children is, however, affected by a variety of factors that can change over time, including the attitudes and decisions of older family members and the social and cultural worlds in which they live. Risk is thus both a feature of interaction with the immediate environment, and a consequence of the political and economic structure of society.

The study of risk and responses to it leads into a consideration of what comprises children's well-being. Although some aspects, such as health and nutrition, can be measured objectively, other dimensions, such as inequality and social exclusion, are not easily measured, still less how people feel about meeting their expectations. Well-being cannot simply be measured in material terms. Children's perceptions of what is good and bad in their lives often refer to relationships with those around them and recent experiences, sometimes belying intuitive assumptions based on abstract norms. In the introduction to this volume we mentioned children's right to be heard in matters that affect them, and the importance of allowing children to speak for themselves in research. In Chapter 4, Stefan Dercon pointed out that the perceptions of caregivers and children differed from more material and objective measures of poverty. The chapter by Gillian Mann illustrates vividly that the social experience of adversity can be far worse than material privation. The main concerns of Congolese refugees in Tanzania are social exclusion, discrimination, and harassment. Their well-being depended on how they responded to these indignities and creatively found ways to enhance and maintain their self-esteem, and how successfully they fought to maintain their dignity. Mann also shows how parents and children within the same households sometimes respond differently to adversity, and that adversity and responses to it carry different meanings for them: poverty was experienced differently even within a single household.

Experiences and perceptions of adversity are central to the chapter by Laura Camfield, which describes different ways in which children and their parents understand a good or bad life in Young Lives sites in Ethiopia, often reflecting particular recent experiences. In particular, well-being is usually assessed in relation to peers and others in the surrounding community. Concerns of both children and parents depend on the environment in which they live and the facilities available to them. Although the concerns of children are usually similar to those of their parents, there are divergences in such things as the importance of school for children and the importance of religion for adults.

In the final chapter in this section, we return to Andhra Pradesh. Gina Crivello, Uma Vennam, and Anuradha Komanduri (Chapter 13) explore children's views on the relationship between social and material aspects of poverty. The survey and group discussions show how children assess their childhood and perceive differences in power and resources between rich and poor. Two case studies illustrate ways in which children are forced by circumstances into particular trajectories, but at the same time exercise some control over the direction of their lives, and therefore over the outcomes of the dimensions of poverty that afflict them. Decisions that close certain opportunities, such as schooling, sometimes open up others, such as travel and work experience.

References

Bolin, Inge (2006) *Growing up in a Culture of Respect: Child Rearing in Highland Peru*, Austin TX: University of Texas Press.

Boyden, Jo (2009) 'Risk and Capability in the Context of Adversity: Children's Contributions to Household Livelihoods in Ethiopia', *Children, Youth and Environments* 19: 111–37.

Rogoff, Barbara (2003) *The Cultural Nature of Human Development*, New York: Oxford University Press.

Sinclair, Ruth, K. Cronin, L. Lanyon, V. Stone and A. Hulsi (2002) *Aim High Stay Real: Outcomes for Children and Young People: The Views of Children, Parents and Professionals*, London: Children and Young People's Unit.

8
Poverty and Developmental Potential

Patrice Engle

Introduction

Longitudinal studies permit us to understand factors influencing an individual's development by observing the impact of changes over time. This chapter outlines key theoretical perspectives from developmental psychology that can be used to understand and interpret longitudinal data from different cultural and economic contexts.

This chapter first discusses the concept of developmental potential and theories that are most commonly used to describe the process of development: the roles of genetic and environmental influences, contributions from brain research, and developmental systems theory. Second, it describes factors known to influence a child's development at the individual and family levels. Third, it uses a developmental approach to examine changes in whether the family fell below the poverty level over the first 10 to 15 years of a child's life and implications of this for his or her development, including the person-centred or profile analysis technique. Finally, findings from developmental psychology relevant to Young Lives are summarized.

A key issue that Young Lives addresses is how families escape from poverty. This chapter presents explanations for two types of factors that influence human development and which account for behavioural trajectories or longitudinal patterns related to emergence from poverty. It is likely that any life course is influenced by several of these factors. These are (a) individual-level factors such as individual capacity due to variations in biological factors (genetics, health, nutrition) and environmental conditions (families, communities, schools) and (b) family, community-level, or societal factors such as opportunities for schooling or productive work due to conditions of economic development or conditions of social exclusion. These are not independent, but interact in each situation. Young Lives should be able to examine both individual-level and community-level factors that contribute to child outcomes and dynamic patterns of poverty.

Individual-level factors

Overall, research suggests that early childhood is the period of maximum risk for children's growth and development but also the period of maximum opportunity for change (Heckman and Masterov 2005). Appropriate inputs in this period will have impacts over the long term, affecting school performance, and adult health and productivity (Walker et al. 2007). Risks such as poor nutrition or high levels of stress can undermine healthy development over the long term, often through direct effects on brain structure and function (Victora et al. 2008; Shonkoff et al. 2009).

Characteristics of the environment and those of the infant influence the emerging trajectory of the child's development (Bradley 1994). The environment is generally described in terms of proximal characteristics such as house quality, educational level of family, or crowding, and distal characteristics, including neighbourhood, services, and economic conditions and cultural factors (Wachs 2000). Child characteristics may include temperament, disability or delay, gender, and perhaps physical appearance.

Developmental potential and environmental influences

Developmental potential is the range within which a child may develop, given limitations of his or her genetic characteristics. This 'zone of modifiability' determines how much the environment can change the pattern of a child's development (Ramey and Ramey 1998). Although the precise importance of genetic and environmental influences on child development has been debated for decades, it is generally recognized that both have similar levels of influence, and they interact in complex ways to determine human development.

Most abilities appear to be quite constant over the developmental period. For example, measures of mental ability tend to be strongly correlated from the age of 3 through to adolescence (see for example, Pollitt et al. 1993, regarding a study in Guatemala). However, when there is change from age to age, environmental factors may play a substantial role. Data from the Colorado Adoption Project suggest that genetic factors account for substantial continuity from age to age, but that when changes from age to age occur, child-specific environmental factors are more likely to be responsible (Wadsworth et al. 2006). For example, randomly assigned interventions to improve a child's early environment through parenting programmes or pre-school experiences have resulted in different life trajectories for those children, compared to children who did not receive the intervention, particularly for children from disadvantaged circumstances (Schweinhart et al. 2005; Reynolds et al. 2007; Walker et al. 2005, 2006). Although long-term effects on a variety of outcomes in adulthood are found in several longitudinal studies in the USA, the pathways for the effects are not well known. An analysis of three longitudinal studies with low-income children in the USA (Reynolds et al. 2010) suggested that there were five paths of influence from pre-school to years of education that were large and consistently significant across all three studies: (1) pre-school had an immediate effect on cognitive skills at age 5; (2) early cognitive skills increased parental involvement; (3) early cognitive skills increased academic motivation; (4) motivation increased retention/special education; and (5) retention/special education was negatively associated with reading achievement at age 14 to 15. These findings indicate that the effects begin with the enhancement of cognitive skills but at a later time, at least in part, motivation makes a difference.

This pattern is also seen with early biological risk conditions such as low birthweight, which is associated with lower levels of cognitive development. Changing the environmental circumstances may reduce the effects of a biological risk, such as low birthweight, as illustrated by long-term assessments of the effects of interventions in Jamaica (Walker et al. 2004, 2010) and the USA (McCormick et al. 2006). Similarly, early interventions to reduce stunting have long-term effects on school performance for women (Lui et al. 2004) and adult wages for men (Hoddinott et al. 2008).

Although the Young Lives datasets do not contain genetic information, the diversity of outcomes at 8 and eventually 12 years old compared to initial nutritional and cognitive levels at 1 and 5 years can help to identify environmental factors associated with changes in performance and productivity.

Linkages of brain and behaviour

The role of brain development in many child development outcomes is currently of great interest. Brain development is genetically influenced, but modifiable by characteristics of the environment. The brain is seen as 'experience expectant' so that it is programmed to receive certain stimuli at certain periods of development (National Scientific Council on the Developing Child 2007). In humans, critical or sensitive periods for input vary by developmental task.

Small initial changes in the 'building blocks' can result in larger changes later on, and the brain is built through these multiple interactions (National Scientific Council on the Developing Child 2007). Under-nutrition, iron deficiency, environmental toxins, stress, lack of stimulation, and social interaction can affect brain structure and function and can have lasting cognitive and emotional effects (for example, Black et al. 1998). In humans and animals, variations in the quality of maternal care can produce lasting effects in stress reactivity, anxiety, and memory function in offspring (Shonkoff et al. 2009).

The process of development requires particular inputs to occur at particular times, although some developmental systems are more sensitive to timing than are others (Thompson and Nelson 2001). For example, vision and audition are most sensitive during the first 3 to 8 months of life, followed by expressive and receptive language from 6 to 8 months through to 3 years. Problem solving and higher cognitive thought begin slightly later and have a longer sensitive period, through perhaps to the sixth year of life. Small perturbations in these processes during these critical periods can have long-term effects on the brain's structural and functional capacity (Grantham-McGregor et al. 2007). Timing is more limited (constrained) for processes such as visual depth perception, moderately constrained for processes such as distinguishing speech sounds (requires input before 3 or 4 years of age), and modifiable over the developmental course for others (for example, learning the vocabulary of another language) (Thompson and Nelson 2001).

Despite the vulnerability of the brain to early negative experiences (for example, malnutrition or neglect), remarkable recovery is often possible with interventions, and generally the earlier the interventions, the greater the benefit (Grantham-McGregor et al. 2007). The brain has considerable plasticity or modifiability in the earliest years.

Biological factors: nutrition

The critical role of nutrition for the development of cognitive skills has been shown in many studies (Victora et al. 2008; Grantham-McGregor et al. 2007). The nutritional conditions most consistently related to poor cognitive development are stunting, iron-deficiency anaemia, and iodine deficiency, although a number of other nutrients probably play a critical role in cognitive development, such as those obtained from breastfeeding (Walker et al. 2007).

The pre-natal environment accounts for a significant amount of the variance in brain development, and the quality of that environment is directly related to maternal health and nutrition. Low birthweight, owing either to small size for gestational age or prematurity, has significant long-term consequences for a child's development although the size of the effects may decrease in adolescence and adulthood. The iron status of the infant has long-lasting effects on a child's development (Lozoff et al. 2006).

Under-nutrition not only has an impact on cognitive development, but it also has been shown to increase a child's emotionality (how easily he/she is upset by external events) and irritability, and to reduce attention, play, and the quality of social relations (Walker et al. 2007). Iron-deficiency anaemia during early childhood is related to later decrements in IQ and poorer social functioning, and more anxiety, depression, and inattention in adolescence (Lozoff et al. 1998; Walker et al. 2007). Victora et al. conclude that 'the damage suffered early in life leads to permanent impairment, and might also affect future generations' (2008: 23).

Psychosocial factors

Cognitive stimulation and opportunities for learning

Stimulation and responsive care, reflected in caregivers' style of interaction with children, result in improved cognitive development in many countries (Eshel et al. 2006). For example, the amount of language a child hears, particularly language used in a meaningful context such as a conversation with the child (rather than on TV), is strongly associated with later language development, which in turn helps school performance and success in later years (Brooks-Gunn and Duncan 1997). Learning materials that provide children with opportunities for touching, manipulation, problem-solving, and control, whether homemade or purchased, exist in many societies and are important supports for learning. Reading books, telling stories, and discussing pictures with children help them build oral vocabulary and become familiar with print, representation, and words (Bradley and Corwyn 2005). Children who do not have these learning opportunities are at risk of not developing their potential.

Experiences of pre-school have been significantly associated with improved cognitive development in many developed and developing countries (Nores and Barnett 2010; Engle et al. 2007) as have community-based interventions to improve parenting skills, such as the provision of books and play opportunities for parent and child together (Maulik and Darmstadt 2009). Bradley and Corwyn (2005) found three key dimensions along which most cultures vary: warmth/responsiveness, discipline/harsh punishment, and stimulation/teaching. Both warmth/responsiveness and stimulation/teaching show strong associations with outcomes in almost every cultural context, the former more consistently with social and emotional development and the latter with child competence, although less with social adjustment.

Attachment and ecological theory

One of the most basic needs of the infant is having a caregiver who is aware of the child's emotions and can respond to them appropriately (often called 'emotional availability'; Bornstein et al. 2008a, 2008b). This emotional availability influences the development of the child's attachment or unique bond with at least one consistent caregiver. Developing an attachment, or an early emotional connection to a caregiver, is critical for an infant's well-being in all cultural contexts (Isabella 1993).

Many patterns of caregiving can meet this need (for example, Keller et al. 2008). However, a marked deficit in the early environment due to lack of stimulation and absence of attachment to a significant other, such as that occurring in a poorly run orphanage, can have significant negative effects on cognitive functioning, growth, and even on brain development (for example, St. Petersburg–USA Orphanage Study Team 2008; Bakermans-Kranenburg et al. 2008).

A risk factor for the development of attachment and a child's development generally is maternal depression. Maternal depression undermines the mother's emotional connection with the infant and can threaten normal development (Rahman et al. 2007). A recent investigation from rural Bangladesh demonstrated that when maternal depressive symptoms occurred in conjunction with the parent thinking that the child was difficult or irritable, infants acquired fewer cognitive, motor, and behavioural skills than when only maternal depression or child irritability/difficultness occurred (Black et al. 2007). Child irritability and maternal depression, either alone or in combination, resulted in lower levels of interaction between the mother and the infant, and less responsive care, both risk factors for poorer cognitive development. Rates of maternal depression are quite high in many parts of the world, particularly in South Asia. For example, these rates were 15–28 per cent in Africa and Asia (Husain et al. 2000), 35–50 per cent in Latin America (Wolf et al. 2002), and 50 per cent in Bangladesh (Black et al. 2007).

Interactions of biological and psychosocial effects

Developmental systems theory is based on ecological theory and conceptualizes interactions across multiple levels, extending from basic biological processes to interactions at the individual, family, school, community, and cultural levels. As with any systems model, interactions are bidirectional, such that changes in one aspect of the system may affect relations and processes throughout the system (Engle and Black 2008).

In a direct effects model (see Figure 8.1), poverty influences children's education and development by increasing risk factors and limiting protective factors and opportunities for stimulation and enrichment. For example, in the USA, children in low-income families are at increased risk for both under-nutrition and obesity, which are often associated with food insecurity (Casey et al. 2005). Both poverty and family patterns have direct effects on child well-being.

A moderated effect depends on characteristics of families or children (see Figure 8.2). For example, in the USA, families who are poorly educated with poor decision-making skills may have more difficulty protecting their children from some of the negative effects of poverty

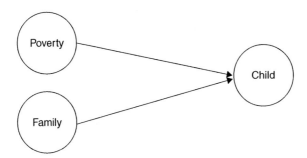

Figure 8.1   Direct effects of poverty on children

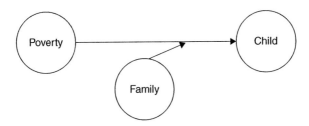

Figure 8.2   Moderated effects of poverty on children

than families who are better educated or have more opportunities for making decisions (Shipler 2005). Parents who are better educated or have access to financial resources can invest in their children through educationally enhancing materials (such as books) and activities (such as reading), thus protecting their children from some of the effects of poverty. A child who is born with a low birthweight can develop well if the family has time and knowledge to provide the appropriate kinds of stimulation and care.

In mediated models, the effects of poverty operate through changes in family functioning, which in turn have repercussions on the children (see Figure 8.3). For example, poverty may lead to family stress and have a negative impact on parental emotional well-being and mental health, undermining parenting behaviour and possibly increasing the likelihood of harsh and controlling parenting (Gutman and McLloyd 2005; Zevalkink and Riksen-Walraven 2001).

In transactional models, the effects of poverty have a continuous impact through the ongoing relations between families and children, incorporating both moderated and mediated processes (see Figure 8.4).

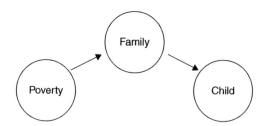

Figure 8.3   Mediated effects of poverty on children

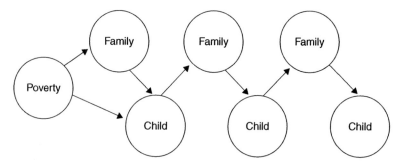

Figure 8.4   Transactional model of the effects of poverty on children

As parental characteristics may moderate the impact of poverty on children's development, children's characteristics, in turn, may affect parental reactions. For example, caregivers of temperamentally difficult children are less likely to exhibit sensitive-responsive caregiving and more likely to report depressive symptoms than caregivers of temperamentally easy children (Wachs 2000). The negative consequences of maternal depressive symptoms on children's development are exacerbated when a child is temperamentally difficult (Black et al. 2007), and the challenge of raising such a child is also likely to exacerbate the negative consequences of poverty. Similarly, caregivers are likely to invest in educational resources, even in times of poverty, if they perceive their children to be bright or academically talented. Then children perform better and in turn parental investment is likely to increase.

Thus, although caregivers may experience stress related to poverty, resulting in mental health problems and interfering with the quality of their interactions with their children, they are also influenced by their perceptions of their children's skills and their children's behaviour. Likewise, children are influenced by multiple processes. In addition to the direct effects of a lack of resources or other risk factors associated with poverty, there are also negative effects of caregiver behaviour, including inconsistent caregiving or harsh parenting, leading to more disorganized child behaviour. A child may become moderately or severely malnourished through parental neglect or poor care practices, and the behaviour changes associated with malnutrition may reduce the parental interest even further. The cycle continues as caregivers react to their children's behaviours that are more difficult to handle.

Social factors: opportunities, social exclusion, and marginalization

Poverty is associated with poor child development outcomes in all parts of the world. The previous sections described individual- and family-level effects. This section describes the effects of social exclusion at community and national levels on opportunities and outcomes for children, and proposes a strategy for examining pathways of change over time.

In low- and middle-income countries, children in poverty are at much greater risk of never attending school than are wealthier children. For example, in UNESCO's dataset of 80 low- and middle-income countries, 12 per cent of children in the top quintile of households never attended school, whereas 38 per cent of children in the poorest quintile never attended school and there are consistent associations between socio-economic status and student achievement (UNESCO 2006). Socio-economic differences in achievement scores, often called socio-economic gradients, exist within most countries, reflecting inequality in educational outcomes (Ross et al. 2005). One of the few countries that has a flat gradient (socio-economic status does not make much difference) is Cuba (UNESCO and LLECE 2008).

A critical factor pushing many families into poverty is a health crisis in the family, particularly when health care costs are high and there are no social safety nets. In a study of three countries, Krishna (2007) identified three factors as critical in moving families into poverty: health care payments, borrowing money at high interest rates, and customary obligations (for example, weddings and funerals). These are related, in that the health crisis may be linked to borrowing funds, to loss of income of a wage-earner, and possibly to death. One of the major impacts of HIV on families has been to increase the likelihood of their becoming poor (Adato and Bassett 2008; Joint Learning Initiative on Children and HIV/AIDS 2009).

Emergencies, both natural disasters and conflict, have a huge cost for infants and children. These costs are normally considered to be health and nutrition risks, but increasingly there is an awareness of psychosocial impacts on caregivers and on young children. Not only is there a risk of depression, but also exposure to violence may be more common in these situations. Lustig (2009) outlines effects of separations and chaotic experiences of refugee children and of interventions that have been shown to make a difference.

The effect of migration on economic well-being depends on the circumstances and opportunities that result from migration. Migration from rural areas, particularly remote areas, to areas with more economic opportunity has resulted in increased incomes and family well-being (Sachs 2005). However, internal migration (of internally displaced persons) and international migration are often associated with emergencies and conflict, and this migration can have detrimental effects on family well-being. Countries that receive the most migrants (for example, countries in sub-Saharan Africa) are often those least able to handle them.

Over 70 per cent of the population in industrialized countries and Latin America live in urban areas, with Central and Eastern Europe and the Commonwealth of Independent States and the Middle East and North Africa not far behind (62 per cent and 58 per cent, respectively). East Asia and sub-Saharan Africa are rapidly urbanizing, although the percentages of the population that live in urban areas are still relatively small (in East Asia, 44 per cent and in sub-Saharan Africa, 36 per cent). The least urbanized area to date is South Asia (29 per cent; UNICEF 2008). In comparisons of urban and rural children, urban children almost always have better outcomes, possibly because of greater wealth in urban families. However, there are other differences between rural and urban families. Urban families tend to be smaller and more edu- cated, and have more access to services; in addition, there are rural–ur- ban differences in caregiver beliefs and rearing practices that can affect productivity (Bornstein et al. 2008b). For example, rural families tend to have a greater belief in parental authority and to emphasize chil- dren's incorporation into a family unit (Keller et al. 2008) rather than individual initiative. However, combining all children in urban areas into a single group disguises the greater risks faced by the urban poor.

Expanding the concept of poverty: poverty as lack of respect, emotional integrity, and choice

Many poverty researchers use a broad definition for 'poor', including not only lack of material assets and health but also capabilities such as social belonging, cultural identity, respect and dignity, emotional integrity (being able to feel and show your emotions), and information and education (Sen 1995). Sen's capability approach proposes that pov- erty alleviation must focus on increasing the capabilities of participants to choose a life that they themselves have reason to value, increasing agency and human potential (Sen 1999). Schischka et al. (2008) demon- strated the effectiveness of the approach in two development projects in the Pacific region.

Tilly (2007) describes the additional barrier that social exclusion places on poverty alleviation. Belonging to a socially excluded group can prevent categories of people from moving out of poverty, and reduc- ing barriers to a social group can be one of the more effective means of poverty alleviation. These complex and multi-faceted concepts of pov- erty, and the complexity of moving out of poverty, are illustrated in 60,000 interviews from 60 countries in *Voices of the Poor* (Narayan and Petesch 2002).

Being a member of a socially excluded group can also affect a per- son's performance through 'stereotype threat'. Simply being a member of a negatively stereotyped group can affect performance on stereotype- relevant tasks (that is, tasks for which the stereotype might apply; Armenta, 2010). When a person has a stereotyped group identity and is taking a stereotype-relevant test (for example, a female taking a maths test) and the stereotype is brought to the attention of the test-taker, performance tends to shift in the direction of the stereotype (Steele 1997); performance that was equivalent between groups without the threat changes for the group, which has been reminded of the negative stereotype. Research shows that children's test scores can be negatively affected just by arousing their expectations that they will be judged on a characteristic such as gender or ethnicity that has been used as the basis for social exclusion (for example, Steele 1997). This occurs similarly for members of positively and negatively stereotyped groups. It applies to ethnic groups in the USA, such as Latinos (negative) (Armenta and Hunt 2009) and Asian Americans (positive) (Armenta 2010). It was also found in three studies in India, in which asking the test-taker what his or her caste was, thereby making caste a 'salient element' resulted in lower test performance for the 'untouchable' caste, whereas there had been no difference when caste was not mentioned (Hoff and Pandey 2004).

Poverty and toxic stress

Mild stress and even moderate stress, when there are supportive attachment figures available, do not have long-term effects on children. However, toxic stress can impair a young child's brain architecture in the first few years of life (Shonkoff et al. 2009; National Scientific Council on the Developing Child 2007), and has been demonstrated to affect directly a child's potential for language development as well as lifelong social competence and physical health (National Scientific Council on the Developing Child 2007).

Shonkoff et al. (2009) found that children from lower socio-economic backgrounds in the USA and Europe had a heightened stress activation response system. They concluded that differences in parenting related to income and education – as mediated through parent–child interaction, exposure to new vocabulary, and stability of responsiveness – could alter the maturation of selected brain areas, such as the prefrontal cortex. These changes can persist into adult life and alter emotional states, decision-making capacities, and bodily processes, all contributing to emotional instability, substance abuse, aggression, obesity, and stress-related disorders.

It is highly likely that similar effects occur in low- and middle-income countries. Chronic poverty, as well as crises within the family such as maternal depression, caregiver illness or death, divorce, and family violence, may cause persistent elevation of stress hormones in children that, without the buffered protection of adult support, disrupt brain chemistry and can lead to impaired learning, memory, social development, and increased susceptibility to physical illness in adulthood (National Scientific Council on the Developing Child 2007). These risks can be minimized and prevented by strengthening the family environment through such means as the provision of consistent, safe, high-quality programmes for early childhood development and child and family educational opportunities (National Scientific Council for the Developing Child 2007; Irwin et al. 2007).

Charting poverty trajectories

Poverty is a dynamic process, with some families moving in and out of poverty in a relatively short time, resulting in intermittent rather than persistent poverty (Duncan et al. 1993). In a study of 30,000 households in India, Kenya, Peru, and Uganda, Krishna (2007) reported that nearly one-third of individuals currently living in poverty were not born poor. Mobility out of poverty has been described as the interaction of (1) changes in the *opportunity structure,* which consists of the dominant institutional climate and social structures within which disadvantaged actors must work to advance their interests; and (2) changes in the capabilities of poor individuals or groups to take purposeful action, that is, to exercise *agency* (Narayan and Petesch 2007). Agency depends on individual assets, such as education and self-confidence, and collective and family assets, such as organization, identity, and having a voice. Many of the risks described in this chapter relate to lack of agency, but the limited opportunity structure may have equal weight.

On the other hand, to assume that life circumstances are totally external to the individual is also incorrect. For example, we cannot assume that a child attends an after-school programme only as a function of external factors unrelated to the individual child (exogenous – as if children were assigned to a programme at random). It is more likely that the child attends not only because the centre is there and available but also because of child characteristics and characteristics of the family who decide that this would be a good idea or is needed for child care. Thus a careful examination of these two problems is needed.

Longitudinal data have been analysed through the study of personal profiles. Participants are clustered into categories of pathways or patterns of behaviour that change over time. These categories can provide new insights into patterns of behaviour that are expected and that are not expected, called 'unexpected pathways' research and illustrated in a special issue of the *Journal of Social Issues* (in 2008). For example, Trost and El-Khouri (2008) examined Swedish females from the age of 10 to the age of 43 categorized by degree of achievement (competence) and whether they had problems such as aggression or depression. Those who were high or low on both dimensions in childhood were two to three times more likely than others to be the same at the age of 43, which the authors interpreted as an integrated system, in which competence protects against problems and lack of problems protects against lowered competence. One unexpected pathway was females with low competence but few problems, who reported higher life satisfaction at the age of 43, suggesting that competence and absence of problems do not always go together. Duncan (2008) lauded the approach as a novel strategy for understanding changes in development, but cautioned against assuming that patterns derived from an after-the-fact analysis are representative. He proposed that the trajectories be coded for some subjects, and then a random sample of additional subjects be selected to see if the same patterns emerge. This approach could provide interesting insights from the Young Lives sample.

Conclusions

A number of research findings are relevant to the analysis of longitudinal data, and the Young Lives data can be used to test the validity of many of these findings in different cultural contexts.

- Genetic factors play a role in children's cognitive development and achievement which appears to increase rather than decrease with age.
- Individual-level and family factors that contribute to a child's long-term well-being include cognitive stimulation and responsiveness, attachment and emotional support, and good nutrition and health.
- The early years are critical for brain development but 'it's all over by the age of 3' does not reflect the current research showing that some skills and capacity such as cognitive functioning and problem-solving continue to develop rapidly until the age of 9 or 10.
- The process of development is not limited to cognitive development alone, but includes emotional development, which depends on parental responsivity and sensitivity to the child's development.
- The developmental systems model illustrates several ways in which risk factors (for example, malnutrition) and protective factors (for example, mother's education) can affect the child's development.

They can be seen as mediating or moderating factors, or as a trans-action between the child and the environment. The transactional model charts the mutual influences of parent on child and child on parent on most domains over time and is generally accepted.

- Poverty is not simply a lack of income but also a lack of choice and people's sense of agency.
- Evidence suggests that families move in and out of poverty, and poverty should be conceptualized as a dynamic variable.
- Both individual- and family-level factors and social- and community-level factors should be considered in understanding families' movements in and out of poverty.
- A possible analytical tool to examine poverty over time in the Young Lives sample is to chart expected and unexpected pathways to identify children who continue an expected pathway and those who deviate from the pattern.

References

Adato, M. and L. Bassett (2008) 'What is the Potential of Cash Transfers to Strengthen Families Affected by HIV and AIDS? A Review of the Evidence on Impacts and Key Policy Debates', Joint Learning Initiative on Children and HIV/AIDS, http://www.jlica.org/resources/publications.php (accessed 1 September 2010)

Armenta, B. (2010) 'Stereotype Boost and Stereotype Threat Effects: The Moderating Role of Ethnic Identification', *Cultural Diversity and Ethnic Minority Psychology* 16.1: 94–8.

Armenta, B. E. and Hunt, J. S. (2009) 'Responding to Societal Devaluation: Effects of Perceived Personal and Group Discrimination on the Group Identification and Self-Esteem of Latinos/as', *Group Processes and Intergroup Relations* 12: 23–39.

Bakermans-Kranenburg, M.J., M.H. van IJzendoorn and F. Juffer (2008) 'Earlier is Better: A Meta-Analysis of 70 years of Intervention Improving Cognitive Development in Institutionalized Children', *Monographs of the Society for Research in Child Development* 73.3: 279–93.

Black, J., T. Jones, C. Nelson and W. Greenough (1998) 'Neuronal Plasticity and the Developing Brain' in N. Alessi, J. Coyle, S. Isaac and S. Eth (eds), *Handbook of Child and Adolescent Psychiatry*, Vol. 6, New York: Wiley.

Black, M.M., A.H. Baqui, K. Zaman, S.W. McNary, K. Le, S.E. Arifeeen, J.D. Hamadani, M. Parveen, M. Yunus and R.E. Black (2007) 'Depressive Symptoms Among Rural Bangladeshi Mothers: Implications for Infant Development', *Journal of Child Psychology and Psychiatry* 48: 764–72.

Bornstein, M.H., M.E. Lamb and D.M. Teti (2008a) *Development in Infancy: An Introduction*, Mahway NJ: Lawrence Erlbaum Associates.

Bornstein, M.H., D.I. Putnick, M. Heslington, M. Gini, J.T.D. Suwalsky, P. Venuti, S. de Falco, Z. Guisti and C. Zingman de Galperin (2008b) 'Mother–Child

Emotional Availability in Ecological Perspective: Three countries, Two Regions, Two Genders', *Developmental Psychology* 44.3: 666–80.

Bradley, R.H. and R.F. Corwyn (2005) 'Caring for Children Around the World: A View From HOME', *International Journal of Behavioural Development* 29.6: 468–78.

Bradley, R.H. (1994) 'The HOME Inventory: Review and Reflections' in H. Reese (ed.), *Advances in Child Development and Behavior*, San Diego CA: Academic Press.

Brooks-Gunn J. and Duncan G.J. (1997) 'The Effects of Poverty on Children', *The Future of Children* 7: 55–71.

Casey, P., K. Szeto, J.M. Robbins, J.E. Stuff, C. Connell, J.M. Gossett and P.M. Simpson (2005) 'Child Health-Related Quality of Life and Household Food Security', *Archives of Pediatrics and Adolescent Medicine*, 159: 51–6.

Duncan, G.J. (2008) 'What to Make of 'Unexpected' Pathways?', *Journal of Social Issues* 64.1: 213–17.

Duncan, G.J., B. Gustafsson, R. Hauser, G. Schmauss, H. Messinger, R. Muffels, B. Nolan and J.-C. Ray. (1993) 'Poverty Dynamics in Eight Countries', *Journal of Population Economics* 6: 215–34.

Engle, P.L., S. Castle and P. Menon (1996) 'Child Development: Vulnerability and Resilience', *Social Science and Medicine* 43.5: 621–35.

Engle, P.L. and M.M. Black (2008) 'The Effects of Poverty on Child Development and Educational Outcomes' in S.G. Kaler and O.M. Rennert (eds), *Reducing the Impact of Poverty on Health and Human Development: Scientific Approaches*, Boston MA: Annals of the New York Academy of Sciences Vol. 1136: 243–56.

Engle, P.L., M.M. Black, J.R. Behrman, M. Cabral de Mello, P.J. Gertler, L. Kapiri, R. Martorell, M.E. Young and the International Child Development Steering Group (2007) 'Strategies to Avoid the Loss of Developmental Potential in More than 200 Million Children in the Developing World', *The Lancet* 369.9557: 229–42.

Eshel N., B. Daelmans, M.C. de Mello and J. Martines (2006) 'Responsive Parenting: Interventions and Outcomes', *Bulletin of the World Health Organization* 84.12: 991–8.

Grantham-McGregor, S., Y.B. Cheung, S. Cueto, P.W. Glewwe, L. Richter, B. Strupp and the International Child Development Steering Group (2007) 'Developmental Potential in the First 5 years for Children in Developing Countries', *The Lancet* 369.9555: 60–70.

Gutman, L. and V. McLoyd (2005) 'Financial Strain, Neighborhood Stress, Parenting Behaviors, and Adolescent Adjustment in Urban African American Families', *Journal of Customer Services* 15: 425–49.

Heckman, J. and D.V. Masterov (2005) *The Productivity Argument for Investing in Young Children*, Chicago IL: University of Chicago.

Hoddinott, John, John A. Maluccio, Jere R. Behrman, Rafael Flores and Reynaldo Martorell (2008) 'Effect of a Nutrition Intervention During Early Childhood on Economic Productivity in Guatemalan Adults', *The Lancet* 371.9610: 411–6.

Hoff, K., and P. Pandey (2004) *Belief Systems and Durable Inequalities: An Experimental Investigation of Indian Caste*, Policy Research Working Paper 3351, Washington DC: World Bank.

Husain, N., F. Creed and B. Tomenson (2000) 'Depression and Social Stress in Pakistan', *Psychological Medicine* 30: 395–402.

Irwin, L.G., A. Siddiqi and C. Hertzman (2007) 'Early Child Development: A *Powerful* Equalizer', Final Report for the World Health Organization's Commission on the Social Determinants of Health, Geneva: WHO.

Isabella, R.A. (1993) 'Origins of Attachment: Maternal Interactive Behavior Across the First Year', *Child Development* 64, 605–21.

Joint Learning Initiative on Children and HIV/AIDS (JLICA) (2009) 'Home Truths: Facing the Facts on Children, AIDS, and Poverty', Summary report, http://www.jlica.org/resources/publications.php (accessed 1September 2010).

Keller, H., M. Abels, B. Lamm, R.D. Yovsi, S. Volker and A. Lakhani (2008) 'Ecocultural Effects on Early Infant Care: A study in Cameroon, India, and Germany', *Ethos* 33: 512–41.

Krishna, A. (2007) 'Escaping Poverty and Becoming Poor in Three States of India, with Additional Evidence from Kenya, Uganda, and Peru', in D. Narayan, and P. Petesch (eds), *Moving Out of Poverty: Cross-Disciplinary Perspectives on Mobility*, Washington DC: Palgrave Macmillan and World Bank.

Lui, H., A.M. DiGirolamo, H.X. Barnhart, A.D. Stein and R. Martorell (2004) 'Relative Importance of Birth Size and Postnatal Growth for Women's Educational Achievement', *Early Human Development* 76: 1–16.

Lozoff B., E. Jimenez and J.B. Smith (2006) 'Double Burden of Iron Deficiency in Infancy and Low Socioeconomic Status: A Longitudinal Analysis of Cognitive Test Scores to Age 19 Years', *Archives of Pediatric and Adolescent Medicine* 160: 1108–13.

Lozoff, B., N.K. Klein, E.C. Nelson, D.K. McClish, M. Manuel and M.E. Chacon (1998) 'Behavior of Infants with Iron-Deficiency Anemia', Child Development 69: 24–36.

Lustig, S. (2009) 'An Ecological Framework for the Refugee Experience: What Is the Impact on Child Development?', in G.W. Evans and T.D. Wachs (eds) *Chaos and Children's Development: Levels of Analysis and Mechanisms*, Washington, DC: American Psychological Association.

Maulik P.K. and G.L. Darmstadt (2009) 'Community-Based Interventions to Optimize Early Childhood Development in Low Resource Settings', *Journal of Perinatology* 29.8: 531–42.

McCormick M.C., J. Brooks-Gunn, S.L. Buka, J. Goldman, J. Yu, M. Salganik, D.T. Scott, F.C. Bennett, L.L. Kay, J.C. Bernbaum, C.R. Bauer, C. Martin, E.R. Woods, A. Martin and P.H. Casey (2006) 'Early Intervention in Low Birth Weight Premature Infants: Results at 18 Years of Age for the Infant Health and Development Program', *Pediatrics* 117.3: 771–80.

Narayan, D. and P. Petesch (2002) *Voices of the Poor: From Many Lands,* Washington, DC: World Bank.

Narayan, D. and P. Petesch (2007) *Moving Out of Poverty: Cross-Disciplinary Perspectives on Mobility,* Washington, DC: Palgrave Macmillan and World Bank.

National Scientific Council on the Developing Child (2007) *The Science of Early Child Development: Closing the Gap Between What We Know and What We Do*, Cambridge MA: National Scientific Council on the Developing Child.

Nores, M. and W.S. Barnett (2010) 'Benefits of Early Childhood Interventions Across the World: (Under) Investing in the Very Young', *Economics of Education Review* 29.2: 271–82.

Pollitt, E., K.S. Gorman, P.L. Engle, R. Martorell and J. Rivera (1993) 'Early Supplementary Feeding and Cognition: Effects over Two Decades', *Monographs of the Society for Research in Child Development* 58.7: 1–99.

Rahman, A., J. Bunn, H. Lovel and F. Creed (2007) 'Maternal Depression Increases Infant Risk of Diarrhoeal Illness: A Cohort Study', *Archives of Disease in Childhood, 92,* 24–8.

Ramey, C. and S. Ramey (1998) 'Early Intervention and Early Experience', *American Psychologist* 53.2: 109–20.

Reynolds, A.J., M.M. Englund, S. Ou, L.J. Schweinhart and F.A. Campbell (2010) 'Paths of Effects of Preschool Participation to Educational Attainment at Age Twenty-one: A Three-study Analysis' in A.J. Reynolds, A.J. Rolnick, M.M. Englund and J.A. Temple (eds), *Childhood Programs and Practices in the First Decade of Life: A Human Capital Integration,* New York: Cambridge University Press.

Reynolds, A.J., J.A. Temple, S. Ou, D.L. Robertson, J.P. Mersky, J.W. Topitzes and M.D. Niles (2007) 'Effects of a School-based, Early Childhood Intervention on Adult Health and Well-being: A Nineteen-year Follow-up of Low-income Families', *Archives of Pediatrics & Adolescent Medicine* 161.8: 730–9.

Ross, K., L. Zuze and D. Ratsatsi (2005) 'The Use of Socioeconomic Gradient Lines to Judge the Performance of School Systems', Paper presented at SACMEQ Research Conference, Paris, 28 Sept–2 Oct 2005.

Sachs, J. (2005) *The End to Poverty,* New York: Penguin.

St. Petersburg–USA Orphanage Research Team (2008) 'The Effects of Early Social-Emotional and Relationship Experience on the Development of Young Orphanage Children', *Monographs of the Society for Research in Child Development* 73.3: 1–262.

Schischka, J., P. Dalziel and C. Saunders (2008) 'Applying Sen's Capability Approach to Poverty Alleviation Programs: Two Case Studies', *Journal of Human Development,* 9.2: 229–46.

Schweinhart, L.J., J. Montie, Z. Xiang, W.S. Barnett, C.R. Belfield and M. Nores (2005) *Lifetime Effects: The High/Scope Perry Preschool Study through Age 40,* Monographs for the High/Scope Educational Research Foundation 14, Ypsilanti MI: High/Scope Educational Research Foundation.

Sen, A. (1999) *Development as Freedom,* Oxford: Oxford University Press.

Sen, A. (1995) 'The Political Economy of Targeting' in D. van de Walle and K. Nead (eds), *Public Spending and the Poor: Theory and Evidence,* Baltimore, MD: Johns Hopkins University Press.

Shipler, D. (2005) *The Working Poor: Invisible in America,* New York: Vintage Books.

Shonkoff J.P., W.T. Boyce and B.S. McEwen (2009) 'Neuroscience, Molecular Biology, and the Childhood Roots of Health Disparities: Building a New Framework for Health Promotion and Disease Prevention', *JAMA: The Journal of the American Medical Association* 301.21: 2252–9.

Steele, C.M. (1997) 'A Threat in the Air: How Stereotypes Shape Intellectual Identity and Performance', *American Psychologist 52,* 613–29.

Thompson R.A. and C.A. Nelson (2001) 'Developmental Science and the Media: Early Brain Development', *American Psychologist* 56.1: 5–15.

Tilly, C. (2007) 'Poverty and the Politics of Exclusion' in D. Narayan and P. Petesch (eds), *Moving Out of Poverty (Volume 1): Cross-Disciplinary Perspectives on Mobility,* Washington, DC: Palgrave Macmillan and World Bank.

Trost, K., and M. El-Khouri (2008) 'Mapping Swedish Females' Educational Pathways in Terms of Academic Competence and Adjustment Problems', *Journal of Social Issues* 64.1: 157–74.

UNESCO (2006) *Strong Foundations: Early Childhood Care and Education*, Education For All Global Monitoring Report, UNESCO: Paris.

UNESCO and LLECE (2008) *Student Achievement in Latin America and the Caribbean: Results of the Second Regional Comparative Explanatory Study*, Santiago: UNESCO and LLECE.

UNICEF (2008) *State of the World's Children 2009: Maternal and Newborn Health*, New York: UNICEF.

Victora, C.G., L. Adair, C. Fall, P.C. Hallal, R. Martorell, L. Richter and H.S. Sachdev (2008) 'Maternal and Child Undernutrition: Consequences for Adult Health and Human Capital', *The Lancet* 371: 9609: 340–57.

Wachs, T.D. (2000) *Necessary But Not Sufficient: The Role of Individual and Multiple Influences on Human Development*, Washington DC: American Psychological Association Press.

Wadsworth, S.J., R.P. Corley, R. Plomin, J.C. Hewitt and J.C. DeFries (2006) 'Genetic and Environmental Influences on Continuity and Change in Reading Achievement in the Colorado Adoption Project' in A. Huston and M. Ripke (eds), *Developmental Contexts in Middle Childhood: Bridges to Adolescence and Adulthood*, Cambridge: Cambridge University Press.

Walker S.P., S.M. Chang, C.A. Powell and S.M. Grantham-McGregor (2004) 'Psychosocial Intervention Improves the Development of Term Low-Birth-Weight Infants', The *Journal of Nutrition* 134.6: 1417–23.

Walker, S.P., S.M. Chang, C.A. Powell and S.M. Grantham-McGregor (2005) 'Effects of Early Childhood Psychosocial Stimulation and Nutritional Supplementation on Cognition and Education in Growth-stunted Jamaican Children: Prospective Cohort Study', *The Lancet* 366.9499: 1804–7.

Walker, S.P., S.M. Chang, C.A. Powell, E. Simonoff and S.M. Grantham-McGregor (2006) 'Effects of Psychosocial Stimulation and Dietary Supplementation in Early Childhood on Psychosocial Functioning in Late Adolescence: Follow-up of Randomised Controlled Trial', *British Medical Journal* 333.7566: 472–4.

Walker, S.P., S.M. Chang, N. Younger and S.M. Grantham-McGregor (2010) 'The Effect of Psychosocial Stimulation on Cognition and Behaviour at 6 years in a Cohort of Term, Low-Birthweight Jamaican Children', *Developmental Medicine and Child Neurology* 52.7: e148–e154.

Walker, S., T.D. Wachs, J. Meeks-Gardner, B. Lozoff, G. Wasserman, E. Pollitt, J. Carter and the International Child Development Steering (2007) 'Child Development: Risk Factors for Adverse Outcomes in Developing Countries', *The Lancet,* 369.9556: 145–57.

Wolf, A., I. De Andraca and B. Lozoff (2002) 'Maternal Depression in Three Latin American Samples', *Social Psychiatry and Psychiatric Epidemiology* 37: 169–76.

Zevalkink, J. and J. Riksen-Walraven (2001) 'Parenting in Indonesia: Inter- and Intracultural Differences in Mothers' Interactions with Their Young Children', *International Society for the Study of Behavioral Development* 25: 167–75.

9

Poverty, Child Risk, and Resilience in Developing Countries

Theodore D. Wachs

Growing up in poverty has been consistently linked to reduced cognitive and social-emotional competence in children from both developed (Klebanov and Brooks-Gunn 2006) and low- and middle-income (LAMI) countries (Grantham-McGregor et al. 2007). Reduced competence undermines young children's school readiness and subsequent school performance, and ultimately contributes to the intergenerational transmission of poverty (Engle et al. 2007). To understand how poverty can undermine the development of child competence requires an understanding of issues involving developmental risks, and how risks driven by poverty translate into deficits in child competence. This chapter provides a framework linking developmental risks, poverty, and child competence.

The nature of child competence and developmental risks

Child competence

Child competence is both multifaceted and multi-determined (Wachs 2000: chs 8 and 9). *Multifaceted* means that children can be competent or deficient in a number of areas (for example, cognitive, language, academic, social-emotional, or physical competence). *Multi-determined* means that there are a variety of biological, ecological, psychosocial, and cultural factors that act to influence individual differences in child competence. As described below, individual differences in children's competence result from the combined action of the number and characteristics of developmental risks and promotive influences the child encounters over time.

Developmental risks

Developmental risks refer to biological and psychosocial influences that are known to compromise children's cognitive, language, academic, social-emotional, or physical development (Sameroff et al. 2003). The relation of developmental risks to outcomes is not straightforward. Exposure to a developmental risk increases the likelihood of compromised development, but does not guarantee that development will be compromised. Whether or not exposure to a specific risk results in compromised development will depend on the context within which the risk occurs, whether the child is also exposed to other risks, and whether the child encounters other influences that attenuate the impact of risk. Thus, while iron-deficiency anaemia is a known risk for subsequent child developmental delay, it would be incorrect to conclude that an anaemic child will inevitably be developmentally delayed. What can be concluded is that an anaemic child is significantly more likely to be developmentally delayed than a non-anaemic child.

Known risks affecting development in young children can be found in both high- (Evans 2004) and low-income countries (Grantham-McGregor et al. 2007; Walker et al. 2007). The underlying mechanisms through which risk translates into impaired developmental competence appear to operate in a similar fashion in both developed (Bradley and Corwyn 2005) and low-income countries (Wachs 2003; Walker et al. 2007). However, a substantial number of developmental risks are more common in LAMI countries (UNICEF 2004), examples of which are shown in Box 9.1.

Box 9.1 Examples of developmental risks that are more prevalent in low- and middle-income countries

- Growth retardation (Walker et al. 2007)
- Diarrhoea–malnutrition cycles (Guerrant et al. 2008)
- Micronutrient deficiencies (Walker et al. 2007)
- Chronic disease (Nugent 2008)
- Reduced access to healthcare (Peters et al. 2008)
- Maternal depression (Wachs et al. 2009)
- Being orphaned as the result of parents dying from AIDS (UNAIDS 2008: ch 6)
- Living in slum areas characterized by a lack of basic services, substandard housing, and overcrowding (Sheuya 2008)
- Societal violence resulting in involuntary family migration (Ernholt and Yule 2006)

Risks that compromise development fall into three categories; examples are shown in Box 9.2. Whether or not the risks listed in Box 9.2 actually translate into impairments in child competence will depend in good part upon 'dosage'. Dosage refers to the number and intensity of risks the child encounters and the length of time the child is exposed to risk. Time-limited or mild levels of exposure to risk or risk-induced stress are not likely to be harmful and in some cases may even facilitate development (for example, positive or tolerable stress: Shonkoff et al. 2009).

Box 9.2 Examples of known developmental risks

Bio-ecological
- Pre- and post-natal biomedical problems (for example, intra-uterine growth retardation, foetal alcohol syndrome, malaria or other parasitic infections)
- Child or parental macro- and micro-nutritional deficits (for example, protein calorie malnutrition or iron-deficiency anaemia)
- Exposure to environmental toxins (for example, lead or other heavy metals)
- Chronic family health problems
- Genotypes that either directly compromise development or increase the detrimental impact of other risks

Psychosocial
- Low maternal education level
- Insensitive or non-responsive parenting
- Harsh physical punishment
- Inadequate opportunities for cognitive stimulation in the home
- Crowded or highly chaotic home environment
- Maternal depression
- Exposure to family or neighbourhood violence
- Poor-quality schools
- Educational or societal discrimination

Individual
While these are often the result of exposure to bio-ecological and psychosocial risk factors, in and of themselves they can also increase the probability of non-optimal developmental outcomes:
- Insecure attachment
- Highly reactive temperament
- Low self-regulation
- Below-average cognitive skills

Sources: Bradley and Corwyn (2005); Evans (2004); Irwin et al. (2007: 19–28); Wachs (2003); Walker et al. (2007); Yates et al. (2003).

Cumulative (high dosage) risk occurs when children are exposed to multiple biological and/or psychosocial risks, whether at a given point in time and/or across time. When a child is exposed to multiple risks at a given point in time, or to cumulative risks across time, or when risk exposure results in highly intense stress, there is a very strong likelihood of adverse long-term consequences. Studies from high-income countries have documented that children exposed to cumulative risks have a far greater likelihood of compromised health (Bauman et al. 2006; Shonkoff et al. 2009) and development than children exposed to only a limited number of risks (Appleyard et al. 2005; Evans 2004; Masten and Obradovic 2006; Sameroff et al. 2003). A similar pattern of findings has also been shown in low-income countries (Walker et al. 2007). Figure 9.1 illustrates the cognitive and academic consequences of cumulative risk in a lower-middle-income country (Guatemala).

A major reason why cumulative risks may be particularly detrimental is illustrated by evidence on the physiological impact of risks that increase individual stress levels. Physiological reactions to stress involving the hypothalamic-pituitary-adrenocortical (HPA) axis function to promote physiological and behavioral adaptation to acute time-limited stress. However, if the stress is cumulative, continued secretion of HPA stress hormones leads to physiological damage, with a substantially increased risk of long-term adverse consequences on health, development, and well-being (Hertzman and Boyce 2010).

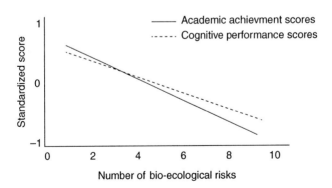

Figure 9.1 Relationship between risk factors in early childhood and adolescent academic achievement and cognition

Source: Adapted from Gorman and Pollitt (1996: 320).

Promotive influences

There are significant numbers of children who are doing substantially better than would be expected, given their level of risk exposure (Luthar et al. 2000). These children are referred to as resilient.[1] The phenomenon of resilience illustrates that a child's level of competence does not depend only on the number of risks the child encounters: it is also necessary to consider the operation of promotive influences. Promotive influences refer to biological, individual, or contextual characteristics that enhance children's competence and thus promote resilience (Sameroff et al. 2003).[2]

Promotive influences fall into three categories. Examples of documented influences from each category are shown in Box 9.3. Promotive factors may operate directly upon the child (for example, vaccinations) or through child characteristics (for example, self-regulation) or indirectly through the actions of primary caregivers (for example, sensitive-responsive parenting). There is nothing necessarily unique

---

Box 9.3   Examples of promotive influences

Bio-ecological
- Provision for sufficient intake of macro- and micro-nutrients
- Adequate preventative medical care (for example, vaccination programmes, growth monitoring) and reactive medical care (available and affordable treatment facilities)
- Genotypes that attenuate the impact of developmental risks

Psychosocial
- Stimulating, sensitive, responsive parenting
- Stable home environment
- Social support to parents and children
- Provision of pre-school programmes and access to quality school programmes

Individual
Again these result from exposure to bio-ecological and psychosocial promotive influences, but can also operate to facilitate development:

- Secure attachment
- Self-regulation
- High positive emotionality
- A sense of competence and motivation to master ones environment
- Above-average cognitive skills

Sources: Irwin et al. (2007: 19–28); Masten and Powell (2003); Rutter (2006); Sameroff et al. (2003); Wachs (2006); Werner and Smith (1992: Ch 9); Yates et al. (2003).

about promotive influences that require special conditions or interventions (Masten has characterized these influences as 'ordinary magic'; Masten and Powell 2003). Much of our knowledge about the nature and operation of promotive influences comes from research in developed countries. However, there is some evidence suggesting that promotive influences similar to those found in high-income countries also operate in low-income countries (Hestyanti 2006).

Promotive influences also operate in a probabilistic fashion. Exposure to promotive influences increases the likelihood of both positive development resilience when encountering risks, but such exposure does not guarantee resilience or more optimal development. For example, evidence from LAMI countries has shown that at-risk young children do not benefit equally from pre-school intervention programmes designed to promote cognitive development. Rather, the degree of benefit from program participation will partly depend on contextual characteristics such as the level of family economic disadvantage (Nores and di Gropello 2009) or the level of maternal education (Umek et al. 2008).

Comparing risk and promotive influences

While risk and promotive influences appear to be distinct concepts, in reality, they may reflect partially overlapping phenomena. Depending upon level, a given bio-ecological or psychosocial influence may operate either to increase risk or to provide protection. For example, low levels of maternal education can act as a risk factor inhibiting cognitive development of offspring, while higher levels of maternal education can act as a promotive influence, facilitating the offspring's cognitive development (e.g., Emond et al. 2006).

Further, as noted earlier, when risks are short term and/or mildly to moderately intense, exposure can promote development, particularly when the child is able successfully to cope with risk-produced frustration or stress. In addition, depending upon contextual characteristics, influences that are commonly regarded as risks may serve to promote more adequate development. For example, high individual reactivity to the environment may promote development when the environment is supportive or nurturing, but may act as a risk factor when the environment is stressful or neglectful (Hertzman and Boyce 2010). Similarly, depending on context, use of multiple caregivers (Weisner 2010), child labour (Boyden 2009), or seasonal labor migration by primary caregivers (Macours and Vakis 2007) may operate either as a risk or a promotive influence for children.

For conceptual reasons, the distinction between risk and promotive influences will be maintained in this chapter. However, it is essential to keep in mind the importance of not labelling a biological, contextual, or individual characteristic as a risk or a promotive factor, without taking into account other important features such as context, duration, and level.

Bringing together risk and promotive influences: an initial model

The interplay of risk and promotive influences is seen in a simplified conceptual model in Figure 9.2. There are several implications that follow from this model. First, neither risks nor promotive influences taken in isolation influence children's development. Rather, it is the interplay among and between risk and promotive influences that promotes developmental competence or vulnerability in children (Luthar et al. 2000). Second, child resilience in the face of risk is not an all-or-nothing phenomenon. Children can show resilience in one outcome domain while doing poorly in other outcome domains (Rutter 2006). Third, reflecting

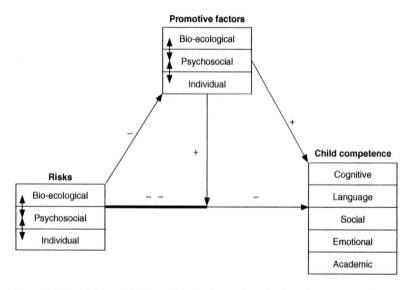

Figure 9.2 Initial model illustrating the interplay of risk and promotive factors in the development of child competence

Note: Plus signs refer to positive associations (e.g. more promotive factors, higher child competence); minus signs refer to negative associations (e.g. more risks, lower child competence). The greater the number of minus signs, the stronger the association.

the multi-determined nature of children's development, there are multiple pathways to resilience or vulnerability (Wachs 2000: ch 10).

Not inherent in Figure 9.2, but of critical importance, is the fact that the relation between risk and promotive influences and child competence operates over time (Yates et al. 2003). Children who display resilience at one time point may show developmental impairments at later time points (Luthar et al. 2000), especially when these later time points are more stressful. Delayed effects may result from early exposure to cumulative risks: (1) increasing the likelihood that a child will subsequently be exposed to later occurring risks (Hertzman and Boyce 2010); (2) compromising the child's ability to benefit from later more supportive environments (Kreppner et al. 2007); and (3) increasing a child's over-reactivity to later stress (Shonkoff et al. 2009). There also are sensitive time points where specific risks are particularly salient. For example, there can be long-term, non-remediable adverse developmental consequences due to changes in certain aspects of early brain development as the result of iron-deficiency anaemia in the first year of life (Lozoff et al. 2006).

Mechanisms underlying the interplay of risk and promotive influences

Co-variance among risks

Bio-ecological and psychosocial risk factors often go together (co-vary). As a result children in both developed (Appleyard et al. 2005; Evans 2004) and LAMI countries (Wachs 2003: table III) are more likely to encounter clusters of risks, rather than single isolated risks.

Co-variance among risks is especially critical for children growing up in poverty in LAMI countries. Evidence from these countries shows that child *malnutrition* co-varies with an increased risk of poor sanitation, polluted water supply, inadequate medical care, crowded homes that are low in stimulation value, and low parental involvement with the child's activities (Grantham-McGregor 1984); *maternal depression* increases the risk of offspring low birthweight (Rahman et al. (2007) and insecure attachment (Cooper et al. 2009), while living in *overcrowded homes* increases the risk of violence between spouses (Jeyaseelan et al. 2007) and maternal depression (Wachs et al. 2009).

As discussed earlier, the higher the number of cumulative risks the child encounters, the more development is likely to be compromised. Because individual risks often co-occur, there is an increased likelihood of exposure to cumulative multiple risks. The developmental impact of co-variance among multiple risks is illustrated by the functional isolation model shown in Figure 9.3. This figure illustrates how the developmental consequences of inadequate nutrition are the result of both impaired central nervous system development, and the co-variance between poor nutrition, less adequate parent–child relations, and reduced child involvement with the environment. While it is likely that the same process of co-variance is also occurring for promotive factors, at present, there is little direct evidence on the validity of this assumption.

Exposure to cumulative risk weakens promotive influences

There is a substantial body of research from high-income countries documenting that when high levels of exposure to cumulative developmental risks occur, the positive influence of promotive factors may be compromised (Masten and Obradovic 2006; Klebanov and Brooks-Gunn 2006; Sameroff and Rosenblum 2006). Two possible mechanisms underlying the weakening of promotive influences are sensitization and blunting (Wachs 2000: ch 9).

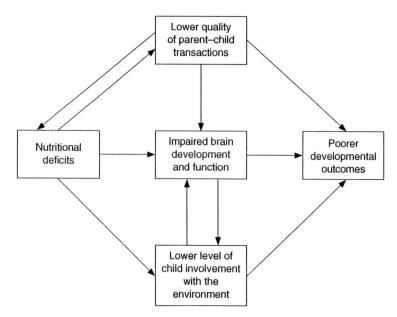

Figure 9.3 Functional isolation from the environment for poorly nourished children

Source: Wachs (2003: 392).

Sensitization occurs when cumulative exposure to high risk levels early in life increases the child's sensitivity to later risks. An example of sensitization is seen for previously malnourished children, who are more sensitive to later short-term nutritional deprivation than are non-malnourished children (Pollitt et al. 1998). Similarly, insecurely attached infants (an individual risk factor) show higher levels of physiological reactivity to a mild stress event than do securely attached infants (Hill-Soderland et al. 2008).

Blunting occurs when previous risk exposure makes a child less able to make use of later promotive experiences. One example of blunting is when children with poor early nutritional status benefit less from later rearing in advantaged circumstances than children with better early nutrition (Winick et al. 1975). Similarly, evidence shows that children with extended rearing in highly depriving orphanages are less likely to benefit from subsequent long-term rearing in high-quality adoptive homes (Beckett et al. 2006).

One critical implication deriving from the operation of blunting or sensitization processes is the need to minimize child exposure to cumulative risk, if promotive influences or interventions are to have a chance of succeeding.

The interplay of risk and promotive influences may not be linear

In a linear model, such as that shown in Figure 9.2, individual differences in child competence reflect the difference between the number of risks and promotive influences the child encounters. However, there also is evidence that the interplay of risks and promotive influences can be non-linear (interactive). In an interactive model the impact of specific risks will depend on the nature of other risks or promotive influences (Rutter 2006).

To the extent that the influence of risk and promotive influences upon child development is non-linear, we should expect to find marked individual outcome differences in children exposed to similar types and levels of risk. One example of such differences is the fact that while a high proportion of children previously reared in severely depriving orphanages show adverse long-term consequences, some previously institutionalized children show few long-term adverse effects (Rutter et al. 2010: ch 1).

Individual differences in reactivity are the likely result of the interplay between multiple biological (for example, genes: Caspi et al. 2002), psychosocial (for example, social support: Cluver et al. 2009) and individual characteristics (for example, temperament: Wachs 2006), which in turn are influenced by the timing (Yates et al. 2003) and intensity of events (Ernholt and Yule 2006). The operation of non-linear processes means that in order to understand fully how risk and promotive influences translate into developmental outcomes, it is necessary to go beyond looking at individual risk or promotive factors taken in isolation. Far more attention needs to be given to the interplay within and between specific multiple risks and promotive influences, operating over a background of time and intensity.

Poverty compromises child competence

Poverty compromises child competence in three interrelated ways. First, poverty compromises competence by increasing the likelihood that children will grow up being exposed to multiple bio-ecological (Evans 2004) and psychosocial risks (Bradley and Corwyn 2002; Irwin et al. 2007; Yates et al. 2003). For example, in both high- and low-income countries, there is a strong association between family poverty and maternal depression (Wachs et al. 2009). Maternal depression is a marker for multiple developmental risks including child undernutrition and impairments in the quality of mother–child interactions (Wachs et al. 2009). The increased risk of maternal depression in low-income women at least partially accounts for the adverse impact of poverty upon children's social-emotional competence (Mistry et al. 2004).

Second, poverty further compromises competence by reducing the likelihood of exposure to promotive factors (Klebanov and Brooks-Gunn 2006), particularly when poverty is chronic, as is more likely in low-income countries. In addition, as discussed earlier, higher levels of cumulative risk associated with poverty can attenuate the impact of promotive influences. Thus, children growing up in poverty are likely to encounter more developmental risks and fewer and less effective promotive influences.

Third, recent evidence also documents that the adverse child consequences associated with poverty are neural as well as behavioural. Neural consequences of exposure to poverty include dysregulation of the HPA system (Fernald and Gunnar 2009), as well as changes in aspects of brain electrical activity related to efficiency of cognitive processing (Hackman and Farah 2009). Poverty-related neural consequences may reflect the increased stress linked to poverty, which in turn can affect brain function and development (Shonkoff et al. 2009).

A model illustrating the links between chronic poverty, risk and promotive influences, and neural and developmental function is shown
in Figure 9.4. When risks associated with poverty are not excessive or
cumulative, promotive factors can attenuate the impact of risk and promote both brain and behavioural development. However, as seen in
Figure 9.4, high levels of chronic poverty and associated cumulative
risk act to reduce the facilitative impact of promotive factors upon both
brain and behavioural development.

Conclusions

Implications for intervention

One implication of the model in Figure 9.4 is that interventions to
reduce poverty may not impact on children's development unless they
can directly impact on poverty-related risks and promotive influences.
Support for this conclusion is seen in economic studies involving allocation of family financial resources. In families where mothers have
some degree of control over family finances, money is more likely to
be used in ways that reduce child risks or increase child exposure to
promotive influences (for example, by providing better nutrition or

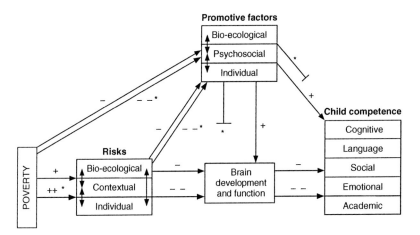

Figure 9.4 Model linking poverty to risk and promotive influences and to child
competence in low- and middle-income countries

Note: *Child exposed to high levels of cumulative risk or chronic poverty.
Plus signs refer to positive associations (e.g. higher poverty, more risks); minus signs refer
to negative associations (e.g. more risks, less adequacy of brain development). The greater
the number of plus or minus signs, the stronger the associations.

promoting better health), than in families where fathers have primary financial control (Kusago and Barham 2001; Pfeiffer et al. 2001). Such findings have clear implications for interventions designed to promote child welfare through cash transfers to families.

A second implication is that for children exposed to multiple poverty-related risks, designing interventions to remediate or reduce just one risk is not likely to have a strong or long-term impact. Even when there are gains associated with reducing one risk, these gains may be relatively modest and less likely to endure. Rather, the goal should be multidimensional interventions to reduce as many risks as is feasible.[3] A major reason for emphasizing multidimensional interventions designed to reduce multiple risks is evidence showing that the impact of promotive influences may be compromised in the context of multiple risks. This may be particularly true with respect to young children growing up in poverty in LAMI countries, where there is a substantially greater likelihood of encountering multiple risks.

A third implication is the critical need to intervene early in a child's life, before a child has been exposed to multiple cumulative risks. The evidence is clear that the longer a child has been exposed to multiple risks, the greater the likelihood of a negative developmental track, and the lower the likelihood that promotive factors will be effective. For example, early exposure to cumulative risks adversely influences the nature of the child's health (Bauman et al. 2006) and quality of interactions with their environment (Appleyard et al. 2005), both of which reduce the likelihood of adequate school readiness (Blair 2002; Walker et al. 2007). Poor school readiness adversely impacts on the child's subsequent school performance (Duncan et al. 2007), which in turn predicts adult economic welfare (Heckman 2006).

A final implication is that we must be careful not to over-promise with regard to the gains that potentially could come from interventions. Not all potential risks are remediable and not all promotive influences can be implemented. Even in the best intervention programmes not all children will benefit to the same extent, and some children may not benefit at all (Wyman 2003).

Implications for future research: contributions from the Young Lives database

Far less is known about the nature and role of promotive influences in low-income countries compared to the information base from high-income countries. Critical questions that need to be answered include: do known promotive influences operate in the same way in low- and high-income countries? And are there unique promotive influences that are particularly salient in some cultures? The Young Lives database could be of critical importance in answering such questions.

For example, even within high-risk populations some children are more at risk than others of impaired development. There is a clear need to develop valid and cost-effective measures to identify young children from LAMI countries who are at particularly high risk for failure to develop needed cognitive and social-emotional skills, which promote school readiness. The use of developmental landmarks for this purpose is problematic, especially in the first few years of life when such measures are often not strongly predictive of school readiness (National Research Council Committee on Developmental Outcomes and Assessments for Young Children 2008: ch 4). The Global Child Development Group (www.globalchilddevelopment.org) has suggested an alternative strategy of focusing on number of risk and promotive influences encountered, as one way to identify children who are at particular risk of compromised development. In this endeavour, the Young Lives database may be uniquely placed to test the validity and utility of a cumulative risk approach for early identification of young children who are likely to show a lack of school readiness and subsequent school failure.

Notes

1. Resilience does not mean total protection against developmental risks. Children can be resilient in the face of risks in one domain of development but display vulnerability in other domains (Luthar et al. 2000). Similarly, children who show resilience at one point in time may show developmental vulnerability at later time points as a result of continued exposure to cumulative risks (Sameroff and Rosenblum 2006).
2. In the developmental literature, a distinction has been made between protective and promotive influences (Sameroff et al. 2003). Protective influences are those that operate primarily when the child is exposed to developmental risks, and act to attenuate the detrimental impact of risk exposure. Promotive influences are those that enhance development regardless of the child's risk status. While the distinction between protective and promotive factors is important conceptually, this distinction may be less critical in the real world. For simplicity I shall use the term 'promotive' to refer to both protective and promotive influences.
3. The necessity for more complex multidimensional interventions rather than simple uni-dimensional interventions is a point that appears to be hard to get across to policymakers. We need to do a better job of making the point that simple solutions to complex problems may be penny-wise, pound foolish.

References

Appleyard, K., B. Egeland, M.H.M. van Dulmen and L.A. Sroufe (2005) 'When More is Not Better: The Role of Cumulative Risk in Child Behavior Outcomes', *Journal of Child Psychology and Psychiatry* 46.3: 235–45.

Bauman, L.J., E.J. Silver and R.E.K. Stein (2006) 'Cumulative Social Disadvantage and Child Health', *Pediatrics* 117: 1321–28.

Beckett, C., B. Maughan, M. Rutter, J. Castle, E. Colvert, C. Groothues, J. Kreppner, T. O'Connor, S. Stevens and J. Sonuga (2006) 'Do the Effects of Early Severe Deprivation on Cognition Persist into Early Adolescence? Findings from the English and Romanian Adoptees Study', *Child Development* 77: 696–711.

Blair, C. (2002) 'School Readiness: Integrating Cognition and Emotion in a Neurobiological Conceptualization of Children's Functioning at School Entry', *American Psychologist* 57, 111–27.

Boyden, J. (2009) 'Risk and Capability in the Context of Adversity: Children's Contributions to Household Livelihoods in Ethiopia', *Children, Youth and Environments* 19: 111–37.

Bradley, R. and R. Corwyn (2002) 'Socioeconomic Status and Child Development', *Annual Review of Psychology* 53: 371–99.

Bradley, R. and R. Corwyn (2005) 'Caring for Children Around the World: A View from HOME', *International Journal of Behavioral Development*, 29: 468–78.

Caspi, A., J. McClay, T. Moffitt, J. Mill, J. Martin, I. Craig, A. Taylor and R. Poulton (2002) 'Role of Genotype in the Cycle of Violence in Maltreated Children', *Science* 297: 851–54.

Cluver, L., D. Fincham and S. Seedat (2009) 'Posttraumatic Stress in AIDS-Orphaned Children Exposed to High Levels of Trauma: The Protective Role of Perceived Social Support', *Journal of Traumatic Stress* 22: 106–12.

Cooper, P., M. Tomlinson, L. Swartz, M. Landman, C. Molteno, A. Stein, K. McPherson and L. Murray (2009) 'Improving Quality of Mother–Infant Relationship and Infant Attachment in Socioeconomically Deprived Community in South Africa: Randomised Controlled Trial', *BMJ* 338: b974.

Duncan, G., C. Dawsett, A. Claessens, K. Magnuson, A. Huston, P. Klebanov, L. Pagani, L. Feinstein, M. Engel, J. Brooks-Gunn, H. Sexton, K. Duckworth and C. Japel (2007) 'School Readiness and Later Achievement', *Developmental Psychology* 43: 1428–46.

Emond, A., P. Lira, M. Lima, S. Grantham-McGregor and A. Ashworth (2006) 'Development and Behaviour of Low-Birthweight Term Infants at 8 years in Northeast Brazil: A Longitudinal Study', *Acta Paediatrica* 95: 1249–57.

Engle, P., M. Black, J. Behrman, M. Cabral de Mello, P. Gertler, L. Kapirri, R. Martorell, M. Young and the International Child Development Steering Group (2007) 'Child Development in Developing Countries 3: Strategies to Avoid the Loss of Developmental Potential in More Than 200 Million Children in the Developing World', *The Lancet* 369: 229–42.

Ernholt, K. and W. Yule (2006) 'Practitioner Review: Assessment and Treatment of Refugee Children and Adolescents Who Have Experienced War-Related Trauma', *Journal of Child Psychology and Psychiatry* 47: 1197–210.

Evans, G. (2004) 'The Environment of Childhood Poverty', *American Psychologist* 59: 77–92.

Fernald, L. and M. Gunnar (2009) 'Poverty-Alleviation Programme Participation and Salivary Cortisol in Very Low-Income Children', *Social Science and Medicine* 68: 2180–9.

Gorman, K. and E. Pollitt (1996) 'Does Schooling Buffer the Effects of Early Risk?', *Child Development* 67: 314–26.

Grantham-McGregor, S. (1984) 'The Social Background of Childhood Malnutrition' in B. Schurch and J. Brozek (eds), *Malnutrition and Behavior*, Lausanne: IDECG.

Grantham-McGregor, S., Y. Cheung, S. Cueto, P. Glewwe, L. Richter, B. Strupp and the International Child Development Steering Group (2007) 'Child Development in Developing Countries 1: Developmental Potential in the First Five Years for Children in Developing Countries', *The Lancet* 369: 60–70.

Guerrant, R., R. Oria, S. Moore, M. Oria and A. Lima (2008) 'Malnutrition as an Enteric Infectious Disease with Long-Term Effects on Child Development', *Nutrition Reviews* 66: 487–505.

Hackman, D. and M. Farah (2009) 'Socioeconomic Status and the Developing Brain', *Trends in Cognitive Sciences* 13: 65–73.

Heckman, J. (2006) 'Skill Formation and the Economics of Investing in Disadvantaged Children', *Science* 312: 1900–2.

Hertzman, C. and T. Boyce (2010) 'How Experience Gets Under the Skin to Create Gradients in Developmental Health', *Annual Review of Public Health* 31: 329–47.

Hestyanti, Y. (2006) 'Children Survivors of the 2004 Tsunami in Aceh, Indonesia: A Study of Resilience' in B. Lester, A. Masten and B. McEwen (eds), *Resilience in Children. Annals of the New York Academy of Sciences* 1094: 303–7.

Hill-Soderlund, A., W.R. Mills-Koonce, C. Propper, S. Calkins, D. Granger, G. Moore, J. Gariepy and M. Cox (2008) 'Parasympathetic and Sympathetic Responses to the Strange Situation in Infants and Mothers from Avoidant and Securely Attached Dyads', *Developmental Psychopathology* 50: 361–76.

Irwin, L., A. Siddiqi and C. Hertzman (2007) *Early Child Development: A Powerful Equalizer*, Final report for the WHO Commission on the Social Determinants of Health, Geneva: WHO.

Jeyaseelan, L., S. Kumar, N. Neelakantan, A. Peedicayil, R. Pillai and N. Duvvury (2007) 'Physical Spousal Violence Against Women in India: Some Risk Factors', *Journal of Biosocial Science*, 39: 657–70.

Klebanov, P. and J. Brooks-Gunn (2006) 'Cumulative Human Capital and Psychological Risk in the Context of Early Intervention', in B. Lester, A. Masten and B. McEwen (eds), *Resilience in Children. Annals of the New York Academy of Sciences* 1094: 63–82.

Kreppner, J., M. Rutter, C. Beckett, J. Castle, E. Colvert, C. Groothues, A. Hawkins, T. O'Connor, S. Stevens and E. Sonuga-Barke (2007) 'Normality and Impairment Following Profound Early Institutional Deprivation: A Longitudinal Follow-Up into Early Adolescence', *Developmental Psychology* 43: 931–46.

Kusago, T. and B. Barham (2001) 'Preference Heterogeneity, Power, and Intra-household Decision-Making in Rural Malaysia', *World Development* 29 1237–56.

Lozoff, B., J. Beard, J. Connor, B. Felt, M. Georgieff and T. Schallert (2006) 'Long-Lasting Neural and Behavioral Effects of Iron Deficiency in Infancy', *Nutrition Review* 64: s34–s44.

Luthar. S., D. Cicchetti and B. Becker (2000) 'The Construct of Resilience: A Critical Evaluation and Guidelines for Future Work', *Child Development* 71, 543–62.

Macours, K. and R. Vakis (2007) *Seasonal Migration and Early Childhood Development*, World Bank Social Protection Discussion Paper 0702, Washington DC: World Bank.

Masten, A. and J. Obradovic (2006) 'Competence and Resilience in Development' in B. Lester, A. Masten and B. McEwen (eds), *Resilience in Children. Annals of the New York Academy of Sciences* 1094: 13–27.

Masten, A. and J. Powell (2003) 'A Resilience Framework for Research, Policy and Practice' in S. Luthar (ed.) *Resilience and Vulnerability: Adaptation in the Context of Childhood Adversities*, New York: Cambridge University Press.

Mistry, R., J. Biesanz, L. Taylor, M. Burchinal and M. Cox (2004) 'Family Income and Its Relation to Preschool Children's Adjustment for Families in the NICHD Study of Early Child Care', *Developmental Psychology* 40: 727–45.

National Research Council Committee on Developmental Outcomes and Assessments for Young Children (2008) *Early Childhood Assessment: Why, What and How*, Washington, DC: National Academies Press.

Nores, M. and E. di Gropello (2009) 'Pre-K Availability in Vietnam: Determinants of Early Attainment and Progress', Symposium Presentation to the Society for Research in Child Development, April 2009, Denver.

Nugent, R. (2008) 'Chronic Diseases in Developing Countries: Health and Economic Burdens', *Annals of the New York Academy of Sciences* 1136: 70–9.

Obradovic, J. and T. Boyce (2009) 'Individual Differences in Behavioral, Physiological and Genetic Sensitivities to Contexts: Implications for Development and Adaptation', *Developmental Neuroscience* 31: 300–8.

Peters, D., A. Garg, G. Bloom, D. Walker, W. Brieger and M. Rahman (2008) 'Poverty and Access to Health Care in Developing Countries', *Annals of the New York Academy of Sciences* 1136: 16–71.

Pfeiffer, J., S. Gloyd and L. Li (2001) 'Intrahousehold Resource Allocation and Child Growth in Mozambique: An Ethnographic Case-Control Study', *Social Science and Medicine* 53: 83–97.

Pollitt, E., S. Cueto and E. Jacoby (1998) 'Fasting and Cognition in Well and Undernourished School Children', *American Journal of Clinical Nutrition* Supplement 67, 779s–85s.

Rahman, A., J. Bunn, H. Lovel and F. Creed (2007) 'Maternal Depression Increases Infant Risk of Diarrhoeal Illness: A Cohort Study' *Archives of Disease in Childhood* 92: 24–8.

Rutter, M. (2006) 'Gene-Environment Interdependence', *Developmental Science* 10: 12–18.

Rutter, M., E. Sonuga-Barke, C. Beckett, J. Castle, J. Kreppner, R. Kumsta, W. Schlotz, S. Stevens and C. Bell, (2010) Deprivation-Specific Psychological Patterns: Effects of Institutional Deprivation, *Monographs of the Society for Research in Child Development*, 75, #295.

Sameroff, A., L. Gutman and S. Peck (2003) 'Adaptation Among Youths Facing Multiple Risks: Prospective Research Findings' in S. Luthar (ed.), *Resilience and Vulnerability: Adaptation in the Context of Childhood Adversities* (pp. 364–91), New York: Cambridge University Press.

Sameroff, A. and K. Rosenbloom (2006) 'Psychosocial Constraints on the Development of Resilience' in: B. Lester, A. Masten and B. McEwen (eds),

Resilience in Children. Annals of the New York Academy of Sciences 1094: 116–24.

Sheuya, S. (2008) 'Improving the Health and Lives of People Living in Slums', *Annals of the New York Academy of Sciences*, 1136: 298–306.

Shonkoff, J., W.T. Boyce and B. McEwen (2009) 'Neuroscience, Molecular Biology and the Childhood Roots of Health Disparities: Building a New Framework for Health Promotion and Disease Prevention', *JAMA* 301: 2252–9.

Umek, L., K. Marjanovic, U. Fekonja and K. Bajc (2008) 'The Effect of Preschool on Children's School Readiness', *Early Child Development and Care* 178: 569–88.

UNAIDS (2008) *2008 Report on the Global AIDS Epidemic*, Geneva: Joint United Nations Programmeme on HIV/AIDS.

UNICEF (2004) *The State of the World's Children 2005: Childhood Under Threat*, New York: UNICEF.

Wachs, T.D. (2000) *Necessary But Not Sufficient: The Role of Individual and Multiple Influences on Human Development*, Washington, DC: American Psychological Association Press.

Wachs, T.D. (2003) 'Expanding Our View of Context: The Bio-Ecological Environment and Development' in R. Kail (ed.), *Advances in Child Development and Behavior:* vol 31 (pp. 365–411), New York: Academic Press.

Wachs, T.D. (2006) 'Contributions of Temperament to Buffering and Sensitization Processes in Children's Development', in B. Lester, A. Masten and B. McEwen (eds), *Resilience in Children. Annals of the New York Academy of Sciences* 1094, 28–39.

Wachs, T.D., M. Black, and P. Engle (2009) 'Maternal Depression: A Global Threat to Children's Health, Development and Behavior and to Human Rights', *Child Development Perspectives* 3: 51–9.

Walker, S., T.D. Wachs, J. Meeks-Gardner, B. Lozoff, G. Wasserman, E. Pollitt, J. Carter and the International Child Development Steering (2007) 'Child Development in Developing Countries 2: Risk Factors for Adverse Outcomes in Developing Countries', *The Lancet* 369, 145–57.

Weisner, T. (2010) 'Well-being, Chaos and Culture: Sustaining a Meaningful Daily Routine', in G.W. Evans and T.D. Wachs (2010) (eds) *Chaos and Its Influence on Children's Development: An Ecological Perspective.* (pp. 211–24), Washington, DC: American Psychological Association.

Werner, E. and R. Smith (1982) *Vulnerable but Invincible: A Longitudinal Study of Resilient Children and Youth*, New York: McGraw-Hill.

Werner, E. and R. Smith (1992) *Overcoming the Odds: High Risk Children from Birth to Adulthood*, Ithaca: Cornell University Press.

Winick, M., K. Meyer and R. Harris (1975) 'Malnutrition and Environmental Enrichment by Early Adoption', *Science* 190: 1173–5.

Wyman, P. (2003) 'Emerging Perspectives on Context Specificity of Children's Adaptation and Resilience' in S. Luthar (ed.), *Resilience and Vulnerability: Adaptation in the Context of Childhood Adversities* (pp. 293–317), New York: Cambridge University Press.

Yates, T., B. Egeland and L. Sroufe (2003) 'Rethinking Resilience: A Developmental Process Perspective' in S. Luthar (ed.) *Resilience and Vulnerability: Adaptation in the Context of Childhood Adversities* (pp. 243–66), New York: Cambridge University Press.

10
Political Economy, Perception, and Social Change as Mediators of Childhood Risk in Andhra Pradesh

Jo Boyden and Gina Crivello

Introduction

Poverty is one of the most significant adversities confronted by children around the world today. Young Lives aims to improve understanding of the dynamics, causes and consequences of childhood poverty and provide evidence to support the development of effective policies for reducing it and breaking enduring poverty cycles. The study of risk and protection in the context of poverty is central to this endeavour and the focus of this chapter.

By examining statistical associations between adverse circumstances in households and outcomes for children, we capture the underlying processes that structure childhood risk. We focus on crime, economic shocks (such as job loss), government regulations (such as forced resettlement or land redistribution), environmental hazards, housing disasters (for example, fire), the illness or death of a household member and other family adversities (for example, separation of family members). Our survey questionnaire also addresses children's aspirations and their sense of agency, self-esteem and self-respect, all of which can help them to confront risk. Qualitative research with a sub-sample of children and adults permits deeper enquiry into children's experiences of and their responses to adversity, and their ideas about risk and well-being. The longitudinal design of the study facilitates exploration of how individual life trajectories are shaped by adversity, and allows attention to be paid to differences in risk exposure levels and outcomes among different social groups. Examination of the resources that children, their families and others bring to bear on their situations, as well as the contribution of social protection and/or child protection schemes, assists understanding of protective processes.

The bulk of research on childhood risk has been conducted within psychiatry, medicine, psychology, genetics and social work studies (for reviews, see Walker et al. 2007; Barton 2005; Cowan et al. 1996; Compas et al. 1995; Rolf et al. 1990).[1] This research has made a significant contribution to understanding the vulnerabilities and strengths of young people living with adversity in the industrialized world. Nevertheless, there are limitations associated with the relevance of findings to diverse contexts; the use of the individual as the unit of observation and analysis and subsequent generalization of conclusions; and the neglect of children's daily experiences of risk. In particular, very little consideration is given to how risk is produced and reproduced by social systems and structures and experienced by social groups (Hart 2008; Schoon 2006).

Within the dominant tradition, risk in childhood is taken to concern the probability of life outcomes having their origins in earlier circumstances, based on statistical associations (Schoon 2006). Thus, in the majority of definitions, 'risk' is associated with future uncertainty (Tulloch and Lupton 2003) and has negative connotations, increasing the probability of some 'undesirable outcome' (Schaffer 2006: 87). Hence, in psychology and psychiatry, the investigation of risk in children has to do with the likelihood of pathology in behaviour, development or mental health arising from the experience of different kinds of physical or social hazard (Gauvain 2001; Schaffer 2006). Most studies employ an a priori definition of risk and use standardized instruments that rate levels of exposure and impacts against a sliding scale.

Research on risk generally shows that negative experiences and deficiencies in early childhood pose a severe threat to development, well-being and adaptation, with lifelong and intergenerational implications (for example, Grantham-McGregor et al. 2007). Several studies derived from Young Lives data support this broad finding (summarized in Boyden et al. 2011). Poverty is one of the environmental risks most commonly cited as undermining individual adaptation across a variety of domains of development (Grantham-McGregor et al. 2007; Schoon 2006). And poverty is commonly found to lead to or be associated with other grave hardships, for example, family crises, such that the development and well-being of poor children are doubly compromised through the interaction of multiple adversities, with cumulative effect (see Chapter 9 by Theodore Wachs). Evidence from this kind of research may seem to present a compelling case with regard to childhood deprivation; yet there is considerable complexity in human responses to risk and outcomes are not all knowable. For example, even though physical outcomes may be relatively easy to gauge, the psychosocial effects of stress and adversity tend to be diagnostically unspecific and therefore very difficult to determine (Rutter 2010). It is increasingly acknowledged that not all boys and girls exposed to adversity experience negative consequences and some may even grow stronger (Rutter 2001).

Many of the boys and girls in the Young Lives sample show impressive courage in the face of what is broadly defined here as risk, even while specific detrimental effects may be clearly discerned. This kind of finding points to the enormous challenge of forecasting risk outcomes for children and the adults they become. Accordingly, in this chapter, we warn against overly deterministic analyses and stress the importance of mediating and contextual forces in human experience and development. We draw on emergent evidence from Andhra Pradesh, India, focusing on survey data for the whole sample and qualitative data collected with children in two communities: 'Polur', a Muslim area of Hyderabad and 'Patna', a rural community inhabited by the Jathapa sub-tribe in Srikakulam district.[2] We conclude by arguing for a revised approach to research in this field.

The political economy of risk

Power and wealth are highly concentrated in India within an extremely complex and formalized social structure in which ethnicity, language, religion and caste are key organizing principles. This chapter focuses on the most economically disadvantaged groups, Scheduled Castes and Scheduled Tribes, and on Muslims, another minority group that experiences much discrimination. Believed to be the original inhabitants of India, Scheduled Tribes (many of whom prefer to be called *adivasis*; Gupta 2005: 419) comprise a minority of ethnic and tribal peoples with diverse languages, belief systems and lifestyles. Historically, these groups were concentrated in remote, forested, hilly areas, showed little allegiance to national religions and were only marginally incorporated within the national economy and polity. However, some have now converted to Hinduism and adopted plains cultivation, with the government applying considerable pressure for their integration in many cases (Gupta 2005).

The concept of caste, on the other hand, originated in the Hindu *varna* system, which divides society into four divinely ordained, heritable categories according to duty and occupation, with Scheduled Castes outside and beneath this hierarchical order. The position of Scheduled Castes has been underpinned by a religiously sanctioned notion of pollution in which members are allocated the most defiling occupations, such as those involving blood, the dead, or human waste. Hence, Scheduled Castes are considered 'unclean' and thereby 'untouchable', this taboo being buttressed by widespread political and economic dominance by more powerful castes and an array of formalized exclusionary practices (Srinivasulu 2002).[3] Backward Castes, currently the largest caste category in Andhra Pradesh, are so designated because they also occupy a low position within the caste hierarchy, there being five groups in this category in the state.[4]

Formed in 1956, the state of Andhra Pradesh comprises three regions: Telangana, coastal Andhra, and Rayalaseema. The three regions have distinct histories which indelibly shape contemporary socio-political formations, relations of production and patterns of social mobilization (Srinivasulu 2002). However, despite considerable regional diversity, Scheduled Castes and Scheduled Tribes consistently experience multiple disadvantages when compared with other social groups (Mukherji 2008; Murray 2008) and this is clearly reflected within our sample.

The distribution of ethnic and religious groups in the Young Lives sample in Andhra Pradesh is not representative of the state as a whole and richer groups are excluded altogether. Even so, inequality based on class, caste, gender and location is very evident (Galab et al. 2008). Scheduled Caste and Scheduled Tribe children are mainly concentrated in the poorest households, a large proportion of the latter being in the bottom quintile. Backward Caste children are generally better off than these groups, although less so than 'Other caste' Hindus and Muslims, who are, mainly, in the wealthier quintiles.

Table 10.1 explores the association between the economic status of Young Lives households and the frequency and type of adversities they reported for the period 2002 to 2006. Overall, poorer households carry a heavier burden of risk than wealthier households; environmental hazards, economic shocks and family adversity are the most prevalent across the sample as a whole. The frequency of environmental hazards is influenced by the prevalence of rural households in the sample and the 2002 to 2004 drought in Andhra Pradesh. There is a lower correlation with poverty for some risks, for example, adverse government regulations like mandatory land redistribution, than others, with family difficulties such as separation or divorce more common in wealthier households.

Table 10.1 Adversities by wealth quintiles

Shocks/adversities	1st (poorest)		2nd		3rd		4th		5th (least poor)		Total	
	No.	%	No.	%	No.	%	No.	%	No.	%	No.	%
Crime	34	5.78	36	6.05	33	5.72	27	4.61	27	4.61	157	5.35
Government regulation	14	2.38	18	3.03	15	2.60	15	2.56	3	0.51	65	2.22
Economic	121	20.58	152	25.55	132	22.88	111	18.94	81	13.82	597	20.36
Environmental	306	52.04	325	54.62	270	46.79	193	32.94	42	7.17	1,136	38.74
Housing	13	2.21	17	2.86	13	2.25	3	0.51	1	0.17	47	1.60
Family illness/death	204	34.69	187	31.43	162	28.08	185	31.57	131	22.35	869	29.64
Family adversity	111	18.88	84	14.12	81	14.04	135	23.04	160	27.30	571	19.47

Table 10.2 shows a clear correlation among Scheduled Castes between household economic status and risk, with those in the bottom two quintiles the most affected. The most common risks for this group are economic shocks, environmental hazards and family illness or death.

The relationship between risk exposure and poverty for Scheduled Tribe households (Table 10.3) is more complex and varied. Economic shocks, environmental hazards and family illness or death are more frequent among poorer tribal households, whereas crime affects those in the third quintile (middle group) more than others, possibly because wealthier groups experience higher rates of theft. Family adversity appears to have no correlation with economic status in this group.

Although further work is needed to enhance understanding of the interaction of low household socio-economic status, other forms of risk and outcomes for children, we already have some evidence of the disadvantages experienced by Scheduled Caste and Scheduled Tribe children as compared to other groups. Higher levels of stunting (low height for age, an indicator of long-term malnutrition) in the Younger Cohort (Galab et al. 2008) is one example, and lower levels of school achievement, as measured by Peabody Picture Vocabulary Scores, another (Nair 2009). In addition, Older Cohort children in these groups are more likely than others to drop out of school, work long hours, miss classes because of work or migrate for work during crises (see Chapter 13 by Crivello, Vennam and Komanduri).

Income shocks at the household level are associated with an increase in the amount of children's work by around two hours per day, with the greatest impacts on girls in rural areas (Krutikova 2009). Similarly, the 2002–04 drought reduced the hours children spent at school and their cognitive scores, which was partly driven by an increase in working hours among rural families (Galab and Outes-Leon 2011). Gender and birth order emerged as influential factors in this analysis, in that eldest boys were the only group to experience a reduction in demand for their labour and increased opportunities for schooling, probably because they are more likely than others to work on family smallholdings, which became uncultivable during the drought.

In summary, preliminary findings on household risk from Andhra Pradesh indicate structural causes, with multiple detrimental outcomes for children in disadvantaged groups. Given that subjective perspectives of affected populations fundamentally shape the impact of adversity (Boyden 2009: 8), this evidence raises the question as to whether or not affected children are aware of the impact of such forces in their lives or concerned about household risk and whether they perceive any

Table 10.2 Adversities experienced by scheduled caste households

Shocks/adversities	1st (poorest)		2nd		3rd		4th		5th (least poor)		Total	
	No.	%	No.	%	No.	%	No.	%	No.	%	No.	%
Crime	9	7.63	12	6.78	9	6.62	3	3.23	2	6.45	35	6.31
Government regulation	3	2.54	10	5.65	3	2.21	0	0.00	0	0.00	16	2.88
Economic	20	16.95	44	24.86	33	24.26	14	15.05	5	16.13	116	20.90
Environmental	56	47.46	91	51.41	58	42.65	20	21.51	2	6.45	227	40.90
Housing	5	4.24	8	4.52	2	1.47	0	0.00	0	0.00	15	2.70
Family illness/death	41	34.75	58	32.77	31	22.79	31	33.33	7	22.58	168	30.27
Family adversity	17	14.41	24	13.56	14	10.29	12	12.90	5	16.13	72	12.97

Table 10.3 Adversities experienced by scheduled tribe households

Shocks/adversities	1st (poorest)		2nd		3rd		4th		5th (least poor)		Total	
	No.	%	No.	%	No.	%	No.	%	No.	%	No.	%
Crime	9	5.36	3	4.29	6	11.32	1	2.56	1	5.26	20	5.73
Government regulation	0	0.00	1	1.43	1	1.89	1	2.56	1	5.26	4	1.15
Economic	40	23.81	18	25.71	12	22.64	9	23.08	2	10.53	81	23.21
Environmental	75	44.64	35	50.00	20	37.74	13	33.33	3	15.79	146	41.83
Housing	1	0.60	1	1.43	0	0.00	1	2.56	0	0.00	3	0.86
Family illness/death	45	26.79	24	34.29	18	33.96	11	28.21	4	21.05	102	29.23
Family adversity	47	27.98	12	17.14	15	28.30	9	23.08	5	26.32	88	25.21

of this as having a bearing on their lives (France 2000: 325). This question is the focus of the next section.

Children's perspectives

Our exploration of children's perceptions of risk draws on qualitative data from the tribal village of Patna and the Muslim community of Polur, respondent households in the former community being largely concentrated among the poorest in our sample and in the latter, the richest. We have shown that wealth is closely associated with religion, caste and ethnicity in Andhra Pradesh and that these structures are central to the risk biographies of Young Lives households. Nevertheless, so far we have found that even though the children in Patna and Polur are conscious of social structures, issues of religion, caste, ethnicity, and even gender, are not much talked about and only came to the fore through purposeful questioning. When asked directly, the children explained that poorer castes and tribes experienced material lack, stigmatization and other adversities, citing extreme hunger, family debt, heat exposure, domestic violence and ridicule by others – especially other children – as examples (see Chapter 13 by Gina Crivello et al.). But less directed conversations seldom revealed a systematic link between broader structural factors and daily experience. From this evidence, we would like to suggest that in these communities the dynamics of political economy appear to be habituated within everyday embodied practice and thereby taken for granted, or naturalized (Bourdieu 1977: 168, 2001).

Overall, illness, injury and death were prominent in children's risk discourses in both Polur and Patna. Children indicated that frequent or chronic ailments such as headaches, fever, malaria and jaundice were common, often associating this with poor environmental quality. In Patna, inadequate hygiene at school hostels[5] was cited as contributory to bad health and some young people returned home or changed hostel as a result. Wider environmental problems like deficient community sanitation, prevalence of mosquitoes and heavy rains were also cited. Poor environment aside, boys and girls in this sub-sample did not otherwise pay much attention to the household adversities, which caregivers had highlighted as most grave in terms of children's well-being.

Social risks

We have seen that in Andhra Pradesh environmental phenomena such as drought and flooding can have devastating effects, as do illness and death. Yet in both Polur and Patna, social factors also came across as a fundamental feature of children's sense of well-being, with gender an important referent in these cases, especially following puberty. Childhood social risk is expressed in many ways, including through young people's ideas about and use of public spaces. In this sense, physical space is as much a social experience as a natural phenomenon and in this context has become an arena for negotiating gendered identities, roles and risk (see also Schildkrout 2002; van Blerk 2005).

In Polur, girls' movement outside the home is heavily restricted, particularly after puberty. The social standing of households is greatly dependent on the modesty of young, unmarried, female members, whose association with unrelated males can pose a significant threat to the family's reputation. Accordingly, girls in Polur ranked befriending and riding bicycles with boys and being on the streets as the main indicators of 'ill-being' for young females of their age. Similarly, boys favoured restricting girls' mobility as a way of preventing them from being exposed to negative peer influences, picking up 'bad habits', losing respect for their parents or seeking a 'love' marriage (rather than an arranged one). Boys also highlighted the disadvantages for girls of such limitations, including how this forces girls to depend on others and provides little opportunity for them to become practised in decision-making. However, despite restrictions on girls' use of public space in Polur, established norms are being challenged by schooling. Education is now such a compelling force in children's life aspirations that attendance by girls has become commonplace, necessitating their use of public spaces. Multiple practices are employed in protecting a girl's reputation in these circumstances, including use of the *burka* (an all-enveloping cloak) to hide the face, and walking to school in groups.

Risks to young males also have spatial implications. Boys perceived regular attendance at school and the *madrasa* (place of religious learning) as central to their well-being, whereas ill-being was associated with 'never being at home', 'always roaming the streets' or 'loitering at the railway station'. Thus, it is not so much that the street is a 'masculine' space, as that boys on the street invoke a specific kind of masculinity, in which they 'roam around here and there. They play games outside – video games. Boys outside smoke cigarettes, eat *gutka* [a mild stimulant].' Such boys are characterized as 'junglee' (uncultured) and stand in stark contrast to school pupils.

Girls from the Jathapa sub-tribe in Patna appear to experience fewer social risks than do girls in Polur and are allowed greater mobility outside the home. Nevertheless they are more constrained than boys, especially following 'maturity' (puberty), when they cease to be as free to go out unaccompanied and may be withdrawn from school. However, as in Polur, school education has brought about certain anomalies between norms and practice. Children of both sexes and from an early age commonly move into hostels outside the village to access schools. Many of the children living in hostels described an assortment of early challenges, from homesickness and loneliness to poor nutrition. But there were also perceived to be certain benefits, and some families saw the relatively regulated environment of the hostels as protection against negative peer influences in the village. Several children highlighted potential developmental gains from managing these difficulties such as increased self-sufficiency and an expanded worldview. In addition, 'migration' for education was understood by a few to offer a developmental opportunity. Thus, 12-year-old Santhi explained that:

> [I]f one remains at home all the time it may not be possible to know anything about the outside world. So I want to go out...We will know about the views of different people...One ought to know about the world outside. So, I want to join a hostel and know much more...I feel I might be able to live.[6]

Hence, deep-rooted ideas about the gendered nature of morality are key to the notion of childhood social risk. Yet, these ideas are not fixed but respond to changes in the institution of childhood and expectations of children. This can lead to complex and conflicting notions about the safety or appropriateness of everyday childhood practices.

Inter-subjectivity

There appears to be a strong inter-subjective dimension to childhood risk in Polur and Patna, in that impacts are very often understood to affect relationships within groups more than individuals. This is evident in the case of girls who, in transgressing norms around modesty, may put whole families in moral and social jeopardy. Boys invest in their sisters' well-being and described a number of ways in which they helped their sisters, by paying their school fees and contributing to their wedding costs, for example. In contrast, girls did not communicate a similar sense of duty towards their brothers. Overall, there is an expectation that children will share, rather than be shielded from, the burden of family difficulties, as, for example, when they seek to protect parents from suffering. Kareena, aged 13, from Polur, attributed her family's deteriorating circumstances to her father's illness. Her mother could no longer afford to provide nutritious food for the family and lamented having to dilute the *dal* stew and repeat the same dishes frequently. Kareena and her sister would try to conceal their poverty from other children by sitting apart during school lunches or covering their lunch box with a book while they ate. She explained that she, her sister and their mother had agreed to try and prevent the sick father from becoming more distressed by keeping their plight from him.

Inter-subjectivity is also evident in the collective effort involved in dealing with household adversity, with children playing an active part. For example, teenage girls reported taking measures to protect themselves and their families from contagious diseases, for example, by separating the sick from the healthy. Family indebtedness was a major concern associated with deterioration in household economic circumstances and was seen to lead older children to assume greater domestic responsibilities. In Polur, 13-year-old Rahmatulla described how, when his father became paralysed after a stroke, he had to undertake a lot more tasks in the home, running errands and doing embroidery, the latter for income. By the same token, children said that the family had 'worked hard' as the main reason for any improvements in household circumstances.

Fulfilment of family obligations is perceived as central to young people's developing morality; again, these ideas are gendered. Boys articulate a stronger commitment to supporting their parents (mothers in particular) in old age than do girls. Thus, Rajesh returned to Patna and resumed working his family's fields after suffering prolonged ill health in a hostel, explaining that: 'They give me something for doing this and that [a tip]... I will still go even if they don't pay me... It is because I am doing it for my own household.' At the age of 12, Rajesh said he wanted to become a doctor, an aspiration he reiterated at the age of 13. But because of household difficulties, he had become less ambitious by the age of 15 and was considering enrolling on a computer course to obtain employment more quickly. He reasoned:

> Well... my parents are taking care of me now and I depend on them and I want to take care of them when I grow up.... Higher education may not be easily accessible to me and I don't want to be a burden on my parents.

Girls do not articulate the same sense of obligation, possibly because brides move to live with their in-laws and transfer their sense of duty to their mothers-in-law at marriage. Thus, Yaswanth said that his sister would 'forget' about her birth family when she married and moved to her in-laws' house.

So, families are heavily reliant on intergenerational and sibling mutuality to protect against both social risk and destitution. These are central organizing principles of inter-subjectivity in the context of adversity, with clear distinctions along gender lines. While boys have very specific obligations towards family, which emphasize their economic contribution, girls have more generalized moral duties.

Well-being and the life course

We have argued that discourses of childhood risk are not fixed but continually changing, as with the introduction of school education. But there is also a life-course dimension. We employ the term 'chrono-risk' to reflect the developmental aspects of risk as they evolve over time as children mature. Chrono-risk encompasses both pressing adversities that have direct impacts on children's well-being and require immediate response, and longer-term threats, which have to be seen within the broader context of the life course. Managing the different elements of risk involves multiple and sometimes competing social goals. For example, Sania, from Polur, revealed that she had been beaten by her mother because she did not wish to learn or carry out domestic chores in the home. Her mother was ambivalent about Sania's time use, for while she wants her daughter to continue with schooling, she is clear that this should not be at the expense of learning the domestic skills required to position her favourably in the marriage market. A role-play exercise performed by a group of girls in Polur highlighted similar issues. Having learnt that she had passed her school exams, the central character, Zeenath, and her parents were keen for her to continue her studies. But when the grandmother was informed of this plan, the following exchange ensued:

> *Grandmother*: No, it's not necessary. Let her be in the home and learn [house]work. If you provide her with more [education] she will be spoiled.
>
> *Father*: No, Mum. Nowadays everyone is particular about the qualifications, not about the [house]work.

The grandmother insisted, 'Otherwise, how could she survive at her in-laws' house?' Zeenath's brother agreed with the grandmother, maintaining, 'There is no need for Zeenath to study further because the boys will tease her on the streets.' But the father retorted, 'You are there to protect her as a brother in case someone does something. Every day you go along with her to school and tell us if anyone misbehaves with her.'

When boys confront risk, this is perceived as developing the self-reliance needed for them to make an effective contribution to their households. Thus, boys in Patna indicated a strong sense of their roles in relation to the family. Ranadeep stated that his 'way of thinking' had improved since he started orienting himself more towards the future and supporting his family; he saw this growing sense of responsibility as a sign of his maturity. For Akshay Khan, who lives in Polur, increased awareness of his responsibilities had motivated him to study harder.

These examples show how immediate and longer-term considerations of protection and well-being may conflict in the context of risk, insofar as pressures on girls to acquire skills for married life may undermine their schooling and employment prospects. Similarly, boys who work to support their families may struggle to attend school, although work may also build crucial competencies and facilitate school access through funding for materials and other school-related purposes. In addition, different generational perspectives can lead to disagreements over what constitutes a risk for children and how it should be managed. Thus, for example, while education is considered an investment in the future of the family, it is but one of many social expectations that young people must negotiate, and different generations may have different views about what matters most for individual children and/or their families.

Forces for change

Clearly, localized ideas about and strategies for responding to risk are key to children's well-being in Andhra Pradesh, as is articulated by the children in our sample. However, our quantitative data show that in this state, risk is not simply an expression of localized values and practices but also has a strong material dimension associated with deep-rooted political and social inequalities. These inequalities may have become naturalized in children's lives, but are hotly contested in some parts of the state. So, even while the localized narratives and practices of children focus on everyday matters and coping strategies, Scheduled Caste activists have been pivotal in the politicization of issues of social injustice and the pressure for reform in Andhra Pradesh (Gupta 2005). Although they have mostly sought to challenge their lowly status within the traditional caste hierarchy rather than reject the caste system outright (Gupta 2005), these groups have spearheaded a proliferation of movements articulating diverse demands for an end to caste/class-based oppression. Together with local agrarian campaigners, they have sought land redistribution, wage increases for agricultural and other workers, the discontinuation of forced labour (Srinivasulu 2002) and 'reservations within reservations' (UNDP 2007: 19) for groups designated by government as disadvantaged.

State government has responded to this discontent by introducing a number of poverty reduction schemes and has been one of the main advocates of the Indian reform process, making explicit its intention to embed economic restructuring within a larger development and governance project (Mooij 2005; Srinivasulu 2002; UNDP 2007). Andhra Pradesh was also the first state to negotiate an independent loan from the World Bank for economic restructuring that involved financing social sector expenditure and economic reform, including cuts in subsidies, reduction of employment in the civil service, improvement of expenditure management, strengthening revenue mobilization and public enterprise reform (Mooij 2005).

Yet moves to bring about political and economic change have little benefited Scheduled Castes and Scheduled Tribes. Overall, land reforms have privileged peasant farmers from the landed *Shudra* castes far more than poorer groups, and old feudal practices such as *vetti*, the collection of fines and debt bondage remain widespread in many areas (Gundimeda 2009; Gupta 2005; Srinivasulu 2002). The impact of popular protest has been constrained by the sheer size and complexity of the social base, with multiple demarcations along lines of ethnicity, religion, caste, class and gender leading to factionalism and political polarization (Banerjee and Somanathan 2001). In addition, complex relations between protest groups and political parties and co-option by the state government has undermined the effect of collective action in some cases (Banerjee and Somanathan 2001; Srinivasulu 2002; UNDP 2007). Continuing inequalities, susceptibility to risk of minority groups and polarization of political views combined with intermittent repression by the state government have been associated with an escalation of unrest and outbreaks of violence in some cases (Mishra 2008). In the tribal regions of Telangana, confrontations between the Naxalite Maoist insurgent group and government forces have been increasing in recent years, such that armed violence (and associated decline in the economy and services) has become a risk for children in these areas. At the same time, there has been unrest among disaffected low-caste Muslims in some places. Hence, in the absence of effective reform, the politicization of inequality, poverty and risk can be seen as an emergent source of risk for children in certain parts of Andhra Pradesh. Some Young Lives communities fall within the area under Naxalite influence and some of the children in our sample, including those in Polur, come from the Muslim minority population. That said, these issues are highly sensitive and difficult to research, and we do not have data on the impact of political unrest on children at this stage.

Conclusion

Most studies of childhood risk are based solely on quantitative data and take little or no account of children's perceptions. But we have argued that subjective understandings are key to well-being in contexts of adversity and have used qualitative data to illustrate the kinds of concerns raised. At the same time, research into responses to risk generally emphasizes individual vulnerability, resilience and coping, attending also to protective environmental processes. While we agree that these definitely are compelling factors in children's susceptibility to risk, we have suggested that risk is not simply a feature of individual interactions with the immediate environment, but an expression also of potent forces which play out at the collective level, where it is unequally distributed across space and between different groups of children depending on their social and economic power. Hence, we stress the centrality of structural features in risk exposure, the dynamics of political economy being particularly salient in circumstances of childhood poverty, with lasting effects into adulthood. In Andhra Pradesh structural inequalities bearing down on specific socio-religious and ethnic groups are associated with a disproportionate burden of risk. While these inequalities have seemingly become naturalized within children's everyday worlds, they are the subject of vociferous contestation and collective political struggle in some quarters. Mainstream research on childhood risk seldom makes this important connection to wider processes of political engagement.

In making the case for greater attention to risk contexts, we contend that not all 'risks' can be described a priori as 'objective' external threats with predictable outcomes for all children; some are inseparable from children's social and cultural worlds and the shared meanings generated within these. Hence, children's views on risk and adversity are fundamental to outcomes, requiring research to give serious consideration to subjective understandings of populations living with adversity. The examples we have offered suggest the inter-subjective nature of risk perception and response. There is a clear social and moral dimension to childhood risk in Andhra Pradesh, gender and age being central organizing principles. The vulnerabilities, capacities and moral ideas children develop in this context are extremely dynamic. Many children experience multiple risks that have both immediate effects as well as implications for life transitions and intergenerational relations. In these circumstances, risk mitigation may become the subject of competing concerns and priorities and consequently, conflicting views on protection (see also Chapter 9 by Theodore Wachs). Appreciation of the multiple dimensions of childhood risk in particular contexts implies careful reflection regarding what might be most appropriate in terms of intervention to support children's well-being, since policy which focuses narrowly on a single issue or group may have unintended detrimental effects on children's relationships or development, or other aspects of their lives.

Notes

1. A very different tradition of scholarship around risk within sociology and anthropology has had far less influence on studies with children (see Crivello and Boyden 2011).
2. Patna and Polur were selected for their contrasting characteristics (rural/urban location, religious and socioeconomic), which offer different settings for exploring the contextual factors shaping risk exposure and experiences among their youngest residents.
3. The Government of India has documented Scheduled Castes and Scheduled Tribes so as to secure 'reservation', or affirmative action, to counteract socioeconomic disadvantage. Untouchability has been outlawed and copious constitutional and legal measures introduced promoting employment in public administration and access to basic services, facilities, and infrastructure for these groups.
4. A significant portion of Muslims and Buddhists have now been incorporated within the caste system.
5. Areas with a high tribal population are covered by the Integrated Tribal Development Agency, which provides scholarships and boarding hostels for Scheduled Tribe children to attend school, and job training and placements.
6. Interviews extracts transcribed here are from the second round of in-depth interviews conducted in 2007/08 as part of the Young Lives qualitative research.

References

Banerjee, A. and R. Somanathan (2001) 'Caste, Community and Collective Action: The Political Economy of Public Good Provision in India', http://econ-www.mit.edu/files/503 (accessed 4 June 2010).

Barton, W. (2005) 'Methodological Challenges in the Study of Resilience' in M. Ungar (ed.), *Handbook for Working with Children and Youth: Pathways to Resilience across Cultures and Contexts*, Thousand Oaks CA: Sage Publications.

Boyden, J. (2009) 'Risk and Capability in the Context of Adversity: Children's Contributions to Household Livelihoods in Ethiopia', *Children, Youth and Environments* 19.2: 111–37.

Boyden, J., A. Hardgrove and C. Knowles (2011) 'Continuity and Change in Poor Children's Lives: Evidence from Young Lives' in Alberto Minujin (ed.), *Child Poverty: A Global Perspective*, New York: Policy Press.

Bourdieu, P. (1977) *Outline of a Theory of Practice*, trans. Richard Nice, Cambridge: Cambridge University Press.

Bourdieu, P. (2001) *Masculine Domination*, Palo Alto, CA: Stanford University Press

Compas, B., B. Hinden and C. Gerhardt (1995) 'Adolescent Development: Pathways and Processes of Risk and Resilience', *Annual Review of Psychology* 46: 265–93.

Cowan, P., C. Cowan and M. Schulz (1996) 'Thinking About Risk and Resilience in Families' in E. Hetherington and E. Blechman (eds.), *Stress, Coping and Resiliency in Children and Families*, Mahwah, NJ: Lawrence Erlbaum Associates.

Crivello, G. and J. Boyden (2011) *Situating Risk in Young People's Social and Moral Relationships: Young Lives Research in Peru*, Working Paper 66, Oxford: Young Lives.

France, A. (2000) 'Towards a Sociological Understanding of Youth and their Risk-taking', *Journal of Youth Studies* 3.3: 317–31.

Galab, S. and I. Outes-Leon (2011) *Schooling and Work in Times of Drought*, Working Paper 73, Oxford: Young Lives.

Galab, S, P. Reddy and R. Himaz (2008) *Young Lives Round 2 Survey Report. Initial Findings: Andhra Pradesh, India*, Oxford: Young Lives.

Gauvain, M. (2001) *The Social Context of Cognitive Development*, New York: Guildford Press.

Grantham-McGregor, S., Y.B. Cheung, S. Cueto, P. Glewwe, L. Richter, B. Strupp and the International Child Development Steering Group (2007) 'Child Development in Developing Countries 1: Developmental Potential in the First 5 Years for Children in Developing Countries', *The Lancet* 369: 60–70.

Gundimeda, S. (2009) 'Dalits, Praja Rajyam Party and Caste Politics in Andhra Pradesh', 29 December 2009, http://socialjusticeanddemocratization.wordpress.com/2009/12/29/dalits-praja-rajyam-party-and-caste-politics-in-andhra-pradesh/ (accessed 15 May 2010).

Gupta, D. (2005) 'Caste and Politics: Identity over System', *Annual Review of Anthropology* 34: 409–27.

Hart, J. (2008) *Business as Usual? The Global Political Economy of Childhood Poverty*, Technical Note 13, Oxford: Young Lives.

Krutikova, S. (2009) *Determinants of Child Labour: The Case of Andhra Pradesh*, Working Paper 48, Oxford: Young Lives.

Mishra, P. (2008) 'Violence runs through this "stable" India, built on poverty and injustice', *The Guardian*, 7 August.

Mooij, J. (2005) *Reforms and Children: Issues and Hypotheses Regarding the Impacts of Reform Policies on the Welfare of Children in India, with Special Emphasis on Andhra Pradesh*, Working Paper 16, Oxford: Young Lives.

Mukherji, A. (2008) *Trends in Andhra Pradesh with a Focus on Poverty*, Technical Note 7, Oxford: Young Lives.

Murray, H. (2008) 'Andhra Pradesh/India: Political Economy Context and Current Policy Debates', internal document, Oxford: Young Lives.

Nair, A. (2009) *Disadvantaged at Birth? The Impact of Caste on the Cognitive Development of Young Children in Andhra Pradesh, India*, Young Lives Student Paper, Oxford: Young Lives.

Rogoff, B. (2003) *The Cultural Nature of Human Development*, Oxford: Oxford University Press.

Rolf, J., A. Masten, D. Cicchetti, K. Nüchterlein and S. Weintraub (eds) (1990) *Risk and Protective Factors in the Development of Psychopathology*, Cambridge: Cambridge University Press.

Rutter, M. (2001) 'Psychosocial Adversity: Risk, Resilience and Recovery' in J. Richman and M. Fraser (eds) *The Context of Youth Violence: Resilience, Risk and Protection*, Westport CT: Praeger.

Rutter, M. (2010) Plenary presentation given at 'Pathways to Resilience II: The Social Ecology of Resilience', Halifax, Canada, 9 June 2010.

Schaffer, H.R. (2006) *Key Concepts in Developmental Psychology*, London: Sage Publications.

Schildkrout, E. (2002) 'Age and Gender in Hausa Society: Socioeconomic Roles of Children in Urban Kano', *Childhood* 9.3: 344–68.

Schoon, I. (2006) *Risk and Resilience*, Cambridge: Cambridge University Press

Srinivasulu, K. (2002) *Caste, Class and Social Articulation in Andhra Pradesh: Mapping Different Regional Trajectories*, Working Paper 179, London: Overseas Development Institute.

Tulloch, J. and D. Lupton (2003) *Risk and Everyday Life*, London: Sage Publications.

UNDP (2007) *Human Development Report 2007: Andhra Pradesh*, http://hdr.undp. org/en/reports/nationalreports/asiathepacific/india/name,18746,en.html (accessed 12 August 2010).

van Blerk, L. (2005) 'Negotiating Spatial Identities: Mobile Perspectives on Street Life in Uganda', *Children's Geographies* 3.1: 5–21.

Walker, S., T. Wachs, J. Meeks Gardner, B. Lozoff, G. Wasserman, E. Pollitt, J. Carter and the International Child Development Steering Group (2007) 'Child Development: Risk Factors for Adverse Outcomes in Developing Countries', *The Lancet* 369.9556: 145–57.

11
On Being Despised: Growing up a Congolese Refugee in Dar es Salaam

Gillian Mann

Introduction

The vast majority of Congolese refugee children living without papers in Dar es Salaam experience extreme hardship and marginalization. The material conditions in which they live are insufficient to meet their daily needs for adequate food, shelter, and health care. Like their parents, most boys and girls regularly speak of feeling hungry, tired, and worn out. They try at every opportunity to stem their chronic hunger and ill health. They work hard to contribute to the survival of their families through household chores, paid work, or exchanging services for food, soap, favours, or money. However, despite the sometimes overwhelming nature of these problems, children from as young as 9 argue that the worst part of their lives is not their material deprivation. Rather, it is the social exclusion, discrimination, and harassment that they experience on a daily basis. As 'illegals', they not only fear deportation, forcible removal to refugee camps, and imprisonment, but they also see signs everywhere that they are not wanted in Tanzania. Such a hostile environment leads most children to feel not only marginalized, but reduced to little else than 'animals' or 'garbage', as Munga,[1] aged 16, put it.

This chapter explores how Congolese boys and girls learn to have dignity and self-respect in an environment in which they are treated as dangerous and morally corrupt. How do they come to understand, and appreciate, their place in a world where they are not only unwanted, but where they feel despised? What strategies do they use to maintain their sense of self and to remain strong in the face of widespread ignorance, prejudice, and marginalization? This chapter examines how boys and girls try to reconcile this tension in their everyday lives and in the futures that they expect, imagine, and hope for. It focuses on the relationships they nurture and the strategies they use to negotiate this challenging task.

These questions are important for both theoretical and practical reasons. In the African context, very little is known about the social and emotional experience of poverty and extreme marginalization from boys' and girls' points of view. Investigations of such questions can provide important insights not only into how they understand and make sense of their lives, but also into how interventions designed to assist these children and their families can be most helpful.

From Congo to Dar es Salaam

Since the outbreak of the First Congo War in 1996, large numbers of Congolese children and adults have been forced to seek safety and survival in Tanzania. The great majority of these displaced people live in the western part of the country, where Tanzanian government policy requires all refugees to live in camps. Many Congolese refuse to live in refugee camps, which they consider to be 'cages' or 'prisons' since residents are forbidden to leave without permission and are rendered dependent on agencies for their basic needs such as food, water, clothing, and housing. Inadequate food rations,[2] concerns about security, and the desire for greater personal freedom motivate many adults and children to leave the camps and others to avoid them altogether. In so doing, they forfeit their right to official refugee status, even if they have fled the very same circumstances as those official refugees who live in camps. While this distinction between 'legal' and 'illegal' refugees is important to policymakers in the region, it is not a significant marker of difference for Congolese themselves. Whether an individual lives inside or outside a camp affects the resources one receives but bears no relationship to one's experience of insecurity, violence, and conflict in Democratic Republic of Congo (DRC). Throughout this chapter, I use the term 'refugee' to apply not only to those who have been legally recognized as refugees by the Government of Tanzania and United Nations High Commissioner for Refugees (UNHCR), but also to those who have not registered as such for personal, practical, or social reasons.

Many of those Congolese who decline to live in camps choose instead to live *sans papiers* in Dar es Salaam. These individuals are usually drawn to the city by the imagined promise of improved opportunities for security, employment, education, and personal freedom. Some come directly from DRC, without passing through official registration procedures; others leave the camps on foot at night or on day passes and never return. A very small number come to Dar with permission to remain for a specified period, but choose to stay after their permit has expired and to live clandestinely. The majority of refugees appear to be young men between the ages of 20 and 30. However, there are also women who migrate to the city on their own, as well as large numbers of single- and two-parent families who come with biological, related, and unrelated children. Some boys and girls also journey to Dar es Salaam without adults, sometimes in the company of siblings or peers, and at other times entirely on their own. Over the course of approximately 27 months' fieldwork in Dar es Salaam (March 2001; September 2001–September 2002; February 2006; December 2006–December 2007), I came into contact with more than 250 Congolese of all ages. The bulk of my time, however, was spent with children and young people between the ages of 7 and 18. Research was conducted in Kiswahili and French.

Given that most Congolese live without permission for legal residence, it is impossible to know how many actually live in Dar es Salaam because they hide their identity. The perceived need to do so means that people live dispersed across the city: I encountered refugees in 36 different urban neighbourhoods. Most Congolese conceal their nationality, preferring instead to live as 'Tanzanians'. Some claim to come from Kigoma, the region in western Tanzania that borders Lake Tanganyika. The strong similarities between the Kiswahili spoken in Kigoma and across the lake in DRC make this claim believable to some. Others say they grew up in any number of other places, such as Mbeya, near the Tanzanian border with Zambia, or Mwanza, on Lake Victoria. For example, Marie-Claire, 17, who came to Dar in 2004 from Goma, has memorized the details of a village near Mbeya, where she has never been. These were provided to her by a young, unknowing female neighbour, whom Marie-Claire asked to describe everything she could remember about her home area, including how many houses there were, how the village was laid out, and how many students went to the local primary school. She also learned some basic vocabulary in the local language.

These 'strategies of invisibility' (see Malkki 1995) are employed by adults and children in a deliberate effort to live as unobtrusively as possible. One such strategy, used by many Congolese, but especially common among older refugee children, is to change their first names. They do this at school,[3] in the neighbourhoods around their homes, and in their interactions with Tanzanian officials, staff members of NGOs, hospital workers, and complete strangers. Some boys and girls have several different names, which they use in different contexts, so that

Marie-Claire, for instance, is called Neema at school, Ruth by the batik sellers whose items she sometimes sells on commission, and Anna in the neighbourhood where she lives. In the past, she has also been called Julia. Her 14-year-old brother, Peter, was called Parfait until the family arrived in Dar, at which point he realized that his name sounded '*trop Congolais*'. Similarly, other individuals with French names have changed them to common Kiswahili or English: Anne-Marie, 20, became Adila; Dieudonné, 19, was renamed James; Grâce, 14, was anglicized to Grace; Jean, 18, to John; and Patrice, 15, became Hamisi. This last example shows also how some Christian Congolese boys and girls and men and women claim Muslim identities through name changes or new styles of dress (such as wearing a long chemise with a *kofia* or, for females, by covering their heads with a *hijab*). While there are some Muslim Congolese refugees in Dar, this is a cultural and religious identity which is usually associated with Tanzanians, in particular the Swahili people of the coast, and is therefore a good disguise.

Being a refugee in Dar es Salaam

Congolese refugees of all ages describe their life in urban Tanzania as one of social exclusion, discrimination, and harassment. These feelings are common for young children, adolescents, and adults in a variety of circumstances. Despite their near-constant efforts to conceal their identity, it is not unusual for the people I have known to walk down the street and have a Tanzanian adult or child call out to them, '*Mkimbizi! Mkimbizi!*'[4] This Kiswahili term for 'refugee' is widely considered to be derogatory, because the public conception of a refugee is that of an idle beggar who lives off the generosity of others. In fact, the term has entered the popular Kiswahili lexicon and is used to connote additional characteristics, especially those of an unreliable, lazy, and untrustworthy person. One steamy April afternoon in 2007, I sat quietly with Marie-Claire, 17, in a roadside bar, drinking Coke and enjoying her company after a long walk through the neighbourhood. Our attention was drawn to a heated telephone conversation between a man in his mid-twenties and someone on the other end of his mobile. The man was angry because the caller had not fulfilled his promise of dropping off a car for the man to use. In a frustrated mixture of Kiswahili and Kichagga, he told the caller he was a 'useless *mkimbizi*'. This was my first experience of hearing a Tanzanian use the term to insult another Tanzanian, and I was surprised. Marie-Claire was not. She and I wordlessly looked at each other. '*Tu vois?*' ('you see?') she asked, quietly.

For Marie-Claire, the overhead comment was not merely an impolite or offensive slip of the tongue; it was typical. From her perspective, it was representative of a general lack of respect and appreciation for the experiences of Congolese and others who had lived through brutal wars and were forced to flee to Tanzania because they were unable to live in their countries of origin. In the opinion of Farida, a 10-year-old girl, 'Even dogs are treated better than *wakimbizi*.' Many children endure insults and mockery on the bus, in the school playground, and in their neighbourhood. Young boys and girls describe being reduced to tears on a regular basis and say their lives are 'miserable' because they can 'never feel at ease'. Older children are equally hurt by such behaviour; as Eva, 14, commented, 'We are just like garbage, thrown away and forgotten.' 'We are considered wild animals,' Munga, 16, told me, reminding me of a comment made by 14-year-old Charles: 'Here, a refugee is not a person.'

These sentiments are reinforced by the larger social and political environment in which refugees have been living for the past years in Dar es Salaam. Since the mid to late 1990s, successive Tanzanian governments – not unlike governments in Europe – have increasingly succumbed to populist discontent about refugees. Repatriation is openly promoted in speeches, interviews with the media, and other public forums (US Department of State 2009). In 2007, it was common for Members of Parliament and others publicly to blame high crime and unemployment rates on refugees and 'illegals', whom they accused of being untrustworthy, morally corrupt, and above all abusive of Tanzanian generosity. Arrests, imprisonment, deportation, and forced removal to the refugee camps are not uncommon, although they are unpredictable and sporadic. While many Tanzanians do not dislike foreigners, xenophobia is an everyday reality for the Congolese whom I knew in Dar es Salaam. On a daily basis, they experienced discrimination, harassment, social exclusion, and at times physical violence. This was as true for children as it was for adults. I knew a 4-year-old girl who was beaten by her adult neighbour when the child's parents were out of the house. The neighbour had asked her where her '*wakimbizi*' parents were. When the girl failed to respond, the woman delivered several smacks and blows to the child. I know another woman who was beaten three times by her male neighbour. Other neighbours watched, but did not intervene or offer support afterwards. Such occurrences were not unusual among people I knew.

Certainly Congolese refugees and those from other countries living in Dar es Salaam have experienced similar abuses over the last ten years or so. However, urban Tanzanians now appear more open in their dislike of refugees and what they see to be not only their ingratitude but also their good fortune in having found a place where everything is given to them for free. In fact, as *'sans-papiers'*, nothing is given to Congolese for free, but the common perception is that refugees are given free food, housing, shelter, education, and health care. Life in Tanzania is thought by Tanzanians to be a good and easy life for refugees, and many people, especially those who are themselves very poor, feel that refugees are treated better than they are. The truth is that extreme poverty is the norm for the Congolese I knew in Dar, as it is for many Tanzanians. The difference is that Congolese who live outside of refugee camps live illegally and in so doing have to hide their identity and forfeit any rights to social services like primary education and health care. Tanzanians at least have the right to work and to access some very basic social services, inadequate as these may be.

Added to this increasingly blatant xenophobia is the fact that the United Nations and the governments of DRC and Tanzania are now actively engaged in efforts to repatriate Congolese. Since 'free' elections were held in late 2006 in DRC, the official position has been that peace has been established in eastern Congo and it is time for everyone to go 'home'. This stance has been maintained even in the face of direct evidence to the contrary. For instance, the Tanzanian government advocated repatriation throughout the period of incursions of the rebel leader Laurent Nkunda, including in September 2007 when more than 170,000 people were displaced in North Kivu.[5] More recently, in the face of renewed conflict and the displacement of at least 250,000 people near the city of Goma in October and November 2008,[6] the UNHCR and the Government of Tanzania continued to promote voluntary repatriation to areas of South Kivu, which they argued were safe and secure for returnees. Refugees from this area, however, are concerned that the conflict will spread south. More generally, among the Congolese I knew in Dar and those with whom I am still in contact, no one is yet willing to return to DRC, for a variety of reasons, summed up in the view so clearly articulated by 19-year-old Adam: 'There will always be clouds on the horizon.' People fear the murderous violence of the small, nascent militias at the local level, the brutal killing and exploitation of the government forces, and the potentially devastating consequences of the on-again-off-again tensions with Rwanda and Uganda. So great are these concerns that some Congolese have recently fled the camps in the western part of Tanzania for fear of being forcibly repatriated.[7]

Being despised

The Congolese boys and girls who participated in this research know about material deprivation and insecurity. Many of those under the age of 15 have experienced or remember little else. Through conversations, role plays, drawing, painting, singing, story-telling, and other activities, I learned from them about the challenges that they faced in their home communities in DRC, as internally displaced people (IDPs) elsewhere in the country, and as refugees in Tanzania. Before coming to Dar es Salaam, many had experienced extreme hunger and other hardships. Nonetheless, when the children I knew spoke of their greatest misery or 'suffering', they would almost invariably talk about their lives in Dar es Salaam. Most said that life was better in DRC, even in the midst of war, than it was in Dar. Claude, 19, for example, told me that he would rather return to his home village near Bukavu, where he had been forced to watch the killings of his parents and younger brother, than be treated like a 'savage' in Tanzania. Similarly, Adam, 18, said that while life in Congo, where four of his siblings have died in the last five years, was difficult, he would nonetheless prefer to live there than to live like a 'caged dog' in Dar es Salaam. 'At least there we are still considered people,' he told me. Such dramatic statements raise important questions about the fundamental human need for respect and understanding. To look back at life in a war zone – a life so difficult that it had to be fled – and think that it was better than life outside may in some cases have been a rhetorical exercise. However, the intolerable character of their present circumstances in Dar has led many older boys to migrate elsewhere in the region, including South Africa, Kenya, Mozambique, and the Comoros. Some, like Adam, said the only reason he had not returned home was because his parents, who had remained in their war-ravaged village, had sent word to him that he was forbidden to do so.

Certainly, children under the ages of about 9 or 10 referred frequently to their hungry bellies, their desire to drink milk, and their lack of money to buy clothes, shoes, or notebooks. Boys and girls older than this also mentioned these and other concerns. But when these older children said, *'tunaishi kwa mateso'* ('we are suffering' or 'we are living with suffering'), they were usually referring to their personal and collective experiences of marginalization and discrimination and the concomitant struggle to maintain their dignity. A growing body of research demonstrates the threats posed by widespread stigma and social exclusion to the development and maintenance of children's self-esteem (Fisher et al. 2000; Foster and Germann 2002; Foster and Williamson

2000; Meursing 1997; Verkuyten 1998). In the context of Africa, most of this research has centred around children affected by HIV/AIDS, in particular, orphans. To my knowledge, few studies have explored these issues as they pertain to refugee children. Yet the boys and girls I knew struggled on a daily basis to rise above their 'suffering', to develop and maintain their self-worth in the harsh social and economic environment in which they were living.

I came to learn about children's experiences and perspectives in a number of different ways. From mothers and fathers, I learned of some of the difficult experiences boys and girls had on a daily basis. Mireille told me through tears one day of the time Amani, 10, came home from school without his shoes on. 'Where are your shoes?' she asked him angrily, certain that he had somehow lost them. He told her that another boy had taken them from him on the way home from school. When she demanded to know why he had not reclaimed them, he explained that the boy was taller and stronger than he was. Mireille sent her eldest son, Deo, 19, to find the boy, which he did. The boy told Deo that if Deo hit him, or took back the shoes, then the boy would tell his father, who would report the '*wakimbizi*' family to the police. Deo came home angry and dejected at his inability to defend his brother from someone as small as a 12-year-old boy. 'We are like garbage,' he told his mother and brother, 'but worse, because at least garbage is collected when it is dropped on the ground.'

Experiences such as these differ from those reported by other researchers who have worked with refugee children in camp settings, some of whom have suggested that children make the transition to life as a refugee more easily than do adults (Atkinson 2007; Hinton 2000). For example, Rachel Hinton (2000: 200) argues that Bhutanese refugee boys and girls living in a camp in Nepal tended to see their hardship as one related to material deprivation, as opposed to feeling a sense of loss or abandonment, as adults tended to do. She suggests that children's 'lifeworlds' (using the term of Nieuwenhuys 1994) changed little in this new context, in part because of their close proximity to neighbours and friends from Bhutan, with whom they were able to play and go to school. Adults, on the other hand, saw the experience of becoming a refugee as one of marginalization, characterized in part by social and psychological strain. Clearly the situation of Congolese children and adolescents in Dar es Salaam is very different from the one described by Hinton. Many of these boys and girls have extremely restricted lives and limited interaction with neighbours, let alone other Congolese, who usually live far enough away that household chores, the constant need to 'find money', and transport costs preclude most children and families from visiting one another except on the rarest of occasions. Outside the immediate household, boys and girls in these circumstances have few people to turn to for assistance and support. The importance of friendship and social relations to children in this context was underscored by several of the children I knew in Dar es Salaam, who said that they would rather have friends than food. This view was evidenced in children's actions as well: 12-year-old Alice, for example, knew that by going to see her old friend on the other side of town she would miss her once-daily meal at home. She nonetheless jumped at every opportunity to go.

'You are not living unless you are fighting'

Refugee life for Congolese boys and girls in Dar es Salaam is a struggle. On one level, it is a struggle to make ends meet, to make it through another day, and, ultimately, to survive. On another level, one that is arguably as important or more important to children themselves, it is a struggle to assert one's humanity, to remain a person, and not to become the lesser being that they believe the host society sees them to be. Michel, 16, articulated this clearly when I met him in March 2007 at a rundown roadside bar on the far edge of his neighbourhood. That morning he had been released from prison, where he had spent the last week. He had been arrested for robbery, a charge he denied. He explained that he had organized the sale of a laptop computer for a Tanzanian businessman. The arrangement was that he would earn US$100 from the US$600 price tag. After Michel brought the buyer to the seller and the sale had taken place, the seller refused to give Michel his $100. Michel complained, at first quietly and respectfully, then more vociferously and unhappily. Eventually the seller, in a fit of anger, called a friend, a police officer, to report that his laptop had been stolen and that he had the *'mkimbizi'* thief on site. Michel, furious yet frightened, fled the building. The men outside stopped and detained him by force until the police arrived. He was then arrested and imprisoned. His mobile phone was confiscated and he was told that he would be deported. As the days passed, he grew less angry and increasingly despondent, until his hoped-for release one week later, by a senior officer with whom he made a deal: that evening the officer would meet Michel near the police station, where Michel would give him 50,000 Tanzanian shillings (approx US$40). He was now on his way home, where he intended to bathe, inform his roommate what had happened, and then to go out to request money from acquaintances and a friend of his late father's. When I asked him how he was holding up, he said, 'I am alive and I am fighting. You are not living unless you are fighting.'

For the refugee boys and girls who participated in this research, this concept of 'fighting' is one they know well. For them, fighting poverty is about more than trying to meet one's material needs. It is about fighting to maintain one's dignity. Doing so may come at a material cost in that there are certain jobs that children, particularly those over the age of 13 or 14, will not do because performing these tasks makes them feel bad about themselves. Adili, 18, and Juliana, 16, for example, said that they would never beg for money, even if they knew that doing so might give them enough to eat an additional meal or to pay for transport rather than walk in the burning midday sun. Peter, 14, said that certain forms of domestic work were out of the question, especially if performed for unrelated families: 'I am not a slave,' he asserted. In these and other instances, children did not want to do things that challenged their own sense of self-worth and self-respect. They did not want to prove their hosts right. They did not want to give in and become the 'animals' or 'garbage' that those who dislike refugees assumed them to be. They preferred to safeguard their sense of self and identity first and foremost.

These efforts to maintain their morals and notions of what is 'good' and 'correct' behaviour are what keeps many Congolese boys and girls – and their parents – feeling strong, even when such choices come at great personal cost. Certainly, there are occasions when these ideals must be suspended, for example, when an individual or family's circumstances are so desperate that they must acquire money in any way possible, such as through transactional sex with older men, a last resort for the adolescent girls I knew. Such actions are considered temporary lapses and are rationalized with the understanding that an individual had no other choice (*'je n'ai pas eu de choix'*). The fight to maintain one's dignity is also a fight to keep feelings of shame and degradation at bay.

Another strategy is to assert their cultural superiority over that of their hosts in Dar es Salaam. Countless hours are spent cataloguing the various signs of Tanzanian inferiority. Among those people I knew, everything was under attack – from the corrupt and unsophisticated education system, through tribalism and women's lack of style, to a general ignorance of the world around them – and Tanzanians were widely agreed to be 'uncivilized' (*'Ils ne sont pas civilisés'*). Boys and girls as young as 7 asserted their teacher's lack of expertise and the nosy and untrustworthy character of Tanzanians. Older girls said that Tanzanian men did not respect their wives, and older boys said Tanzanian girls only appreciated men with money. Everyone balked at what they argued to be Tanzanians' lack of pride in their appearance. For every Congolese I knew in Dar, the clothes one wore and how one carried oneself were real points of pride, so much so that people who worked for refugee-serving agencies would sometimes remark, 'But you don't *look* like a refugee.' Such comments infuriated those I knew because of the implication that to be a refugee was to be a person without self-worth and self-esteem.

Children tried to maintain their sense of self and to elevate themselves from their 'suffering' not only through their behaviour and interactions in their social worlds, but also through the use of their imagination. Some boys and girls would sometimes refer to dreams they had for their future, and plans they had for themselves. Grégoire, 12, spoke to me, and others, about his uncle in South Africa, and the man's intention to come to Dar to fetch him and take him back to Johannesburg. Yet Grégoire had no such uncle and his mother did not know to whom he was referring when he made these comments. Fabrice, 13, practised football for hours every day, in preparation for his audition with the scout whom he heard would soon be coming from Kinshasa. Fabrice's parents and siblings shrugged off these claims, saying that there was no way such a person would come all the way to Dar. In both these cases, while parents tried to set their children straight, they did not labour their points. They recognized, as did those children mature enough to understand, that dreams such as these were what kept hope alive for many boys and girls by giving them the feeling that their suffering was not going to be everlasting. Several authors have argued that imagination is a critical resource for children because it enables them to remove themselves from the often stressful reality of everyday life (Bruner et al. 1976; Dunn 1993, 2004; Singer and Singer 1990; Sutton-Smith 1972). By imagining alternative lives, or ways out of their current lives, the children I knew were able to create a space for themselves in which they could become the people that they wanted to be. In a context where one determines one's worth in part through future possibilities – both real and imagined – dreams and future hopes can serve as important supports for children who are otherwise experiencing great hardship and marginalization.

Finally, boys and girls fought to maintain their dignity by trying to focus on the needs of others who were worse off than they were. Many were attentive to the experiences and emotions of those around them and tried to assist them whenever possible. For instance, Chantal, 6, a great mimic, often performed for her mother when she saw that she was upset or overwhelmed. Other young children tried to make their parents laugh, in the hope that they would smile and forget their troubles. Some school-going boys and girls worked hard to get good grades to impress and please their troubled parents. Older girls, like 14-year-old Eva, would cook the family's meal according to their overburdened fathers' specific tastes, and would allocate their portion to him. These same girls would also clean the house, sweep the yard, and do all the chores they could in order to minimize their mothers' stress. Boys like Peter, 14, drew skilful, smiling portraits of family members whose photographs had been lost, so that his mother could abate her loneliness by looking at the faces of loved ones on her walls. Despite her lack of credit on her mobile phone, Lucie, 14, would 'beep'[8] a sad or lonely friend across town to let her know she was thinking of her. These acts of kindness were attempts to help those in need, but they also served to affirm the humanity and substance of those who reached out to others, particularly to those in similar circumstances. They helped individuals to feel that, despite their 'suffering', they were still able to empathize with others, an important quality of a 'good' person in this context.

These strategies for maintaining one's dignity are the weapons Congolese children use to fight against the effects of their marginalization and exclusion. While these weapons are more or less successful at different times and in different circumstances, they serve an essential function in their well-being and coping. Parents' strategies, however, are not always respected or appreciated by children. This is especially the case when children feel that parents have forfeited their dignity in order to access resources needed, for instance by begging or by not responding to mockery or harassment on the street ('Have they no pride?' Deo, 19, asked me). Boys and girls often spoke to me of the shame and humiliation they felt when they saw their parents doing 'demeaning' things, like digging through garbage or behaving in a sycophantic manner to unkind people. At times, however, parents may be willing to swallow their pride because they fear the potential ramifications of not doing so – being unable to provide the basic necessities for their families – make it impossible to behave otherwise. On an intellectual level, most of the children I knew understood their parents' actions to be necessary under the circumstances. But many felt angry and resentful when it seemed their parents had actually become the 'useless *wakimbizi*' that ignorant Tanzanians already thought them to be. Alain, 17, for instance, told me that the father he used to know would be ashamed to know the man that he had now become. In such circumstances, children were highly judgemental of their parents' conduct, suggesting, as Munga, 16, did, that it would be better to go hungry or to speak out and risk creating a public scene than to allow oneself to be subjected to degrading treatment. As a result of these intergenerational differences, the fight for dignity became a central component in an 'economy of meaning' at the household level, in which different meanings were produced by different members of the family, which then competed for special status (Wenger 1998). Claiming ownership over meaning is thus a locus of struggle between Congolese parents and children in many households in Dar es Salaam. It calls into question the degree to which the experience of poverty can be said to be shared by those who appear to live in similar circumstances, even households.

Conclusion

When I initially set out to research Congolese refugee children in Dar es Salaam, I was interested in how boys and girls in these circumstances were able to access the resources that they needed. I knew that extreme poverty was the norm for many children, and when lived with alongside the challenging social and economic conditions of displacement, I wondered how they were able to survive. I thought that understanding these issues from the perspectives of children and families would give rise to important insights that could contribute to the development of policies and programmes to meet their needs. Over time, however, I came to realize that my initial research question, pragmatic as it may have been, was missing the point. As I came to know boys and girls of different ages, living in different circumstances, I began to understand that for these children, survival meant more than making it through the day with enough to eat and drink and a place to sleep at night. Their struggle for survival was an existential endeavour as much as it was a practical one.

The discrimination, harassment, and social exclusion with which large numbers of Congolese children live in Dar es Salaam led many I knew to question their own humanity, to ask themselves if they were actually people. They asked themselves these profound questions not, as one might expect, on the basis of the violence or extreme hardships that they had experienced in DRC or in flight. Instead, they were driven to do so because their treatment as unwelcome migrants in a largely hostile environment had fundamentally challenged their sense of self and self-worth. Making it through the day involved much more than 'finding money': it meant finding and holding onto dignity and self-respect.

To say that poverty is more than material deprivation is to state the obvious. But recognizing the extent to which the experience of poverty can challenge children's developing sense of self and personhood is to acknowledge its pervasive impact – a necessary step towards the development of creative and enduring ways to combat it in the first place.

Boys and girls of different ages employ numerous strategies in their efforts to combat poverty. They try at all times to reconcile the humiliations and adversities of their everyday lives with the futures that they imagine and hope for. They try to maintain personal codes of conduct which defy the stereotypes they have been assigned. They develop and nurture relationships with siblings, parents, and friends, and doing so reminds them of their humanity. Ultimately, they try in concrete and imaginative ways to act and think like the individuals they believe themselves to be or wish to become.

Notes

1. All names have been changed to protect individuals' anonymity. Ages remain unchanged.
2. Frequent funding shortages to the World Food Program have resulted in ration cuts of up to one-third of recommended daily intake in refugee camps in western Tanzania (http://www.wfp.org/stories/us-donation-stems-cuts-refugee-rations-worldwide).
3. Despite the fact that their undocumented status meant that enrolling in public school was against the law, many boys and girls (and their parents) went to great lengths to try to secure an education.
4. *Mkimbizi* is the word for refugee (singular); *Wakimbizi* means refugees (plural).
5. http://news.bbc.co.uk/2/hi/africa/3786883.stm – article dated 2 October 2007.
6. http://news.bbc.co.uk/2/hi/africa/7754258.stm – article dated 28 November 2008; http://news.bbc.co.uk/2/hi/africa/7839510.stm – article dated 20 January 2009.
7. To date, there has been no indication that UNHCR or the Government of Tanzania will undertake forcible repatriations of Congolese. However, for many refugees such actions are not beyond the scope of their imagination: in December 1996 the Government of Tanzania, with logistical and financial support from the UNHCR, expelled at least 100,000 Rwandan refugees living in Tanzanian camps in *OpLAST resheni Rudisha Wakimbizi* (Operation Return Refugees – Whitaker 2002). Many were killed upon return to Rwanda (Amnesty International 1997).
8. To 'beep' someone is to call their mobile telephone, let it ring once, and then hang up before the recipient answers the call, thereby avoiding incurring any charges for the call.

References

Amnesty International (1997) 'Great Lakes Region Still in Need of Protection: Repatriation, *Refoulement* and the Safety of Refugees and the Internally Displaced', internal report, ref: AI Index: AFR 02/07/97, London: Amnesty International.

Atkinson, Lucy (2007) 'Living, Eating and Learning: Children's Experiences of Change and Life in a Refugee Camp', PhD dissertation, Department of Social Anthropology, University of Edinburgh.

Bruner, Jerome., A. Jolley and K. Sylva (1976) *Play: Its Role in Development and Evolution*, New York: Basic Books.

Dunn, Judy (1993) *Young Children's Close Relationships: Beyond Attachment*, Newbury Park CA: Sage.

Fisher, Celia, Syatta Wallace and Rose Fenton (2000) 'Discrimination Distress During Adolescence', *Journal of Youth and Adolescence* 29.6: 679–95.

Foster, Geoff and Stefan Germann (2002) *AIDS in Africa*, New York: Kluwer Academic.

Foster, Geoff and John Williamson (2000) 'A Review of Current Literature of the Impact of HIV/AIDS on Children in Sub-Saharan Africa', *Aids* 14(suppl 3): 275–84.

Hinton, Rachel (2000) 'Seen but not Heard: Refugee Children and Models for Intervention' in C. Panter-Brick and M. Smith (eds), *Abandoned Children*, pp. 199–212, Cambridge: Cambridge University Press.

Malkki, Liisa (1995) *Purity and Exile: Violence, Memory and National Cosmology Among Hutu Refugees in Tanzania*, Chicago: University of Chicago Press.

Meursing, K. (1997) *A World of Silence. Living with HIV in Matabeland, Zimbabwe*, Amsterdam: Royal Tropical Institute.

Nieuwenhuys, Olga (1994) *Children's Lifeworlds: Gender, Welfare and Labour in the Developing World*, London: Routledge.

Singer, D.G. and J.L. Singer (1990) *The House of Make-Believe: Children's Play and Developing Imagination*, Cambridge MA: Harvard University Press.

Sutton-Smith, B. (1972) *The Folkgames of Children*, Austin TX: University of Texas Press.

United States Department of State (2009) '2008 Human Rights Report: Tanzania' http://www.state.gov/g/drl/rls/hrrpt/2008/af/119028.htm (accessed 12 December 2009).

Verkuyten, Maykel (1998) 'Perceived Discrimination and Self-Esteem Among Ethnic Minority Adolescents', *Journal of Social Psychology* 138.4: 479–93.

Wenger, Etienne (1998) *Communities of Practice: Learning, Meaning and Identity*, Cambridge: Cambridge University Press.

Whitaker, Beth Elise (2002) 'Changing Priorities in Refugee Protection: The Rwandan Repatriation from Tanzania', *Refugee Survey Quarterly* 21.1,2: 328–44.

12

'Pen, Book, Soap, Good Food, and Encouragement': Understandings of a Good Life for Children among Parents and Children in Three Ethiopian Communities

Laura Camfield[1]

Introduction

Confronting the 'universal' with the 'local' has become an important theme within development, contesting growth-led development strategies and uniform approaches to policy and programming. From an empirical perspective, however, the local appears multiple and contested, and the universal equally local, given that all ways of thinking are specific to particular times, places, and purposes. This understanding presents a challenge to interventions to reduce child poverty, which are typically underpinned by models of good childhoods drawn from Euro-American contexts and may neglect crucial aspects of children's experiences. This chapter contributes to this debate from the bottom-up by reporting the diverse opinions of Ethiopian children and their caregivers on what constitutes a good or bad life for children, elicited primarily through group interviews and activities.

Worldwide there have been many studies about understandings of well-being (reviewed in Alkire 2002: 203-6; Camfield 2006: 6–10; Camfield et al. 2009). These represent a paradigm shift towards holistic, person-centred, and dynamic understandings of people's lives that are nonetheless embedded in particular socio-cultural contexts. People's values, aspirations, and experiences of happiness or unhappiness are now measured directly within some large surveys of individuals and households (for example, South African Quality of Life Trends Study; see Moller 1987) rather than inferred from proxies such as income. These experiences are also explored in participatory studies that identify pathways to particular outcomes (for example, chronic poverty) and the perceived possibilities for change in the future.

The inclusion of subjective experiences and meanings is part of a move within international development and research on poverty from economic to multidimensional understandings of people's lives (Sumner 2007). However, multidimensional approaches can fail to acknowledge the interpersonal and recursive aspects of well-being such as the shaping of people's experiences and evaluations of their lives by their own perception of their environment and themselves, in the context of what they value and aspire to. Group exercises of the sort reported in this chapter can, through a process of collective reflection, shift the focus from what people have or are able to do to how they think, feel, locate themselves, and relate to others. This moves the discussion beyond the 'visible inventory of wants' often elicited in Participatory Poverty Assessments (PPAs) to explore 'the "intermediate norms" that structure these particular wants through local ideas about arranged or love marriages; joint or nuclear family structures; honourable and dishonourable forms of work, and how these vary for men and women; and so on' (White 2010: 162).

Previous research with children in Ethiopia, described later, demonstrates considerable diversity in understandings of well-being, and these differences may be more pronounced between adults and children. For this reason, the chapter contrasts qualitative data from different exercises involving children, caregivers, and community informants who explore what constitutes well-being or a good life for children in their community. It provides a brief overview of findings from previous studies of understandings of well-being among adults and children in Ethiopia and of aspects of children's lives identified as central to their well-being. It then describes the methods used and reports differences in expressed understandings of a good life and what is needed to achieve this, primarily by location, gender, and age.

Poverty and well-being in Ethiopia

Ethiopia is one the poorest and most donor-dependent countries in Africa, with a history of centralized and authoritarian rule dating back to the rule of Emperor Haile Selassie I (1917–1974) (Vaughan and Tronvoll 2003; Bevan and Pankhurst 2007). Poverty in Ethiopia has a complex socio-political history, which incorporates patron–client relationships and subordination of different forms. In Ethiopia, adult understandings of poverty and well-being have typically been collected through PPAs (Rahmato and Kidanu 1999; Ellis and Woldehanna 2005), open-ended qualitative research (reviewed in Camfield 2006), and more recently using subjective measures such as the Global Person Generated Index (Ruta et al. 2004) and the WeD-QoL (Woodcock 2007).[2] Although the different types of study show common elements (see Table 12.1) – health, economic independence, behaving well, having religious faith, and respectful and supportive relationships within family and community – they also demonstrate considerable diversity by location, gender, religion, socio-economic status, and life stage. This is rarely captured in global summaries such as the 'Consultations with the Poor' series (critiqued by Cornwall and Fujita 2007). The diversity in understanding becomes more apparent when the data behind the headings are reported. For example, while well-being is almost always seen as involving the family, there may be different understandings of 'good' families in different contexts, or even of what counts as a family. Table 12.1 also shows a clear difference between the results of the PPAs and the two other studies in the other studies' inclusion of (1) relationships (the only PPA heading connected to relationships is 'lending money to the poor'); (2) personal characteristics in so far as they support good relationships; (3) religious faith; and (4) value contestation within communities where opposing models of a good life are presented.

In relation to children, the main areas identified by the studies in Table 12.1 are material security, schooling, appropriate work, and good family relationships. However, child-centred studies of children in Ethiopia (reviewed in Poluha 2007: 1–41; Tekola 2009: 28–31) also highlight the importance to children of health and access to health care, being able to fulfil basic needs without depending on others, and good behaviour as the key to respectful and supportive relationships. The Young Lives study has found that, for children in early adolescence, the age of the Older Cohort, the interrelated experiences of schooling, work, and for girls, an increasing sense of physical vulnerability in public spaces, have become more prominent. For example, despite high expectations of education and future employment reported by children and caregivers in Young Lives (74 per cent of caregivers want their children to complete university), less than 50 per cent of older children in rural areas are in the correct school grade for their age. Reasons for this include late enrolment, irregular attendance, brevity of the school day, and quality of schooling, including teacher absenteeism. The cost

Table 12.1 Adults' understandings of a good life, elicited through participatory and qualitative research

	PPA 1999/00	PPA 2004/05	WeD–QoL[a]	WeD exploratory
Rural	Size of farmland Livestock, including oxen Food security Access to fertilizer and agricultural equipment Lending money to the poor	Land and labour for farming Livestock holdings Food security Non-farm activities/enterprises Access to vocational training Access to fertilizer, enabling on-farm diversification Salaries/remittances Children's enrolment in school Children working at an appropriate level for their age/capabilities	*Considered 'very necessary' by >70% of respondents, listed in rank order* Health Economic independence Peace of mind Food Behaving well Room or house Faith Land	Fertile land, livestock, including oxen Modern agricultural equipment Material sufficiency, especially food Economic independence Education and knowledge Health Housing Marriage and children Having a good appearance/sociable and hospitable/able to celebrate the holidays Reciprocal relationships with family (including birth family) and friends
Urban	Food security ('able to eat as much as they want') Own business and/or permanent, pensionable employment 'Living in good houses with good-quality furniture' 'Can afford to send their children to good schools' Addis Ababa only: Owning commercial trucks, stores, hotels or bars Running grain mills 'Living in nicely furnished houses that they own'	Education and skills Business or assets and credit to start businesses Salaries and remittances, ideally international Household assets, including house quality Utilities and sanitation	Community peace Wealth Good family relationships Personal progress Good living environment	Religion Respectful, respected – seen as advice giver/communicator/altruist Observes traditional cultural forms OR progressive, 'modern' Practises conspicuous consumption OR moderation, temperance Disciplined, hard-working, ethical & family-oriented Happy, satisfied, has peace of mind

[a] Conducted by the Well-being in Developing Countries ESRC Research Group (WeD) on people's values and aspirations in the context of their understandings of a good life.

of schooling, including materials such as uniform and exercise books, presents a further barrier and this increases with children's age owing to the greater distance from second-cycle primary schools (grades 5 to 8) and secondary schools, which are usually located in urban centres.

In most Young Lives communities, children are expected to work according to their capacity from the age of 5, and girls should be able to perform all household tasks by the age of 12. While there are a range of paid and unpaid activities in different communities, by the age of 10, most children work to support their families in the family farm or business, and provide for their own clothing, schooling, and occasionally leisure. Children and adults usually report that they consider work to be beneficial, unless it exposes children to physical or social risks (for example, 'heavy' labour such as quarrying, or working in bars). However, work may affect children's schooling, particularly during key agricultural periods, and poorer children described being too tired to follow their lessons or missing school through work-related health problems. While marriage, often through abduction,[3] is not yet a reality for children in this age group, it is a concern for parents and children and is starting to affect girls' access to education, especially in rural areas.

Little research has been undertaken with children in Ethiopia on their understandings of well-being, relative to adults in Ethiopia or children in other countries, although two recent studies by Tekola et al. (2008) and Tafere (2007) produced interesting insights. Tafere's comparative analysis of two urban communities from Young Lives demonstrated the perceived importance of social relationships, personal characteristics, engagement with environment, and spirituality, which reflect many of the themes that emerged from focus groups with adults (Table 12.1). Tekola's use of community maps with children in Addis Ababa generated interesting information about well-being and ill-being in relation to education. For example, many children liked the school flag, which they described as a symbol of belonging, and the trees and flowers in the school compound. A nation-wide UNICEF study in 2005 on Ethiopian children's understandings of well-being combined individuals' written and pictorial responses to four questions addressing 'dreams in life for yourself, your community, and your country' with task-based group responses on the same theme led by youth facilitators (Conticini et al. 2005). Education was the main 'dream' as it was seen as 'key to having a better life, getting out of poverty, "becoming someone", and being able to help other vulnerable children' (ibid. p. 11), although respect, representation, and rights were also important. This brief review suggests that children's understanding of what it means to live well shows many similarities to that of adults, as might be expected, given children's early engagement with adult activities. For example, children and adults concur on the importance of relationships and the personal characteristics that support these, although adults place a greater emphasis on religious faith. However, the contexts of these understandings differ, with a stronger focus among children on school as a social space, location of work and pleasure, source of identity, and guarantor of the future. Children, especially in urban areas, also appeared to be more ready to challenge the views of other participants, which may indicate that they were less constrained than adults by norms of respect and politeness and an awareness of hierarchies within the groups.

Research methods

Sites and sampling

The data for this chapter come from three of the five sites chosen for longitudinal qualitative research: Atkilit tera (urban, Addis Ababa region), Leki (near-rural, Oromia), and Semhal (remote-rural, Tigray), which are described below (pseudonyms have been used throughout to protect the identities of children and their communities).

Atkilit tera, situated in the national capital, is a densely populated community (14,066 inhabitants), which is diverse in terms of ethnicity, religion, and socio-economic status. It is near the city's fruit and vegetable market, which provides economic opportunities for adults and children, but is dirty and unsafe for girls. With easy access to secondary and high schools, it has higher educational participation and a greater range of schools than the other sites.

With a population of 2,835, Leki is a comparatively small and ethnically homogenous community. It has good natural resources (including irrigated fields for growing vegetables to be sold in the markets of Addis Ababa and a lake for fishing, which provide economic opportunities for girls and boys respectively) and a temperate climate, but is nonetheless materially poor. The education provided within the community is of low quality: in the school year 2007/08, the school lacked three of the ten teachers it needed to function and it lost a further four during the year because of health problems.

Semhal is similar in size to Leki and is also ethnically homogenous; however, it is more remote: to reach the nearest town takes two to three hours on foot and the road is only usable in the 'dry season'. Respondents were materially poor and had limited access to electricity and piped water. While every hamlet had a school providing education up to Grade 4, children needed to walk for over an hour to access the higher levels of primary school.

Equal numbers of boys and girls were sampled in each site ($n = 20$): 12 children who became 'case studies' and participated in group and individual activities and eight children who acted as 'reserves' and were interviewed briefly in the first and second rounds of qualitative research to provide a baseline for future data collection if any of the case studies dropped out.

Methods and ethical considerations

The qualitative research used a toolkit of methods developed for application in diverse cultural contexts, including methods based on conversation, drawing, and writing (Crivello et al. 2009). The data analysed in the following section comes from two sources. First, separate group interviews were conducted with caregivers and male and female community informants (for example, government employees and elders) on understandings of well-being and transitions for children aged 11 to 13. These interviews used focusing questions such as, 'How are children expected to spend their time?' or, 'Tell me some local sayings/proverbs that relate to children.'

Second, a group activity called the Well-Being Exercise was conducted with children, in which they were asked to think about and draw 'a girl or a boy of their age in the community and living a good or bad life' (in translation, good life incorporated living well in a material and a moral sense). Children drew pictures individually and explained their meaning to the group, often eliciting critical or challenging responses (for example, debates over whether a 12-year-old child was too young to chew *chaat*, a mild narcotic). This was followed by a collective discussion with children's suggestions written on a flip chart divided into columns for 'good life' and 'bad life': these could easily be turned into 'indicators', which the participants ranked. Individual children's ideas and rankings were recorded and followed up in individual interviews (not reported here).

The exercise was conducted independently with five boys and five girls aged 11 to 13 in each site (six case studies and four reserves), typically in a meeting hall or space within the local administration's offices or compound. Fieldwork took place between September and November when children had returned to school, so activities were scheduled around school and other commitments. Careful attention was paid to the composition of the research team and the nature and scheduling of activities to enable respondents to relax with the researchers. Informed consent was obtained from caregivers at the start of the project; however, the team regularly checked the willingness of participating adults and children and reminded them that they could refuse or stop whenever they wanted to, a right which was exercised on several occasions (see Chapter 2 by Virginia Morrow for a discussion about informed consent in Young Lives).

The data reported in the next section address whether it is possible to identify cohesive and distinctive models of a good life that reflects the priorities identified in other Ethiopian studies, namely health, economic independence, behaving well, having religious faith, and respectful and supportive relationships within family and community. It asks whether children's understandings are the same as those of adults (for example, is education valued to the same extent and in the same way by children and adults) and identifies cross-cutting effects of gender and location. Finally, it provides evidence that group interviews capture relational aspects obscured by individual methods and enable the exploration of 'individual' values and frames of reference.

Results

Group activities with children

The analysis reported in this sub-section focuses on differences between the responses of groups of girls and boys, and groups taking place in rural and urban areas, using data from the Well-Being Exercise.

While this exercise raised common themes, such as education, these were specified differently in different sites and by different groups of respondents. In Semhal and Leki, the main concern was access to education, especially for girls (or boys with no younger siblings to herd cattle) and to a lesser extent educational materials. In Atkilit tera, however, the focus was on educational quality in many different dimensions (teaching, sanitation, class sizes, and so on). This led to a lively debate in the girls' group about the relative merits of private and government schools. One girl who had been removed from the private school she was attending after her mother lost her job ranked 'having to attend a government school' as the second most important indicator of ill-being, which is a poignant example of the influence of individual biographies on understandings of well-being. Educational materials were ranked second only to education and were seen as symbolizing parents' care for their children, similar to the perception of clean clothes and oiled hair in the rural sites (hair that has been oiled, and therefore is not 'big', 'dry', or 'dreadlocked', demonstrates that parents have either cattle for

butter or cash income to purchase hair oil). Parents who made sacri-
fices so children could have what they needed were greatly respected,
including single mothers who washed clothes in order to pay for their
children's school materials.

Children's behaviour was also a common theme, for example, being
obedient, not fighting. Their comments were highly moral in tone, illustrated by the vivid description of the destitute child who has a bad life
because he 'lives by wandering from house to house to steal' and after
a period of imprisonment '[becomes] rich because of theft' (Afework,
12-year-old boy, Semhal). This perhaps reflects a need to bolster their
own identities by distinguishing themselves from both poor people and
from rich ones whose wealth had not been gained honestly. Comments
from the urban site related mainly to how children's behaviour might
affect their interactions with others. One boy described a child who
had no one to buy him polish to shine shoes on the street (a popular
way for children to earn money), or to vouch for his poverty status to
the *Kebele* [local administrative unit] to ensure his access to government
support, as: 'He is not liked by his neighbours; he has no relatives, [and]
he cannot keep his personal hygiene well, so that people ostracize him'
(Addisu, 12-year-old boy, Atkilit tera). Another described how a boy who
fought with his parents would not be supported in continuing his education, or even if he became sick: 'His parents do not pay school fees for
him because they don't like him; it is not because they don't have the
money but because of lack of good family relations' (Berhanu, 13-year-
old boy, Atkilit tera). In Atkilit tera, relationships outside the family
were considered important for social mobility. Many children emphasized the importance of having friends from school, rather than the
local residential area: 'His friends are from his surroundings and have
bad behaviour. His friends are not clever so he is not clever either…He
and his friends are lazy in their education' (Bekele, 13-year-old boy,
Atkilit tera).

Other common themes were work and its relation to education, food,
shelter, access to health care, and having a good appearance ('[having]
no clothes means it becomes difficult to leave the house and you cannot
go anywhere for work' – well-being indicator identified by boys from
Leki). Having a biological relationship with your caregivers was also
mentioned as this was seen as giving a child '[the] right to get what
she wants from her guardians' (Abebe, 13-year-old girl, Atkilit tera).
Children's material ambitions seemed to be higher in Atkilit tera than
in the rural localities, which reflect its location at the centre of the
Ethiopian capital. An example is '[having] a table full of a variety of

food like a buffet' rather than simply 'sufficient food'. Goods such as cars and DVDs were also mentioned, which were not part of the aspirations of rural children or visible in the rural sites. The aspirations of respondents in rural areas related more to productive assets such as irrigated land or cattle, and in Leki, a boat for fishing. While all respondents were aware of status differentiation, children in Atkilit tera seemed to feel this more keenly and described experiences of inequality with great insight:

> [The well-being girl] has a pen, an exercise book, good living conditions, a uniform, can get adequate food, and can attend a private school. Her parents can afford the school fees and can fulfil what she wants to have. However, the ill-being girl cannot get a pen, a pencil, a bag, clothes or food. She is attending a government school...A girl who is not doing well may join the private school but she cannot get what she needs like her well-being friends since her family is poor economically but they can only afford her school fees. But the well-being girl can get what she wants to have [the same] as her friends. (Abebe, 13-year-old girl, Atkilit tera)

Once children had generated indicators of well-being or ill-being from the discussions, they were asked to rank these in order of importance. The recording researcher noted any differences in opinion (for example, in Atkilit tera, where respondents could agree on the five most important indicators, but not the order in which they should be placed). Unlike the other two communities, in Leki, education was only mentioned once as an indicator of well-being (by girls) and was ranked sixth. There were few differences between girls' and boys' indicators, although girls in Semhal mention having a separate kitchen (which would reduce eye irritation caused by cooking over wood in a poorly ventilated room), sufficient clothes, and access to means of communication such as television, radio, and the telephone.

Although girls and boys in Semhal agreed on the importance of good clothing, attending school, and cleanliness as indicators of well-being and ill-being, there was a greater divergence in their views of a good life than in other communities, suggesting differentiated trajectories for girls and boys with associated differences in concerns. Girls mention getting sufficient food (for example, not having to go to school without breakfast), being encouraged to study, having time to play, and being asked their opinion, and being shown respect as signs of a good life, which may indicate that these things are uncommon or absent from their lives. Boys are more concerned about good behaviour (for example, not stealing, fighting, being 'foolish', or disobedient), health, and having a loving and peaceful family.

Education appears to be a more important component of a good life in Atkilit tera than in the other localities since both boys and girls ranked it as the main indicator of well-being or ill-being. Older girls gave a detailed account of the experiences of girls whose parents either could not send them to school or could not afford to support them while they were there: 'Unable to get what her friends have, even if she learns, she doesn't understand properly.' Consequently she feels she is falling behind her friends: 'When she is learning rather she thinks about her life. She faces different problems and her mind becomes full of tension.' The result of this is that she becomes pregnant at an early age and 'watches when other children are going to and from school', 'too fearful' to approach them.

Boys and girls mentioned having sufficient food and not being an orphan, which reflects the large number of orphans within Young Lives sites (25 per cent of the Older Cohort), and particularly in urban areas (all of the older children selected in Atkilit tera are orphans). Girls also mention shelter. As in Semhal, boys mention not getting advice or 'follow up' from their family which is implicitly linked to having good or bad behaviour.

Group interviews with adults

The group interviews with adults explored understandings of well-being and ill-being for boys and girls aged 5 to 6 and 11 to 13. Valued dimensions of well-being in all sites for children of any age and gender were (1) having material security, specifically being able to satisfy basic needs such as food and clothes; (2) experiencing good and harmonious family relationships, characterized by love, affection, and care; (3) receiving advice and moral guidance; (4) having access to education and appropriate work that does not interfere with this; (5) living in a good physical environment (that is, clean and with plentiful natural resources); and (6) having personal characteristics, such as confidence, sociability, and cleanliness, that enable children to relate well to others.

Site-specific dimensions included the importance of clean water in the rural sites, having educated parents who can advise and teach their children in Atkilit tera, and divergent attitudes to early marriage[4] for girls. In Semhal, early marriage was characterized as becoming enlightened (*berhan*) and fruitful (*abebe*) and seen as a blessing only rich girls could enjoy because their families had the resources to arrange wedding ceremonies and attract good sons-in-law; in Leki, it was seen as a risk to health and education; and in Atkilit tera, youth pregnancy outside marriage and illegal abortion were more pressing concerns. For example, when the researcher asked participants in Atkilit tera at what age children in this community married, the respondents laughingly replied, 'These days we never see any wedding ceremony in the community. Girls may have love affairs with boys and start living together without having legal marriage.' Despite this variation in attitudes towards early marriage, there was consensus among adults in rural and urban sites that marriages by abduction or pregnancy outside marriage were greater threats.Gender differences in adult responses were few, and reflected different spheres of activity for males and females and expectations about how they would use their time (Table 12.2). Male respondents in all sites mentioned play – having materials, space, and time for recreation – which was not mentioned by women. Conversely, women highlighted the importance of access to health care while men mentioned health only in the sense of a resource to achieve goals, suggesting that they saw health as instrumentally rather than intrinsically valuable.

Common understandings of ill-being included (1) the absence of the dimensions of well-being listed above (such as food and parental care); (2) ill-health or disability, which incurred large medical expenses; (3) feeling inferior to or resentful of others; (4) inability to learn because of poor-quality tuition, lack of time, or physical weakness through overwork or lack of food; (5) large, disharmonious families; (6) poor parenting leading to mutual disrespect between parents and children and a lack of role models; (7) living and working on the street, leading to exposure to drugs, crime, violence, prostitution, and so on (Atkilit tera only); and (8) corresponding risks of overwork, beating, and sexual abuse at home.

The differences between men and women (Table 12.3) were largely the converse of those described for well-being, with the addition of concerns relating to education among women in two of the three sites: whether religious education is a genuine alternative for girls in communities where there are no pre-schools (Semhal); how children have become distracted from education by new economic opportunities such as picking tomatoes and onions (Leki); and the high price of educational materials (all).

The only dimension of well-being mentioned by an adult group that was not mentioned by children was having the opportunity to practise religion and attend religious education, something that came out strongly in earlier work by WeD (religious education was only mentioned

Table 12.2   Differences in adult understandings of children's well-being between male and female groups in different sites[a]

	Atkilit tera (urban)	Semhal (remote rural)	Leki (near rural)
Men	Being calm and broad in their perspective Time to study and play	Plays well with others Good academic performance Plump and physically mature (girls), physically strong (boys) Boys should feel equal to peers, perhaps even start to feel 'proud' and 'look down on others' (enhanced confidence through starting to farm)	Local places and materials for recreation Having well-behaved friends and learning from them Early religious tuition and participation in church activities Becoming a good citizen Girls being supervised to avoid early intimacy with boys and having early marriage discouraged
Women	Not being an orphan Health care	Having both parents Health care Girls should be able to (1) keep clean during puberty and be prepared for menstruation; (2) marry and have children, even if this involves leaving school; (3) make choices in their lives and not be pressurized by parents	Having both parents Health care Family wealth

[a] Common understandings are given in the text.

by children as an inferior form of general schooling). Perhaps related to this, adult groups talked about the importance of maintaining a particular approach towards life; for example, having a peaceful mind or being broad and calm, which are characteristics that might develop with maturity. Children were also aware of the importance of personal characteristics such as confidence and sociability, but this was framed in terms of what it would help them to achieve, or how it would hinder achievement, in their social relationships (see also Tekola 2009).

Table 12.3   Differences in adult understandings of children's ill-being between male and female groups in different sites[a]

	Atkilit tera (urban)	Semhal (remote rural)	Leki (near rural)
Men	No long-term support from government or community Resentment at not having what their friends have	No places for recreation No kindergarten (women also identify lack of care as problem) Preference for traditional medicine over modern (indicates poor parenting) Husbands waste family resources	No recreational spaces
Women	Parents separated or children orphaned by HIV/AIDS Poor sanitation, difficult for girls to keep clean Elderly household head Unemployed adults setting bad example in household No TV or money to watch TV Education – no time to study, going to govt. rather than private school, no extra tuition Limited access to healthcare, having to use traditional healers	No parents Effect on education of burdensome work within and outside household, for example, young children herding instead of going to school, girls working too hard to study	Orphan or without a father Shyness, difficulty relating to others Effect of comparing self with rich children on subjective well-being

[a] Common understandings are given in the text.

Discussion

There was a high level of consensus between children and adults within particular communities (see also Tafere and Camfield 2009); differences by gender, cross-cut by differences across communities, were more pronounced. For example, girls and women in Atkilit tera and Semhal emphasized that girls needed time to study, which was not mentioned by respondents in Leki, suggesting that in Leki schooling is given a lower priority.

While the research described here supported dimensions found in earlier participatory assessments (Table 12.1), it found a stronger emphasis on parental provision of advice and moral guidance and children's personal characteristics. Children and adults valued characteristics such as patience, confidence, and sociability because they enabled children to relate well to others. They also valued 'good behaviour', or 'living in a good way', which they attributed to teaching by parents or religious teachers (interviews carried out in Semhal). A similar emphasis on behaviour has been found by other qualitative studies in Ethiopia (for example, Tekola 2009), but not in Participatory Poverty Assessments. The omission of behaviour from PPAs may reflect the implicit focus of the participatory poverty assessments on material poverty and livelihoods and the expectations set up by the exercise of material assistance from outside. Appearance, for example, having good, clean clothes and shoes, and neat hair, was another aspect that is rarely included in international definitions of poverty. This was valued as a concrete expression of family prosperity and care; for example, dressing children's hair. Similarly, although 'material security' emerges in all poverty assessments, its value is seen as self-evident. In this case, respondents explained that it enabled children to appear or feel equal to others, and parents to express their care by buying them 'everything they needed'.

While at the level of frameworks or summary tables, the qualitative data appear to do little more than underline the importance of relationships and the attitudes and behaviour that support these, closer investigation brings out the subtle, contextual, and dynamic aspects of people's understandings of well-being, particularly well illustrated in relation to early marriage. As both adults and children addressed good lives for boys and girls aged 11 to 13 in particular contexts, the data should not be read as a general prescription for the well-being of children in Ethiopia. However, taking a specific and concrete focus has arguably produced data that is more reliable and useful than anything relating to an ageless and context-free 'Ethiopian Child'. Although not the focus of this paper, there is a need to use group and individual methods to go beyond the a-contextual lists generated by PPAs and embed notions of well-being in the lives of individuals and communities. For this reason, I endorse the position of Stefan Dercon in Chapter 4 of this volume in advocating not a single, static list of dimensions of poverty or well-being, which might form the basis of a measure, but a deliberative

process that recognizes the importance of 'identifying and prioritis-
ing the freedoms people value' (Alkire 2007: 2). For example, Robeyns
(2005: 198–9) warns that even 'by engaging in appropriate cross-cultural dialogue...it is very hard, and indeed often impossible, to truly
understand people who live in a very different situation...Instead, we
need a process of genuine listening and deliberation until a list, which
will necessarily be collective, can be constructed...[Otherwise] even a
good idea may in the end turn into a politically illegitimate proposal.'
This process should retain an awareness of questions such as which
judgements are informed, how and by whom are values determined,
and how conflicting value claims resolved (ibid.). It should also be sensitive to the material and political barriers to attaining well-being, even
though the latter are rarely articulated in group settings. In Ethiopia,
the barriers reflect a history of centralized and authoritarian rule dating
back to the time of the Ethiopian Empire, expressed through patron–
client relationships and different forms of subordination (Bevan and
Pankhurst 2007). These extend into everyday power relationships in
homes and communities, impacting particularly strongly on children.

Notes

1. The author thanks Young Lives participants and researchers, in particular
   my colleague Yisak Tafere, who led the research in Ethiopia and shares an
   interest in understandings of well-being.
2. Conducted by the Well-being in Developing Countries ESRC Research Group
   (WeD) on people's values and aspirations in the context of their understandings of a good life; see www.welldev.org.uk and www.wed-ethiopia.org. The
   findings of the exploratory study are reported in Camfield (2006) and the
   WeD-QoL in Woodcock (2007).
3. Abduction is the practice of taking a wife without the consent of her parents,
   either by force, for example, while she is on her way home from school, or
   through seduction ('voluntary abduction').
4. Early marriage is marriage below the customary age of 15, rather than below
   the statutory age of 18.

References

Alkire, S. (2002) *Valuing Freedoms. Sen's Capability Approach and Poverty Reduction*,
    Oxford: Oxford University Press.
Alkire, S. (2007) *Choosing Dimensions: The Capability Approach and Multidimensional
    Poverty*, Working Paper 88, Manchester: Chronic Poverty Research Centre.
Bevan, P. and A. Pankhurst (2007) 'Power Structures and Agency in Rural Ethiopia:
    Development Lessons from Four Case Studies', Paper prepared for the empow-
    erment team in the World Bank Poverty Reduction Group, 14 June 2007.

Camfield, L. (2006) *Why and How of Understanding "Subjective" Well-Being: Exploratory Work by the WeD group in Four Developing Countries*, Working Paper 26, Bath: Well-being in Developing Countries Research Group.

Camfield, L., N. Streuli and M. Woodhead (2009) 'What's the Use of "Well-Being" in Contexts of Child Poverty? Approaches to Research, Monitoring and Children's Participation', *International Journal of Children's Rights* 17.1: 65–109.

Camfield, L. and Y. Tafere. (2009) *'Children with a Good Life Have to Have School Bags': Understandings of Well-being among Children in Ethiopia*, Working Paper 37, Oxford: Young Lives.

Conticini, Kui and Tsadik W. (2005) *We Have a Dream: Children's Visions, Vulnerabilities and Rights in Ethiopia*, Addis Ababa: UNICEF.

Cornwall, A. and M. Fujita (2007) 'The Politics of Representing the Poor' in: J. Moncrieffe and R. Eyben (eds), *The Power of Labelling: How People are Categorized and Why It Matters*, London: Earthscan.

Crivello, G., L. Camfield and M. Woodhead (2009) 'How Can Children Tell Us About Their Well-Being? Exploring the Potential of Participatory Approaches within the *Young Lives* Project', *Social Indicators Research* 90.1: 51–72.

Ellis, F. and T. Woldehanna (2005) 'Ethiopia Participatory Poverty Assessment 2004–05', Addis Ababa: Ministry of Finance and Economic Development (MoFED).

Moller, V. (1987) *Quality of Life in South Africa*, Dordrecht: Kluwer Academic Publishers.

Poluha, E. (2007) *An Annotated Bibliography on Children and Childhood in Ethiopia*, Stockholm: Save the Children Sweden.

Rahmato, D. and A. Kidanu (1999) 'Consultations with the Poor: A Study to Inform the World Development Report 2000/2001 on Poverty and Development. (National Report, Ethiopia)', Addis Ababa: World Bank.

Robeyns (2005) 'Selecting Capabilities for Quality of Life Measurement', *Social Indicators Research* 74: 191–215.

Ruta, D., L. Camfield and F. Martin (2004) 'Assessing Individual Quality of Life in Developing Countries: Piloting a Global PGI in Ethiopia and Bangladesh', *Quality of Life Research* 13: 1545.

Sumner, A. (2007) 'Meaning versus Measurement: Why do "Economic" Indicators of Poverty Still Predominate?', *Development in Practice* 17.1: 4–13.

Tafere, Y. (2007) 'Children's Understanding of their Well-being: Evidence from Young Lives Qualitative Research in Two Urban Communities in Ethiopia', Paper presented at the 6th Conference of the Ethiopian Society of Sociologists, Social Workers and Anthropologists (ESSSWA), Addis Ababa, 14–15 December 2007.

Tafere, Y and L. Camfield (2009) *Community Understandings of Children's Transitions in Ethiopia: Possible Implications for Life Course Poverty*, Working Paper 41, Oxford: Young Lives.

Tekola, B., C. Griffin and L. Camfield (2008) 'Using Qualitative Methods with Poor Children in Urban Ethiopia: Opportunities and Challenges', *Social Indicators Research* 90.1: 73–87.

Tekola, B. (2009) 'Making Sense of Childhood Poverty: Perceptions and Daily Experiences of Poor Children in Addis Ababa, Ethiopia', unpublished dissertation, University of Bath.

Vaughan, S., and K. Tronvoll (2003) *The Culture of Power in Contemporary Ethiopian Political Life*, Stockholm: Swedish International Development Cooperation Agency.

White, S.C. (2010) 'Analysing Well-being: A Framework for Development Practice', *Development in Practice* 20.2: 158–72.

Woodcock, A. (2007) 'Validation of WeDQoL-Goals-Ethiopia: Goal Necessity and Goal Satisfaction scales and individualised quality of life scores', Report to the WeD Team, unpublished.

13
'Ridiculed for Not Having Anything': Children's Views on Poverty and Inequality in Rural India

Gina Crivello, Uma Vennam, and Anuradha Komanduri[1]

Introduction

This chapter reports on research carried out with boys and girls, aged 12 to 15, participating in Young Lives in the southern Indian state of Andhra Pradesh. It focuses on young people's descriptions, explanations, and experiences of poverty and inequality in two contrasting rural communities and highlights implications for research, policy and practice, and rights. Young people growing up in poor communities are generally alert to inequalities and injustices, and to their own disadvantaged situations (see for example, Chapter 11 by Gillian Mann; Bissell 2009; Camfield 2010; or Witter 2002). The research presented here indicates that children perceive material inequalities as indicative of wider differences in power and position, of which they are very much a part. Children's concerns, explanations, and experiences of the effects of poverty may differ from those of adults, and children often have distinct roles and responsibilities within their families for managing hardship and risk related to household poverty (for example, caring for siblings, carrying out essential household chores, working for pay, and going to school). There may also be important differences in patterns of children's awareness and understanding of inequality, reflecting their varied positioning in the social hierarchy and the range of social expectations they manage (related, for example, to age, gender, class, and ethnicity, or caste).

There is a growing body of research documenting young people's accounts of poverty in both developed and developing contexts (for example, Camfield 2010; Middleton et al. 1994; Ridge 2002, 2003; Tekola 2009; Van der Hoek 2005; Witter 2002). A study of child poverty in India, Belarus, Kenya, Sierra Leone, and Bolivia found that for children 'the personal and immediate effects of poverty, such as the shame of wearing patched shoes, are frequently articulated more strongly than the broader structural trends, like chronic ill health or insecurity of tenure, which adults often tend to emphasize' (Boyden et al. 2003: 109). Across these studies, and echoed in recent research in Europe (for example, Attree 2006; Redmond 2008, 2009; Ridge 2007), what children often find most distressing about the lack of material goods is the sense of shame that comes with 'not having' or not 'fitting in'; they worry about not being able to participate in valued activities (for example, because they might not be able to pay for transportation to see friends) or about their ability to display the symbols that mark them as 'somebody' amongst their peers and in their communities (for example, wearing a clean and correct school uniform). This can be especially important for children's evolving sense of identity, belonging, and self-efficacy, which are strongly shaped by their everyday social interactions.

This chapter draws on information collected through surveys and qualitative research with rural children in Andhra Pradesh to explore their views on the relationship between the material and social aspects of poverty, and the implications of inequalities for children and their families. There are two fundamental reasons for this analysis. The first is to take account of the distinct (yet diverse) contribution that children make to research and to the generation of knowledge. Capturing poor children's 'standpoints' respects their capacities to think, feel, and aspire beyond 'survival' (Ben-Arieh 2005), and acknowledges that they may do so differently from poor adults. In most societies, children lack social power in relation to adults and may be more vulnerable to poverty and other adversities as a result (Harper et al. 2003: 535). Their views and experiences of poverty have important implications for the ways in which policies and services represent and intervene in their lives and communities (cf. Bissell 2009: 538).

The second reason relates to children as bearers of rights (see Beazley et al. 2009; Robson et al. 2009). Key to this is their right to have a say in matters affecting their lives, based on Article 12 of the United Nations Convention on the Rights of the Child (1989). Their participation in research may provide an opportunity for them to negotiate priorities and make choices in the research process with adults and other children (Jabeen 2009: 417). It is especially important in contexts with marked child–adult hierarchies to find ways of increasing children's participation, while also respecting their right to be researched in accordance with high academic standards.[2]

Organization of the chapter

The next section briefly describes where the research took place, how it was carried out, and who participated. This is followed by an analysis of a selection of survey variables capturing children's views and aspirations. The subsequent section is an overview of qualitative research findings, which are explored in detail through two case studies. The final discussion highlights the importance of children's social relationships, both as a factor shaping their experiences of poverty, and as a resource for dealing with economic hardship.

Background to the research

Around one-third of the population of Andhra Pradesh is under the age of 14, and over 70 per cent of the population live in rural areas, which have the highest incidence of poverty (Mukherji 2008: 17). Andhra Pradesh has done well in terms of reducing income poverty, but concern remains over inequalities: Scheduled Tribes and Scheduled Castes continue to be the poorest groups and this is reflected in different outcomes for children (CESS 2008; Galab et al. 2008; Mukherji 2008).[3] The state has also achieved considerable progress on child development indicators since the mid-1990s, but despite this, significant disparities remain, based on sector (rural versus urban), caste, and region (Galab et al. 2008: iii). Young Lives survey data on 12-year-olds show that school dropout rates 'are higher in rural areas (10 per cent) than in urban areas (3 per cent), among the poorest households (16 per cent), among Scheduled Tribe children (possibly because of distance to school), and among girls (11 per cent)' (ibid.: vi).

This chapter draws on the 2006 Young Lives survey data, collected from 651 rural children aged around 12–13 (and on their caregivers), and on qualitative data, collected in 2007 and 2008. Young Lives collected the latter to explore child well-being, important turning points in childhood ('transitions'), and children's experiences of programmes and services. This involved children and adults, and combined individual and group-based interviews. Group discussions with children were aided by creative techniques, including mapping, drawing, storytelling, and video work.

We focus on two communities. Patna[4] is a rural tribal village in Srikakulam district with some 1,056 resident families. Although it is predominantly tribal, there are also Backward Caste families (less poor than Scheduled Castes), and some Scheduled Caste families in the immediate area. Katur, a (non-tribal) rural community, is situated in Anantapur district with around 400 local families. In Katur, most families belong to the Boya caste (traditionally a hunter group, which later shifted into agriculture, and is now classified as a Backward Caste). There are around nine households belonging to the Kamma caste (the dominant caste in the community and classified as 'Other Castes'), and others belonging to a Scheduled Caste.

From these communities, twelve children (six boys, six girls) were selected for case studies, representing a mix of caste and poverty backgrounds, but most belonging to either Scheduled Tribes (five) or Backward Castes (six): one of the children is from the Scheduled Castes and none are from the Other Castes. There is a balance between children in the poorest households (three) and those in the least poor (three) and a good spread in between.[5] In Patna, all of the case study children were enrolled in school and the poorest children worked on family farms and in the household, mostly during school breaks. In Katur, two of the three girls had dropped out of school! (one because seasonal family migration to Mumbai disrupted her studies and the other because the high school was located outside the community). Boys there tended to combine work and school.

In 2008, a further exercise elicited 'children's understandings of poverty'. Twenty-one children participated in four gender-specific groups.[6] They were asked to think about the different families and socio-economic groups in their communities and to describe what makes them different from each other, how they relate to each other, and how (or if) families move from one category to another (that is, can they move out of poverty). The group discussion aimed to be general, focusing questions on community dynamics and not personal experiences, in part because of ethical concerns around poverty as a sensitive issue (see Chapter 2 by Virginia Morrow).[7] However, children sometimes recounted their personal experiences.

Children's views and experiences of poverty and inequality: the survey

In general, rural children placed a high value on formal schooling: they felt that it was 'essential' for their future lives (97 per cent, including *all* those in the poorest households). Most of them were still enrolled in school (88 per cent) and very few wanted to stop before reaching the tenth grade (1 per cent). However, seventy-eight of our rural sample had left school and the most common reason was because they had to work (28 per cent), either at home or for paid work outside the household. The second most common reason was truancy (21 per cent). Children also left school because their families could not afford school-related costs, because of ill-treatment from teachers, or because they had family problems. However, most children managed to combine school with their work obligations. Nearly one in five of them reported working for pay in the past year and most working children said that the job they did made them feel proud, even though a third of them felt they had little choice in the work they did.

When the analysis is disaggregated by children's gender, caste, and poverty levels, some notable patterns emerge (see Table 13.1). First, the differences by gender appear unremarkable on the selected variables, except in relation to aspirations for attending university (more boys than girls) and the slightly higher rates of school dropout by girls. However, it is clear that poverty and caste background are important factors shaping childhood inequalities. For example, children from the poorest households and from marginalized caste groups were more likely to drop out of school, to be working for pay, and to have missed school because of work. The poorest and most marginalized among working children were also more embarrassed and less proud of their jobs than were working children from richer households. They were more likely to describe their households as 'struggling to get by' or as 'poor'.

Common to children across these categories was the value of education. There have been many efforts to achieve universal primary education under the Government of India's flagship programme, *Sarva Shiksha Abhiyan* ('Education for All' in Hindi). Formal schooling is increasingly becoming a key feature of what is considered a 'good childhood' for boys and girls in Andhra Pradesh, and even the poorest families aspire to send their children to private, English-medium schools in the hope that this will be a pathway out of poverty.

Although the poorest children placed a high value on their formal education, they reported lower educational aspirations than did children in the richest homes. In Europe and the USA, some poor children learn to 'make do' with their limited resources and opportunities, and lower their expectations for the future (see Attree 2006; MacLeod 1987). Tracking these children's opinions on this issue will be of interest to the next Young Lives survey, when these children (the Older Cohort)

Table 13.1 Rural children's opinions on work, school, and poverty by wealth level, caste, and gender (%)

	Expenditure quintile		Caste/ethnicity				Gender		All
	Poorest	Richest	Scheduled caste	Scheduled tribe	Backward caste	Other caste	Male	Female	
Not enrolled in school	19	5	14	11	11	4	10	13	12
Worked for pay in past year	24	10	20	37	20	10	19	19	19
Missed school in last 4 years because of work	18	3	11	13	9	3	8	9	8
Embarrassed by the work have to do (agree/strongly agree)[a]	21	7	27	15	20	3	24	23	24
Job done makes child feel proud (agree/strongly agree)[a]	79	93	80	86	83	87	82	80	81
Believe school will be useful for future life ('essential')	100	97	94	96	98	99	99	96	97
Would like to go to university	52	81	65	74	62	67	73	56	64
Child describes household as 'struggles to get by'	57	30	59	50	38	21	41	46	43

[a] Questions asked of children who reported paid work.

Source: Round 2 Older Cohort Child Questionnaire.

will be aged 15–16, and this sort of information is crucial for policy intervention with this age group. We turn now to the results from the qualitative research.

Children's perspectives in qualitative research

Children listed the attributes that distinguished 'poor', 'middle-class', and 'rich' families in their communities (see Table 13.2). There were three broad bases of difference, relating first to material goods and services; second, to social relationships; and third, to childhood and families. The second of these includes issues of social inclusion and exclusion, and of the interdependence between poor people who have few resources and rich people who need labour.

Material goods and services

Children's descriptions characterized poverty as inadequate resources and constrained opportunities. Children's descriptions of material difference reflected a continuum of quantity, quality, and access across the three types of families. For example, children's descriptions of varied access to services suggested that wealthy families had more choices and greater access to quality services, whereas poor families had little choice. Middle-class families were 'worse than rich, better than poor', yet still found it difficult to lead a 'smooth life' (Patna). Wealthy families were not only characterized as being of good health: they were also able to use private multi-speciality hospitals if they fell ill. Middle-class families went either to private or government hospitals depending on the seriousness of the illness. Poor families were described as 'mostly ill', yet limited to government hospitals or traditional healers. They were both more vulnerable to ill health and least able to afford access to good-quality services, and often went into debt trying to cover costs. Material differences were therefore important to children because they reflected and reproduced entrenched relationships of interdependence between those who 'have a lot', 'have some', and 'have nothing', and children saw themselves as very much a part of these relationships and power structures.

Children, childhood, and families

In each of the study communities, certain castes or ethnic groups were associated with specific socio-economic categories (see Tables 13.3 and 13.4). In the tribal community in Patna, poverty was associated with the Savara tribe, who live in interior parts of the forest and on hilltops.

Table 13.2 Children's indicators of inequality: material goods and services

Rich	Middle class	Poor
Material possessions		
Big, neat, multi-storey houses	Own small, thatched or tiled, 'pukka' houses (p/k)	No house or live in huts or rented homes ('not neat'); some live in
Money (k)	Own less land than the rich / small gardens (p/k)	new drain pipes on building sites or at rail
Land and factories (varied land, inherited from ancestors) (p/k)	Less money & property than rich, but more than poor (p/k)	stations, bus stops, etc. (p/k)
Bullock cart and animals (k)	No assets (k: g); some livestock and a cart (k)	No money or assets (p/k)
Cars, tractors, scooters	Small cars (p)	No land (k); most sold their small lands for their urgent needs (p)
Good, fresh and adequate food (p/k)	Have grain and rice to eat but not always enough (k); variety of food not as good as rich, but better than poor (p)	Not enough food or clothes (p/k); young children may die from heat and hunger (p)
Good clothes and jewellery (k)	Good clothes (k)	Clothes are not good (k)
Home appliances, colour TV, mobile, etc. (p/k)	Only have black and white TV, one fan, bicycle (k)	
Cook on gas stove (k)	Cook on earthen or electric stove (k)	
Service access and quality		
Servants do all household work, care for children (p/k)	Children go to government schools (p/k); some may attend private schools (p)	No money to send their children to schools (p/k); go to government schools (p/k); use welfare hostels (p)
Children study in highly reputable schools and live in hostels with all facilities; some of them are living abroad (p); use private English-medium schools (k)	No servants so must do household work themselves (p)	
Children get extra tuition if they need it (p)	Depending on seriousness of illness, may go to government or private hospitals (p)	If no electricity, use kerosene, oil or street lamps (p)
When ill, use private multi-speciality hospitals (p)		Most are ill and use government hospitals or traditional healers (p)

Note: p = Patna, k = Katur.

Table 13.3 Children's indicators of inequality: social relationships and marginality

Rich	Middle-class	Poor
Status and inclusion/exclusion		
Well respected, recognized, have political contacts and influence people (p)	Cannot influence higher authorities and politicians (p)	Excess debt may drive them to suicide and to kill family (p)
Feared by others and people listen to what they say (p)	Deposit money in banks for their children's marriages and education (p); their children marry good people (k)	Many do undignified jobs like scavenging or domestic work, near landlords and in rich houses (p)
Treat others as 'cheap' (p) / treat other groups poorly and refer to them by caste (k) (examples: If poor or middle-class people are smoking and rich person comes along, smoker has to put out cigarette (k); they say, 'Veetikintha kovva?' ('How dare they? They have a lot of "flesh" [galli]') if poor or middle class do not obey them (k); they make servants use separate plates and glasses and don't allow them in the house (k)	Only buy clothes for important festivals (k)	Must save money to celebrate festivals (k)
Have money for celebrations and leisure (cinemas, picnics); visit big towns (p/k)		
Jobs and opportunities		
High-level jobs, good pay (in tribal site, ITDA job)* (p); don't do daily labour (k)	Few jobs, may work own land or work for others on wage basis or in small government jobs (p/k)	Ca nnot even get wage labour so often 'sleep without food' (p/k)
Can eat, buy, and do whatever they want, no matter what the cost (p)	Small-scale businesses (p); in vegetable business, tailoring, or woodworking (k); take care of own cattle (k)	Ad ults & children may not get work in some seasons (p)
Have business opportunities to earn money (p); lease their land and take half the yield so they don't go to the fields (k)		If no work, may turn to begging or migrate (p)

Deposit money in the bank and give loans to poor at high interest rates; may keep poor children as bonded labour (k)	May migrate to earn money (p) Get loans for children's education as have assets (p) No one helps them, except the government, a little, but not as much as government helps the rich (p)	Cannot get loans because lack assets (p)

Dependencies

Rich depend on poor for their labour; poor get financial help from rich (k)	Do not work under the Kammas but cultivate their own land (k)	They always depend on rich people (k); may be cheated by the rich (p)
Help release poor and middle class if jailed; lend tractors and carts (k)	Will not work as bonded labour at Kamma family (k) Poor and middle class help each other out, share bullock carts (k)	May sell body parts or organs to rich for low price to get food (p) Some kidnap children for ransom to cover basic needs (p)

*Integrated Tribal Development Agency. This agency was set up by the Government of India to promote the socioeconomic development of tribal communities through income-generating schemes, infrastructure development, and protection of tribal communities against exploitation. Provision of boarding hostels for boys and girls to attend school, scholarships, training for jobs, job placements, etc., are some of the special services available to tribal children.

Table 13.4   Children's indicators of inequality: families and childhood

Rich	Middle class	Poor
Families and childhood		
Small families (p)	Boya (k)	Savara people who live
Look very neat and smart, speak well and have good lifestyle (p/k)	Difficult to lead life smoothly; worse than rich, better than poor (p)	in interior parts of the forests and on hilltops (p); Scheduled Caste (k)
Children wear clean clothes, attend private English-medium school; may not study if financially secure; don't do household work (p/k)	Children attend government school (p/k); they do housework and work in fields (p); have less leisure time and work hard (p); parents cannot afford school costs (p); some families are educated, some illiterate (p)	Have many children (p); children work for wage labour and may drop out of school (p/k); go to government schools (p/k); stay at welfare hostels (p) Eldest child may care for younger siblings (p)
Arrogant and proud because of wealth; speak harshly (p/k)	Not healthy but not very ill (p)	They don't apply oil to their hair (k)
Alcoholism (p)	Alcoholism due to a lot of loans and natural disasters (p)	Bad habits and addictions (p); beat wives and may murder their women and children (p); household head always pre-occupied (k) They don't have money but they have more affection (g)

In Katur, people from the Scheduled Caste were associated with the poor category, and the Boya caste with the middle class (which included farmers). Children used the term *kammavallu* to refer to rich people (Kamma being the dominant caste).

There were other markers that distinguished groups of children and their families (see Table 13.4). More than the other two groups, children in poor households were characterized by vulnerability and were targets of ridicule by other children and abuse by adults. They confronted a variety of risks such as extreme hunger, family debt, exposure to heat, and domestic violence. One of the girls' focus groups said, 'Even when they [poor people] go to work in the fields, they are asked by the rich to sit separately and eat their food. They're ridiculed for not having anything.'

Children's accounts of differing childhoods indicated that shame and humiliation was a particular risk and concern for poor children. One of the boys in Katur described his own experience of fetching milk from a Kamma household; he said that before he was given the milk he was made to sweep and fetch water for them. In both communities, children were portrayed as some of the main perpetrators of the ridicule and exclusion of other children (see also Redmond 2009). Poor children faced 'ridicule from classmates because of their way of dressing and speaking', for not having books and for falling behind in their studies. In Patna, the tribal village, the boys said that poor children were treated differently – 'cheaply', and they 'kept aside' at functions and parties, suggesting self-exclusion to avoid stigma and shame.

Case studies exploring the material and social aspects of poverty and inequality

Generally, children did not represent themselves as 'victims' of poverty, nor did they represent themselves as wholly in control of their lives. They emphasized the importance of family, of 'belonging', of balancing their different obligations, and the constraints posed by material poverty.

The case studies of Ravi and Preethi explore these themes further. Fifteen-year-old Ravi is from Katur and his story illustrates the way children make decisions about their lives. Fourteen-year-old Preethi is from Patna and is living in a student hostel while she attends school. Her narrative illustrates how children's aspirations and expectations are shaped within the familial context and constrained by poverty. Both cases highlight the importance of family and friendship for children's well-being.

Ravi

Ravi's family belong to the Scheduled Caste and are classed as being in the fourth Young Lives 'expenditure quintile' (among the less poor in terms of expenditure). His parents, elder brother, and nephew live together; his two sisters recently moved out to their in-laws' houses. The family rents their house from an uncle because heavy rains destroyed their previous home. When Ravi was in the fourth grade, aged 10, his parents migrated for work and he was left in his grandmother's care. He often missed school and eventually dropped out.

Ravi worked as a farmhand, mostly weeding in the fields of the dominant high-caste families. At home he also worked: he swept, fetched water and firewood, and 'took care' of his parents when they returned. He explained, 'I took good care of my parents and protected my mother... If there were any debts I tried to clear them'. Ravi's father had taken a loan from a Kamma family, which he had been working off through bonded labour, but his worsening arthritis made it difficult to work. Ravi recalled the day his father's 'master' came to their home and shouted at his father for not repaying the loan. Ravi worried that 'everyone will laugh at me', and decided to take over from his father to clear the family debt.

Ravi described being mistreated by the Kamma family. For example, the 'master' beat him with a broomstick if he did not show up for work. He was made to stay at work even when the rains were bad. He explained:

> It was nauseating to pile up the garbage, the dung and the worms... It was filthy over there... I just could not work there... It was repulsive. I had to remain there... I wasn't allowed to come home. I was made to run all the errands... They kept on harassing me... They were telling me to do 'this and that'... even on the days of festivals I was made to herd cattle and I was made to work from dawn to dusk. They even wanted me to remain during nights at their place. I had to sleep there during nights...

But he felt he had little choice. When the Kamma family came to his house they said, 'Either pay or we will have him [Ravi] as a farmhand under us and he will serve us.'

After a short while, Ravi told his mother he could not bear the mistreatment and she agreed he could stop. But the family still owed 6,000 rupees, which Ravi planned to pay off by working elsewhere. At the age of 14, through his uncle, he got a job at a stone quarry in Anantapur (about 20 km away), earning 2,500 rupees each month. He set aside 500 rupees for himself, and gave the rest to his mother, who used it to pay back loans she had taken from the Self-Help Group.[8] He lived with his uncle and went home to celebrate a harvest festival and the festival of the local deity.

Ravi enjoyed his days at the quarry, especially since he befriended two boys of his age who worked with him. They played tops and marbles and played 'snakes' on one of the boys' mobile phones. At weekends they swam in the well together and went to the cinema. Ravi did not find the work very difficult, and he liked the way his uncle's wife cared for him, insisting, 'They took good care of me... They gave me all their love and affection... like my mother and my father.'

Ravi went home for a month and then left again, this time to learn masonry in Kadapa (about 420 km away), where his eldest sister lived. 'I used to mix sand and cement and hand it over... They used to tell me to do this and that. In that way I learnt the work by observing them.'

Although he earned 150 rupees per day,[9] he did not like Kadapa as much as he liked working at the quarry. He missed his friends. And instead of going to the cinema, he stayed home in the evenings to watch Chiranjeevi, his favourite film star, on DVD.

Earning money is important to Ravi and the way he sees his role within his family: he can buy new clothes on festival occasions and also support the education of his elder brother and nephew. He explained, 'When someone makes some money... they are really proud to show it off.'

He still worries about the stigma associated with his family debt and the possibility that when he returns home, villagers will point to him and say, 'He did not repay the loan, that's why he left the village.' There is also some regret about his dropping out of school. His mother noted how other children talked about Ravi rearing cattle, calling him 'shepherd' and 'poor boy'. When reflecting on his time as a bonded labourer, Ravi said, 'I always feel sad about it. I think about why I am like this, when all the others are going to school.' Nonetheless, he finds value in the skills he acquires through his work and believes that if he were at school he would not have the opportunities to see new places outside the village: work closed some choices, but opened up others (see Bissell 2009: 538 on Indonesian children). Ravi did not mention going back to school, but did say he would like to farm in his village. His mother hopes he can purchase at least two acres of land, which he could lease out to someone else and cover his basic needs. She said this would be good, otherwise 'forever they live on labour alone'.

Preethi

Preethi is the third of four children: her elder brother and sister still live at home with her parents, who are farmers. The family are in the second Young Lives 'expenditure quintile' (below average). At the time of the first qualitative research visit (2007), Preethi was studying at a school run by the ITDA (see note 8) and staying in the residential hostel 25 km from her home. She saw her family around once a month. Graduation to the eighth grade (in 2008) meant a change in schools and after passing the entrance exam to a new residential school 3 km from her home, she relocated there. Preethi described how at first she was very lonely and wanted to return home. Her mother did not visit her and Preethi did not return to her village, despite her hostel being located near her home. Her father came to the school a few times, drunk, which made her feel sad and want her mother even more. Eventually she became good friends with three girls at the hostel, which helped her settle. In the four months after changing schools, she only returned home once, at the death of her grandfather – for only one day for his funeral, to avoid falling too far behind in her classes.

Preethi's grandfather had cared for the family's cattle and he received a pension of 2,000–2,500 rupees per month. After his death, the responsibility for caring for the cattle fell to Preethi's mother and they lost his pension. When Preethi's mother announced she that she wanted to sell the cattle because she could not care for them, Preethi asked where they would get money to celebrate the festivals. Her mother recounted Preethi's complaints but explained that she was unable to visit her at the hostel because she was so busy with the cattle.

There were also heavy rains, bad crops, and a significant rise in food prices. Like all families in the village, Preethi's family have a white ration card (indicating they are 'below the poverty line') with which they are able to get kerosene and sugar. They also get other food at subsidized prices, but it has still been difficult. Preethi's mother described how she made food stretch, how the 'thick' sauces she used to cook are now thinned: 'It should be served for two meals, what we ate for one meal now we are eating for two.'

Preethi believes that their economic difficulties will have social repercussions and that they might not be able to celebrate festivals as they had done in the past. She described in detail her cousin's recent celebration to mark her 'maturity' (called *Pedda Manishi*, a rite of passage acknowledging the attainment of menarche). This involved an elaborate family party, which Preethi attended.

She had not yet reached 'maturity' and said for herself:

> It makes no difference whether such a thing [a big celebration] happens or not... I want it to be a simple affair...
>
> We haven't much money... if grandfather were alive it would have been different. When grandfather was alive he brought home five thousands or at times ten thousands. It would have been possible then with that money, in a grand way. My sister's ceremony was done in a big way...

She believes her parents want hers to be a small event and has lowered her expectations in recognition of her family's strained economy. It is nonetheless important for Preethi that she has a ceremony to mark her change of status: children's celebrations are important opportunities to strengthen family ties, as well as to mark individual change.

Discussion

A crucial theme emerging from children's views is the importance of their social relationships, their families, and their friendships for shaping their experiences of poverty. Strong social relationships may be especially important in situations of marked material deprivation, and should therefore be taken account of in children-centred policies and programmes. Ravi's network of family and friends protected him from some of the risks often associated with migration. Preethi's experience of moving to a new residential hostel was difficult because her mother was unable to visit her, and she attributed her finally settling to the friendships she made.

Children's experiences also often fall short of the dominant models of 'good' childhoods in their communities. While formal schooling was appreciated as an essential experience for young people in Ravi and Preethi's communities, the case studies show how the ideal of going to school may clash with children's obligations to their families: it may also clash with their preference or need to work or to get married, or with the poor quality of their schooling environments. The surveys pointed to some of the diverging trajectories among rural children in the study. Poverty and caste or tribal background accounted for many of these inequalities. The qualitative research showed how children perceived these inequalities and their place within them.

Children also demonstrated awareness of the intergenerational transfers of advantage and disadvantage, as they contextualized child poverty within household poverty and social background (for example, tribe or caste). We have illustrated the general phenomenon that poorer households lack insurance resources and are therefore more vulnerable to shocks such as job loss or illness (cf. Davis 2006: 32; Wood 2003: 455). In poorer Young Lives households, young and old shared the burdens of debt and poverty. Children, therefore, had responsibilities for managing economic hardship and for breaking the intergenerational transfer of poverty. Ravi is a clear example of this: his relationship to his family was based on interdependence and sharing of responsibilities (cf. Punch 2002). Expanding social protection programmes for marginalized families may buffer such shocks and provide children with more options for dealing with them.

In conclusion, young people offer a distinct vantage point from which to understand the effects of poverty in their communities. Their knowledge and experience should therefore be considered a valuable source of information for the design and evaluation of policies and programmes aimed at improving their lives and the life chances of children marginalized by poverty. This requires acknowledging the validity of children's knowledge, respecting their right to contribute views on matters affecting their lives, and ultimately taking what they say seriously.

Notes

1. The authors are grateful to the Young Lives children, families, and community members who make our research possible. Our thanks to the very able team of fieldworkers who assisted in data collection: Dr Kongara Hymavathi, M. Madhavilatha, Udaya Duggani, and V. Latha Krishna. Naureen Karachiwalla provided excellent research assistance. We benefited from several comments on the chapter, some of them anonymous.
2. 'Participatory' approaches have been used with adults in Andhra Pradesh to identify 'the poor' and to measure poverty (for example, The Andhra Pradesh Human Development Report 2007), but it is still unusual to involve children in these efforts.
3. 'Scheduled Tribes' and 'Scheduled Castes' are legal terms for population groupings in India. Scheduled Tribes consist of indigenous tribal groups and are outside the traditional caste system. Scheduled Castes are the lowest in the caste system and, like Scheduled Tribes, have been historically marginalized (Galab et al. 2008: 6). Legislation to protect these groups is in place, and there are special government schemes to promote opportunities for them. Nevertheless, they are mostly poor and disadvantaged. The 'upper castes' in our sample are primarily captured in the 'Other Castes' category.
4. The names of communities and children are pseudonyms to preserve their anonymity.
5. With the poorest households classified as quintile 1 and the least poor as 5, two children were in quintile 2, three in quintile 3, and one in quintile 4.
6. This included both Young Lives and non-Young Lives children, aiming at five or six participants per group.
7. One of the concerns was in relation to the sensitivities around asking 'poor children' about their experiences of poverty, especially in group settings in which children from differing socioeconomic backgrounds participated.
8. In this context, a Self-Help Group is a small group of people, often women, who come together to work on a common problem, such as livelihood generation, with a degree of self-sufficiency.
9. Note that a day's work through the Indian National Rural Employment Guarantee Scheme (NREGS) earned 80 rupees, recently increased to 100 rupees. The scheme was rolled out nationally in 2008 and guarantees up to 100 days unskilled manual labour for every adult available to work on that day.

References

Attree, Pamela (2006) 'The Social Costs of Child Poverty: A Systematic Review of the Qualitative Evidence', *Children and Society* 20: 54–66.

Beazley, H., S. Bessell, J. Ennew and R. Waterson (2009) 'The Right to be Properly Researched: Research with Children in a Messy, Real World', *Children's Geographies* 7.4: 365–78.

Ben-Arieh, A. (2005) 'Where are the Children? Children's Role in Measuring and Monitoring their Well-Being', *Social Indicators Research* 74: 573–96.

Bissell, S. (2009) 'Indonesian Children's Views and Experiences of Work and Poverty', *Social Policy and Society* 8.4: 527–40.

Boyden, J., C. Eyber, T. Feeny and C. Scott (2003) *Children and Poverty: Experiences and Perceptions from Belarus, Bolivia, India, Kenya and Sierra Leone*, Virginia: Christian Children's Fund.

Camfield, L. (2010) ' "Stew Without Bread or Bread Without Stew": Children's Understandings of Poverty in Ethiopia', *Children and Society* 24.4: 271–81.

CESS (2008) *Andhra Pradesh Human Development Report 2007*, Centre for Economic and Social Studies, Hyderabad, India: Government of Andhra Pradesh and Centre for Economic and Social Studies.

Davis, P. (2006) *Poverty in Time: Exploring Poverty Dynamics From Life History Interviews in Bangladesh*, CPRC Working Paper 69, Manchester: Chronic Poverty Research Centre.

Galab, S., P. Prudhvikar Reddy and R. Himaz (2008) 'Young Lives Round 2 Survey Report Initial Findings: Andhra Pradesh, India', http://www.younglives.org.uk/pdf/publication-section-pdfs/country-reports/YL_CR_Rnd2_India.pdf (accessed 23 July 2009).

Harper, C., R. Marcus and K. Moore (2003) 'Enduring Poverty and the Conditions of Childhood: Lifecourse and Intergenerational Poverty Transmissions', *World Development* 31.3: 535–54.

Jabeen, T. (2009) ' "But I've Never Been Asked!" Research with Children in Pakistan', *Children's Geographies* 7.4: 405–19.

MacLeod, J. (1987) *Ain't No Makin' It: Leveled Aspirations in a Low-Income Neighborhood*, Boulder CO: Westview Press.

Middleton, S. K. Ashworth and R. Walker (1994) *Family Fortunes: Pressures on Parents and Children in the 1990s*, London: Child Poverty Action Group.

Mukherji, A. (2008) *Trends in Andhra Pradesh with a Focus on Poverty*, Technical Note 7, Oxford: Young Lives.

Punch, S. (2002) 'Youth Transitions and Interdependent Adult–Child Relations in Rural Bolivia', *Journal of Rural Studies*, 18.2: 123–33.

Redmond, G. (2008) *Children's Perspectives on Economic Adversity: A Review of the Literature*, Innocenti Discussion Paper IDP 2008-01, Florence: UNICEF Innocenti Research Centre.

Redmond, G. (2009) 'Children as Actors: How Does the Child Perspectives Literature Treat Agency in the Context of Poverty?', *Social Policy and Society* 8.4: 541–50.

Ridge, T. (2002) *Childhood Poverty and Social Exclusion: From a Child's Perspective*, Bristol: The Policy Press.

Ridge, T. (2003) 'Listening to Children: Developing a Child-Centred Approach to Childhood Poverty in the UK', *Family Matters* 65: 4–9.

Ridge, T. (2007) 'Negotiating Childhood Poverty: Children's Subjective Experiences of Life on a Low Income' in H. Wintersberger, L. Alanen, T. Olk and J. Qvortrup (eds), *Childhood, Generational Order and the Welfare State: Exploring Children's Social and Economic Welfare*, Odense: University Press of Southern Denmark.

Robson, E., G. Porter, K. Hampshire and M. Bourdillon (2009) ' "Doing It Right?" Working with Young Researchers in Malawi to Investigate Children, Transport and Mobility', *Children's Geographies* 7.4: 467–80.

B. Tekola Gebru (2009) 'Looking Beyond Poverty: Poor Children's Perspectives and Experiences of Hazard, Coping, and Resilience in Addis Ababa', Unpublished Doctoral thesis, Department of Psychology, University of Bath.

Van der Hoek, T. (2005) *Through Children's Eyes: An Initial Study of Children's Personal Experiences and Coping Strategies Growing Up Poor in an Affluent Netherlands*, Innocenti Working Paper 2005-05, Florence: UNICEF Innocenti Research Centre.

Witter, S. (2002) *The Silent Majority: Child Poverty in Uganda*, London: Save the Children.

Wood, G. (2003) 'Staying Secure, Staying Poor: The "Faustian Bargain" ', *World Development* 31.3: 455–71.

Part IV

Learning, Time Use, and Life Transitions

The third central theme in Young Lives is 'Learning, Time Use, and Life Transitions'. Longitudinal research is able to reveal factors shaping children's cognitive and psycho-social development, and how they learn both in school and elsewhere; their experiences of school, work, and caring for others in their families; changing ways in which boys and girls spend their time as they grow up; and how all these relate to children's pathways from early childhood into adulthood. Much of this material will appear in later rounds of research and subsequent volumes of this series. Here, we consider some aspects of pre-schools, schools, and work.

Significant growth in formal education in the last 50 years has resulted in the vast majority of children receiving at least some schooling. Economic growth in developing countries has been accompanied by a massive increase in available education, and it is reasonable to assume that schooling can help break the poverty cycle by providing children of poor people with the knowledge necessary to earn higher incomes. This is supported by many studies showing correlations between years of schooling and higher income (for example, Psacharopoulos 1997).

There is, however, need for caution about such correlations on two principal grounds. First, they rarely take account of the quality of schools or children's ability (Glewwe 1996; Glewwe and Kremer 2006). Second, the potential of schooling to increase incomes also requires an appropriate economic environment that can provide employment for school leavers, particularly when increasing numbers attending school take away the competitive edge of schooling in the job market. Third, schooling is not homogeneous, nor of standardized quality. Equity issues are central, since children access (or are excluded from) 'quality education' according to their ethnicity, gender, individual and household circumstances, the accessibility of schooling, and parents' ability to cover the costs of schooling – especially in countries with a growing private sector. Longitudinal research is able to offer a more nuanced account of how poverty interacts with school trajectories to shape children's educational outcomes in terms of literacy and numeracy. Moreover, the UN Convention on Rights of the Child (CRC) does not confine education to numeracy and literacy, but demands that it be directed at the development of children to their fullest potential. Apart from the material advantages of earning power, education should provide skills and knowledge to enable people to have more control over their own lives, providing capabilities that are the converse of restrictive poverty. The question arises as to whether too heavy a focus on formal schooling might detract from learning important life skills outside the classroom.

Schooling is central to enabling most children to develop socially and economically. Moreover, school attendance, and to a lesser extent numeracy and literacy, are easier to measure in large-scale surveys, than are other aspects of learning. So these factors usually dominate consideration of educational systems. The qualitative research of Young Lives is able also to look at schooling in the contexts of children's lives and experience, as illustrated in the chapters by Woodhead (Chapter 14) and Orkin (Chapter 17) in this section. It examines different ways in which children and families relate to their schools, and how schooling affects them. Moreover, the qualitative work picks up ways in which children can learn social and life skills outside school. One of the narratives emerging from Young Lives research points to the danger that poor-quality schooling can remove from children opportunities for learning outside the classroom, giving them very little in return. That material will be seen in later volumes of this series, and here is hinted at in Chapter 16 about learning agricultural skills from work in South Africa.

We present four chapters: one on early childhood development, one on the problems of equity in Peru's schools, and two on relationships between school and work.

In Chapter 8, Patrice Engle shows that the years before primary school age are very influential in child development and that the disadvantages experienced by poor children need to be addressed at this stage. Other chapters point to the importance of nutrition in particular. In Part IV, Martin Woodhead (Chapter 14) uses both survey data and detailed case studies from three of the Young Lives country sites to examine the roles of early childhood care and education in children's development, pointing to the ways availability of government and private pre-school shapes children's opportunities and transitions to school. Provision of early learning opportunities is only a first step towards improving school outcomes for poor children. Differing quality of institutions and differing access to them threaten to increase inequalities within poor communities. Breaks in continuity between the home and the institutions, and between institutions as young children progress through them, can hinder progressive development of the child.

Santiago Cueto et al. (Chapter 15) consider Peru's attempts to cater for children whose first language is an indigenous one rather than Spanish, basing his analysis mainly on national survey data and school censuses. While they commend the country's policy of trying to incorporate and strengthen indigenous language skills in schools, children from areas where indigenous languages are dominant find themselves at a disadvantage in the school system, for both physical and socio-cultural reasons. They point to the need to attend to the quality of schools in rural areas, and the importance of attending to particularly disadvantaged children within these schools.

It is frequently assumed, especially in economic models, that work and schooling are in direct competition for children's time and effort. The chapters by Camfield (Chapter 12) and by Crivello et al. (Chapter 13) in the previous section show work to be a significant feature in children's lives in Young Lives research sites. Generally, it has been argued that work comprises an important component of child development in many contexts, and it is not necessarily incompatible with schooling (see Bourdillon et al. 2010: 88–132). The remaining chapters in this volume consider children's work.

Kate Orkin (Chapter 17) combines Young Lives qualitative research with data from its surveys to discuss the relationships between children's work and their schooling. Economic models rarely consider the characteristics of either work or school, but qualitative data from Ethiopia suggest that work and school are sometimes competitive and sometimes complementary, and that children can benefit from work experiences. Using this data from a site in which a large proportion of children attended school and also engaged in paid work, she discerned characteristics of work and school that made the two either complementary or competitive. She then used Young Lives survey data to suggest that at least some of these characteristics have wider application.

Andrew Dawes, Judith Streak, Susan Levine, and Deborah Ewing (Chapter 16) report on a survey on children's agricultural work in South Africa, which links into themes emerging from Young Lives research.

Although children's work is often driven by poverty, the most frequent reason for unpaid agricultural work on family farms is responsibility to the family. Poverty and responsibility are not exclusive reasons for working: several of the chapters in the previous section point to the importance of children's work to families, especially in response to shocks that affect their economic status. Another common reason for both paid and unpaid work is to learn agricultural skills, which may be more useful to the children in the future than the poor quality of schooling that is available to many of them. A common use of paid work is to earn for school expenses, in which case school and work complement each other even though they may compete for time.

References

Bourdillon, Michael, Deborah Levison, William Myers and Ben White (2010) *Rights and Wrongs of Children's Work,* New Brunswick NJ: Rutgers University Press.

Glewwe, Paul (1996) 'The Relevance of Standard Estimates of Rates of Return to Schooling for Education Policy: A Critical Assessment', *Journal of Development Economics* 51: 267–290.

Glewwe, Paul and Michael Kremer (2006) 'Schools, Teachers, and Education Outcomes in Developing Countries' in Eric A. Hanushek and Finis Welch (eds), *Handbook of the Economics of Education, Volume 2,* Amsterdam: Elsevier.

Psacharopoulos, George (1997) 'Child Labour Versus Educational Attainment: Some Evidence from Latin America', *Journal of Population Economics* 10.4: 377–86.

14
Pathways through Early Childhood Education in Ethiopia, India, and Peru: Rights, Equity, and Diversity[1]

Martin Woodhead

Introduction

This chapter summarizes research within Young Lives into early child-hood transitions,[2] looking at children's experiences within early child-hood and primary education in three of the four Young Lives study countries. Numerous lines of research have converged to produce a compelling case for prioritizing early childhood care and education (ECCE) services. Research demonstrates that the earliest years of a child's life are a crucial period of biological, neurological, psychological, social, and emotional growth and change; that poverty and other disadvantages can impact in numerous (and in some respects irreversible) ways on 'developmental potential' and that well-planned early interventions can have long-term positive outcomes for children. Economic analyses have shown that access to high-quality early childhood care and education is not only good for children's development, it is also an important pro-poor strategy capable of increasing equity. It can also be cost-effective, with some well-designed programmes calculating high rates of return from early 'investment in human capital'. Underlying all these persuasive lines of analysis is the principle on which all initiatives should be built – that young children have a right to development and to education in their best interests, without discrimination (summarized in Woodhead 2006; and Siraj-Blatchford and Woodhead 2009: see also Chapters 6, 8, and 9 in this volume).

Growing global recognition of the potential of programmes to improve and change young lives provides the backdrop for this chapter. This chapter is based on data from the Younger Cohort in Young

Lives, namely 6,000 children and their families in three of the Young
Lives countries: Ethiopia, India (Andhra Pradesh), and Peru, who were
around 5 to 6 years old and at the point of transition to primary school
when they were studied in 2006–07. In reviewing both quantitative and
qualitative data, the key policy question is how far promises about the
potential of early childhood programmes are currently being translated
into practice, in terms of accessible, equitable, quality ECCE, and successful school transitions.

Rights, equity, and diversity

The UN Convention on the Rights of the Child (UNCRC) is now a
significant starting point for policy development on behalf of the
world's young children. General Comment 7 (UNCRC 2005) confirms
that 'young children are holders of all the rights enshrined in the
Convention.... [and] that the Convention on the Rights of the Child
is to be applied holistically in early childhood, taking account of the
principle of the universality, indivisibility and interdependence of all
human rights' (Paragraph 3).

   Framing early childhood policy in terms of children's rights departs
radically from many formerly influential images of young children.
Children are no longer envisaged merely as the recipients of services,
beneficiaries of protective measures, nor subjects of social experiments.
Genuinely child-centred policies recognize each child's entitlement
to care, education, and comprehensive services; to quality of life – in
their best interests – as the underlying principle. Other justifications
build on this foundation, including the importance of promoting social
equity, respecting cultural diversity, and achieving economic benefits,
and they are underpinned by scientific evidence about the formative
significance of the early years, the consequences of early adversities,
and the long-term benefits of quality programmes.

Early Education For All?

The Dakar Framework for Action for Education For All (EFA) prioritized early childhood care and education as Goal 1: 'Expanding and
improving comprehensive early childhood care and education (ECCE),
especially for the most vulnerable and disadvantaged children' (World
Education Forum, Dakar, 26–28 April 2000).

   The case for quality ECCE, especially targeted towards disadvantaged groups, is indisputable. Many high-quality programmes have

been established throughout the world. Yet inability to access such pro-grammes adds to the multiple disadvantages of the poorest groups in many country contexts, especially in rural locations (UNESCO 2007). Globally, and within many regions and countries, current arrangements for ECCE are at risk of reinforcing rather than combating inequalities. Moreover, in some countries, inequities in early childhood are ampli-fied by inadequacies of primary education, perpetuating intergenera-tional poverty cycles.

Young Lives data confirm global evidence of rapid growth in early education opportunities in our four study countries. Children aged 5 to 6 were reported as having attended pre-school at some point since their third birthday by 94 per cent of caregivers in Vietnam, 87 per cent in Andhra Pradesh, and 84 per cent in Peru, with very little difference in overall participation rates for girls and boys. Pre-school is a minority experience in Ethiopia (just 25 per cent of the sample). Here, the gender imbalance favours boys, but only by 2 per cent.

In the rest of the chapter, I elaborate on some of the major challenges facing young children and their families in three of these countries. The chapter begins with Ethiopia, where primary education is still being consolidated and pre-school has to date been a minority urban experience, mainly offered by the private sector. Peru is very different, with a well-established government primary and pre-school system, but with concerns about quality and coordination between sectors. Andhra Pradesh offers the most complex set of challenges, with a long-estab-lished government system of ECCE, but an increasing trend towards use of private services, including among the poorest communities.

Early childhood in Ethiopia

Ethiopia was identified in the Education For All (EFA) Global Monitoring Report 2008 as one of the countries that has seen the most rapid progress towards the Dakar goals, notably universal enrolment and gender parity at the primary level (UNESCO 2007). For example, the net enrolment ratio in primary education increased from 33 to 68 per cent between 1999 and 2005, and gender equity has improved (38 per cent of boys versus 28 per cent of girls in 1999 to 71 per cent of boys versus 66 per cent of girls; UNESCO 2007: 291). Meanwhile, the role of government in providing pre-school services has until recently been minimal. To help fill the vacuum at pre-primary level, the government has passively encouraged the involvement of other partners, including the private sector.

Young Lives research confirms that opportunity to attend pre-school is almost entirely restricted to urban children. Nearly 58 per cent of children in urban communities had attended pre-school at some point since the age of 3. In contrast, less than 4 per cent of rural children had attended pre-school, and for many rural communities, even basic primary schooling remains elusive. Also, in those few cases where rural children did access pre-school, they did so later (aged on average around 55 months) than their urban counterparts (aged 48 months).

Figure 14.1 shows different types of pre-school attended by children in urban areas, with the sample equally divided into five poverty quintiles (where children in quintile 1 are from the poorest households, and quintile 5 are the least poor in the sample).[3] It confirms that private pre-schools are the main option for all groups, and that levels of access strongly favour the more advantaged groups.

The policy implication seems clear enough. If early education is to fulfil its promise, especially in offering educational equity to disadvantaged and vulnerable groups, then this will require major targeted

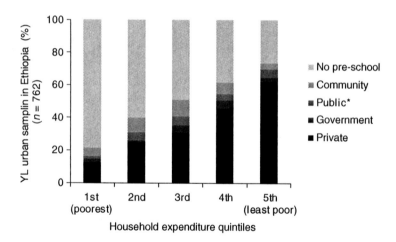

Figure 14.1 Attendance by pre-school type and poverty levels: urban sample in Ethiopia

Note: For Ethiopia, this analysis is given only for children in urban areas because the sample of rural children with pre-school experience was too small (*n* = 43).
* Public schools refer to schools that are funded partly by the government and partly by fees paid by students' families.

investment in quality programmes, and giving attention to disadvantaged communities in rural as well as in urban areas. At the same time, these policy challenges need to be set in the broader context of children's earliest learning experiences in Ethiopia.

Beniam: early transitions in rural Ethiopia

I illustrate these challenges through one of the rural communities selected by the Young Lives team for in-depth study, and the particular case of Beniam who was 6 years old when the research team visited his village in 2007. Like most young children, Beniam is already expected to take on a variety of responsibilities, both at home and in the fields. He takes care of his 1-year-old brother, fetches water, and cleans the house. In the morning, he helps his mother clean out the cattle dung and then during the daytime, he looks after the cattle in the field.

This has been Beniam's early education. There is no organized preschool programme available to his community, even if his parents could afford to send their children to it. But Beniam's parents do want their son to go to primary school. His father thinks schooling 'is useful for the child', especially in a context where agricultural work is not as promising as in the past. However, it is unlikely this father's educational aspirations for his son will work out in practice. Even when Beniam does get access to school, Young Lives' classroom observations draw attention to the very low levels of resources available for his education. For example, one fieldworker reports:

> The rooms are poorly built, and the floor is made of loose stones. Children were observed sitting either on the stones or long wooden benches made from whole tree trunks. Others sit on the floor and use their knee as a table for writing. Students share textbooks. Children complained that some teachers were repeatedly absent from schools. All these factors contributed a lot to drop out and absenteeism.

Additional obstacles to access to primary school included the costs involved, even where education is provided by the government. According to a primary school teacher, most of the households in Beniam's village are 'very poor' and find it difficult to cover the cost of school-related expenses, such as educational materials. There are also the 'opportunity costs' for households where income only marginally meets the family's basic needs, and children like Beniam are expected to play an active role in their family's economic activity, which they must combine with attending school. This is particularly

the case for boys. As one parent put it, a child is called a 'good shepherd when he is 8'.

Finally, even gaining admission to primary school can be a challenge
for poor children. Beniam's father expected him to start school in 2007,
but the teacher said he was too young to be admitted. Many children in
rural areas do not have a birth certificate, and without the required documentation, families are unable to prove their age. Even when Beniam
does start school, it is unlikely that formal large-group teaching methods will take any account of the many skills he brings to the classroom.
However, Beniam was not too concerned because he sees his future very
differently from his father. He wants to 'become a shepherd' and 'look
after the cattle'. Boys like Beniam have found a way of balancing work
and school: around 15 children organize the herding by turns. All children bring their animals to a specific location and then one of them
looks after them so the others can go to school.

The challenges facing children like Beniam draw attention to a major
policy dilemma about the priority given to expanding early education
in situations where the infrastructure and quality of primary education
are relatively weak and few resources are available. Put simply, expanding early childhood education in low-resource contexts may make
UNESCO EFA statistics look more impressive, but may also entail a risk
to children – of being required to spend even more time in low-quality
schooling. Besides being a violation of children's right to education, it is
a very inefficient way to build human capital through education. More
fundamental questions are also raised, about how narrow contemporary expressions of school education connect with children's broader
right to development, in ways that are meaningful now and sustainable into the future. On a more positive note, a major education quality improvement programme (GEQIP) is being implemented in primary
schools. The government of Ethiopia has recently developed an ambitious policy for ECCE, with four strands covering child health, parental
education, pre-school classes attached to primary schools, and a child-
to-child programme (Orkin et al. forthcoming).

Early childhood in Peru

Peru has experienced a rapid expansion of early childhood education,
building on near-universal provision of primary education, with a net
primary school enrolment ratio of 96 per cent in 2005 (UNESCO 2007,
Table 12). Already in 1972, early education became a high priority for
the government and pre-school was renamed 'Initial Education'. It is

estimated that gross enrolment rates in pre-school education in Peru more than doubled from 30 per cent in 1991 to 68 per cent in 2006 (www.uis.unesco.org). Early education provision in Peru has been mainly government-funded, with two major types of pre-schools: low-resource, community-based programmes known as PRONOEIs (Programas no Escolarizados de Educación Inicial, non-school programmes for initial education) and better-resourced professionally staffed programmes, known as CEIs (Centros de Educación Inicial, initial education centres). The most disadvantaged, especially rural children and those living in the outskirts of the cities, are more likely to access PRONOEIs while the CEIs are more often found in urban and more advantaged areas.

Overall levels of early childhood provision are high in Peru; indeed the percentage of the age group accessing pre-school is among the highest in the region. But official statistics disguise differences in access to, resources for, and character and quality of both public and private provision. Of greatest concern is that the 'most vulnerable and disadvantaged children' (prioritized by EFA Goal 1) are at risk of being excluded from quality pre-school education.

These concerns are reinforced by data from Young Lives when the 2,000 Younger Cohort children were aged around 5 to 6 and their parents were asked whether their child had attended pre-school at any point since their third birthday. Although overall participation rates were remarkably high (84 per cent), with only a small gender difference (85 per cent boys and 82 per cent girls), other inequalities were quite marked. Twenty-nine per cent of 6-year-old children from the poorest households had no experience of attending pre-school, whereas only 4 per cent of children from more advantaged households had not attended pre-school at some point since they were 3 years old.

As in most countries, pre-school services in Peru have evolved most rapidly in urban communities. More than 92 per cent of the urban Peru sample is reported to have attended pre-school at some point since age 3, compared to 78 per cent of rural children.[4] Figures 14.2 and 14.3 show substantial differences in pre-school attendance between the 'poorest' and 'least poor' in both urban and rural areas and confirm that rates of attendance at pre-school are linked to poverty.

Figure 14.3 also suggests that for rural children, inequalities relate to differential access to private sector pre-schools. These are only of marginal significance as a provider for the 'poorest', but they account for 30 per cent of the children in the 'least poor' households. Figure 14.2 shows that in urban settings, the picture is more complex. Participation rates in government-run pre-schools are highest among households in

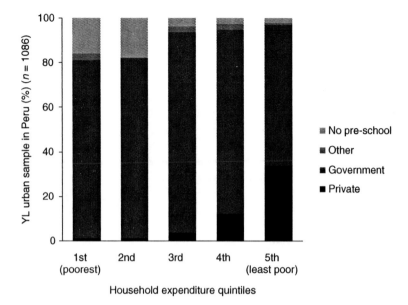

Figure 14.2 Attendance by pre-school type and poverty levels: urban sample in Peru

the mid-range. Children living in the 'poorest' households have less access to government pre-schools. At the other end of the scale, 'least poor' households also make less use of government pre-schools, but this is mainly because 34 per cent of children are attending a private pre-school.

Young Lives research shows overall participation rates are high, but nonetheless, it is the poorer households that have the lowest participation rates, even though these children might be expected to gain most from pre-school in terms of preparation for the transition to school. The differentials also relate to parental education levels. Virtually all children with highly educated mothers (with more than ten years of schooling) have attended pre-school, whereas over 30 per cent of children whose mothers have low levels of education (0 to 4 years) will have begun first grade without any experience of a pre-school programme, which risks perpetuating intergenerational poverty and inequalities.

Ensuring equity of access is not the only or even the major challenge for early education in Peru. The major emphasis of Young Lives qualitative research has been on the relationship between early childhood

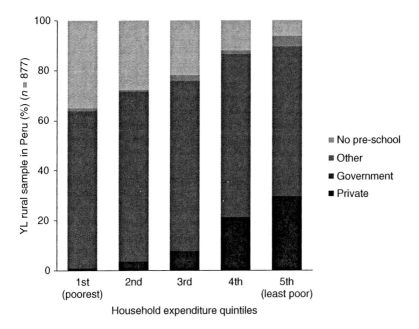

Figure 14.3   Attendance by pre-school type and poverty levels: rural sample in Peru

education and primary education. Peru, in common with many countries, shows a marked organizational, professional, and pedagogic divide between early childhood education and primary education. This translates into issues of continuity and discontinuity for children (Woodhead and Moss 2007) and shifts the question from 'are children ready for schools?' to 'are schools ready for children?' (Arnold et al. 2007). See Ames et al. (2009, 2010) for details.

Lupe: Early transitions in urban Peru

A brief case study of 6-year-old Lupe illustrates these issues. She lives in a well-established shanty town in Lima. This district is not among the poorest in the city, and basic services such as water and electricity, schools, hospitals, and public transportation are available for most people. However, families in this area experience other difficulties, such as living in overcrowded households, high unemployment, and high levels of criminality and insecurity. Lupe lives with her parents, grandparents, and two siblings. She was enrolled in a government-run pre-school from the age of 3 and is now in primary school.

Lupe's case illustrates the many different experiences and feelings that parents and children go through while children make their transition into primary school. This transition is not a straightforward process: it involves active adaptation by both parents and children. For example, while in pre-school, Lupe was surrounded only by children of her own age, because the two buildings were independent (although located within the same compound). Now that she is in first grade, her parents are concerned about her spending time alone with older children during break time and in the toilets, and with boys in particular. Another issue is the suitability of the playground for young children as this is used by other children in the school. The following quote from Lupe's mother illustrates the fears that some parents experience when their children change schools:

> It's like she's on her own, not like in pre-school, it's completely different... In pre-school they also take care of her, they looked after her. Here [in primary school] they don't, here the teacher stays in the classroom, she looks at them for a while but when all the children are together in the playground, then she [Lupe] could tumble and fall, she might be pushed and hit...

The differences between pre-school and primary school are not related only to the physical environment, but also to the teaching philosophy and practice in the classroom. Lupe associated the beginning of primary school with the 'end of holidays', buying new school-related materials and having a 'bigger school bag', which may symbolize the fact that she has more things to do now, more rules to follow, and more responsibilities to fulfil.

Among parents and teachers, there is also an idea of primary school as a more rigorous place where children should learn 'to behave properly', 'work independently', 'to follow instructions', and 'to respect others'. This seems to be associated with tougher discipline. According to one of the teachers, children who are about to join first grade often say to her, 'Miss, next year we're going to have a mean teacher who is going to hit us with a ruler,' or, 'We're going to school... there they're going to pull our ears.'

All this points to the need for better coordination between pre-school and primary school systems. Teachers from this community also agreed that a better link between them would help children and their caregivers in their transitions. At present, when children go to first grade they only bring their pre-school enrolment form. There is no exchange of information about children's adaptation process, learning skills, or anything like this. Everything starts from scratch.

In short, ECCE in Peru appears to be facing the same challenges that have been confronted by school systems throughout the world, in coordinating pre-school and primary sectors. There is little evidence from these data of a 'strong and equal partnership' between sectors planned with the child's interests as the primary focus (OECD 2001, 2006). Indeed, the research team's conclusion is that 'the main burden of adaptation (to school) rests on children, who show a positive attitude and abilities to cope with it. However, this is not necessarily easy for them and causes some stress' (Ames et al. 2009).

Early childhood in Andhra Pradesh (India)

In India, it was expected that the goal of universal primary education would be achieved by 1960 for all children up to the age of 14. Fifty years later, this final goal remains elusive (net enrolment ratio 89 per cent in 2005; UNESCO 2007), although there was a 5 per cent increase in enrolments in primary schools between 1999 and 2005 (which amounts to 35 million extra enrolments; UNESCO 2007). With each new generation achieving higher levels of school participation, and in the context of rapid growth in the Indian economy, parents increasingly recognize the potential of education to alter their children's fortunes and they actively seek early admission to pre-school and primary school.

Although government schools are still the major provision at primary level, India, including Andhra Pradesh, has witnessed rapid growth in private schools, and this growth is largely at the expense of government school enrolment, rather than contributing to increases in overall enrolment. Thirty-seven per cent of children enrolled in primary education attended a private school in 2006–07 according to state government records (www.ssa.ap.nic.in). One of the major attractions of the private sector is that English is often offered as the medium of instruction. This is especially true for high schools, but the pattern percolates down through the primary sector. Indeed, 44 per cent of Young Lives Younger Cohort children were reported to be attending a private school at the age of 8, compared with fewer than 25 per cent of the Older Cohort when they were 8 years old, only six years previously. These trends are in turn impacting on early childhood education, with high parental demand for English-medium kindergartens within private schools.

The growth of private pre-schools is taking place in the context of a long-established government early childhood care system, based on *anganwadi* centres (literally 'courtyard shelter' in Hindi), under the umbrella of Integrated Child Development Services (ICDS). The world's largest national early childhood programme, in terms of children enrolled, ICDS aimed 'to provide adequate services to children, both before and after birth and through the period of growth to ensure their full physical, mental and social development ... so that within a reasonable time all children in the country enjoy optimum conditions for their balanced growth' (National Policy for Children 1974, cited in CIRCUS 2006).

The original vision for ICDS was as a comprehensive early childhood intervention including immunization, growth monitoring, health and referral services, as well as pre-school education. But ICDS depends largely on individual states for implementation through the establishment of a network of *anganwadi* (pre-school) centres in both urban and rural areas. The quality of provision has depended on the skills and commitment of the individual *'anganwadi* worker' who, along with the designated *'anganwadi* helper', is responsible for most aspects of management, enrolment of children, and the daily programme. *Anganwadi* workers are mostly married women from within the community. Most have completed basic secondary education (up to Class 10) and have received some training for working with young children. By contrast, more than 50 per cent of *anganwadi* helpers are either uneducated or received only basic primary schooling (up to Class 4 only) (CIRCUS 2006).

Figures 14.4 and 14.5 highlight striking rural–urban differences within the Young Lives sample, notably in the take-up of government (mainly ICDS) versus private provision. In rural communities, ICDS *anganwadis* dominate and are used by the poorest households. It is only for more advantaged groups that private pre-schools are a significant option, accounting for 31 per cent of the children in the 'least poor' rural group. In urban Andhra Pradesh, by contrast, private pre-schools are the main option chosen by parents. Poverty levels are strongly predictive of whether children attend private pre-school education, but a surprising 34 per cent of the poorest households opt for a private pre-school, compared to 46 per cent attending government pre-schools.

Selective enrolment in private kindergartens is also linked to gender differentiation, with girls more likely to be educated within the government sector and expected to leave school earlier than their brothers. Evidence for these different trajectories comes from the Young Lives Older Cohort (12 years old in 2006/07), with 10 per cent more boys than girls enrolled in private schools, and 68 per cent of boys anticipating

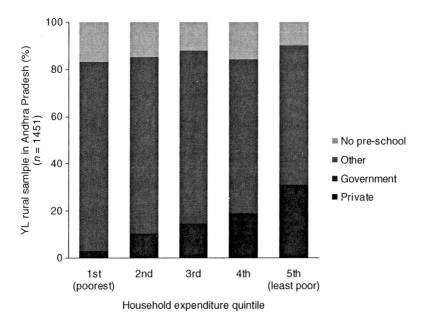

Figure 14.4 Attendance by pre-school type and poverty levels: rural sample in Andhra Pradesh

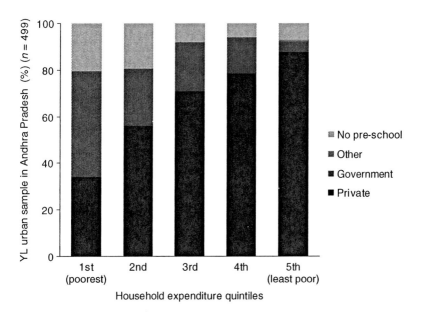

Figure 14.5 Attendance by pre-school type and poverty levels: urban sample in Andhra Pradesh

university education compared to 54 per cent of girls (and only 42 per cent of girls' caregivers).

One of the major influences on parents' choice of early education in Andhra Pradesh is, as mentioned above, that most private schools advertise themselves as offering English as the medium of instruction from kindergarten level, tantalizing parents with the prospect of getting their children on track towards participation in the new global labour market. By contrast, the language of instruction in government primary schools is traditionally Telugu, although that policy has been under review and recent reforms encourage increased English-medium instruction within the government school system. The Right to Education Act (2009) also requires that 25 per cent of places in private schools be reserved for disadvantaged children, with the fees being reimbursed by government (Government of India 2009; see Streuli et al. 2011).

The strong trend towards private schooling as the preferred option even during the pre-school years is confirmed by 123 cases in the Young Lives sample where caregivers reported that their children had attended more than one pre-school since the age of 3. In 82 per cent of these cases, the caregiver reported the child had been moved from a government *anganwadi* pre-school to a private kindergarten class.

These statistics, drawn from the Young Lives 2007 survey, suggest that young children in Andhra Pradesh experience very early differentiation in their transition experiences and educational opportunities, which are strongly shaped by where they live (urban versus rural), by household poverty levels, by levels of maternal education and by access to government versus private educational provision.

To illustrate this, I will offer (as for Ethiopia and Peru) one case study drawn from Young Lives qualitative research based around a sub-sample of 25 young children from four (out of the 20) Young Lives sites (see Vennam et al. 2009).

Revanth: Early transitions in Andhra Pradesh

Revanth is growing up in the Mahaboobnagar district, in a village with a population of around 2000, a majority of whom speak the official state language of Telugu. This is a drought-prone district on an inland plain, where poor people in the community face food shortages during the months of June to August. The community has two *anganwadis* and a government primary school, which most children attend. No private schools are available in Revanth's village, but several parents have chosen to send their children to a private English-medium school about 30 km from the village. Revanth is one of these new recruits to the private system.

Revanth used to attend one of the *anganwadis* in the village but his parents were very disappointed with the poor quality:

> ...She [the *anganwadi* worker] doesn't know anything. She doesn't know which children are registered in the *anganwadi* and which are not. ...She comes to *anganwadi*, stays for some time with the children who turn up on that day, and then leaves. Sometimes she doesn't come. Only *ayah* [the helper] manages...They don't even look after the children. If she comes that's it, they sit...and both of them talk with each other.

Initially, Revanth transferred to the village primary school, but by then his parents already had a more ambitious plan to enrol him in a private school as soon as possible:

> [The village primary school] is not at all good. In our village the teachers are not good. We just send them so that they get used to the routine of going to school...If he goes [to private school] and studies further he will become very wise – that is why we are sending him there...

Revanth is now attending a private, English-medium school which has a hostel, serving children in the surrounding 15–20 villages. The hostel is located on the school premises and therefore children are not required to travel long distances each day to access a private English-medium school. There is a small playground with limited equipment, but better than the one in the government school in the village.

Revanth proudly talks in English about what he has learned:

> *Interviewer*: What do they teach you?
> *Revanth*: A,B,C,Ds
> Uh...E, F, G,...H, I, J, K, L, M, N, O, P [taking a deep breath] Q, R, S, T, U, V, W, X, Y, Z.
> *Interviewer*: And, what else do they teach you?
> *Revanth*: A, P, P, L, E [he goes on to recite short poems, and numbers up to a hundred].

Although Revanth's family are among the 'less poor' groups in the Young Lives sample, paying for even low-cost private schooling is a very significant expense. However, it is one they are willing to bear as an investment in their son's future:

> We are ready to spend; we want him to study well, that is why we sent him there... There is no one [to help with payments]. Our parents don't give... we don't ask anyone. We take as debts... He should not do agriculture, that is why we are spending so much on his education. That means we will make him study, come what may!

The costs of the private school for Revanth's parents are Rs. 9,000 a year (approximately US$175). This includes the fees towards education, the hostel, and food. Other costs relate to the textbooks which cost about Rs. 400–500 a year (approximately US$8–9), plus notebooks, pens, pencils, slates, and slate pencils as and when required. These have to be replaced whenever any are lost, as private school teachers insist on children having these materials. Children in government schools manage with a slate and a notebook. Moreover, the textbooks are provided free of charge in government schools for Scheduled Castes, Scheduled Tribes, and Backward Classes. Further costs include about Rs. 500 per year towards uniform (approximately US$9).

However, these investments are not spread evenly within the household. There are hard choices to be made, which for this family are made along traditional gender lines:

> Two of my girls attend (government) school in the village... We are not buying for them; they are here only [at the village school]... when he is old enough, we will also send our younger son to the [private] school.

Following the original interview with Revanth's parents in 2007, the fee at this private school was increased to Rs. 12,500 per year owing to inflation (that is, from approximately US$175 to US$240). Some parents have therefore shifted their children to another school and hostel where the fee is Rs. 8,500 per year (approximately US$160). The rising costs of schooling is a major factor that risks disrupting educational pathways for boys like Revanth, even though he is on a more privileged trajectory than his sisters.

Realistic promises for early childhood?

These brief portraits of early childhood in three contrasting country contexts draw attention to the numerous challenges of implementing the Dakar Education For All (EFA) Goals for early childhood and primary education. Ethiopia, Peru, and Andhra Pradesh represent very different economic, political, and cultural contexts, with quite different educational traditions and progress towards EFA goals. In Ethiopia, universal primary education is still being consolidated, pre-schools are few, and for some rural children, there may still be doubts among parents about following the schooling option at all. In Peru, government pre-schools and schools are well established, and parents are most concerned about the lack of coordination and continuity in children's transitions. Andhra Pradesh has a well-established but under-resourced government ICDS system, but parents are increasingly turning towards private alternatives, especially for boys. All three countries are faced with issues of equity, related to gender and ethnicity, but especially related to poverty, with the most disadvantaged least likely to have access to quality early education and primary education.

The findings reported in this chapter are mainly based on household surveys and qualitative research around the time when most Young Lives Younger Cohort children were making the transition from pre-school to primary school. We did not make an independent assessment of the quality of the pre-schools attended by the children. Nonetheless, qualitative sub-studies draw attention to the huge variation in buildings, resources, care, and teaching at pre-school. The poorest pre-schools are very poor indeed, by any standards (Woodhead et al. 2009).

Some indication of quality is available from caregivers' answers to the question, 'In your opinion, how good is the quality of the care and teaching at this pre-school?' In both Peru and Andhra Pradesh, a higher percentage of caregivers using private schools judged them to be 'good' or 'excellent' than did caregivers judging their children's public pre-schools. These judgements are very likely shaped by users of private education wishing to believe that they are getting quality for their financial investment in their children's schooling. However, one highly significant finding for Andhra Pradesh is that differences in quality judgements between public and private pre-school users is greatest among the poorest quintile, with less than 50 per cent judging the public *anganwadi* their child attends to be good or excellent, compared with over 90 per cent of private kindergarten users. This finding is also consistent with national reports into the shortcomings of *anganwadis* (CIRCUS 2006).

These findings point to the emergence of new inequalities *within* poor groups, between those with and those without personal and economic resources and opportunities sufficient to make educational choices for their children that they calculate will result in improved outcomes and long-term social mobility. A likely consequence seems to be increased differentiation in children's trajectories within households (along gender lines) and within communities (along caste and poverty lines), with inevitable risk of increased long-term inequality. If EFA goals are to be realized – *for all* – then improving equity of access and quality of public pre-schools and primary schools becomes a high policy priority.

Several general conclusions are offered from Young Lives research.

Ensuring quality in early education. Early childhood programmes are playing a major (and increasing) role in young children's lives, even in countries where primary education systems are still being consolidated. But early education services are often of very variable quality, as are the school classrooms to which children progress. Identifying cost-effective and sustainable ways to improve quality in early childhood and primary classes is a high priority.

Better coordinated pre-school and school systems. Even in countries with well-developed early education services, transition experiences into first grade are frequently stressful for children and parents because of a lack of communication and coordination between two sectors that have different management structures, organization and financing, professional training, curricula, and pedagogy. Ensuring effective coordination of transitions between pre-school and primary classes has been a major ECCE theme among the world's richest countries over many decades. Addressing these issues is now a global challenge.

Focusing on the most vulnerable and disadvantaged children. Current arrangements for early childhood care and education appear in many cases to run counter to the requirements for implementing the rights of every child, and are equally incompatible with achieving social equity. While some government services in the countries studied are explicitly intended to be pro-poor, all too often they do not function effectively to achieve that goal in practice. At the same time, the impact of a growing private sector is to reinforce rather than reduce inequalities of access to quality education. In order to reverse these trends, governments along with international donors and other agencies have a central role to play.

More effective governance, including governance of the private sector. The three countries offer contrasting experiences of the impact of the private sector. In urban Ethiopia, private pre-schools have to some extent filled an ECCE vacuum. Both Peru and Andhra Pradesh have well-established government systems, but there is also a significant private pre-school and primary sector. The situation in urban Andhra Pradesh is extreme, with largely unregulated private providers dominating and displacing traditional *anganwadis* as the pre-school of choice for parents. While some individual children may benefit, quality is highly variable, and inequities at risk of being amplified.

Addressing equality at micro as well as macro level. Efforts to improve equity understandably focus on relative household poverty, urban or rural location, and so on. It is important to recognize the ways that early education opportunities combine with parental choices to reinforce inequities within as well as between households, notably where families make choices about which child to educate privately, which to send to a government school, which to withdraw early, and so on. Unregulated ECCE can amplify rather than reduce these inequalities. The poorest families are at an inevitable disadvantage compared to better-off parents and forced to make hard choices among household members. These disadvantages are often compounded by differences in quality between poor schools and rich schools, especially in the private sector.

Notes

1. The early transitions stream within Young Lives has been supported by the Bernard van Leer Foundation, which funds and shares knowledge about work in early childhood development and child rights (www.bernardvan-leer.org). Many Young Lives colleagues contributed to the research reported in this paper, especially Yisak Tafere and Workneh Abebe (Ethiopia); Uma Vennam and Anuradha Komanduri (Andhra Pradesh, India); Patricia Ames and Vanessa Rojas (Peru); and Gina Crivello, Laura Camfield, Natalia Streuli, Lita Cameron and Karin Heissler (Oxford).
2. Young Lives early transitions research is reported in greater detail in Woodhead et al. (2009); Ames et al. (2009, 2010); Murray (2010); Orkin et al. (forthcoming); Streuli et al. (2011); Vennam et al. (2009); Vogler et al. (2008).
3. Household expenditure is the most appropriate poverty indicator, based on data from the Young Lives survey of individual households and calculated as the sum of the estimated value (approximated to the past 30 days) of food (bought + home grown + gifts/transfers) and non-food (excluding durables such as furniture, gold jewellery, and one-off expenditure). This monthly figure is then divided by household size.
4. Young Lives followed the same definition as that outlined by the Peruvian National Statistics Office (INEI), which defines a rural community as one that has less than 100 dwellings and is not the capital of a district.

References

Ames, P., V. Rojas and T. Portugal (2009) *Starting School: Who is Prepared? Young Lives' Research on Children's Transition to First Grade in Peru*, Working Paper 47, Oxford: Young Lives.

Ames, P., V. Rojas and T. Portugal (2010) *Continuity and Respect for Diversity: Strengthening Early Transitions in Peru*, Working Paper 56, The Hague: Bernard van Leer Foundation.

Arnold, C., K. Bartlett, S. Gowani and R. Merali (2007) *Is Everybody Ready? Readiness, Transition and Continuity: Reflections and Moving Forward*, Working Paper 41, The Hague: Bernard van Leer Foundation.

CIRCUS (2006) *Focus on Children under Six*, New Delhi: Citizen's Initiative for the Rights of Children under Six.

Government of India (2009) 'The Right of Children to Free and Compulsory Education Act, 2009', New Delhi: Ministry of Human Resource Development.

Murray, H. (2010) *Early Childhood Care and Education as a Strategy for Poverty Reduction: Evidence from Young Lives*, Policy Brief 9, Oxford: Young Lives.

OECD (2001) *Starting Strong: Early Childhood Education and Care*, Paris: Organisation for Economic Cooperation and Development.

OECD (2006) *Starting Strong II: Early Childhood Education and Care*, Paris: Organisation for Economic Cooperation and Development.

Orkin, K., W. Abebe et al. (forthcoming) *Delivering Quality Early Learning in Low-resource Settings: Progress and Challenges in Ethiopia*, Working Paper, The Hague: Bernard van Leer Foundation.

Siraj-Blatchford, I. and M. Woodhead (2009) *Effective Early Childhood Programmes*, Early Childhood in Focus 4, Milton Keynes: Open University.

Streuli, N, U. Vennam and M. Woodhead (2011) *Increasing Choice or Inequality? Pathways through Early Education in Andhra Pradesh, India*, Working Paper 58, The Hague: Bernard van Leer Foundation.

UN Committee on the Rights of the Child (2005) 'General Comment No. 7: Implementing Child Rights in Early Childhood', CRC/C/GC/7/Rev.1., Geneva: Office of the High Commissioner for Human Rights.

UNESCO (2007) *Education For All by 2015: Will We Make It? Global Monitoring Report 2008*, Paris: UNESCO.

Vennam, U., A. Komanduri, E. Cooper, G. Crivello and M. Woodhead (2009) *Early Childhood Education Trajectories and Transitions: A Study of the Experiences and Perspectives of Parents and Children in Andhra Pradesh, India*, Working Paper 52, Oxford: Young Lives.

Vogler, P., G. Crivello and M. Woodhead (2008) *Early Childhood Transitions Research: A Review of Concepts, Theory, and Practice*, Working Paper 48, The Hague: Bernard van Leer Foundation.

Woodhead, M. (2006) 'Changing Perspectives on Early Childhood: Theory, Research and Policy', *International Journal of Equity and Innovation in Early Childhood* 4.2: 5–48.

Woodhead, M. and P. Moss (2007) *Early Childhood and Primary Education*, Early Childhood in Focus 2, Milton Keynes: Open University.

Woodhead, M., P. Ames, U. Vennam, W. Abebe and N. Streuli (2009) *Equity and Quality? Challenges for Early Childhood and Primary Education in Ethiopia, India and Peru*, Working Paper 55, The Hague: Bernard van Leer Foundation.

15
Explaining and Overcoming Marginalization in Education: Ethnic and Language Minorities in Peru[1]

Santiago Cueto, Gabriela Guerrero, Juan León, Elisa Seguin, and Ismael Muñoz

Introduction

In the past few decades, education in Peru has shown increased enrolment, especially in primary schools, but low achievement as measured by national and international standard tests in reading comprehension and mathematics. However, averages hide wide disparities in educational outcomes, which are often influenced by individual and family characteristics. Among these, coming from a family that speaks an indigenous language has been shown to be a significant predictor of low educational outcomes as compared to coming from a Spanish-speaking family (Cueto 2007: 425–6).[2] In this chapter, we present and discuss evidence of this trend in Peru, suggesting policies to overcome existing inequalities.

Characteristics of indigenous and Spanish-speaking populations in Peru

In Peru, while the number of people with an indigenous mother tongue has increased in the past 20 years, its percentage among the national population has decreased.[3] There are over 40 indigenous languages spoken in Peru, most by people living in the jungle and with a relatively small number of speakers (Zúñiga 2008: 16–17). Quechua is the most common indigenous language and is spoken widely in the Andes. Aymara is the second most common, spoken mostly in the southern part of the

261

Peruvian Andes.[4] In the 2007 census, around 15.6 per cent of Peruvians reported having an indigenous language as their mother tongue, while 84.1 per cent reported Spanish to be their mother tongue.

According to the Peruvian Constitution[5] (Article 48, issued in 1993), Spanish is the official language of the country but indigenous languages are also official in the places where they are 'predominant' (no operational definition for this term is provided).[6] The language used by the president to address the country, by most newspapers and TV stations, in official documents, and in political forums such as Congress is almost always Spanish. It has become increasingly unlikely to find a school-age person who speaks no Spanish at all (this would be more likely in older adults or infants in relatively isolated rural areas). Spanish is clearly the dominant language in a country that still has a significant occurrence of indigenous languages.

In the remainder of this chapter, we merge all speakers with an indigenous mother tongue (that is, reported as having an indigenous language as the first one learned at home) into a single 'indigenous' group. Although there could be some significant differences in the characteristics of children from different indigenous groups, the databases available are not usually able to capture a representative sample of each group.

Table 15.1 uses the National Household Survey (ENAHO) dataset to show the distributions of indigenous-language and Spanish speakers by region and area of residence (urban or rural). The highest proportion of indigenous households is located in rural areas, especially in the Andes, although many live in urban areas (as a result of migration). As in many developing countries, rural areas are poorly connected to capitals of districts and provinces because of lack of roads or poor road conditions. Rural areas tend also to lack not only electricity, running water, and a

Table 15.1   Distribution of households by region and area of residence

	Coast		Andes		Jungle	
	Urban	**Rural**	**Urban**	**Rural**	**Urban**	**Rural**
Indigenous	426,862	39,719	379,498	935,026	30,202	118,416
	6.2%	0.6%	5.5%	13.5%	0.4%	1.7%
Spanish	2,804,032	321,226	527,676	635,710	363,521	325,275
	40.6%	4.7%	7.6%	9.2%	5.3%	4.7%

Source: Based on ENAHO survey (2007).

public sewage system (see Table 15.3), but also public services such as hospitals, secondary schools, and universities.

This information is consistent with other studies. Trivelli (2000) has shown that over time the population in rural areas had higher indices of poverty than their urban counterparts, and so indigenous-language speakers are more likely to be poor than their Spanish-speaking counterparts. While the percentages of poor and extremely poor decreased between 1997 and 2007, the gap favouring Spanish speakers is still wide (see Table 15.2). In a later study, Trivelli (2005: 83) found that indigenous-language populations were 11 per cent more likely to be poor than their Spanish-speaking counterparts, and this was especially the case in rural areas and for older women. The econometric analysis of Escobal and Ponce (2007) suggested that there were direct and indirect social exclusion mechanisms operating in Peru for indigenous populations, especially when they lived in areas with a high concentration of indigenous-language speakers: these mechanisms limited economic opportunities, including access to public services and the job market.

Here, and for the purposes of considering educational opportunities in the next section, we classified schools into four types. First are schools managed under private administration (with mostly urban, Spanish-speaking students). Schools managed under public administration are differentiated into urban (with mostly Spanish-speaking

Table 15.2   Households by mother tongue and level of poverty (%)

	1997	2007
Indigenous		
Extremely poor	28.8	22.5
Poor	32.5	29.6
Not poor	38.7	47.9
Spanish		
Extremely poor	8.4	6.2
Poor	27.2	19.2
Not poor	64.4	74.6

Note: Although ENNIV and ENAHO are nationally representative surveys, they have different sample designs and different methodologies for the collection of information on consumption, and so are not strictly comparable. Nevertheless, we present poverty estimates from both sources as a reference for the relative standings of each group in given years.

Source: Data from ENNIV (1997) and ENAHO (2007).

students) and rural.[7] Rural schools are further divided into indigenous and Spanish; here indigenous rural schools are defined as those where more than 50 per cent of the students speak an indigenous language. This classification covers all schools in Peru and is based on the school census.[8]

School resources, enrolment and outcomes for indigenous and Spanish-speaking students

School resources

Information on school resources indicates the educational opportunities of children from different groups. Policies favouring equality would require that children from poorer backgrounds (including indigenous children) receive public resources similar to or greater than their richer (usually Spanish-speaking) peers. While it would be difficult to establish a direct causal link between any of the resources and specific educational results from cross-sectional data, we have chosen a few resources that have face validity as desirable characteristics of a school. Table 15.3 shows the results for some resources in the four types of schools, as defined above.

As shown above, libraries and computer laboratories are far more likely to be present in urban than in rural schools, with the language spoken by students making little difference.[9] Private schools are less likely to report having a court or field than urban public schools; many of them operate in a locale that was not designed as a school but has been adapted (such as a large house). In terms of public services, private schools and urban public schools are very similar, with rural schools less likely to have electricity, running water, or sewage, and there is little difference between the two types of rural schools. Private schools are much more likely than public schools to have administrative support staff. There are almost no differences in the percentage of teachers with a tertiary-level teacher qualification, owing to government incentives in the 1990s (although there is no empirical evidence on whether or not teacher performance improved as a result of this). Primary rural schools in general are more likely to be multigrade: this means that in a single classroom students from different grades (occasionally including all six grades) will be placed under the supervision of one teacher. Multigrade schools are widely considered to be of poor quality, at least in terms of the achievement of the students, but this could be due to a combination of poor educational services and the characteristics of the students that attend these schools.

Table 15.3 School resources in primary education by type and location of school

	Private schools (n = 7,558)		Public urban schools (n = 5,694)		Public rural schools (Spanish) (n = 16,499)		Public rural schools (indigenous) (n = 6,255)	
	n	(%)	n	(%)	n	(%)	n	(%)
Infrastructure								
Library	3,889	(51)	2,742	(48)	4,695	(28)	1,279	(20)
Computer lab	4,718	(62)	2,343	(41)	595	(4)	201	(3)
Court or field	1,406	(19)	2,221	(39)	1,421	(9)	694	(11)
Basic services								
Electricity	6,448	(85)	4,805	(84)	4,880	(30)	2,277	(36)
Running water	6,059	(80)	4,307	(76)	5,184	(31)	1,835	(29)
Sewage	6,721	(89)	4,426	(78)	6,166	(37)	2,231	(36)
Teachers and staff								
Administrative staff available (1 or more)	1,492	(20)	119	(2)	72	(0)	38	(1)
Teacher's education (tertiary – pedagogical studies)	44,224	(96)	73,459	(99)	41,516	(98)	16,244	(98)
Teacher's education (tertiary – other studies)	1,729	(4)	524	(1)	442	(1)	195	(1)
Teacher's education (secondary)	121	(0)	203	(0)	268	(1)	157	(1)
Multigrade schools	1,444	(19)	900	(16)	8,354	(51)	3,514	(56)
Students per teacher	15		24		22		23	
Total enrolment	754,370	(19)	1,908,459	(48)	930,057	(23)	374,411	(9)
Percentage of students with an indigenous mother tongue	2		6		1		98	

Source: Based on School Census data (2007).

In 2003, a government programme with World Bank support, called PEAR (Educational Programme for Rural Areas), was approved. The programme covered rural education in general, but had a specific component for indigenous children to be implemented from 2004 to 2013. The budget was US$94.20 million, US$41.7 million from the government of Peru and US$52.50 million from the World Bank. However, the programme was discontinued in December 2008. The main reasons reported by the World Bank (2008) were changes in Peruvian education policy priorities and weak management from the Ministry of Education (including frequent changes in the high-level staff in charge of the programme; insufficient technical, personnel, and institutional resources; poor coordination among relevant departments within the Ministry, its regional offices, and local government; and lack of sufficient external evaluations of progress), which in turn led to significant delays in implementation of the programme and in disbursement of funds for specific activities. PEAR has not been followed by a similar programme.

Student enrolment

For a few years now, Peru has achieved almost universal primary coverage, with small differences between indigenous and Spanish-speaking populations. However, in secondary schools, the situation is quite different. While enrolment has increased, there is still a considerable gap between indigenous and Spanish-speaking populations (see Figure 15.1 which covers selected years where enrolment information was complete for both primary and secondary schools).

School enrolment rates tell only part of the story. It is also important to know how much children learn. The next section presents information on several outputs for indigenous and Spanish-speaking children.

Educational results

In this section, we present some indicators for indigenous and Spanish-speaking children. Figure 15.2 shows that promotion rates are higher for private and urban public schools. Rural schools that include a higher proportion of indigenous children have the lowest promotion rates. Dropout rates (not presented here) also show poorer results for rural schools, especially those with concentrations of indigenous children.[10]

Below we present information on over-age indigenous and Spanish-speaking schoolchildren. A child is over-age when she or he is older than would be expected for the grade in which they are enrolled: in Peru children are expected to be enrolled in first grade by the age of six.

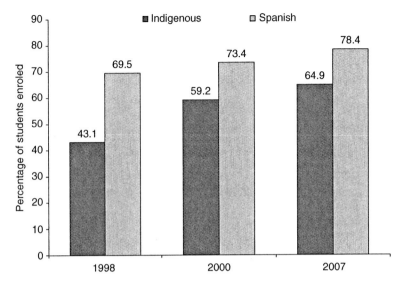

Figure 15.1   Net enrolment in secondary education by mother tongue, 1998, 2000, and 2007

Source: Data from ENAHO (2007).

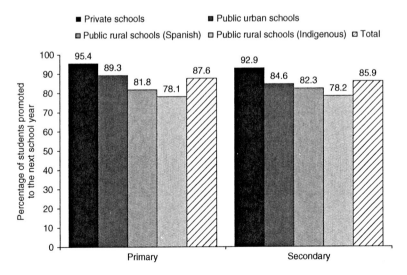

Figure 15.2   Promotion rates in primary and secondary education, 2006

Source: Data from School Census (2007).

The causes for being over-age could be late enrolment, grade repetition, or temporary dropout. For this analysis, we present information from Young Lives, concentrating on children born in 1994.

Beyond grade in school, it is important to analyse how much children learn. For this we used the 2001 and 2004 national assessments.[11] For each evaluation, the national means were set at 0 and the standard deviations at 1, to show gaps as differences between the two groups in SD. The results are shown for the sixth grade (end of primary school) and the fifth year (end of secondary school); both levels are mandatory in Peru according to the Constitution, although as shown before, many children drop out early. In all cases, children with Spanish as their mother tongue score above the mean and children with an indigenous mother tongue score below the mean. The gaps are quite large: the smaller difference is in mathematics in 2004 with seniors in high school, but proportionately more children from the indigenous group would have dropped out by the end of secondary school, making the composition of groups to compare different in primary and secondary schools.

Hernandez-Zavala et al. (2006: 31), using data collected in 1997 with third and fourth graders, found gaps of 0.83 SD for language and 0.58 SD for mathematics achievement between Spanish-speaking

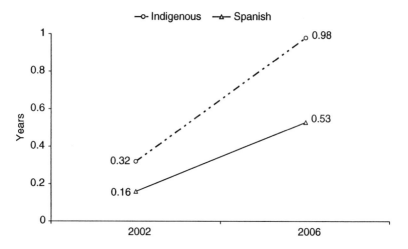

Figure 15.3   Over-age indigenous and Spanish-speaking children in school (in years)

Note: The numbers of children in this analysis are 43 for indigenous children and 631 for Spanish speakers. Even though the sample size for indigenous children is small, it was collected from 20 sites around the country.

Table 15.4 Achievement in mathematics and language in two national assessments (by mother tongue)

	National Assessment 2001		National Assessment 2004			
	6th grade – Primary		6th grade – Primary		5th year – Secondary	
	Maths	Language	Maths	Language	Maths	Language
Gap in SD (Spanish speakers – indigenous-language speakers mean)	−0.91	−0.85	−1.22	−1.07	−0.64	−0.95
Number of students	9,605	8,510	11,535	11,533	11,937	12,617

Source: Analysis done by authors using National Assessments 2001 and 2004.

and indigenous students in Peru. For rural Guatemala, McEwan and Trowbridge (2007) found gaps between 0.39 and 1.03 SD (larger in language skills than in mathematics) favouring Spanish-speaking over indigenous students (third and sixth graders). Also, the authors warn that the higher dropout rates among indigenous-language speakers may be also underestimating the size of the gap. McEwan and Trowbridge also summarize the size of the gaps between indigenous and Spanish-speaking students for different Latin American countries, which vary from −0.33 SD in Bolivia (third graders) to −1.11 SD in Guatemala (third and fourth graders) for language and from −0.2 in Ecuador (fifth graders) to −0.9 in Guatemala (third and fourth graders) for mathematics, all favouring Spanish speakers. Thus the gaps we report for Peru are among the largest reported for Latin America.

Determinants of achievement and the gap between indigenous-language speakers and Spanish speakers

A next step in the analysis is to show the weight of having an indigenous language versus Spanish as the mother tongue in explaining achievement. The analysis presented below decomposes the achievement gap into three portions: a portion explained by individual and family characteristics, a portion explained by school factors, and a portion not explained by any of these. The specific variables included in the models were selected based on a review of previous studies of determinants of school achievement in Peru (Cueto 2007).

For this analysis, the dataset from the National Assessment 2004 (EN 2004) was used. The tests were administered to second and sixth

graders in primary school and third- and fifth-year students in secondary school. Information on family and school variables was also collected. Our analysis will be limited to the results of sixth graders, given
that (1) this is the end of primary school and should show an accumulation of learning; (2) indigenous children should be fluent in Spanish
(all tests were administered in Spanish); and (3) the dropout rates are
relatively small. The mathematics and language tests were designed to
be aligned with the national curriculum: the test of language skills is
primarily on reading comprehension. The definition of the variables
used in the model and descriptive statistics for these are presented in
the Appendix.

Table 15.5 presents several multivariate models for language tests.[12]
The first model presents the gap between indigenous-language speakers
and Spanish speakers without adjusting for any variables. Model 2 controls for some individual and family variables, while model 3 controls
for some school variables. Finally, model 4 presents the fixed-effects
model. Table 15.6 presents the decomposition of the variance in the
three groups of variables of interest for the four models.

The results show that having an indigenous mother tongue is statistically significant in explaining achievement, but its coefficient diminishes when other individual and school variables are included in models
2 and 3 and becomes non-significant when fixed effects for school are
included in model 4. The most likely reason for this, as shown in other
parts of this chapter, is that indigenous-language speakers also tend to
be poorer, live in rural areas, and attend public schools, where they
gather with peers who are from similar backgrounds (especially in rural
indigenous schools). The low achievement of indigenous-language
speakers would be a result of an interaction of several of these factors.
The variance decomposition shows a higher weight of individual and
family variables over school variables in explaining achievement in
model 3. However, in the final fixed-effects model, the higher weight
is for school variables. This does not mean that it is only the school's
quality that explains achievement; it could also be that there are some
effects of the composition of the student body that influence achievement. There are some studies in Peru showing the importance of effects
of the peer group in explaining achievement: for example, Agüero and
Cueto (2003) analysed peer-group effects and found they had a significant influence, suggesting that increasing the variability in the composition of student classrooms might increase overall performance.

These results are similar to those of Hernandez-Zavala et al. (2006:
22) using data from a UNESCO evaluation (in 1997) for third and fourth

graders in Peru. They found that: 'In Peru, having more books at home, having a father with post-secondary education, and attending a private paying school increases test scores, while poor classroom conditions decrease test scores.'

McEwan and Trowbridge (2007) used a fixed-effects model to decompose the gaps in achievement in Guatemala and found a high weight of both individual and school factors, but the latter explained between 50 and 69 per cent of the gap. However, as the authors warn, school fixed effects may capture instructional inputs and educational quality as well as the school's social context (for example, the characteristics of students who attend schools plus the communities where they are located). In a study for Chile and Bolivia, McEwan (2004) found that the school fixed effect explained between 51 and 71 per cent of the gap between indigenous and Spanish speakers. In our analysis the weight of school fixed effects is even larger (79 and 78 per cent for mathematics and language, respectively). In the next section, we turn to specific educational policies targeting indigenous children in Peru.

Intercultural Bilingual Education[13] policies in Peru

Internationally, there is usually agreement among researchers that young children should learn to read and write in their mother tongue, moving on to a second language gradually if this is a goal to be pursued (Padilla 2006). In Peru, this would imply the need to develop bilingual education programmes, at least for indigenous students.

The first national policy for bilingual education in Peru was established in 1972, the first of its kind in Latin America (Zúñiga 2008: 45), by a military revolutionary government that aimed to reduce poverty and increase social inclusion.[14] The Peruvian programme targeted mostly speakers of indigenous languages and had the goal of helping indigenous populations in the transition to speaking Spanish, which was considered the main language, but preserving indigenous languages and cultures.

In the 1980s and 1990s, the policy of the Ministry of Education included an intercultural component alongside bilingual education (Zúñiga 2008: 48–51). Educación Intercultural Bilingüe (EIB) was conceived as a cross-sectional topic of the curriculum, targeting all children and not only speakers of indigenous languages: in practice, however, teaching and learning of indigenous languages occurred almost exclusively in EIB schools, although schools with predominantly Spanish speakers were encouraged to promote intercultural socialization and

Table 15.5 Multivariate analysis of language achievement

	Model 1		Model 2		Model 3		Model 4 (school fixed effects)	
	β	se (β)	β	se (β)	β	se (β)	β	se (β)
Indigenous mother tongue	-73.30	(4.62)***	-35.31	(4.04)***	-27.41	(4.18)***	-5.23	(4.45)
Individual and family variables								
Female			4.03	(2.05)+	4.21	(1.97)*	3.06	(2.03)
Age (years)			-5.57	(0.93)***	-5.22	(0.90)***	-4.89	(0.93)***
Number of siblings			-1.68	(0.48)***	-1.04	(0.47)*	-0.30	(0.43)
Nuclear family			-4.71	(2.00)*	-4.52	(1.94)*	-1.64	(1.81)
Child works outside home			-15.80	(2.64)***	-11.43	(2.64)***	-4.93	(2.46)*
Child works at home			-17.80	(7.03)*	-13.41	(7.08)+	-4.63	(5.71)
Educational materials at home			-2.17	(1.08)+	-2.25	(1.06)*	-1.53	(1.03)
More than 50 books at home			12.43	(2.58)***	9.68	(2.44)***	8.47	(2.44)**
Mother's education (secondary or higher)			7.23	(2.58)**	5.05	(2.64)+	5.32	(2.44)*
Father's education (secondary or higher)			10.81	(2.31)***	8.13	(2.19)***	7.07	(2.16)**
Socioeconomic index			1.27	(0.10)***	0.68	(0.11)***	0.00	(0.10)
School variables								
Public					-18.69	(3.21)***		
Full grade					10.61	(5.67)+		
Urban					8.89	(5.58)		
Infrastructure index					0.08	(0.02)***		

	(1)	(2)	(3)	(4)
EIB school			−9.96 (4.51)*	
Teacher's education 2 (higher technical education)			−2.93 (3.35)	
Teacher's education 3 (higher university education)			5.14 (3.36)	
Teacher's education 4 (post-graduate)			9.99 (6.14)	
Teacher's experience (in years)			0.24 (0.22)	
Constant	302.14 (2.39)***	248.39 (15.71)***	275.58 (16.08)***	306.02 (15.32)***
R-square	0.11	0.32	0.35	0.48
Students	8878	8878	8878	8878
Schools	537	537	537	537

***$p < .001$, **$p < .01$, *$p < .05$, +$p < .10$

Robust standard errors adjusted by clustering of the students are in parenthesis.

Table 15.6   Mother tongue gap decomposition

	Language			
	Model 1	Model 2	Model 3	Model 4
Gap decomposition (%)				
Unexplained	−73.30 (100)	−35.31 (48)	−27.41 (37)	−5.23 (7)
Individual factors	–	−38.00 (52)	−24.75 (34)	−10.86 (15)
School factors	–	–	−21.14 (29)	–
Fixed effect	–	▪		57.21 (78)
Total gap	−73.30	−73.30	−73.30	−73.30

practices. Currently EIB is an official programme administered by the Ministry of Education, which over the past few years has printed around three-and-a-half million textbooks in mathematics and language in five varieties of Quechua, in Aymara, and in nine Amazon languages (Zúñiga 2008: 83), despite the difficulty of establishing a way of writing intelligibly in languages with no written tradition. The EIB model is supposed to teach indigenous-language speakers to read and write first in their mother tongue and then move on to Spanish, while strengthening their mastery of language skills in their mother tongue. While there are a few universities and teacher education institutes with a special programme on EIB, these do not seem to be enough to serve the indigenous population.

In 1993, the new Constitution stated in Article 17 that: 'The State guarantees the eradication of illiteracy. Also it promotes bilingual and intercultural education, depending on the characteristics of each zone. It preserves the diverse cultural and linguistic manifestations in the country. It promotes national integration.'[15] The reference to characteristics of zones suggests a conception of bilingual education targeting indigenous children only, in rural areas where the indigenous population is concentrated. The justification for bilingual intercultural education seems to be based more on national objectives, such as the preservation of cultural and linguistic diversity, than on adapting education models and practices to the culture of children in specific contexts. This type of justification would seem more appropriate for a museum or national historic site than for educational practices based on social interactions. In 2002, the National Agreement, a group formed by representatives of some of the main social and political groups, included in its 12th State Policy the importance of providing EIB to indigenous populations.[16] This has not been achieved. In 2003, a new General Law of Education was issued, again stating the importance of providing EIB nationally (this time not only for indigenous populations). This has not been implemented.

Zúñiga (2008: 12) identifies several limitations of the EIB model as currently implemented in Peru:

> In general, EIB is only implemented in primary education, not at pre-school or secondary; EIB is implemented for the most part in rural areas; EIB is usually thought of as education for indigenous people... In many places EIB is used as a policy of Spanish assimilation: there is great lack of capacity to implement efficient programs to teach Spanish and indigenous languages as secondary languages... Within civil society, with few exceptions, there is no commitment yet to the construction of EIB proposals.

EIB policy calls for all children with an indigenous mother tongue to attend an EIB school. However, targeting indigenous children with EIB schools is still a problem (Table 15.7 shows that almost 120,000 – about 40 per cent – of the children who attend an EIB school say their mother tongue is Spanish).

According to the 2007 school census, school principals reported 3,804 schools to be EIB schools (although the programme may not actually be implemented). The majority are public, multigrade, and in rural areas. A few EIB schools are run by non-governmental organizations (NGOs) or private organizations in agreement with the government.

There are few studies of the impact of bilingual intercultural policies with rigorous designs. Any evaluation would need to take into account

Table 15.7 EIB schools and indigenous student population (primary only)

	Mother tongue		
	Indigenous	Spanish	Total
Enrolment (%)			
EIB	175,282 (35%)	119,167 (3%)	294,449 (7%)
Non-EIB	332,220 (65%)	3,340,628 (97%)	3,672,848 (93%)
Total	507,502	3,459,795	3,967,297

Source: Data from School Census (2007).

if indeed EIB policies are implemented at school and if the programme is accepted by parents, teachers, and students, among other issues. The few studies available suggest that EIB is often not practised as claimed. For instance, Cueto and Secada (2003: 15–16), in a study of fourth and fifth graders, found that in many EIB schools in Puno, in the south of Peru, bilingual policies were not implemented, as less than half of the teachers could read or write in the indigenous languages: in fact some teachers assigned to EIB schools declared that they did not even speak the local language. The language of instruction in the classroom was almost exclusively Spanish and bilingual materials and texts from the Ministry of Education were piled up in a corner and not used. In many of the EIB schools, the majority of parents did not want their children to learn to read and write in Quechua or Aymara. This is probably based on their personal experience of the usefulness of Spanish as opposed to an indigenous language.

Recently, there has been some indication that this may be changing: for instance, the regional government of Puno has translated and displayed publicly the names of streets in the two indigenous languages spoken there, as well as Spanish. This is a small start to indicate that inclusion of indigenous languages in mainstream life may be starting, at least in some regions. The National Agreement mentioned above has a website in Spanish and three indigenous languages.[17] Also, Zavala (2007) and Zúñiga (2008) have described, some case studies of bilingual intercultural programmes in different regions of Peru that seem to be promising, and also pointed out some challenges these face. However, we believe that there is a long way to go before intercultural bilingual policies become an important component of the social agenda of Peru.

Discrimination based on ethnicity seems to be still strong in Peru. A recent incident illustrates this: the personal notes of Quechua Congresswoman Hilaria Supa were photographed from a distance by the press, who presented them as evidence that she was not qualified to be in Congress because of her poor writing in Spanish.[18] This has led to a public discussion on civil rights, education, and discrimination. While most analysts have stated that poor writing in Spanish does not disqualify a person from being in Congress, nor is it evidence of her intellectual abilities, it is likely that many citizens in Peru still believe that indigenous people, who tend to have lower levels of education than Spanish speakers and speak and write Spanish in non-standard ways, should not assume public offices such as Congressman or Congresswoman.[19]

Discussion and policy recommendations

The problems that indigenous populations face in Peru are not unique. At the end of the UN's Indigenous Peoples' decade (1994–2004), Hall and Patrinos (2006) analysed social indicators for the five countries in Latin America with the largest indigenous populations: Bolivia, Ecuador, Guatemala, Mexico, and Peru. They found that in spite of increased attention from diverse institutions and better political and social representation, indigenous people still show a wide disparity from their Spanish-speaking counterparts in several indicators of poverty, including educational outcomes and access to diverse services.

The analyses presented above suggest that children with an indigenous mother tongue in Peru face a variety of challenges: they usually have less educated parents, are more likely to be poor, and are more likely to live in rural areas, especially in the Andes and jungle, where they are likely to lack public services such as running water, electricity, and sewage at home. Given these conditions and the fact that Spanish language and culture are clearly dominant in the country, it is no surprise that many indigenous people have migrated to urban areas and that the proportion of indigenous-language speakers in the country has decreased in the past two decades. Nevertheless, there are still around 4 million people in Peru who declare one of the over 40 indigenous languages to be their mother tongue.

Our data show that children with an indigenous mother tongue are more likely to repeat grades and drop out of school than their Spanish-speaking peers. Also, they attend largely rural schools, which are more likely to have poorer infrastructure than urban public schools or private schools (there are only a few differences between predominantly Spanish-medium rural schools and predominantly indigenous-language-medium rural schools: most rural schools are attended by poorer children). This is an important fact for a country that according to the General Education Law[20] should be trying not only to raise its average educational quality but also to reduce educational inequalities associated with the students' individual characteristics and family background. Currently the Peruvian education system is not reducing inequalities but promoting them, by giving fewer educational resources to poorer students in rural areas (including indigenous children) and failing to provide education safety nets for those who start lagging behind their peers.

Intercultural bilingual education programmes are available for fewer than half of rural schools. Furthermore, there is some evidence that even where EIB programmes exist, they are often not implemented. This is educational violence that goes against children's right to receive high-quality education that is appropriate for each student. One reason why EIB programmes are not implemented is that indigenous parents sometimes wish their children to learn in Spanish, which they perceive as more useful than learning in their mother tongue. Current EIB policy is isolationist in that it is conceived as a policy for indigenous children in rural areas and not a programme implemented wherever children with an indigenous mother tongue go to school (even pre-school but also high school). Finally, indigenous language and culture need to be felt by the population as part of the mainstream. This would require political will and the combined efforts of different social actors.

Considering the disadvantages faced by indigenous children, it is not surprising that their achievement scores in mathematics and language are considerably lower than those of their Spanish-speaking peers. These gaps are among the largest we have found reported in Latin America. School characteristics explain much of this gap, and suggest two possibilities: schools might not be providing the best-quality education; and/or students from relatively similar backgrounds gather at schools, creating a clustering effect. This chapter provides evidence for both of these explanations, and the analysis suggests the need for policies at the school level, concentrating on rural schools and planning interventions that tackle both the institution as a whole and the individual students who attend. In many cases, the implementation of an improved bilingual intercultural programme seems to be needed; in others, children who need more individual attention to catch up with their peers should be targeted; and in others still, schools need more resources. Such interventions certainly do not exclude other policies that depend on specific local needs, such as policies to fight extreme poverty.

In 2006, the Peruvian government started a programme to measure achievement for all second graders nationally, plus a sample of fourth graders in EIB programmes. With this information and that from the national census, school census, and a variety of national surveys, there is enough information to identify predominantly indigenous areas, schools, and even students with the poorest performance. Knowing and not responding, with the near certainty that many of these children will fail in school, is poor educational policy and also shows little respect for the right of these children to receive an appropriate high-quality education that allows them to achieve their potential.

Appendix: Definition of variables included in multivariate analysis

Variable	Definition
Maths achievement	Mathematics test score
Language achievement	Test score in language arts
Indigenous	1 = Child has an indigenous mother tongue; 0 = Otherwise
Female	1 = Female ; 0 = Male
Age (years)	Child's age
Number of siblings	Number of siblings
Nuclear family	1 = Child lives with both parents; 0 = Otherwise
Child works outside home	1 = Child work outside home; 0 = Otherwise
Child works at home	1 = Child work inside home; 0 = Otherwise
Educational materials at home	Sum of selected educational materials (dictionary, maths books, language books, calculator) at home
More than 50 books at home	1 = Number of books present at home is higher than 50; 0 = Otherwise
Socioeconomic index	Index constructed based upon material of the house, access to basic services and assets at home
Mother's education (secondary or higher)	1 = Mother completed at least secondary school; 0 = Otherwise
Father's education (secondary or higher	1 = Father completed at least secondary school; 0 = Otherwise
Public	1 = Public school; 0 = Private school
Full grade	1 = Full grade school; 0 = Multigrade school
Urban	1 = Urban; 0 = Rural
Infrastructure index	Index constructed based upon the number of school facilities and condition of infrastructure
EIB school	1 = Intercultural Bilingual Education Programme is implemented at school; 0 = Otherwise
Teacher's education 1	Level of education completed by the teacher: 1 = Completed secondary education or incomplete higher education; 0 = Otherwise
Teacher's education 2	Level of education completed by the teacher: 1 = Completed higher technical education; 0 = Otherwise
Teacher's education 3	Level of education completed by the teacher: 1 = Completed higher university education; 0 = Otherwise
Teacher's education 4	Level of education completed by the teacher: 1 = post-graduate education; 0 = Otherwise
Teacher's experience	Main teacher's years of experience

For descriptive statistics of the variables included in the model and results for the mathematics analysis and additional information related to this topic, and for the specification of the statistical model supporting the multivariate analysis, see Cueto et al. (2009).

Notes

1. This chapter is a revised version of a background paper commissioned by UNESCO for the 2010 *Education For All Global Monitoring Report, Reaching the Marginalized*. The original paper includes additional statistical information and is available at http://unesdoc.unesco.org/images/0018/001865/186589e. pdf. The authors wish to thank the UNESCO EFA team and Bill Myers for their thoughtful comments.

2. Although mother tongue is not a comprehensive indicator of ethnicity, it is a proxy for being a member of an indigenous group that is usually available in databases and used in empirical studies in Peru and Latin America.

3. Source. Authors' calculations from the databases of the National Census 1993 and the National Census 2007.

4. For a map of Peruvian indigenous languages, see http://portal.perueduca. edu.pe/boletin/boletin24/mapa.htm.

5. Consulted at http://www2.congreso.gob.pe/sicr/RelatAgenda/constitucion. nsf/constitucion on 10 April 2010.

6. The Public Law 28106, approved by Congress in 2003, declares of national interest the preservation, promotion, and dissemination of indigenous languages.

7. The classification of schools as urban or rural comes from the Ministry of Education and depends on the number of persons living in the site where the school is located.

8. The school census is a survey completed annually by all school principals at the pre-school, primary, and secondary levels, and is not independently verified. Historically, between 2 and 4 per cent of schools do not complete the census. The 2007 report refers to data for 2006, when 2.6 per cent of schools did not complete the census.

9. In 2008 and 2009, the Peruvian government started distributing computers to rural schools under the One Laptop per Child (OLPC) programme, although in 2010 the programme will shift from its rural emphasis to cover all schools.

10. The promotion rate is the percentage of students who were promoted to the next grade at the end of the school year. The repetition rate is the percentage of students who failed and were not promoted to the next grade. The dropout rate is the percentage of students who were enrolled but left the school before the end of the school year.

11. The tests were designed and analysed by the Quality Education Measurement Unit at the Ministry of Education. External field workers were hired to administer them in schools. For more information on the procedures and evaluation reports, see http://www2.minedu.gob.pe/umc/index2. php?v_codigo=51&v_plantilla=2.

12. According to the Collin Test, Vector of Inflation Factor (VIF) values vary around 2 for all independent variables, suggesting acceptable levels of multi-colinearity. We ran a similar analysis for mathematics achievement and the results were essentially the same.

13. EIB stands for Educación Intercultural Bilingüe.

14. Bilingual education policies in Peru were started by the government, while in neighbouring Bolivia and Ecuador they came through indigenous

movements, which are more vigorous in these countries than in Peru. In Peru alone among the three countries, EIB programmes are not managed by representatives of the indigenous populations (Zavala 2007: 31–5 and 193–6).
15. Translated by the authors.
16. See http://www.acuerdonacional.pe/AN/politicas/textoe12.htm.
17. http://www.acuerdonacional.pe
18. *Correo* newspaper: http://www.correoperu.com.pe/correo/nota.php?txtEdi_id= 4&txtSecci_parent=0&txtSecci_id=80&txtNota_id=43706.
19. See http://www.correoperu.com.pe/correo/columnistas.php?txtEdi_id=4& txtSecci_id=84&txtSecci_parent=&txtNota_id=43799 for the editorial piece by *Correo* director, stating that citizens with 'low education levels' such as Congresswoman Supa should not be in Congress; Congresswoman Supa did not go to formal school and has said that she taught herself to read and write in Spanish.
20. Consulted at: http://www2.congreso.gob.pe/Sicr/Congresistas/2001/0311/ si05des_0311.nsf/vf08p/FB1DD772F0DEF467052570ED006E65A8/$FILE/28 044.pdf on 10 April 2010.

References

Agüero, J. and S. Cueto (2003) *Dime Con Quién Andas y Te Diré Cómo Rindes:* Peer Effects *Como Determinantes Del Rendimiento Escolar,* unpublished report, Lima: Consorcio de Educación Económica y Social.

Cueto, S. (2007) 'Las Evaluaciones Nacionales e Internacionales de Rendimiento Escolar en el Perú: Balance y Perspectivas' in Grupo de Análisis para el Desarrollo (ed.) *Investigación, Políticas y Desarrollo en el Perú,* Lima: GRADE.

Cueto, S., G. Guerrero, J. León, E. Seguin and I. Muñoz (2009) 'Explaining and Overcoming Marginalization in Education: A Focus on Ethnic/Language Minorities in Peru', Background paper prepared for the UNESCO Education For All Global Monitoring Report 2010, Paris: UNESCO.

Cueto, S., and W. Secada (2003) 'Eficacia Escolar en Escuelas Bilingües en Puno, Perú', *Revista Electrónica Iberoamericana sobre Calidad, Eficacia y Cambio en Educación* 1.1: 1–12.

Escobal, J. and C. Ponce (2007) 'Economic Opportunities for Indigenous Peoples in Rural and Urban Peru', background paper for H. Patrinos and E. Skoufias, *Economic Opportunities for Indigenous Peoples in Latin America,* Washington, DC: World Bank.

Hall, G. and H.A. Patrinos (2006) *Indigenous Peoples, Poverty and Human Development in Latin America,* Basingstoke: Palgrave Macmillan.

Hernandez-Zavala, M., H.A. Patrinos, C. Sakellariou and J. Shapiro (2006) *Quality of Schooling and Quality of Schools for Indigenous Students in Guatemala, Mexico and Peru,* Policy Research Working Paper 3982, Washington, DC: World Bank.

McEwan, J. (2004) 'La Brecha de Puntaje Obtenidos en las Pruebas por los Niños Indígenas en Sudamérica' in D.R. Winkler and S. Cueto (eds), *Etnicidad, Raza, Género y Educación en América Latina,* Santiago: PREAL.

McEwan, J. and M. Trowbridge (2007) 'The Achievement of Indigenous Students in Guatemalan Primary Schools', *International Journal of Educational Development* 27.1: 61–76.

Padilla, A.M. (2006) 'Second Language Learning: Issues in Research and Teaching' in Eric Anderman, Philip H. Winne, Patricia A. Alexander and Lyn Corno (eds) *Handbook of Educational Psychology*, 2nd edn, Mahwah, NJ: American Psychological Association and Lawrence Erlbaum Associates, Inc.

Trivelli, C. (2000) 'Pobreza Rural: Investigaciones, Mediciones y Políticas Públicas' in Isabel Hurtado, Carolina Trivelli and Antonio Brack (eds), *Perú el Problema Agrario en Debate*, Lima: SEPIA and IRD.

Trivelli, C. (2005) 'Una Mirada Cuantitativa a la Situación de Pobreza de los Hogares Indígenas en el Perú', *Economía* 55–6: 83–158.

World Bank (2008) 'Implementation Completion and Results Report (IBRD-71760) on a Loan in the Amount of (US$52.5 million) to the Republic of Peru for a Rural Education Project in Support of the First Phase of the Rural Education Program', Report No: ICR0000862, Lima: World Bank.

Zavala, V. (2007) *Avances y Desafíos de la Educación Intercultural Bilingüe en Bolivia, Ecuador y Perú*, Lima: IBIS and CARE.

Zúñiga, M. (2008) *La Educación Intercultural Bilingüe. El Caso Peruano*, Lima: FLAPE and Foro Educativo.

16
Child Agricultural Work in South Africa: A Contested Space[1]

Andrew Dawes, Judith Streak, Susan Levine, and Deborah Ewing

The contested developmental space of children's work[2]

Children grow up in multiple socio-cultural spaces that structure activities and learning according to local notions of what is appropriate for their development (Super and Harkness 1986; Miller and Goodnow 1995; Rogoff 2003: 18–24). Contradictions across these spaces may be particularly sharp in modernizing societies where long-standing local 'traditional' practices and ideologies, such as the duty to contribute to family economic well-being, confront modern rights-based ideologies embedded in instruments such as the Convention on the Rights of the Child and the African Charter on the Rights and Welfare of the Child. While they seek to advance the rights of all children to protection and development, these instruments are also forces for the globalization of the state of childhood and child rights (Myers 2001: 39; Boyden 1990: 194). The purpose of this chapter is to explore the experience of children who engage in agricultural work in South Africa as they grapple with the challenges of rural poverty, obligations to support kin and community, and the demands of school (Bourdillon 2009).

In the poor communities of the global South, significant numbers of children engage in paid and unpaid work. Poverty is a common factor in the lives of working children; however, it is by no means the sole reason for working (Bourdillon 2009; Jensen and Nielsen 1997: 423).

As Myers (2001: 43) notes, it is not children's work per se that is at issue in concerns about its impacts: rather it is the form and organization of their work activities. Primary concerns include potential negative impacts on schooling, health, and psychosocial well-being (see for example, Dorman 2008; Jensen and Nielsen 1997; Myers 2001; Patrinos and Psacharopoulos 1995; Woodhead 2004). At the same time, potential benefits to children working under non-hazardous conditions have come to be recognized (Myers 2001; IPEC 2002: 3). Children may learn skills valued in the local community and may take pride in assisting with tasks that support the economic well-being of the household, thereby enhancing their self-esteem (Woodhead 2004).

There is in much of the literature greater focus on the risks to children than the possible benefits of working. The limited number of developing country studies available point to inverse relationships between the extent of children's economic work and their school performance. Also, economically active children are also more likely to repeat grades, drop out, and miss school (Orazem and Gunnarsson 2003: 21; Allais et al. 2008: 15). However, as Basu and Tsannatos (2003) note, working children may not be pushed out of school by work, but may drop out after repeated failure, and the cost of fees, uniforms, and books may promote exclusion. Schools themselves may be so dysfunctional that children either do not progress or leave (Anker 2000; Brown 2001).

Research on the health impacts of different forms of child agricultural work is limited. However, use of dangerous equipment, exposure to pesticides, long hours, transport risks, extreme temperatures, excessive noise, and large animals have been identified as significant risks (Dorman 2008: 30).

Little attention has been paid to psychosocial outcomes, one of the concerns that underpin child labour policy (Piotrkowski and Carrubba 1999). Some studies suggest that this should be a concern. For example, in Ethiopia, Fekadu et al. (2006) found child workers more likely to warrant a psychiatric diagnosis than their non-working counterparts. However, the causal relationship is not clear as it is not known whether their mental condition may have resulted in their being put to work. Physical and sexual abuse have been identified in several studies of working children (for example, Hadi 2000; Gharaibeh and Hoeman 2003). Abusers include adult supervisors and fellow workers.

There is a need for more research on psychosocial outcomes – research which balances risks with the potential benefits of children's work. Such an approach is illustrated in Table 16.1, which is drawn from Woodhead (2004), whose formulation recognizes that both positive and negative outcomes may be possible (depending on the age of the child and the nature of the work), and that the two can co-occur (but where they do, benefits cannot cancel out harm).

Table 16.1 Indicators for psychosocial outcomes of children's work

Domains	Positive indicators	Negative indicators
Cognitive abilities cultural competencies	Intelligence; culturally valued competencies	Compromised development; poor skill base
Personal security, social integration, social competence	Positive relationships; positive moral conduct	Insecurity, inhibition, anti-social behaviour
Personal identity and valuation	Positive self-concept, high self-esteem	Worthlessness, fear of failure, shame, stigma
Sense of personal agency	Self-efficacy, autonomy, responsibility	Helplessness, External locus of control (ELC; lack of agency); hopelessness
Emotional and somatic well-being	Subjective well-being and health	Stress, anxiety, depression

Source: Adapted from Woodhead (2004).

We turn now to discuss findings of a South African study to illustrate both negative and positive consequences of children's agricultural work, and the dilemmas they face as they respond to cultural and economic demands. In this chapter we examine the manner in which South African children living in rural areas negotiate tensions between compulsory schooling and work in commercial, subsistence, and agricultural settings, and how they experience the risks associated with their agricultural activities. We also explore perceptions of the causes of child work by children, parents, and other adults. The data for the chapter are drawn from a study that included survey and qualitative data; our focus is on the qualitative findings (Streak et al. 2008).[3]

Child agricultural work in three South African communities

Following ILO Convention 138, South African law forbids employment of persons under 15 years of age and restricts involvement in hazardous agricultural activities to adults. Schooling is free and compulsory until the age of 15. However, schools are permitted to charge fees for expenses not covered by the state, and all schools use this opportunity. A 'no fee' policy allows for schools serving the poorest communities to waive fees and receive additional state funding. Children are required to wear uniforms and, while text books are free, other equipment must be provided by the child.

The child agricultural labour literature in South Africa is sparse. Bourdillon (2009) provides a review of the legislation and research. We will highlight key aspects here. Apart from policy reports and commissioned studies, one thesis (Levine 2000) and two peer-reviewed journal articles are evident (Levine 2006; Duncan and Bowman 2008). There are also several reports based on the Survey of Activities of Young People (SAYP), which covered children aged 5 to 17 years and was conducted in South Africa in 1999 (Orkin 2000; Statistics South Africa 2000). The SAYP found that 45 per cent of working children were in agriculture, and that the subsistence form predominated over employment in the commercial sector. Most of the children carrying out many hours of work in unpaid subsistence agriculture were located in former black 'homeland' areas, to which most persons classified as African under the apartheid system were restricted. Poverty was identified in the survey as the major driver for children's involvement in agricultural work.

Methods

The study was conducted in three sites identified as typical of the major types of South African agricultural activity and in which child agricultural work is known to be common.

The Worcester area in the Western Cape has a long history of exploitive labour practices and use of child workers to produce grapes for the wine industry and for export fruit markets. There is no subsistence agriculture other than small family gardens. The political economy of the area reflects the deep structural inequalities in the wine industry and the historical rural apartheid economy. The discrepancy between rich and poor in the area is striking, with wealthy farmers living a few metres from workers who commonly live in abject poverty. Prior to the end of apartheid, workers were paid in part with tots of wine (known as the 'dop system'). While the practice is now outlawed, alcohol abuse is rife in the area. The dominant language of children living on wine farms in this study site is Afrikaans.

A second sample of children resides in the rural and traditionally oriented area of Msinga Kwazulu-Natal. Msinga has been identified as one of the four most deprived areas in this region (Noble et al. 2006: 41). Unemployment is high and migration for work is common. Commercial mixed farming (predominantly white-owned) and subsistence agriculture are undertaken. According to local informants, acceptance of child participation in subsistence and commercial agriculture is long established and part of traditional life. IsiZulu is spoken in this area.

The third study site is located south of the Kruger National Park in the Nkomazi Municipality of Mpumalanga Province. Both commercial and subsistence farming occur, with the majority of commercial farms owned by whites. According to the Nkomazi Integrated Development Plan (Nkomazi Municipality 2005/06: 12), the main product is sugar cane followed by fruit and forestry plantations. Subsistence agriculture plays a key role in providing income and food for the poor rural black population in the area. There is significant income inequality between blacks and white farmers, with the former living well below the poverty line (Provide 2005). Adult participants indicated that most of the child participants came from households that had a plot on which they produced food for the household. The main language of the area is siSwati.

A convenience sample of 1,030 boys and girls aged 12 to 16 years participated in a survey during school hours. The samples are not random although likely to be fairly typical for the areas studied.

Items in the survey instrument included questions on work in the past year, and its frequency and length and time of spell. Participants were asked whether school was affected by work (for example, whether they were late, had insufficient time for homework, or missed school), and why they worked (for example, to earn money as a community duty, or to learn skills). The nature of the work (for example, herding cattle, pruning vines), the conditions (heat, cold, use of dangerous implements, abuse, and so on), and the outcomes (injuries and psychological outcomes) were covered.

Psychosocial impacts were measured using five items drawn from the Social and Health Assessment (SAHA) that captured anti-social behaviour (substance use and assaults perpetrated), as well as anxiety and depression (Ruchkin et al. 2004). The number of items was restricted in order to reduce the length of the instrument.

In the absence of directly supplied data on adult economic status, child deprivation was assessed by summing the number of items checked from a list of 12 assets that children had agreed were basic necessities for their age group. The checklist was based on a study of perceived necessities of both adults and adolescents conducted in similar communities (Barnes 2009; Wright 2008). Hunger was measured by asking whether the family had had to go without food because of lack of money in the past month. In addition, children reported on whether or not their parents were employed, and whether or not one or both parents were alive.

Qualitative data was derived from child focus-group interviews and adult interviews. In each study area, group discussions were held with an average of ten randomly selected school children from those who were identified in the survey as working in agriculture. Out-of-school working children (between the ages of 11 and 18) participated in separate sessions.

Two techniques were developed to gather information on perceptions of work, its benefits and hazards. In a body-mapping exercise (Solomon and Morgan 2007: 8–9), children drew outlines of each other's bodies on newsprint and then wrote or drew on their pictures in response to questions about their lives, including: 'Where do you feel safe? Who is the most important person in your life? What kind of work do you do? What is the best/worst thing about working? What injuries have you experienced?' Photographs of working children were also used to generate discussion of participants' experiences.

Adults, including commercial farmers, parents, teachers, social workers, and other professionals, were also interviewed to obtain their views on the appropriateness of children's work in agriculture, its causes, and its effects on schooling and health.

Ethical procedures were followed with adults giving consent to their children's participation, and children giving their assent.

Findings

Incidence

We report briefly on the incidence of children's agricultural work. Seventeen per cent of the children in the Western Cape site, 59 per cent in the Mpumalanga site, and almost the all those in the KwaZulu-Natal site (92 per cent) participated in some form of agricultural activity. It was not uncommon for children to work in both family subsistence and community-owned agriculture. Only 27 per cent of the sample worked exclusively for pay in privately owned commercial agriculture.

Girls and boys were equally likely to report work in subsistence agriculture (which differs from the SAYP findings, according to which boys were more likely than girls to undertake this form of work), but boys were more likely to be employed in the commercial agricultural sector. Sixty-two per cent of girls as against 57 per cent of boys had undertaken domestic work outside their own families in the past year; 45 per cent of this group were paid for their time.

Ninety-four per cent of the sample had undertaken domestic work in their own homes in the past year, with cooking, cleaning, and collecting firewood being most common tasks. Girls (98 per cent) and boys (90 per cent) showed similar rates of participation but in different tasks.

The complexity of causes and consequences

Children were asked why they worked in agriculture.

Participants who said they worked without pay in subsistence agriculture on family or community plots were provided with three options to indicate their reasons (they could check more than one option): to learn things they needed to know; out of duty to family; out of duty to the community. Seventy per cent indicated that they undertook this activity out of duty to family or community, and 46 per cent wanted to learn agricultural skills.

Children working for pay were asked why they needed to earn money (they could give more than one reason). Seventy per cent worked in order to have cash in order to meet their own needs, while 36 per cent were working in order to support their families. Twenty-eight per cent saw paid work as an opportunity to learn agricultural skills.

In this sample, economic work was as much a solution to personal deprivation as it was undertaken to support the family. As will be evident below, it was common for children to use their earnings to purchase uniforms and items for school.

Focus-group conversations revealed a positive aspect of their work in children's awareness of the importance of their activity to the development of practical abilities relevant to their living environment and possible future employment.

Unsurprisingly, poverty emerged as a prominent cause of children working to support themselves and their families. Statistical analyses (see: Streak et al. 2008 for full details) showed that working children possessed significantly fewer assets than children who did not work, and children working in *both subsistence and commercial agriculture* reported significantly fewer assets than those working in subsistence activities alone.

A further indicator of economic distress is that more working children experienced household hunger because of a lack of money (47 per cent) than those that did not (21 per cent) and again, more children working in both subsistence and commercial agriculture experienced hunger (64 per cent) than those working in subsistence farming alone (35.5 per cent), or in commercial agriculture only (45.6 per cent). And finally, those who reported parental unemployment were more likely to be working in agriculture. On all these points, differences between the categories are statistically significant (see Streak et al. 2008). The data from the survey indicate that overall, children who work in agriculture (of any kind) are more deprived than those who do not, and that children from subsistence farming areas who *also* work in commercial agriculture are the worst off.

Food insecurity is illustrated by a teacher's observation: 'Children are taking home food from school feeding schemes to feed their families.'

The impact of poverty is reflected in the comments of a farmer about parents' inability to finance schooling:

> At one school, you may have 50 per cent not paying. Even if you ask parents to pay R10 [US$1.25], they can't. Some are getting a [social] grant but need all that money to buy food.

Working children's comments are instructive:

> We don't have enough money for food and clothes... Some of us give all our money to our mothers for food when we work.
>   Because we are suffering and we need money, we go and work on a farm, but it is not a nice job.
> We are able to support our families and our brothers and sisters.
> [I work] so I can buy a uniform for school.

Despite the hardship, there is a sense of positive identity and pride gained from working evident in the last two quotes, which illustrate the positive indicator of self-esteem as a psychological outcome from work in Woodhead's (2004) 'personal identity and valuation' psychosocial domain. There is also a sense of social competence, moral maturity, and personal agency in these accounts. They suggest self-efficacy rather than hopelessness in the face of a very difficult situation.

The fourth quote illustrates the paradox faced by a poor child in a country within which education is a fundamental right, but where barriers to access are raised by the costs of uniforms.

Adult comments, listed below, illustrate the manner in which reasons for children working reflect multi-layered repertoires of traditional obligation, learning relevant skills, moral development, and contributing to family survival. Woodhead's *culturally valued competencies* are present, particularly in the final quote from a rural subsistence farmer and parent:

> They are learning but they are also helping us... They are taught respect.
>   They learn skills to make gardens – dirty hands bring them a beautiful plate of food on the table but they don't like to see themselves getting dirty.

It teaches them important skills [that] will not leave them ... even without a job they can still produce food.

It is about a boy's future ... building a kraal, taking responsibilities as an adult man.

Negative impacts

Negative consequences were also reported (Table 16.2). Hazards were present in 90 per cent of cases; and 63 per cent of participants reported a negative health impact.

Commonly reported hardships, regardless of the type of agriculture were excessive heat, thirst, long hours, physically and psychologically abusive treatment by employers or fellow workers, and working with dangerous substances.

Children said they felt conflicted about work and its impact. On the one hand, there is the benefit of economic or community contribution together with opportunities to learn skills. On the other, there is the high probability of injury and abuse. A child commented, 'I don't like it when they treat me bad, like shouting at me while I'm working and using harsh words.' Another youth explained, 'If you get cut or hurt, they ask you why – are you stupid?' An example of an injury depicted on a body map is shown in Figure 16.1.

Humiliation was reported by children living and working on white commercial farms: 'When the farmer's children drive past they shout, "*Plaasjapies*" [farm idiots] and we cannot say anything back because they are the Boer's child.' The term 'boer' is standard Afrikaans for 'farmer'. However, it is also used by black South Africans to signify relationships of power and white oppression, as in this example.

Relevant here is Woodhead's (2004) construct of psychosocial domains in terms of *personal identity and valuation*. As much as working children

Table 16.2 Negative work impacts

	Negative impact on school N (%)	Negative impact on health N (%)	Hazardous conditions N (%)
Subsistence agriculture	54 (35%)	74 (49%)	129 (85%)
Community-owned commercial agriculture	13 (21%)	46 (77%)	55 (91%)
Privately owned commercial agriculture	14 (32%)	27 (63%)	41 (95%)

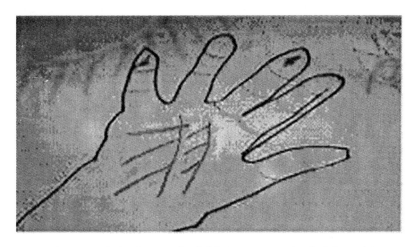

Figure 16.1   Part of a body map of a child's injuries sustained while working

Note: The heavy marks on the palm and the mark at the end of the middle finger were depicted in black.

gain self-respect through work, among the negatives is stigmatization of being a poor (stupid) farm worker's child.

Statistical analysis of the survey data revealed patterns in the psycho-social impacts. Taking all types of agricultural work together, working children reported significantly higher levels of anxiety and depression than those not working at all. However, we cannot be sure that these outcomes are solely a function of their work situation. These children may come from more problematic family backgrounds (with alcohol abuse, for example). There were no differences in regard to anti-social behaviour items.

When we examined sub-types of work, children who *only* worked in subsistence agriculture reported significantly *less* anxiety and depression than those working only in commercial agriculture or in both types. We cannot be sure of the causal pathways here, but those with negative outcomes may be coping with a triple burden of schooling, work for kin, and wage labour. Subsistence work alone may be less troubling because it is coupled to a normative expectation to do such work in the service of kin and community.

In addition to speaking about their psychological stress related to treatment by farmers (of them or their parents), children highlighted that they felt bad about how they were treated by their parents and other adults when the adults drank. One boy said, 'On the farms when the adults get drunk they start fighting with children ... It causes me a lot of stress to see my mother drunk. I get beaten when I ask my mother why she drinks.'

Impact on schooling

The participants were asked approximately how much time they spent working in a week. Responses indicated that children's estimation of hours worked was not reliable, with many saying that they had worked more hours than were possible in an average week when other demands on their time – such as school – were factored in. Given this problem, hours worked were not used for purposes of analysis. The consequence was that unfortunately, we were not able to examine relationships between time spent on work and on schooling and resultant impacts.

The survey established that children mainly worked in agriculture before or after school, over weekends, and during school holidays. Seasonal work affected these patterns. We were unable to examine the effects of agricultural work on child outcomes as we did not have access to the necessary information. However, we found that work interfered with school in 25.6 per cent of cases (missing school; arriving late; too tired to do homework; and so on). Statistical analyses showed that work impacted to the same degree on schooling regardless of the type of schooling. Of those who reported a negative impact of work on school, 25 per cent were girls and 32 per cent were boys.

When asked about the impact of their work on schooling in group discussions, children said that their agricultural work often caused them to be late and absent and did not comment on what this implied for their education outcomes. They missed school most at harvest time and work before school made them late. Work also interfered with leisure activities. For some, the only negative outcome occurred when they were not paid on time (when they worked during holidays): they were then unable to buy uniforms and were refused entry to school.

It is not only enrolment or attendance that can affect school outcomes. Children can be in school, but, having worked in the early morning or over the weekend, there is little time for the homework that is necessary to progress through higher grades. According to one teacher:

It makes them tired ... They don't have enough time ... It can interfere with their school. When it is time for cattle to be disinfected, a lot of children are absent. It is the older ones and around 30–50 are away for dip day on a Monday or Tuesday. It happens all year round.

Teachers noted that many children live in homes where alcohol abuse and violence co-exist with poverty, and where the family shares one room. It is not surprising under such conditions that children are likely to fail grades and drop out. And when they do, it is not only to go and work on farms.

Reflections

These findings, while not based on a random sample, are likely to be a fair reflection of the situation of children living in similar circumstances. Three central points are evident.

First, while poverty is clearly a fundamental cause of children's involvement in agricultural work, particularly in paid work, obligations to kin and community are important contributors. In this study, we find that when subsistence and commercial agriculture are compared, rates of exposure to work hazards and compromised schooling are similar. More children working in commercial agriculture reported that work impacted on their health, although nearly half of those working in subsistence agriculture also experienced an impact on their health. Focusing on exploitation in paid employment has led to a lack of attention to the abuses and hazards for children working on family plots or communal lands.

Second, while work interferes with schooling, our evidence suggests that wider contextual factors such as home conditions and poor school environments are also significant barriers to being able to benefit from education. For example, in one high school classroom we observed 80 pupils with one teacher – a very challenging educational environment for both teacher and students.

Third, the study confirms that from child and adult perspectives, participation in agricultural work (paid or not) has both risks and benefits. In particular, for children who work in both unpaid subsistence and paid commercial settings, the psychosocial costs appear significant. That said, it is important to recognize that negative psychological states are unlikely to be a function of work alone. Conditions at home are very likely to contribute to the incidence of anti-social behaviour, anxiety, and depression. In addition, unpaid domestic work is not necessarily benign and may involve exploitation that is hidden and leads to negative child outcomes.

On the positive side, children and adults value children's work as much for its social function as for its economic contribution. Participation is valued for the transfer of important skills, in many ways more important perhaps than what is being learnt in poorly resourced and overcrowded schools.

However valuable that may be, poor rural South African children are placed in a contested set of developmental spaces. They are caught three ways: by the dictates of legislation and policy that criminalizes their employment and speaks more to the cultural practices of post-industrial societies of the North than to local rural realities; by compulsory schooling that often does not deliver quality; and by a family environment that undermines the possibility of benefiting from school, while making both paid and unpaid work (mainly in subsistence settings) a rational survival solution.

A child participant saw the contradictions: 'We are pushed by the situation, not by our parents.'

Notes

1. This chapter is based on research contracted to the Human Sciences Research Council of South Africa by the International Labour Organization's 'Towards the Elimination of Child Labour (TECL)' South African programme. The authors are grateful for the financial support of the ILO. We also wish to express our thanks to the child and the adult participants who gave us hours of their time to share their views on child work in South African agriculture. Without the dedication of our field staff and those who helped us gain access to relevant communities, this work would not have been possible. We thank the reviewers for their helpful comments on an earlier draft of the chapter.
2. In this chapter we use the term 'work' to include light or heavy agricultural activity undertaken by children in order to contribute their time or earnings to the family or community economy. It includes those classes of work prohibited in law unless otherwise specified.
3. Full details of the research are available at: http://www.hsrc.ac.za/Research_Publication-21019.phtml

References

Allais, F. B. and F. Hagemann (2008) *Child Labour and Education: Evidence from SIMPOC Surveys,* Working Paper, Geneva: International Labour Organization.
Anker, R. (2000) 'The Economics of Child Labour: A Framework for Measurement', *International Labour Review* 139: 257–80.
Barnes, H. (2009) *Child Poverty in South Africa: A Socially Perceived Necessities Approach,* Measures of Child Poverty Project Key Report 2, Pretoria: Department of Social Development, Republic of South Africa.
Basu, K. and Z. Tzannatos (2003) 'The Global Child Labour Problem: What Do We Know and What Can We Do?', *The World Bank Economic Review* 17: 147–73.

Bourdillon, M. (2009) 'Children's Work in Southern Africa', *Werkwinkel* 4.1:18–36.

Boyden, J. (1990) 'Childhood and Policymakers: A Comparative Perspective on the Globalization of Childhood', in A. James and A. Prout (eds), *Constructing and Reconstructing Childhood*, London: Falmer Press.

Brown, D. K. (2001) 'Child Labour in Latin America: Policy and Evidence', *World Economy* 24: 761–78.

Dorman, P. (2008) *Child Labour, Education and Health: A Review of the Literature*, Geneva: International Labour Organization.

Duncan, N. and B. Bowman (2008) 'Educational Aspirations, Child Labour Imperatives and Structural Inequality in the South African Agricultural Sector', *Perspectives in Education* 26: 29–43.

Fekadu, D., A. Atalay and B. Hägglöf (2006) 'The Prevalence of Mental Health Problems in Ethiopian Child Laborers', *Journal of Child Psychology and Psychiatry* 47, 954–9.

Gharaibeh, M. and S. Hoeman (2003) 'Health Hazards and Risks For Abuse Among Child Labor in Jordan', *Journal of Pediatric Nursing* 18: 140–7.

Hadi, A. (2000) 'Child Abuse Among Working Children in Rural Bangladesh: Prevalence and Determinants', *Public Health* 114: 380–4.

IPEC (2002) *Combating Child Labour: A Handbook for Labour Inspectors*, Geneva: International Programme for the Elimination of Child Labour.

Jensen, P. and H. Nielsen (1997) Child Labour or School Attendance? Evidence from Zambia, *Journal of Population Economics* 10: 407–24.

Levine, S. (2006) 'The "Picaninny Wage": An Historical Overview of the Persistence of Structural Inequality and Child Labour in South Africa', *Anthropology Southern Africa* 29: 122–31.

Levine, S. (2000) 'In the Shadow of the Vine: Child Labour in South Africa's Wine Industry', PhD thesis, Temple University, Philadelphia, Pennsylvania.

Miller, P.J. and J.J. Goodnow (1995) 'Cultural Practices: Toward an Integration of Culture and Development' in J.J. Goodnow, P.J. Miller and F. Kessel (eds), *Cultural Practices as Contexts for Development*, San Francisco CA: Jossey-Bass Publishers.

Myers, W.E. (2001) 'Can Children's Work and Education Be Reconciled?', *International Journal of Educational Policy, Research and Practice* 2: 307–30.

Nieuwenhuys, O. (1996) 'The Paradox of Child Labor and Anthropology', *Annual Review of Anthropology* 25: 237–51.

Nkomazi Municipality (2005/06) 'Nkomazi IDP, 2005/2006 Revision' http://www.idp.org.za/documents/IDP/Mpumalanga/MP324/2005/MP324_2005_Nkomazi%20IDP.pdf (accessed 15 May 2010).

Noble, M., M. Babita, H. Barnes, C. Dibben, W. Magasela, S. Noble et al. (2006) 'The Provincial Indices of Multiple Deprivation for South Africa 2001: Technical Report', http://www.casasp.ox.ac.uk (accessed 1 January 2010)

Orazem, P. F. and V. Gunnarsson (2003) *Child Labour, School Attendance and Academic Performance: A Review*, ILO/IPEC Working Paper, Geneva: International Labour Organization.

Orkin, M. (2000) *Surveys of Activities of Young People*, Pretoria: Statistics South Africa.

Patrinos, H.A. and G. Psacharopoulos (1995) 'Educational Performance and Child Labor in Paraguay', *International Journal of Educational Development* 15: 47–60.

Piotrkowski, C.S. and J. Carrubba (1999) 'Child Labor and Exploitation' in J. Barling and E.K. Kelloway (eds) *Young Workers: Varieties of Experience,* Washington DC: American Psychological Association.

Provide (2005) 'A Profile of Mpumalanga: Demographics, Poverty, Inequality and Unemployment', Provide Background Paper 2005. 1.8, www.elsenburg.com/provide (accessed 6 April 2010).

Rogoff, B. (2003) *The Cultural Nature of Human Development,* Oxford and New York: Oxford University Press.

Ruchkin, V., M.E. Schwab-Stone and R. Vermeiren (2004) *Social and Health Assessment (SAHA): Psychometric Development Summary,* New Haven, CT: Yale University.

Solomon, J. and J. Morgan (2008) *Living With X. A Body-Mapping Journey in the Time of HIV and AIDS. A Facilitator's Guide.* Johannesburg: REPSSI. Available at http://www.repssi.net/index.php?option=com_content&view=article&catid=39%3Arepssi-publications&id=49%3Abody-mapping&Itemid=68 (accessed 10 May 2010).

Statistics South Africa (2000) *Survey of Activities of Young People (SAYP 1999),* Pretoria: Statistics South Africa.

Streak, J., A. Dawes, D. Ewing, S. Levine, S. Rama and L. Alexander (2008) *Children Working in the Commercial and Subsistence Agriculture in South Africa: A Child Labour-Related Rapid Assessment Study,* TECL report no. 52, Pretoria: Department of Labour.

Super, C. M. and S. Harkness (1986) 'The Developmental Niche: A Conceptualization at the Interface of Child and Culture', *International Journal of Behavioral Development* 9: 545–69.

UNESCO (2007) *Education For All by 2015: Will We Make It?,* Education For All Global Monitoring Report 2008, Paris: UNESCO.

Woodhead, M. (2004) *Psychosocial Impacts of Child Work: A Framework for Research, Monitoring and Intervention,* Understanding Children's Work Working Project Paper Series, Rome: University of Rome.

Wright G. (2008) *Findings from the Indicators of Poverty and Social Exclusion Project. A Profile of Poverty Using the Socially Perceived Necessities Approach,* Key Report 7, Pretoria: Department of Social Development, Republic of South Africa.

17
Are Work and Schooling Complementary or Competitive for Children in Rural Ethiopia? A Mixed-Methods Study[1]

Kate Orkin

In Ethiopia, most children work and attend school. The most recent Child Labour Force Survey (2001) showed that 52 per cent of children of primary school age in rural areas combined paid or subsistence work with schooling (Guarcello and Rosati 2007: 5).[2] For policies to cater for these children, it is important to understand when children's work competes with education and when it complements it (cf. Boyden et al. 1998: 251). If work and school are complementary, children can participate in each activity at different times of day. At best, engaging in work makes it more possible to engage in school, or vice versa. In contrast, activities can compete with each other: working may make it impossible or more difficult for children to attend school or prevent them from benefiting fully from it.

Anthropology and childhood studies have used qualitative methods to uncover a range of characteristics that make work and school complementary or competitive, which have been largely ignored in survey work. I draw on literature from these disciplines and on my own qualitative research in a Young Lives survey site to question the exclusive focus of many economists on the hours taken by activities. I argue that whether work and schooling are complementary or competitive depends not only on the time each activity takes, but also on the characteristics of the activity. With variables from the Young Lives survey as proxies for these characteristics, I then undertake exploratory quantitative analysis across all 13 rural survey sites. Some correlation between these proxies and decisions about children's schooling and work suggest that the characteristics of activities are generally relevant.

Economic models of children's work

Early economic literature assumed that work and school are mutually exclusive: children either attend school all day or work full time for pay in petty trade or industry (Psacharopoulos 1997; Ray 2003). A more recent strand argues that whether a child enrols in school, whether they work, and how much leisure they have is a single, jointly determined allocation of the time and budget available to the household, so it is artificial to isolate the effect of work on school (Edmonds 2007).

Cigno and Rosati (2005) nest the two most widely used models of child time allocation (Baland and Robinson 2000; Basu and Van 1998) within a general model. Families choose the child's mix of activities to optimize household utility, trading off between the child's current income and future returns to their education. Choices are constrained by parents' budget and the amount of time in a child's day. Depending on which constraints are binding, children work full time, combine work with school, attend school full time, or (if there are costs to schooling) do nothing. Based on this model or variants of it, empirical papers examine determinants of child time allocation, among them schooling price changes (Ravallion and Wodon 2000), household shocks (Beegle et al. 2006), and household composition (Fafchamps and Wahba 2006).

These models emphasize the household budget as the binding constraint on decision-making. However, the models have in common another constraint: the number of hours in a day. Some authors argue that the time constraint should be adjusted to capture that particular activities take a fixed amount of time (Ravallion and Wodon, 2000: C163); for example, the model could specify that children attending school can only take on part-time work (de Janvry et al. 2006: 353). But even with these adjustments, the time constraint assumes that the amount of time activities take is the only influence on the extent to which children can participate in both.

No models found in my literature search consider characteristics of work and school. Schools are assumed to be similar: most studies assume all schools occupy the whole day, except de Janvry et al. (2006), who assume schools teach for half the day. There is also limited recognition that different tasks have different characteristics. Studies find strong heterogeneity in determinants of time allocation across genders (Admassie and Bedi 2003; Cockburn and Dostie 2007) and ages (Duryea et al. 2007; Wahba 2006) but do not discuss reasons for it. One plausible reason is strict gender and age differentiation in characteristics of tasks.

Insights from anthropology and childhood studies on children's work

Researchers in sociology, anthropology, and childhood studies are critical of the view that work and schooling are mutually exclusive, arguing that this perspective is rooted in culturally specific notions of childhood as a time for leisure and learning (Boyden et al. 1998: 246–7). Research uses children's descriptions of how they balance work and schooling to elucidate characteristics that make their activities complementary or competitive. Shift schooling enables children to work and go to school, and work enables schooling when children's wages meet its expenses (Nieuwenhuys 1994). Work may also teach children many relevant skills, and should be considered part of 'education' (Bourdillon et al. 2010: 94–105).

However, work can disrupt schooling (Boyden et al. 1998: 249). Children may be too tired to concentrate in class or do homework. School may be scheduled at times of day difficult for working children and children may be punished for arriving at school late after working at home (Nieuwenhuys 1994: 70). If children miss classes or days because of work, they may fall behind and become discouraged (Boyden et al. 1998: 256).

Methodology

I used survey data collected by Young Lives, in collaboration with the Ethiopian Development Research Institute, on 1,000 Older Cohort children. They and their caregivers were surveyed in 2002/03, when the children were aged between 7 and 8, and again between October 2006 and April 2007.

For qualitative data, I conducted a case study of children's time allocation in Leki, a rural Young Lives site,[3] between July and September 2008. This was one-and-a-half years after the Round 2 survey; so children were between 12 and 13 years old. I selected 24 of the 50 Young Lives children in Leki for focus groups based on their gender, working status, and schooling status. Each group participated in two exercises run by a research assistant, one (from Woodhead 1998) asking children to rank activities they did on various criteria, and one based on protocols for the Young Lives qualitative component (Camfield et al. 2009), where children discussed the characteristics of those who did well or badly at school. With an assistant, I conducted semi-structured interviews with 17 children, and follow-up interviews with ten children, together with home observations and interviews with parents. I also interviewed two teachers, the elected chairperson of the village governing committee, the manager of an NGO providing irrigation, and managers of vegetable farms.

Data collection and analysis was sequential and iterative: findings from one method of analysis suggested issues for investigation by the alternative method in the next stage. Quantitative analysis before fieldwork suggested that qualitative work should focus on rural areas, where children's work was more prevalent. It also enabled the selection of respondents and suggested some themes for interview protocols and child-specific questions. Initial qualitative analysis based on field notes encouraged me to reshape my research questions and generated the conceptual framework of the characteristics of work and school. I then applied this framework in the third stage, a detailed quantitative analysis, and the fourth stage, detailed qualitative analysis of transcripts. Finally, the combination suggested questions for further surveys.

I used qualitative descriptions of work and school in a particular village to develop theoretical propositions about how particular characteristics of the two affect children's allocation of time. Children's descriptions provided 'a map' (Ritchie and Lewis 2003: 269) of the characteristics of school and work that could make schooling complementary or competitive. Bina Agarwal (1997: 6), an economist, argues that such 'analytical descriptions' are useful when the factors being considered are not captured adequately in current models.

Econometric analysis explored which of the relationships described in qualitative work were present across the sample of 633 rural children. Since the 13 sites in the sample were purposively selected, the sample was not nationally representative. However, the sample was random within villages, so I drew conclusions about 12- and 13-year-old children in the sample and similar villages.

I used an econometric specification based on Cigno and Rosati's (2005) theoretical model. The specification, assumptions, and results are presented in Orkin (2008). I examine seven outcome variables using independent probit equations. Work variables are equal to one if a child allocated more than an hour on a typical day to the work. Four types are considered: paid work, subsistence work, chores, and care. There are three school outcome variables: enrolment, regular attendance (that is, missing fewer than 20 days), and spending more than an hour a day studying.

All regressions included controls for household composition, parental education, whether children were stunted, children's religion, gender and birth order, and whether or not children were recent migrants, of a minority ethnic group, or the biological children of the household head. I use village-level fixed effects (Fafchamps and Wahba 2006) to control for omitted village-level variables, but do not use household fixed effects because of data limitations. Omitted variable bias is likely, so I merely note when correlation is present and do not attribute causality to relationships.

Since the Young Lives survey does not capture information on characteristics of work and school, I used the insights of qualitative work to select proxies for children undertaking work or attending a school with particular characteristics, with some but limited success. If one of these proxies correlated with children attending school less and working more, I concluded that that the characteristic of work (or school) made work and school competitive.

Children's work and school in Leki: qualitative evidence

Leki is a lakeside village of 410 households, two hours' walk from the nearest town. In this village, 285 households own land, on which they grow maize, wheat and *teff* (a cereal that is made into *enjera*, the staple flat bread). Ninety-nine families belong to an irrigation scheme, and can grow and sell a second harvest of peppers, tomatoes, or onions. There are also five commercial vegetable farms.

Paid work

Vegetable farming is labour-intensive. Children work unpaid for their own families if they have irrigated land. Both commercial vegetable farmers and families with irrigated land and often hire children as casual labourers for transplanting and harvesting. Even children whose families have irrigated land work for pay. The duration, intensity, and flexibility of work vary depending on the employer.

On both family and commercial farms, a rate is paid for a piece of work. On commercial farms, pieces take a woman or child roughly a day to complete. Girls described planting seedlings:

> Children wake up early in the morning to start their work. They are given 20 rows to put onion seeds. They prepare openings and put the seeds in each opening [and] cover them with soil. It takes a day to complete the 20 rows. This may keep students from going to school. (Girls Group Two, 15 August 2008)

Children are expected to finish a piece of work in one day, or else they are not paid. Only 3 of 17 children interviewed said they would not leave work to go to school before they had finished work. Buzu, a girl, said, 'If we fail to finish the work we are assigned to, the organization does not allow us to go home. Sometimes they beat us and instruct us to finish the work.' In contrast, on family-owned farms, 'If you fail to finish, you come back to doing it the next time.' One boy prefers to work for individual farmers because 'you can earn whatever you do, half day or full day'. The system on commercial farms prevents work from being divided into small chunks of time, which makes work particularly competitive with schooling.

Work on commercial vegetable farms was particularly tiring. Girls said planting onions was their most tiring activity: 'You do it stooped over so you feel pain in your back' (Girls Group One, 13 August 2008). Some boys said, 'Paid work has a huge impact. It is heavy and beyond our capacity' (Boys Group Two, 24 August 2008). Dasse, a boy, said, 'The work in the commercial farms is difficult, and you can't take a break, you have to work all the ten hours in the sun. But with the individual farms you can take breaks and go home earlier.'

Performing tiring tasks made it difficult to participate fully in school: 'Whenever we go to school after doing heavy tasks, we cannot easily follow the lecture in the class' (Boys Group One, 22 August 2008). Senayit, a girl, said, 'When I come home from the place of work I feel tired and fail to do assignments.' A boy said, 'If we have to work on the farm weeding, we go to bed early so that we may wake up in the night to study. We ask our parents to wake us up.' One of the teachers agreed: working children 'come without doing their homework…When we ask their friends after class, they tell us that the student was working on some vegetable farm the previous day.'

Many children used their wages to buy school materials, which makes work and schooling complementary. The school at Leki demanded no fees or uniforms. However, children had to buy exercise books, stationery, and adequate clothes and shoes. Two children interviewed had dropped out of school because their parents could not afford these materials. They worked and saved money and returned to school the next year.

'Children whose parents don't have land and are economically poor need to do paid work to survive and to attend school' (Boys Group Two, 24 August 2008). But work is scarce: the boys said, 'We cannot even get the job opportunity even when we want to do it.' The foreman at one farm reported that children beg to work there.

Thus children worry about finding jobs, which in turn can affect their concentration. Senayit said, 'I think about my payments while I am in class or studying; this definitely affects my learning.' Beletu, another girl, described a child doing badly at school: 'She cannot study because she has to worry about many things... She has to look for a job.'

The scarcity of jobs also meant children missed school if it conflicted with work (Girls Group Two, 15 August 2008). Teachers sometimes allowed children to leave school early for paid work. One of the boys said, 'If we get one [a job], we work. We ask teachers for permission and go to work. The teachers may ask us to bring them some onions and we do accordingly.' But children who were often absent without permission were 'fired' by their teachers (Girls Group One, 13 August 2008).

Work in family enterprises

Most children whose families owned land helped their families to farm. Boys assisted with weeding, ploughing, guarding crops, harvesting, and building fences and barns. Girls and women assisted with harvesting and sowing seed.

Work for families could be divided into small chunks of time, which made it less competitive with schooling: 'Concerning the household work... parents don't refuse to send you to school though you don't finish the work. You can finish the work after school. That is not the case with the paid work' (Boys Group Two, 24 August 2008).

Children started herding smaller animals at around the age of 5. From the age of 7, boys herded cattle. Grazing land was two hours' walk from the village. In dry weather, cattle were taken further away to graze, which took the whole day (Boys Group Two, 25 August 2008). However, if grazing was plentiful, herding took place after school. Children could study while herding: one boy said: 'When my father tells me to look after the cattle, I feel happy because I can read my books.'

Children with few siblings of their gender missed school more often to help their families. One boy, Ramato, had no brothers, so his father often needed him on the farm and would tell him to get permission to miss school. Ramato was unhappy about these absences: 'If I miss a class and friends tell me that they learned many things and took some homework, I really feel upset since I lose marks.' Such children also enrolled at a later age: Dasse, a boy from one of the richer families in the village, was already 'a little grown-up' by the time he started school at 9. He said, 'There was no one to look after the herd, and I was doing that.' When his younger sisters were old enough, they took over herding and he went to school.

Work in the home

Both girls and boys fetched water from the pump and collected fire-wood. In addition, girls cleaned the house, went to market, washed clothes, and made *enjera* (flat bread) and *wot* (sauce). Girls said they did more work than boys. One, Ganat, said, 'Boys work for longer hours than girls in paid work. But girls must also do household chores when they come home.'

Tasks that children said were bad for schooling needed a long and continuous block of time and could not be balanced with studying. These tended to be assigned to girls:

> Girls are mostly busy and consequently get weak in their education. The boys may take their exercise books when they go to herd cattle. But if girls try to study while they bake *enjera*, they may forget and the food may burn. (Girls Group Two, 24 August 2008)

Another girl agreed, saying, 'Making *enjera* has a lot of processes. It requires collecting firewood, mixing the flour with water and a lot more processes all at once.' Similarly, collecting firewood required travelling to the forest some way from the village. Fetching water, however, was quick and could take place before or after school (Girls Group One, 12 August 2008).

Girls struggled to study at home, because they could be asked to work at any time: Senayit said, 'If they order me to work, I work. I cannot disobey them.' When asked how parents should support their children's education, she said, 'Parents should give ample time to their children to read books and prepare themselves for the next class.' Boys felt more in control of their time: 'They [teachers] teach us to use our time economically and finish the work we need to do so that we can have time for study' (Boys Group Two, 25 August 2008).

Girls were also responsible for caring for sick family members. A girls' group described girls doing badly at school: 'They engage in paid work. When their mothers are sick they say, "I have to work and with the money I have to buy medicine"' (Girls Group Two, 14 August 2008). Boys said of girls, 'If her mother is sick, she focuses on work, quitting her education' (Boys Group Two, 24 August 2008).

If women were ill, girls took on all their domestic chores. Senayit, whose mother was sick, said:

> When she was healthy she did all household tasks and cooked my meal. I used to come from school and eat my meal. But now I do

all chores without anyone's assistance. I collect firewood, clean the house, make coffee, fetch water, go to market, and bake bread for the household.

The school

Nearly all children in the Young Lives sample in Leki (93 per cent) were enrolled in school. Many children had started school after the age of 7, the compulsory age of enrolment, because their parents could not pay schooling costs or needed the children for work. Teachers reported high rates of dropout: by halfway through the 2007/08 school year, enrolment in Grades One and Two had decreased by roughly a third.

Illness often caused dropout: two girls stopped school for a year to look after sick parents, and four children dropped out for a year or more because they fell seriously ill. Socioeconomic constraints were another reason. One teacher said, 'The produce from last year gradually depletes in the second semester. Sometimes students come without eating their breakfast; this makes them weak and hopeless; and they quit.' Another teacher agreed, 'The children do paid jobs to get money; they become very money-enthusiastic and their parents do not push them to go to school as they value the daily money the children earn. There could be lack of food, exercise books, and clothing.'

Children often return to school the year after dropping out and thus progress slowly through grades. Only 23 per cent of children in the sample of 633 had passed four grades between 2002 and 2006. Ten per cent of children were in school for some period in these four years but did not complete one grade.

The school operates in only one shift, from 8:00 a.m. until 12:15 p.m. If only school hours are considered, schooling is compatible with some work. Even so, children did not attend regularly. Many students came in the morning and left after the 10:00 a.m. break. Some children reported studying three or four hours a day besides, even waking up early to study, but many did not report any studying.

Children often missed school to work. Senayit said this affected her results: 'If we support ourselves by working as daily labourers, we may lose the lessons the other students have been taught...and score less in tests.'

Children also missed school if they were late because of work. The school hired a guard, who often shut the gate against latecomers. Senayit said, 'Teachers close the gate against us so that we cannot disturb the class. We kill two or more periods just wandering in the fields. Sometimes teachers beat us...order us to collect rubbish and clean the compound.'

Schooling is structured to accommodate children's work. The Leki school management committee, in consultation with farmers, moves the times of the school day according to the cycle of subsistence activities. In October, there is a two-week break so children can help with harvesting, and when school resumes, it is moved from morning to afternoon. In November, school is moved back to the morning. In April, school is moved to the afternoon for tilling.

Orthodox Christians in Ethiopia fast before Easter but are allowed to eat fish. During this period, boys attend less than girls because they can earn money from fishing. Teachers made an informal arrangement with boys and 'told them to come to school at 9:00 a.m. after they have finished fishing... It is better to come late than to quit school.'

However, the calendar does not change around the vegetable harvests, when many poorer children work on commercial vegetable farms. Moreover, the school is not as flexible as parents and children would like it to be. The chairperson of the village governing committee said parents asked for two shifts for schooling, because they could not send all their children to school at the same time, but the school has not complied.

The school is sometimes inflexible in accommodating children who are seriously ill. Five of 17 children interviewed had missed two or more months of school because of illness. Two were allowed to return, although one had to repeat the grade the following year. Three were not allowed to re-enrol until the following school year. This happened to one girl, Shonah, in two consecutive years, once when she got malaria and once when she had worms.

Time allocation to work and school in quantitative data

Across all 13 rural sites, children's activities are very similar to those in Leki. Ninety-three per cent of children are enrolled. Only 5 per cent are enrolled and do less than two hours of chores or caring on the average day, and most children combine school and subsistence work. Leki has unusually high levels of paid work, probably because of commercial vegetable farming.

Qualitative data indicate characteristics of work and school that make them complementary or competitive in children's plans for each day. These describe the situation in Leki, but also provide empirical expectations which can be tested more generally in quantitative research through proxy variables.

Table 17.1 12-year-old children's combination of activities, Ethiopia, 2006

Variable		In all 13 sites (n = 633)			In Leki (n = 49)
		Girls	Boys	Girls and boys	Girls and boys
% not in school		5.56	9.17	7.42	4.08
% in school	and doing paid work[a]	6.86	11.31	9.16	46.94
	and doing subsistence work and more than 2 hours of chores/care	25.82	18.35	21.96	10.20
	and doing subsistence work but less than 2 hours of chores/care	12.42	43.73	28.59	14.29
	and doing no subsistence work but more than 2 hours of chores/care	45.75	10.40	27.49	18.37
	and doing no other activities	3.59	7.03	5.37	6.12
		100.00	100.00	100.00	100.00

[a] They may also spend time on other types of tasks.

Source: Young Lives Older Cohort rural sample, 2006.

Results on gender were similar across qualitative and quantitative work. Qualitative research found that younger boys and girls did similar work – herding smaller animals, fetching water and wood, and looking after siblings – but by the time the children were 12 tasks were clearly differentiated between genders. It also found no differences in enrolment between boys and girls, although girls complained they found it difficult to find time to study. Quantitative research supported these conclusions. When children were 8, being male or female did not make them more likely to engage in particular types of work. When children were 12, boys were more likely to engage in paid and subsistence work and less likely to engage in chores and caring work. There was no gender-based difference in the likelihood of boys and girls enrolling in school, attending regularly, or studying. Perhaps girls studied despite distractions at home, or perhaps boys had other reasons for not studying.

Schooling costs

Qualitative research found that schooling costs were a barrier to enrolment. I do not examine variation in schooling costs between children, because the majority of children in the survey sites attended the government village school and regressions compared children in the same village.[4]

Instead, I investigated variation in households' ability to pay schooling costs. Survey data showed that children in wealthier families (measured by household durables) were more likely to be enrolled, and less likely to do more than two hours of chores in a day. Likewise, as family land size increased, children were more likely to attend school regularly and less likely to do subsistence work.

Worrying about finding paid work

Children said worrying about finding work made them more likely to work for pay when they had the chance and less likely to attend school. The proxy used is whether families would be unable to raise 150 birr in a week. Since each regression already controlled for household wealth, this proxy captured differences in how credit-constrained families were compared to families with the same level of wealth.

The argument is that worrying about finding work to pay schooling costs in qualitative research mapped onto whether parents were credit-constrained. Richer children sometimes did paid work, but not if it affected schooling. In contrast, children from families burdened by illness and extreme poverty had to find work to pay schooling costs and were more likely to worry about finding work. As expected from qualitative research, quantitative research showed that worried children were likelier to take on work and less likely to be enrolled and attend school regularly. Worrying about finding work also led to lack of concentration in class and while studying, but this was difficult to capture using available data.

Inflexible schooling

Qualitative research showed that the formal schooling system was somewhat flexible regarding work but less flexible regarding lateness, children caring for ill household members, or children's own illness. School flexibility to work is difficult to quantify directly with this round of data, although it is a major focus of more recent data collection. I therefore only examined the effect of child and family illness on children's schooling.[5]

The first proxy for school flexibility to illness was whether children had had a serious illness in the last four years. If schools were flexible, children who had been sick might have been less likely to attend regularly but should have been as likely to be enrolled. However, as expected from qualitative data, schools were not accommodating of sick children: children who had been ill were less likely to be enrolled and less likely to be attending regularly. The effect is not strong, probably because children's enrolment and attendance was not always measured in the year they fell ill.

The second proxy is the percentage of household members who had been ill for more than 30 days in the last year. The proxy is crude: regressions already control for differences in family wealth that may result from illness in the household, but there may be other effects of household illness on school participation not related to school flexibility. Children whose households were burdened by illness were somewhat more likely to do caring work and much more likely to work for pay, possibly to pay for medicine, as raised in qualitative work. They were less likely to be enrolled and attending regularly.

Indivisible work

In qualitative research, children indicated that piece-work tasks on commercial farms, herding, fishing, collecting firewood, and making *enjera* were difficult to balance with school attendance and studying. They could not be divided into small chunks of time or combined with other activities. This finding proved difficult to test in quantitative research.

Herding was competitive with schooling when cattle had to be taken far away from home, so in quantitative analysis, I examined children whose families had larger herds. There was strong probability that these children would do subsistence work, but they were not more likely to miss school. On average, herding and schooling were complementary.

The second proxy examined was whether irrigation was available in the research site. In the qualitative work, irrigated agriculture increased opportunities for indivisible paid work. I used a variety of cluster-level variables as an imperfect substitute for cluster fixed effects. As expected, availability of irrigation in the area increased the probability that children participated in paid work. However, irrigation in the site unexpectedly increased the probability that children attended school. Perhaps children were using money earned in agriculture to subsidize their schooling costs. Alternatively, in other sites work in irrigation agriculture may have been divisible and complementary to schooling attendance.

Tiring work

Qualitative research found that tiring work prevented concentration during school and decreased studying. Lack of quantitative data on the nature of work prevented examination of tiring work, but the variable has been included in Round 3 of the survey.

Conclusion

Across qualitative and quantitative research, a picture emerges of characteristics of activities that make them competitive. Findings, although preliminary, inform a number of debates relevant to policy.

First, minor adjustments to existing schooling systems, such as synchronizing school calendars with agricultural calendars or providing shorter school days, would help children to combine school with work and could greatly improve enrolment and attendance.

Second, illness among children and families has major effects on participation in schooling. Flexible policies about absence and structures to assist children to catch up would prevent drop out when children or their parents were ill. Better access to health care for parents and children would both improve health and increase school attendance.

Third, despite education being nominally free in Ethiopia, the costs of books, clothes, and stationery reduce enrolment. Interventions targeted at poor families to reduce the cost of schooling, such as provision of schooling materials or grants, would probably improve school enrolment and attendance. They might also prevent children worrying about finding work and so improve concentration in class.

Fourth, many interventions in developing countries to improve school participation also aim to reduce children's participation in work (Ravallion and Wodon 2000). This chapter suggests that, if the aim is to improve participation in schooling, intervention should target not all work, but only work that competes with school.

Fifth, work in the home or work supervised by family should be considered together with work for pay. Feminists and others have long argued that to deny that chores and caring are work denigrates and makes invisible the contribution of children (and women) to families (Agarwal 1997; Levison 2000). In addition, I show that some chores and caring share characteristics with work that is competitive with schooling, and are equally important in any analysis of children's work.

The research also makes a methodological point. This analysis is an 'analytic description' (Agarwal 1997: 2) of characteristics of work and schooling which affect time allocation. The most obvious theoretical extension is to construct a formal economic model that goes beyond the linear time constraint as the main parameter of child decision-making. Qualitative conclusions stand independently, gathering children's perspectives on their lives to advance knowledge and improve policy. But they can also enable economists to improve their economics.

Notes

1. The interviews described in this chapter were conducted for my MPhil dissertation, which was supervised by Professor Stefan Dercon and Dr Laura Camfield. The Skye Foundation, Young Lives, OReNGA and St Antony's College funded fieldwork. The author thanks Young Lives participants and researchers.
2. Analysis on the Ethiopian Rural Household Survey generates a similar statistic (Admassie and Bedi 2003; Cockburn and Dostie 2007). Qualitative work (Poluha 2004) suggests most rural Ethiopian children work.
3. All names of children and study sites have been changed to protect the children and their families' confidentiality.
4. No government schools charge fees, but children pay for stationery and clothing and schools ask for 'contributions' for new facilities, hiring guards, or teachers' salaries.
5. Household shocks were found to be exogenous (the values of the outcome variables when children are 8 predict shocks between when children are 8 and 12 Beegle et al. 2006). It can be argued that household shocks cause particular time allocation choices.

References

Admassie, A. and A.S. Bedi (2003) *Attending School: Two R's and Child Work in Rural Ethiopia*, Working Paper Series 387, The Hague: Institute of Social Studies.
Agarwal, B. (1997) '"Bargaining" And Gender Relations: Within and Beyond the Household', *Feminist Economics* 3.1: 1–51.
Baland, J. and J.A. Robinson (2000) 'Is Child Labour Inefficient?', *Journal of Political Economy* 108: 663–79.
Basu, K. and P. Van (1998) 'The Economics of Child Labor', *American Economic Review* 88: 412–27.
Beegle, K., R.H. Dehejia and R. Gatti (2006) 'Child Labor and Agricultural Shocks', *Journal of Development Economics* 81: 80–96.
Bourdillon, M., D. Levison, W. Myers and B. White (2010) *Rights and Wrongs of Children's Work*, New Brunswick, NJ: Rutgers University Press.
Boyden, J., B. Ling and W. Myers (1998) *What Works for Working Children*, Stockholm: Radda Barnen.
Camfield, L., G. Crivello and M. Woodhead (2009) 'Wellbeing Research in Developing Countries: Reviewing the Role of Qualitative Methods', *Social Indicators Research* 90.1: 5–31.
Cigno, A. and F. Rosati (2005) *The Economics of Child Labour*, Oxford: Oxford University Press.
Cockburn, J. and B. Dostie (2007) 'Child Work and Schooling: The Role of Household Asset Profiles and Poverty in Rural Ethiopia', *Journal of African Economics* 16.4: 519–63.

de Janvry, A., F. Finan, E. Sadoulet and R. Vakis (2006) 'Can Conditional Cash Transfer Programs Serve as Safety Nets in Keeping Children at School and from Working When Exposed to Shocks?', *Journal of Development Economics* 79.2: 349–73.

Duryea, S., D. Lam and D. Levison (2007) 'Effects of Economic Shocks on Children's Employment and Schooling in Brazil', *Journal of Development Economics* 84: 188–214.

Edmonds, E.V. (2007) 'Child Labor' in T.P. Schultz and J. Strauss (eds), *Handbook of Development Economics, Volume 4*, Oxford and Amsterdam: North-Holland.

Fafchamps, M. and J. Wahba (2006) 'Child Labour, Urban Proximity and Household Composition', *Journal of Development Economics* 79: 374–97.

Guarcello, L. and F. Rosati (2007) *Child Labor and Youth Employment: Ethiopia Country Study*, World Bank Social Protection Working Paper Series, Washington DC: World Bank.

Levison, D. (2000) 'Children as Economic Agents', *Feminist Economics* 6.1: 125–34.

Nieuwenhuys, O. (1994) *Children's Lifeworlds: Gender, Welfare and Labour in the Developing World*, London and New York: Routledge.

Orkin, K. (2008) 'The Relationship between Child Work and Schooling in Rural Ethiopia', MPhil dissertation, University of Oxford.

Poluha, E. (2004) *The Power of Continuity: Ethiopia through the Eyes of Its Children*, Uppsala: Nordic Africa Institute.

Psacharopoulos, G. (1997) 'Child Labour Versus Educational Attainment: Some Evidence from Latin America', *Journal of Population Economics* 10: 337–86.

Ravallion, M. and Q. Wodon (2000) 'Does Child Labor Displace Schooling? Evidence on Behavioral Responses to an Enrollment Subsidy', *The Economic Journal* 110: 158–75.

Ray, R. (2003) 'The Determinants of Child Labour and Child Schooling in Ghana', *Journal of African Economics* 11: 561–90.

Ritchie, J. and J. Lewis (2003) *Qualitative Research Practice: A Guide for Social Science Students and Researchers*, London: Sage.

Wahba, J. (2006) 'The Influence of Market Wages and Parental History of Child Labour and Schooling in Egypt', *Journal of Population Economics* 19: 821–52.

Woodhead, M. (1998) *Children's Perspectives on Their Working Lives: A Participatory Study in Bangladesh, Ethiopia, the Philippines, Guatemala, El Salvador and Nicaragua*, Stockholm: Rädda Barnen.

Index